Predictocracy

Predictocracy
Market Mechanisms for Public and Private Decision Making

MICHAEL ABRAMOWICZ

Yale University Press

New Haven and London

Set in Adobe Garamond by Binghamton Valley Composition

Printed in the United States of America.

Library of Congress Cataloging-in-Publication Data

Abramowicz, Michael.
Predictocracy : market mechanisms for public and private decision making /
Michael Abramowicz.
p. cm.
Includes bibliographical references and index.
ISBN 978-0-300-11599-4 (cloth : alk. paper)
1. Business forecasting.   2. Economic forecasting.   3. Decision making.
4. Forecasting.   I. Title.
HD30.27.A27 2007
658.4'0355—dc22   2007020340

A catalogue record for this book is available from the British Library.

The paper in this book meets the guidelines for permanence and durability of the
Committee on Production Guidelines for Book Longevity of the Council on
Library Resources.

10 9 8 7 6 5 4 3 2 1

For my parents

Contents

Preface

"Wanna bet on that?" This playground challenge attests to the sincerity of the questioner. Acceptance of the challenge attests to the sincerity of the target as well. A refusal to bet, meanwhile, suggests insincerity. In the absence of any information about the merits of the dispute, at least, such a refusal gives onlookers some reason to favor the challenger's claim. The actions of others who hear the challenge can also give information to onlookers. An onlooker who has information about the matter could intervene, offering to take the bet. Should that not occur, then it will be apparent to all that one person in the group projects greater confidence than anyone else. It may still be that this confidence is a bluff or that it is built on misinterpretation and mistake. But it would be difficult to construct a better procedure for identifying the most sincere belief. And over the run of questions and challenges, sincere beliefs tend to be more accurate than insincere ones.

Prediction markets, sometimes called *information markets, idea futures,* or *virtual stock markets,* are elaborations of this simple device for identifying sincere belief. By insisting that individuals back their views with money, they eliminate cheap talk. At bottom, the simplest form of prediction market is a forum for repeated challenges of this type. Someone who thinks that an event has more than a 75 percent chance of occurring offers to place three quarters against the single quarter of any challenger. Someone else who thinks that an event has less than a 25 percent chance of occurring would have a financial incentive to take that bet. The acceptance of such a bet indicates the apparent existence of genuine disagreement.

Still more useful than such bets in conveying probability estimates to the outside world are the challenges that go unanswered. Suppose that no one responds to the challenge described above. Meanwhile, someone who thinks that the event has a less than 80 percent chance of occurring offers to place $0.20 on the event's not occurring against anyone else's $0.80. No one responds to this offer, either, not even the first challenger. There are then two unanswered challenges. No one is sufficiently confident that the event has a less than 75 percent chance or a more than 80 percent chance of occurring to take either of the bets. One could infer no one sincerely believes that the probability is outside the 75 percent to 80 percent range. At the least, anyone who initially would have guessed the probability to be outside that range does not think it sufficiently clearly outside that range to be worth accepting a challenge. The actual probability, based on information known to potential bettors, thus may be between 75 percent and 80 percent. A probability of 77.5 percent might be a good guess, if a precise number is required.

Prediction markets do not merely show that those who make bets are sincere but identify the most committed predictors in a group. At any time, these are the predictors who have made forecasts that have not yet been challenged. Admittedly, the most committed challenger will not always be the most sincere, but at least he or she will appear to others to be the most sincere. For if it is obvious that a challenge is bluster, perhaps intended to influence a decision or simply to make a point, others can be expected to counter the challenge. This is especially so for prediction markets in which anyone is permitted to participate. If, after repeated challenges, no one agrees to accept a bet and meet a challenge, then even those who initially had different views must have developed sufficient doubt that they no longer think it in their interest to bet. In part, prediction market participants revise their views on the basis of the willingness of others to advance contrary positions.

In a recent book titled *The Wisdom of Crowds* James Surowiecki identifies a variety of contexts, including prediction markets, in which crowds perform better than their best members.[1] The strongest case for a prediction market, however, is not that it simply aggregates knowledge by averaging beliefs. Prediction markets do tend to allow individuals within a crowd to learn about the beliefs of others, but this will not always be important. There are some contexts in which the errors of individual intuition tend to cancel each other out, but there are others in which errors are correlated and the masses are wrong. What a prediction market excels at is identifying the wisdom in crowds, identifying the individual challenger (or group) that is so committed to a particular view that no one remains willing to accept a challenge. This will not always be the individual who in fact has the most wisdom and knowledge. But the procedures of prediction markets generally do a better job of identifying that person than do the alternatives.

This book argues that organizations in the private and the public sectors ought to use this procedure, as well as more sophisticated procedures building on this basic design. Prediction markets can serve as general-purpose prediction mechanisms, and although one can debate how they best should be designed, they generally are superior to alternative procedures for generating predictions not involving direct financial incentives. A counterargument is that someone who learns of the results of a prediction market might still be able to improve on the prediction by scrutinizing the evidence directly, and so institutions, too, ought to make a prediction market forecast just one of many decision-making inputs. Someone who does independent research, however, could participate in a market and change its forecasts in that way. A refusal to do so suggests lack of sincerity, especially if the market is heavily subsidized to make predictions attractive.

Even if there is a plausible alternative explanation for such a refusal—perhaps someone with information has a low tolerance for risk—there are reasons to prefer market predictions to those of individuals. In general, individuals who are asked to make predictions as part of a decision-making process have many conflicting incentives. One incentive might be to preserve one's reputation by announcing predictions that turn out to be correct, but other incentives might skew the announcement of a prediction. The predictor may alter a prediction in order to make a desired consequence more likely, modify a genuine prediction to please a third party such as a boss or a friend, or make a prediction on the basis of hopes and fears rather than hard analysis.

A prediction market forces someone making a prediction to bear the financial consequences of allowing extrinsic factors such as these to influence a prediction. What is more, it gives third parties incentives to assess the sincerity of the predictor, bringing to bear all their knowledge about the incentives that might be driving that individual. One might still argue that some individuals can be trusted to make accurate predictions yet somehow cannot be induced to participate in a prediction market, and so we might obtain better predictions by relying on these individuals. But developing reliable mechanisms for selecting them is not easy. And even if we could do so, we could induce these individuals to announce predictions and then allow third parties to take these predictions into account in their own prediction market bets. To prefer predictions that are untested by the competition of a market is to believe that only by granting power to designated decision makers can we achieve uncorrupted analysis.

A prediction market, then, is a decision-making device for excluding from consideration predictions that no one appears willing to back with money. Only with the development of the Internet has creation of prediction markets become economical, and regulatory obstacles have slowed their development. Nonetheless, as this book documents, prediction markets are becoming increasingly common. Preliminary empirical evidence confirms that they generally make accurate predictions, and if later research confirms this, there is every reason to believe that they will gradually replace alternative means of making predictions. Moreover, prediction markets are sufficiently cheap that they can be used to make predictions that are not now made. Many decisions are made without explicit quantification of various relevant projections. Prediction markets can improve decision making by creating a useful procedure for making those projections explicit.

It might appear that prediction (including the implicit kind) is but a fringe element of public and private decision making. This book argues, however, that prediction is central. This is perhaps more obvious in a private entity such as a corporation, where many decisions are aimed at achieving concrete goals, most notably (though not exclusively) making money. Public decision making, in contrast, involves a balancing of various private rights and interests, rather than straightforward maximization of specified variables. Even so, representative government itself can be viewed as an implicitly predictive exercise. We delegate power to legislatures, agencies, and other institutions largely because we believe that the decisions that they reach will accord more closely than alternatives with the decisions that the citizenry as a whole would reach, if only the citizenry had the time to become fully informed about particular issues.

We know, however, that the impossibility of all voters' becoming fully informed on every issue means that the democratic process often fails to achieve this modest goal of aggregating hypothetically informed preferences. Some-times it fails because relatively uninformed people are given too much of a voice. Policy becomes the voice of the mob. At other times it fails because the public's lack of information means that appointed decision makers are able to advance their own interests at the expense of the public's. Policy becomes the voice of special interests. Governmental design can be seen in large part as re-flecting attempts to balance these and other problems, to steer decision mak-ing to the institutions and individuals who seem likely to come closest to reflecting a hypothetical majority sentiment.

More populist institutions, such as juries and referenda, decrease the risk that decision makers will act against the will of the people, but they are costly and increase the risk that decisions will not reflect the best available informa-tion and analysis. This helps explain and justify the use of legislative commit-tees, administrative agencies, and courts. By channeling decisions to a rela-tively small number of individuals with a comparatively large amount of expertise, we ensure that decisions are made by those in the best position to assess the consequences of those decisions. The law of small numbers, how-ever, means that their decisions are not always representative. Institutional de-sign faces a fundamental trade-off between representativeness and expertise.

The project of government and political science has proceeded on the reason-able assumption that there is no objective way of ascertaining what the people would decide if only they were fully informed. The technology of prediction markets changes this assumption. Prediction markets can be used to predict, for example, the probability that a randomly selected person, after having an oppor-tunity to consider an issue fully, will conclude that a proposed policy would be beneficial. If market participants do not know who will be selected, they will try to divine what an average decision maker would conclude. The market will help to identify the most sincere predictor, likely to be someone who has a great deal of information about both the underlying issue and the underlying population from which the randomly selected individual will come.

Prediction markets do not eliminate the tradeoff between representative-ness and expertise altogether; we must still decide, for example, whether to pick a person at random from the population as a whole, or from a smaller body such as the legislature or the judiciary. But relative to alternatives, they enable decisions that are both relatively representative and relatively informed. We will also see that prediction markets can enable more principled decisions. Someone announcing how that person would resolve an issue may be more inclined to consider higher-order principles, such as fairness to minorities and consistency with precedent, when the decision will merely resolve a prediction market, in the sense of determining payouts, than when the decision will actually affect policy. Prediction market evaluations of policy alternatives can thus be faithful to a society's highest ideals.

My aim, of course, is not to suggest that we should discard institutions developed over hundreds of years in favor of unproven alternatives. We should not. But nor should we close our minds to the possibilities of democratic institutions structured in radically different ways from the ones that we now have. If these alternative institutions have advantages, then they can provide useful contributions in particular contexts. This book seeks to describe some relatively modest possible reforms using prediction markets, but it also envisions the most radical possible reforms. Only by comparing the most central of our existing institutions to prediction market alternatives can we identify most clearly the strengths and limitations of prediction markets. For today, this can and should be only an academic exercise; many of the ideas developed are theoretical and untested, although the book also discusses empirical evidence of existing prediction market designs. Much more experimentation would be necessary to refine these designs.

We cannot identify alternatives to complex institutions merely by repeated use of playground challenges. This book will show, however, how bets can serve as a foundational alternative to votes in the construction of institutions. For example, a principal goal of many institutions is to encourage deliberation that may sway the votes of, for example, jurors or senators. We will see how prediction markets can similarly encourage deliberation by requiring individuals to bet on whether they will be able to persuade others of their views. Similarly, we will see how combined series of bets can be used to produce not merely numeric predictions but also consensus "texts," much as governmental procedures lead to the creation of statutes, regulations, and judicial opinions. We will also see how prediction markets can be combined into a kind of "web" so that every assumption and calculation that underlies a prediction or policy evaluation can be explicitly identified and challenged.

The prediction market designs described in this book build on one another, with more complex designs generally introduced later in the book than more basic designs. Each chapter focuses primarily on a different institution or group of individuals that could benefit from prediction markets, with hypothetical prediction markets replacing the central institutions of government in the later chapters. The final chapter imagines predictocracy, a form of government in which prediction markets serve as the foundation for all decision making. My intent is not to endorse this form of government, and I occasionally note the dangers associated with abandoning the status quo. Prediction markets offer the possibility of a new way of thinking about structuring decision making, and this approach can be used for problems large and small.

Acknowledgments

Like prediction markets, this book was a group project. I thank those who have read the manuscript and offered comments: Amitai Aviram, Scott Baker, Donald Braman, Naomi Cahn, David Bernstein, Robert Hahn, Robin Hanson, Peter Siegelman, Maxwell Stearns, and Geoffrey Woglom. I have also benefited from the editorial support of Michael O'Malley, from the secretarial support of Padmaja Balakrishnan and Carrie Davenport, from research assistance by Greg Leon, Nancy Hoffman, and Daniel Stabile, and from the institutional support of the George Washington University Law School. For information about corporate prediction market projects, I thank Ilya Kirnos of Google, David Pennock of Yahoo! Laboratories, Todd Proebsting of Microsoft, Emile Servan-Schreiber of NewsFutures, and Adam Siegel of Inkling Markets. For data, I am grateful to Mike Knesevitch and Margaret Cruise O'Brien of TradeSports and to Justin Wolfers. Most of all, I am grateful to my family.

Although all of the writing in this book is new, it builds on a number of articles about prediction markets that I published previously: Michael Abramowicz, *Market-Based Administrative Enforcement*, 15

YALE J. ON REG. 197 (1998) (providing an early version of the market-based adjudication proposal discussed in Chapter 8 of this book); Michael Abramowicz, *The Law-and-Markets Movement,* 49 AM. U. L. REV. 327 (1999) (offering a general overview of the use of market mechanisms in legal institutions, including auctions, self-assessment, and exchange mechanisms); Michael Abramowicz, *Cyberadjudication,* 86 IOWA L. REV. 533 (2001) (discussing hypothetical institutions that resemble the market-based adjudication proposal described in Chapter 8 and the market web proposal and the self-resolving prediction markets described in Chapter 10); Michael Abramowicz, *Information Markets, Administrative Decisionmaking, and Predictive Cost-Benefit Analysis,* 71 U. CHI. L. REV. 933 (2004) (explaining how administrative agencies might use prediction markets, e.g., in conducting cost-benefit analysis, as discussed in Chapter 6); Michael Abramowicz, *Predictive Decisionmaking,* 92 VA. L. REV. 69 (2006) (introducing the concept of predictive decision making, discussed in Chapter 5); Michael Abramowicz, *Deliberative Information Markets for Small Groups,* in INFORMATION MARKETS: A NEW WAY OF MAKING DECISIONS 101 (Robert W. Hahn and Paul C. Tetlock eds., 2006) (explaining how prediction markets can encourage deliberation, as discussed in Chapter 4); Michael Abramowicz and M. Todd Henderson, *Prediction Markets for Public Corporations,* 82 NOTRE DAME L. REV., 1343 (2007) (assessing the applicability of prediction markets to public corporations, as discussed in Chapter 7); Michael Abramowicz, *The Hidden Beauty of the Quadratic Market Scoring Rule: A Uniform Liquidity Market Maker, with Variations,* J. PREDICTION MARKETS (forthcoming).

Chapter 1 The Media

If democratic institutions are tools for translating public opinion into public policy, then the most important institution might be the one that contributes most to forming public opinion in the first place: the media.[1] Constitutional protections for free speech and a free press such as the First Amendment to the U.S. Constitution seem to reflect a view that allowing uncensored speech will promote truth and, indirectly, good governance.[2] Perhaps the most articulate expression of this view is Oliver Wendell Holmes's famous statement, "The best test of truth is the power of the thought to get itself accepted in the competition of the market."[3] The metaphor of the marketplace draws its appeal from the premise that competition in the economic sphere generally works, with superior products emerging from the choices of consumers. Yet even those who accept the general claims of such market enthusiasts as Adam Smith and Friedrich Hayek recognize the existence of market failures. Markets for ideas can fail, too, and the result can be broader failures in democratic governance.

Why might markets for ideas fail? A simple answer is that many members of the public will generally be ignorant about particular issues and underlying theoretical frameworks, often rationally so.[4] Acquisition of information requires time and money. Just as economic markets can lead to suboptimal results because of imperfect information,[5] so, too, can limited background knowledge make accurate evaluation of new claims about the world extraordinarily difficult. So it is not surprising that surveys indicate that the public's views about issues often differ from the views of those who might be considered experts. For example, survey evidence suggests that economists generally believe that trade agreements between the United States and other countries have helped create more jobs in the United States, whereas the public generally believes that such agreements have cost American jobs.[6] The direction of this discrepancy should not be surprising. Stories about people losing jobs are more engaging than stories about people gaining jobs from trade, and so some doses of media may make people more ignorant than they would be in the absence of any media.[7]

The media, of course, cannot be expected to fix all cognitive errors among the public. When the media accurately report information, the public may pay little attention. For example, although the media presumably accurately report the identities of congressional candidates, in many elections the vast majority of voters cannot name a single congressional candidate in their district,[8] let alone give information about voting patterns. And if the media could succeed in informing the public with facts of this type, they cannot hope to replace the educational system in providing background knowledge and skills necessary for making relatively informed voting decisions. All is not lost, and some political scientists argue that voters still are able to make rational decisions.[9] Nonetheless, it should not be too idealistic to hope that the media, though constrained by the need to entertain, would generally seek to improve the knowledge of the viewing and reading public.

The media, however, may be hesitant to provide information about the consensus views of experts concerning particular issues because there may be controversy about what the consensus is. Ironically, a desire to promote objectivity sometimes may interfere with attempts to provide accurate information. When an issue is contested, a media outlet perhaps can best achieve the goal of objectivity by presenting both sides of the issue. The public, however, often cannot identify which argument is more true and compelling. Suppose, for example, that a news program about crime features one expert who contends that crime rates in a particular city will soon rise and another who contends that crime rates will soon fall. Even a criminologist or a statistician might need to spend hours evaluating the literature to assess the relative strength of the competing arguments. The public might benefit from a statement by the news program that three-quarters of the experts contacted subscribed to one view. Understandably, however, journalists are reluctant to report the results of such unscientific polls, yet lack the resources to conduct more sophisticated polls of experts, assuming that they could find an objective definition of who should count as an expert.

With regard to some issues, "just the facts" may be all the public needs, but in many cases an important fact may be what the consensus opinion about the issue is or whether such a consensus exists. This chapter suggests that prediction markets can provide objective gauges of expert consensus for the media to pass along to the public. My claim is not that prediction markets provide the best possible predictions, overcoming all irrationality. Indeed, individual experts sometimes might be able to beat markets. But experience suggests that prediction markets are generally fairly accurate, and at least they provide incentives for those who could beat the market to push predictions in a sensible direction.

I begin by describing a relatively simple structure for a prediction market that can be used to estimate the probability that a particular event will occur. After recounting the experiences of perhaps the most famous prediction market, the nonprofit Iowa Electronic Markets (IEM), I describe a more general type of numeric prediction market that the IEM also uses. Although it has focused primarily on predicting the outcomes of elections, prediction markets conceivably can be used to predict virtually any outcome, and the for-profit Web site Tradesports.com has used them to predict the results of athletic contests and a range of other events. A prediction market is not the only possible prediction technology—pari-mutuel wagering has long been shown to produce predictions about horse racing—but this chapter argues that prediction markets offer considerable advantages. They also present unique challenges, and I assess the danger that they might be manipulated. Finally, I suggest how the media might use prediction markets to provide better information to readers and viewers.

THE PROBABILITY ESTIMATE
PREDICTION MARKET

Prediction markets may take many forms, and some of the designs for prediction markets that this book considers might not merit being described as markets at all. The term *prediction market*, however, is descriptively accurate at least as applied to the design most prevalent today, which I call the "probability estimate prediction market." As the name suggests, its purpose is to produce a certain type of information, in particular, an estimate of the probability of a designated event. In most markets goods or services are exchanged for money, and the price provides a kind of information, specifically about the value of the good being exchanged relative to the value of other goods. The real purpose of the market, however, is to facilitate the exchange, with the price simply a by-product of the actions of market participants. In a prediction market, by contrast, the exchanges themselves will generally have no economic function (except in some cases for hedging purposes; see Chapter 3). A prediction market's purpose is to produce a price that the creator of the prediction market finds useful.

Consider, for example, a subject that recently was of great import: whether the actress Angelina Jolie and the actor Brad Pitt will marry. Suppose that *Us Weekly* wished to provide its readers with the most accurate information possible about the probability that a marriage would result by January 1, 2010. Of course, *Us Weekly* presumably wants to present its readers with a range of relevant information, such as reports of supposed friends and analyses by body language experts who scrutinize photographs of celebrities as they seek to escape from the paparazzi. But it might also want to provide a concrete number, an estimate of those in the know of the chance that the marriage really will happen. This would be useful both for readers in a hurry and for readers who are unsure of their own ability to weigh the different pieces of evidence. Of course, *Us Weekly* might simply make up a number, but such numbers might seem arbitrary or sensationalistic. If it wanted to produce a more credible estimate, it might launch a probability estimate prediction market.

Here is how such a prediction market might work, placing aside for now concerns about whether creation of such a market in the United States would be legal (see Chapter 2): *Us Weekly* would sell two different kinds of tradable contract to the public, a marriage tradable contract and a no-marriage tradable contract. For example, it might hold an on-line auction for one hundred of each type of share. It would promise to issue a fixed payoff, say, one dollar, on January 1, 2010, depending on whether Jolie and Pitt in fact become married by that date. So, should they become the Jolie-Pitts by that date, each marriage tradable contract would be redeemable for one dollar on that date, but the no-marriage tradable contract would be worthless. On the other hand, should Jolie and Pitt not be married to each other by that date, then the no-marriage tradable contract would be redeemable for one dollar on that date, but the marriage tradable contract would be worthless. In announcing the prediction market, *Us Weekly* presumably would seek to limit the possibility of ambiguities, such as whether a marriage followed by a divorce would count. But if there were ambiguities, then *Us Weekly* would resolve them either after or before the payoff date.

The initial auction of such tradable contracts itself would produce some information that could help assess the tradable contracts. For example, suppose that the marriage tradable contracts sold for an average of about sixty cents, and the no-marriage tradable contracts sold for an average of about thirty cents. That would seem to indicate that the marriage share is considerably more likely than the no-marriage share to be redeemed for one dollar. Hazarding a specific probability from such information would be difficult, however. Perhaps the purchasers of the marriage tradable contracts are sentimentalists, willing to indulge their romantic notions for a collective total of sixty dollars. This is not a fully satisfactory answer, for it does not explain why the no-marriage tradable contracts did not sell for more. After all, if marriage seemed unlikely, at thirty cents each, the no-marriage shares would have been a bargain, and someone should have had an incentive to bid more for them. But given the inherent uncertainty of celebrity love lives, playing in the market carries some risk and demands some transactions costs, which include at least the time it takes to purchase and redeem shares. These factors can explain why the combined auction prices might be less than one dollar. Meanwhile, the possibility that individuals might obtain pleasure from holding tradable contracts independent of their financial value will tend to push prices up.

Whether the initial tradable contracts are distributed by auction or by some other means, the key to the prediction market is that holders of tradable contracts can sell them. Typically, an on-line exchange serves to facilitate such transactions. Someone interested in purchasing the marriage tradable contract could submit a "bid price," the price the potential purchaser would be willing to pay for that tradable contract. Someone interested in selling it could submit an "ask price," the price at which an owner of the tradable contract would be willing to sell it. Whenever a bid or an ask is submitted, the exchange would seek to pair the offer with another. For example, if I offer to sell a marriage share for sixty cents, and then you offer to buy a marriage share for up to sixty-five cents, the on-line exchange could then complete a transaction, presumably at sixty cents, since the offer to sell came first. When an offer does not immediately find a match, it is placed in a queue, with the best offers placed at the front of the queue. At any given time, the on-line exchange maintains a "bid queue" and an "ask queue." At the front of the bid queue is the most generous offer to buy, and at the front of the ask queue is the most generous offer to sell. The ask price will always be greater than the bid price, because when a new offer matches an existing one, a transaction is immediately completed. In economics, this arrangement is known as a continuous double auction.[10]

Just as the auction prices provide some indication of the probability of the Jolie-Pitt union, so, too, can the bid and ask prices provide some hint. For example, suppose that the bid price is fifty-five cents and the ask price is sixty cents. That would indicate that no one is willing to sell the tradable contract for less than sixty cents but that there are people willing to buy the tradable contract for fifty-five cents. If the event were viewed as having a significantly more than 60 percent chance of occurring, then one would think that someone would be eager to purchase the tradable contract for more than sixty cents. If the event were viewed as having a significantly less than 55 percent chance of occurring, then one would think that someone would be willing to sell for less than fifty-five cents. The midpoint of the bid and ask prices might thus provide at least a rough probability estimate, and this estimate may be averaged with the corresponding estimate from the no-marriage tradable contract. An alternative approach to deriving a probability estimate would be to base it on the most recent transaction or possibly on an average of several recent transactions. Either way, a significant advantage of a prediction market is that it will produce data that change over time as new information becomes available.

THE THEORETICAL CASE FOR
PREDICTION MARKETS

Risk and transactions costs might affect not only the amount that individuals will be willing to pay at auction but also their bid and ask prices in the subsequent market. But there is a strong theoretical reason to believe that prices derived from market activity will provide more reliable probability estimates than prices derived from the result of auctions. In an auction, sentimental considerations might easily bid up the marriage tradable contract, but such sentiment is unlikely to last over the long term in a market. If some market participants are merely unsophisticated sentimentalists, then more sophisticated players will bet against them, placing them at a disadvantage. Even if the sentimentalists have purchased all the Jolie-Pitt shares, the market could allow a third party to offer to sell additional shares. Such a third party would merely need to show the ability to pay one dollar per new share if in fact the shares are redeemed. Eventually, the unsophisticated parties will run out of money or, more likely, reach the limits of their celebrity affection. It is one thing to lose a few dollars, another to pour one's life savings into a bet against eager speculators. The result is that after a while, the bid and ask prices are increasingly likely to be determined by the actions of informed, rather than uninformed, parties.

This reflects a key aspect of prediction markets. Prices do not simply reflect an average assessment by a group but also reflect the degree of confidence that different members of the group have in their estimates.[11] Simply taking the average estimate of a group may work well for some problems but not for others. For example, Francis Galston studied a competition in which contestants guessed the weight of an ox; the average guess of the 787 contestants, 1,197 pounds, was only one pound short of the actual weight.[12] But when Cass Sunstein, a law professor, asked his colleagues to estimate the weight of the fuel that powers space shuttles, they gave a median answer of two hundred thousand pounds, far short of the actual answer of four million pounds.[13] People may on average systematically misestimate certain numbers, and even if a few people in a group know the correct answer, those people may have only a small impact on the average.

Because no one is forced to participate in a prediction market, those who participate tend to be those who have information relevant to the particular prediction or at least those who can obtain the information at low cost. Among participants, individuals who have the most information should be willing to place the most money at risk. It will not always work out this way, of course. Sometimes, someone who has relatively little information or erroneous information might nonetheless be bold and wager a great deal of money on a particular position. For example, someone might invest heavily after overhearing a conversation in which Pitt refers to Jolie as his wife, when others who heard the conversation realized that Pitt and Jolie were merely discussing their roles in the movie *Mr. and Mrs. Smith*. Other market participants might surmise wrongly that this trader has some valuable information and change their own initial probability assessments on the basis of this individual's trading.

Meanwhile, someone with excellent information will face some constraints on liquidity. For example, suppose a friend learned that Pitt and Jolie had agreed that they would flip a coin to determine whether to marry. Assuming the reliability of this information and the fairness of the coin, the friend could be sure that the correct probability is 0.5. This friend would probably want to purchase some no-marriage shares for thirty cents, and gradually that would move the price toward fifty cents. But unless the friend can credibly reveal the information to the world and liquidate the resulting financial position, this strategy is not guaranteed to produce profit. A purchase of the no-marriage share for thirty cents produces a 50 percent chance of a seventy-cent profit and a 50 percent chance of a thirty-cent loss. A risk-averse individual might take this deal but decide to stop buying once the no-marriage share reached forty-five cents. Willingness to invest depends both on a trader's assessment of the quality of the trader's information and on the trader's liquidity, so mistaken self-assessments and liquidity constraints can lead market prices astray.

The case for a probability estimate prediction market thus cannot be that it will somehow produce perfect information. Such a market cannot tell us for sure whether Pitt and Jolie will marry. And we cannot even be sure that the probability estimate that the market produces will be the best one possible based on existing information. Theory suggests, however, that a probability estimate prediction market can serve as a relatively simple technology for aggregating individual probability assessments. Self-assessments of information quality seem likely to be at least correlated with actual information quality, and so a prediction market in effect provides a mechanism for weighing the estimates of a group of individuals based on the information that members of the group possess. The financial incentives of prediction markets ensure that forecasts will reflect genuinely held beliefs. Prediction markets reflect the intuition that when someone puts his money where his mouth is, he has greater credibility than when he does not.

The question remains: How good a technology for producing probability estimates is the probability estimate prediction market? There are, after all, competing approaches. One could seek to identify a group of individuals who might have relevant information or who are experts in the field and survey them. Perhaps a few phone calls to friends of Pitt and Jolie would produce more accurate estimates. Of course, a prediction market participant might make such calls, but there is no guarantee that the market prediction will take this information into account to the optimal degree. Even if prediction markets are superior to alternatives such as surveying experts, another prediction market design might be preferable to the probability estimate prediction market. If *Us Weekly* ever were to accept such markets, they would likely need to become far more commonplace, but for this to occur, there must be empirical evidence that the probability estimates that they produce are accurate.

Generating reliable evidence about the accuracy of probability estimate prediction markets, however, is not easy. The occurrence of an event cannot show that a probability estimate of that event was correct or incorrect. Suppose, for example, that the Pitt-Jolie market predicts with 99 percent confidence that they will marry. If they do marry, that provides some reassurance, but perhaps the result is a mere coincidence. And if Pitt and Jolie do not get married, that might appear to cast substantial doubt on the market. But it could be that the 99 percent estimate was reasonable based on information available at the time, and the 11 percent possibility has come to pass. Probability estimate prediction markets are not able to miraculously anticipate that events that would seem unlikely to anyone with the relevant information in fact will come to pass. The best hope for them is that their probability estimates will be better than alternatives'. We can only reliably gauge the accuracy of probability estimate prediction markets after much experience with them.

IOWA ELECTRONIC MARKETS
AND TRADESPORTS

We can obtain an approximate sense of the accuracy of probability estimate prediction markets by eyeballing them. Let us consider the most venerable collection of prediction markets, the Iowa Electronic Markets, created by professors at the business school at the University of Iowa. Although the IEM features a range of prediction markets, the most famous involve elections. Perhaps most interesting are the "winner-take-all" markets for presidential elections, which work essentially in the same manner as the hypothetical Pitt-Jolie market described above. The only difference is that shares are not distributed via an initial auction. Rather, anyone who wishes to participate may pay one dollar in exchange for a collection of tradable contracts corresponding to all possible outcomes. For example, in the 2004 presidential election, paying one dollar would entitle a participant to a Democratic share (in effect, a John Kerry share) and a Republican share (in effect, a George W. Bush share).[14] The market promised to pay one dollar on whichever share corresponded to the candidate who won a majority of the popular votes received by the two parties.[15] In economic jargon, the market involved trading of Arrow-Debreu securities, that is, securities that pay off if and only if a particular event occurs.

Figure 1.1 illustrates the prices at which contracts last traded in the market at the end of each trading day.[16] It is clear that the prices of the Bush and the

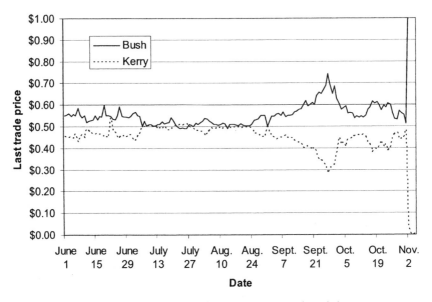

Figure 1.1. Prediction market assessments of the 2004 U.S. presidential election

Kerry shares are virtual (though not perfect) mirror images of each other. This alone is not enough to validate the results, of course, but if the Bush and the Kerry shares appeared to move inconsistently, that might furnish an argument that prediction market predictions appear irrational or random. The price lines also appear rational when compared against actual events in the election campaign. Although they cover only four months of the election cycle, the price lines appear at least roughly to correspond to the candidates' chances of victory as indicated by the polls. Figure 1.2 shows Bush's polling share (excluding undecided or third-party voters) for all major national polls.[17] The race appeared to be quite close until Bush began to take a lead at about the beginning of September, possibly in part as a result of aggressive advertising by a group called Swift Boat Veterans for Truth that questioned Kerry's record in the Vietnam War, though this lead dwindled through mid-October. The spikes in figure 1.1 are greater than the spikes in figure 1.2 because a small difference in poll numbers can result in a large difference in probabilities. Had Bush been leading Kerry 60 percent to 40 percent in the polls, after all, his victory would have been virtually certain on Election Day. Electoral trends are somewhat easier to deduce with the prediction market forecasts of figure 1.1 than with the polls of figure 1.2, because trends are accentuated and because there is less noise from anomalous polling results.

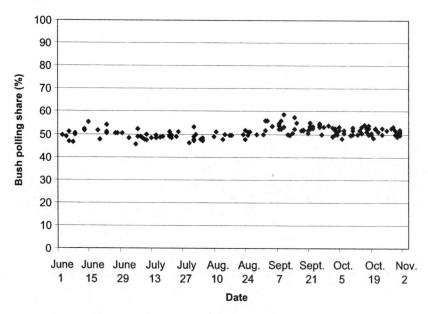

Figure 1.2. Polls taken during the 2004 U.S. presidential election campaign

A better assessment of overall predictive accuracy can be obtained by comparing predictions with results across a range of markets. Figure 1.3 reports results from twenty-five winner-take-all markets sponsored by the Iowa Electronic Markets. Wolfers and Zitzewitz collected data about the last trade each day for each tradable contract in each of these markets, producing a total of more than twenty-three thousand observations.[18] For each one-percentage-point market price interval, they then counted the proportion of times the event being predicted in fact occurred. For example, if prediction markets are accurate, then one would expect contracts priced at about fifty cents to result in payoffs about 50 percent of the time and contracts priced at about eighty cents to result in payoffs about 80 percent of the time. The data appear to reflect this expectation. Higher contract prices appear to bear an approximately linear relationship to probabilities. For comparison purposes, figure 1.3 includes a forty-five-degree line that would represent perfect prediction accuracy.

Figure 1.3 does show a variety of anomalies. But this is because in a sample of only twenty-five elections, a few unexpected election outcomes or dramatic shifts mid-election can affect a relatively large number of data points. Figure 1.4 thus shifts from the Iowa Electronic Markets to TradeSports, a for-profit exchange that includes trading on a wide variety of events, including athletic

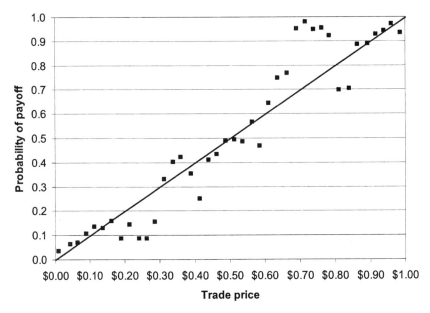

Figure 1.3. Trading in 25 Iowa Electronic Markets (adapted from Justin Wolfers and Eric Zitzewitz, *Five Open Questions About Prediction Markets, in* INFORMATION MARKETS: A NEW WAY OF MAKING DECISIONS, at 24 fig. 2–2)

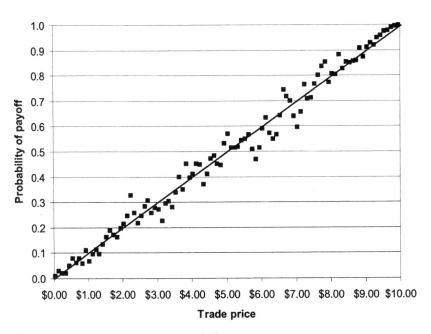

Figure 1.4. Trading on Major League Baseball games in 2005

and political contests. For example, for a particular baseball game, TradeSports might include contracts concerning whether a particular team will win, whether the total score will exceed a particular number, and whether a particular team will win by at least a specified number of points. It thus serves as a market alternative to more traditional forms of sports betting. Figure 1.4 reflects 145,388 trades on a total of 1,508 contracts determined by the outcome of Major League Baseball games that TradeSports decided to feature in 2005. With this larger sample, the data appear to reflect more consistently the forty-five-degree line that one would expect if prices can be interpreted as probabilities.[19]

Two significant caveats are worth making. First, we cannot guarantee that the regularities observed in this case will be perfectly replicated in other markets. In an analysis of 384,655 trades on National Football League games over the course of three seasons, Richard Borghesi found some small but systematic anomalies.[20] Borghesi found that on average, prices decreased from early values by approximately 3.42 ticks (34.2¢ on a $10 contract), indicating that bettors generally are overly optimistic about the probability that the contract will pay off, that is, that the named team will win. By combining TradeSports data with play-by-play football data, Borghesi shows that the market tends to underreact to information. In the minute following a touchdown, the market continues the rise caused by the touchdown itself, and, indeed, the trend continues for another nine minutes, with additional average increases in price for a touchdown for the named team of 0.14 ticks. Although these findings are statistically significant, they imply only small deviations from accurate probability estimates, so prices still can be said at least roughly to reflect probabilities. One possible explanation for the poor performance of these markets relative to the markets illustrated in figure 1.4 is that the figure includes only "featured games," which may have higher liquidity and receive more careful attention from traders.

Second, that the prices of contracts reflect probabilities does not mean that the prediction market is particularly accurate. If for each of a large number of athletic contests I made a trade at fifty cents on a randomly selected team, then I would win about 50 percent of the time (and lose a great deal of money on a Web site that charges commissions). Although it could be said that my trades reflect accurate probabilities, they reflect guesses or no information at all. Given prices that correspond closely to probability estimates, the higher the proportion of trades on the extremes of a probability distribution, the more confidence a prediction market will inspire. For example, if the predictions implied by prices for a season's baseball games were almost all below five cents or above ninety-five cents a day before the games, and those prices still turned out to reflect actual probabilities, that would either be truly impressive or reveal an unusually imbalanced level of baseball competition. It is possible to derive formulas that can be used to compare sets of probability predictions (see Chapter 4), but in the absence of a set of predictions from some other source to compare to those used by TradeSports, one cannot say whether these are particularly good or particularly bad.

What one can say with confidence is that if there are methodologies that can produce predictions considerably better than those used by TradeSports, the gap should narrow over time. The reason is that someone with a superior methodology has a profit incentive to trade on TradeSports. If the methodology is superior, then it should be profitable. The trading on the methodology might have at least some effect on prices of transactions not involving the party practicing the methodology, if third parties take the trades into account in formulating their own probability assessments. If trades have no effect on prices of transactions by other traders, then the individual with the better methodology will make more and more money over time and presumably will be willing to risk progressively higher amounts in the market. Eventually, then, this trader would be responsible for a high volume of trading. Betting pursuant to a successful methodology will nudge market predictions in the direction suggested by that methodology.

This does not mean that at any given time the predictions of TradeSports will be better than what any given person could produce. Because of commission charges and the costs of risk, one will only have an incentive to place bets when one's methodology allows for a considerable improvement in the market price. It will not be worth paying a commission of four cents per tradable contract to improve a prediction by less than four cents per tradable contract. But given current commission levels, a risk-averse participant will generally trade on information when the bet will improve the probability by 0.8 percentage points or more.[21] This suggests that, at least if trading on a prediction market actually occurs at regular intervals, the prices at which the trades occur should be close to the best that can be produced by any other known method, on average and in the long run. Sometimes, someone might be hesitant to trade because of uncertainty about whether the market price already incorporates insights from the methodology, but at least those with the best information will trade when they have reason to believe that market prices appear markedly wrong.

The strongest theoretical defense of prediction markets is that traders can profit from information suggesting that the market price is wrong, yet at any given time they have not done so. Current trading prices in prediction markets in which considerable trading occurs provide roughly accurate estimates of the probability that a designated event will occur. One caveat is that at any given time, some traders might be able to beat the market with careful analysis. But there may be no uncontroversial way of identifying the people who are most likely to do so, and a prediction market allows these market-beaters to push the market price in the right direction up to the limits of their risk tolerance. Another caveat is that prediction markets are superior only to *known* methodologies, and it is possible that other predictive institutions might produce better results. But prediction markets provide at least a modest financial incentive for individuals to identify better methodologies and apply them.[22]

It is interesting that prediction markets have proved successful even in the absence of a financial incentive. Some prediction markets use "play money" or virtual currencies rather than real cash, in part because of regulatory obstacles to real-money markets. And yet many of those play-money markets have been shown to have considerable success. For example, four economists compared the accuracy of NewsFutures, which uses play money, with TradeSports in predicting the outcome of National Football League games in 2003 and found that neither performed better than the other.[23] Similarly, the Hollywood Stock Exchange, a play-money market that predicts the box office returns of various Hollywood movies, has been shown to fare well in comparison with expert predictions.[24] Of course, this success might be attributable in part to the intrinsic interest of football and movies and might not be replicable for issues without substantial interested populations. For participants on these exchanges, play money had real value. Where it is not feasible to create a real-money prediction market, a play-money prediction market under certain circumstances might provide an equivalent means of aggregating public opinion. It seems doubtful that this will work, however, for boring or mildly interesting issues.

PARI-MUTUEL WAGERING

The probability estimate prediction market represents an improvement over what might have been the best earlier approach for aggregating bets on a particular outcome: pari-mutuel wagering, commonly used in horse racing. In pari-mutuel wagering, a bettor can place money on any possible outcome. For example, in a horse race, a bettor could place $1 on a particular horse that the bettor predicts will win the race. All bets are pooled, and after the race sponsor takes a percentage commission, the remaining money is distributed to the individuals who bet on the correct outcome. For example, suppose that $10,000 was bet in all, but only $500 was bet on the winning horse. If the commission rate is 10 percent, then $9,000 remains to be distributed among the individuals who collectively paid $500, so $18 is paid out for every $1 invested, producing a profit of $17.[25]

Pari-mutuel wagering provides incentives similar to those provided by the probability estimate prediction market. In the latter, one can profit by buying low or selling high–that is, by identifying tradable contracts that are mispriced. In pari-mutuel wagering, one may profit by betting on an outcome that too few people have bet on. For example, if a horse player expects that there is a 10 percent chance that a horse will win but less than 10 percent of the money in the pool has been placed on that horse, then the horse player might have an incentive to bet on the horse, depending on whether the difference is sufficiently large to outweigh the expected commission. If pari-mutuel wagering works sufficiently well, less money will be gambled on long shots than on favorites. Given any particular commission, it is straightforward to convert odds into probability estimates; they are two different ways of expressing the same information.

Economic studies have shown that pari-mutuel wagering, indeed, is relatively efficient.[26] That is, just as probability estimate prediction markets provide numbers that, experience suggests, truly can be interpreted as probability estimates, so will odds tend to correspond to the expected probability that any particular horse will win. This is true also for more complicated bets involving relatively large numbers of outcomes, for example, the trifecta. In order to win the trifecta, a bettor must correctly predict the first-, second-, and third-place winners of the race. At least one anomaly, however, is apparent, even in bets on a single race. In general, favorites tend to produce better payoffs than long shots, controlling for the fact that more money will be wagered on favorites than on long shots.[27]

Some evidence suggests that this is the result of some type of human cognitive bias,[28] but there is also a relatively simple possible partial explanation.[29] Bettors with relatively good information, based on either superior analytical abilities or particular facts known only to a few, often bet at the last minute. Otherwise, other bettors might see heavier-than-expected betting on a particular horse and add their own bets on that horse to the pool, thus reducing the horse's odds. The horses that remain long shots after such last-minute betting can then be expected to return less per dollar bet than horses that attracted last-minute betting. A related point is that some bettors may be far more sophisticated than others. If a certain percentage of people bet on horses based on caprice or on flawed methodologies, more sophisticated bettors will have incentives to bet against them. The activity of the more sophisticated bettors should move the odds closer to true probability representations. Because of commissions, however, sophisticated bettors will not have an incentive to bet enough to compensate entirely for the actions of unsophisticated bettors.

There is an additional incentive to place pari-mutuel bets at the last minute: information can change, so one might as well make a final decision at the last possible moment. A particularly important type of information is the amount that other bettors will place on a particular outcome, so even if one is confident that one's probability assessment will not change before the start of a race, it may make sense to wait to determine which outcomes are relatively good bargains. This incentive to place bets at the last minute, however, suggests a significant weakness of pari-mutuel betting relative to prediction markets. Traders in a prediction market will generally have an incentive to trade on information at the earliest possible time, before the market has fully priced the information. As a result, probabilities in a prediction market should come close to reflecting all available information at any time. Moreover, the ability to buy and sell in a prediction market allows someone to profit on information without waiting for the conclusion of an event that might depend on many subsequent pieces of information as well. Someone who acquires information early can buy tradable contracts and then sell them once the information becomes generally known. With pari-mutuel betting, by contrast, some available information will not be priced efficiently until later, and bettors must wait for the event to conclude in order to profit on sound bets.

We will see that one could design a pari-mutuel betting scheme that, like a probability estimate prediction market, produces incentives for information aggregation over time (see Chapter 3). There is relatively little incentive, however, for race tracks to adopt such a scheme, because it does not matter to race tracks whether the odds at any given time are as accurate as they can be. The media, however, generally have an interest in reporting the best available information, even for topics such as horse racing. It is interesting that prediction markets for horse racing also exist (for example, on TradeSports), and so the information from such markets might well be valuable to bettors. I do not know of any study comparing early betting on TradeSports to early odds, but it seems possible that TradeSports might be a slightly more accurate predictor well before a race. Of course, because the total amount bet on such prediction markets is relatively small, bettors with private information still might choose not to reveal their information by participating in the prediction market, and so the final odds at the track might still better reflect the outcomes of the race than those offered by TradeSports.

At the least, newspapers that publish odds and betting lines for sporting events might consider publishing prediction market forecasts, especially when significant trading has occurred sufficiently in advance of the event to make the late edition. Newspapers sometimes claim that they publish odds for entertainment purposes. However dubious this claim, a sports fan might derive some value from obtaining predictions of upcoming events. Of course, prediction markets may suffer from a chicken-and-egg problem; newspapers will not publish prediction market results when readers do not understand what they mean or think them relevant, and readers will not learn when newspapers will not publish. Someday, though, it is quite possible that prediction market predictions will earn a place in the morning sports pages beside the scores and the standings.

Sports pages might also include prediction market trading on past events. TradeSports allows betting not only before but also during athletic contests; pari-mutuel wagering, by contrast, cannot occur during the event. In a graph representing prediction market trading, the price lines show the progress of a game. Consider, for example, figure 1.5, which reports the TradeSports prices from a basketball game in which the favorite initially fell behind and then staged a comeback, winning in overtime. In contrast, a game in which the favorite performs about as expected can be visualized as more or less a straight line rising slightly to the maximum payoff (which, in TradeSports, is ten dollars rather than one dollar per contract). The more ups and downs the line has, the more exciting the game. In the game represented in figure 1.5, the excitement began only shortly before the two-hour mark. It may be a long time before readers of the sports pages do what readers of the business pages often do: look at a price graph for a snapshot of the day's news. But such graphical representation can leave the media to focus on what the graph cannot convey: the individual plays and performances that make sports more interesting to watch than stock tickers.

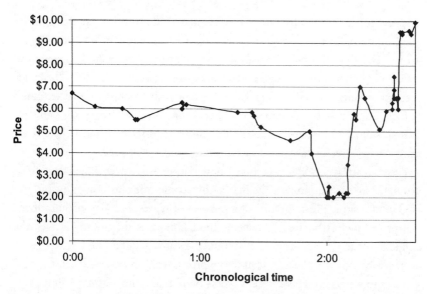

Figure 1.5. Trading on a basketball game (Phoenix Spurs vs. Sacramento Suns, November 8, 2006)

THE PROBLEM OF HEURISTICS AND BIASES

Consistent reporting of prediction market predictions and trends could demystify the sports pages, reducing events that require much attention today to mere blips on a market chart. Some prediction markets on TradeSports, for example, predict not the result of individual games but the outcome of entire seasons. For example, before the beginning of the Major League Baseball season, a contract is issued for each baseball team, to pay off only if the team ultimately wins the World Series. The prices at which these contracts are traded thus provide estimates of the probabilities that individual teams will win. Observing the line reflecting the price at which any team trades provides a snapshot of the season as a whole, but the lines may suggest less drama than fans might expect. Sports reporting tantalizes readers with suggestions that a dramatic comeback victory or unexpected collapse might be turning points in a season, but to prediction markets, these are often ho-hum.

This provides at least informal support for the proposition that prediction markets might help overcome heuristics and biases that ordinarily might distort human probability estimates. When a team has a winning streak, each of the wins matters in the standings, and one's estimate of the team's quality should correspondingly increase. But some fans might believe that streaks are more significant than they are. Conventional wisdom in sports, after all, has long supported the notion that a player with a "hot hand" will be more likely to succeed than the player's season and career numbers would suggest, but economists appear to have debunked this with statistical research.[30] The belief in the hot hand, as well as the related overemphasis among fans of the significance of a streak, is an example of what is sometimes known as the "clustering illusion,"[31] a tendency among some humans to see a pattern where none exists, where really there is nothing more than a sequence of independent events. The relative stability of prediction market prices over time provides informal evidence that in part the market overcomes the clustering illusion.

The clustering illusion is one of a number of biases that may affect individual probability estimates. Among the most famous is the hindsight bias, the tendency of individuals to see actual outcomes as more likely ex ante than they in fact were.[32] Other biases include the primary and recency effects, the tendencies to weigh initial and recent events more than other events. Another fallacy to which sports fans might be particularly susceptible is the illusory correlation bias, the tendency to infer causation from a correlation, for example, giving a new coach credit for a team's changing fortunes. Many of these biases may be related to what is perhaps the most important bias, the availability error,[33] the tendency to place too much weight on events that are easily accessible in memory. A baseball fan, for example, is more likely to remember a player's dramatic home run than the many instances in which the player grounded out to the shortstop. As a result, the fan might overestimate the probability of another home run. Although a fan knows that a player with a .350 batting average and a .400 on-base percentage is more likely than not to make an out in any given plate appearance, it does not seem that way.

Overcoming biases afflicting sports fans might not promote the welfare of news consumers. But overcoming biases can be of greater importance. Timur Kuran and Cass Sunstein have argued that the availability error leads to bad policy consequences and that the media play a major role.[34] For example, Kuran and Sunstein claim that the publicity surrounding Love Canal, a neighborhood built on a landfill containing chemical waste, had no basis in science. Residents and other observers placed too much weight on individual instances of health problems, disregarding studies indicating that the overall level of health problems was not statistically anomalous. The media then reported the concerns, raising the availability of the health problems in public discourse and furthering mistaken risk perceptions by the public. Kuran and Sunstein label the effect an "availability cascade." Whether or not they are right about

Love Canal, the example demonstrates how the media can aggravate public misperceptions. Potentially aggravating availability cascades are reputational cascades, in which media and other experts conclude that agreeing with the consensus will promote their career prospects.[35]

Journalists generally admit to having at least one bias: a preference for stories with news to stories without news. The local evening news thus reports on several incidents of fire and crime but rarely on people who emerged from a given day comparatively unscathed. The evidence for the availability heuristic suggests that the public as a result will overestimate the probability and prevalence of the events that tend to lead to news reports. The media, of course, sometimes might counteract this tendency by reporting hard facts. Sometimes hard facts will make a less vivid impact than more sensational news stories, but they tend to move individual probability assessments in the right direction. There are not always hard facts to report, however, especially when the media report on the possibility of future risks. If prediction markets help overcome individual cognitive biases, consistent reporting on prediction market predictions might help.

The empirical question is the extent to which prediction markets do overcome cognitive biases. Early evidence suggests that prediction markets do not succeed altogether in vanquishing them. Paul Tetlock, for example, analyzed pricing in TradeSports markets to determine whether the market overcame the favorite–long shot bias. He also tested for what is known as the reverse favorite–long shot bias, an observed tendency of baseball and hockey wagering markets to underprice teams that are not favored to win.[36] He found both. The favorite–long shot bias dominated for very unlikely events, and the reverse bias occurred in middle probability ranges.[37] He also found evidence of "return reversals."[38] That is, after the market initially moves in a particular direction following the appearance of new information, it is likely to move partway in the opposite direction afterwards. This indicates overreaction to new information, which might be attributable to the availability heuristic.

Such evidence disproves any claims that prediction markets are completely free of cognitive biases. Nonetheless, it is possible that other methods of deriving consensus probability estimates—such as asking sports fans their opinions—might be more prone to error. There is at least a theoretical reason to believe that prediction markets should help alleviate biases. Individuals with more sophisticated models for assessing probabilities generally have greater self-confidence about their predictions and thus greater willingness to place bets on prediction markets when those models suggest that current prices are inaccurate. Indeed, some sophisticated market players might focus consciously on the specific types of cognitive errors that are likely to produce poor probability assessments and trade against them. Tetlock's analysis suggests a particular betting strategy to take advantage of the reverse favorite–long shot bias that, he estimates, would produce phenomenal positive returns of 10 percent after commissions. The strategy requires buying contracts that have recently experienced bad news and selling those that have recently experienced good news. If Tetlock is correct, then someone who is persuaded by his analysis will implement this betting strategy, and prediction market pricing should improve. This may not happen overnight, because every trader must worry that others are already trading using the strategy, but it seems likely to occur eventually.

If prediction markets do help counteract biases, it will be a long time before media reporting of the results of prediction markets will significantly affect public policy. For starters, only a relatively small number of prediction markets currently exist, at least outside the area of sports. These may do little to correct important public misperceptions. The many markets predicting the results of elections, for example, may have little public value aside from testing prediction market mechanisms. Consumers of media might invest a great deal of time reading about election contests, but biases in predictions of the outcomes of such contests likely have relatively little consequence for the world. Ultimately, if the media are to play an important democratic function, it cannot be merely by telling the public who will win elections; it must be also by telling the public what it can expect in the future.

Prediction markets forecasting the probabilities of different possible news events might be considerably more useful if the public learned to understand both their abilities and their limitations. For example, figure 1.6 reports the trading prices in prediction markets used to predict whether weapons of mass destruction would be found in Iraq at various points after the U.S. invasion of that country.[39] On one hand, the graph shows that probability estimates can lead people astray. At the beginning of May, the market expected that such weapons probably would be found by the end of September, yet they were not. This should not, however, necessarily be seen as an indictment of prediction markets, for the general reason that prediction markets are not wrong merely because low-probability events end up occurring. Although the market would have been more impressive if it had bucked the conventional wisdom and proved correct, at least the market approximately conveyed the conventional wisdom of people who were relatively well informed, based on the information then publicly available.

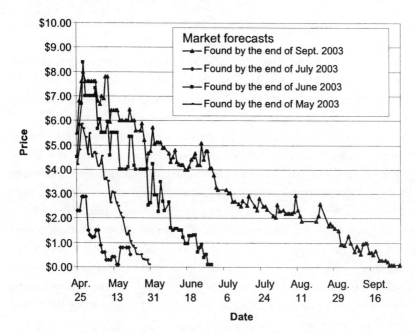

Figure 1.6. Probability that weapons of mass destruction would be found in Iraq

More important, at any given time, both the graph of trading prices and the current trading price tells a concise story. A reader, to be sure, might wish to read all of the publicly available information in order to develop an independent prediction of the probability that weapons would be found, and a reader willing to devote a great deal of effort to the task might expect to be able systematically to earn profits by trading on the information on the market. But some readers, if convinced that prediction markets provide at least approximate probability estimates, might prefer to consider the prediction market summary rather than all of the underlying information. When partisans on all sides of contested issues can be expected to seek to sway public opinion by offering confident predictions about the future, the media often have trouble objectively indicating what the expert consensus on the issue is, leaving readers to sort through an awesome quantity of data. These readers will be subject to the usual assortment of heuristics and biases, and they may therefore make systematic errors. By seeking objective means of aggregating expert views, the media can help overcome such errors. Reporting of prediction market results in particular will leave readers not only with probability estimates that in general should be more accurate than their own deductions but also with more time to read analyses of appropriate policy responses.

THE NUMERIC ESTIMATE PREDICTION MARKET

The prediction markets illustrated so far are designed to predict probabilities, but sometimes it is useful to aggregate individual predictions of numbers that are not probabilities, for example, how many games the New York Mets will win this year or how many people in Love Canal will die of cancer over the next ten years. A very simple solution is to divide the plausible range of numbers into intervals and to calculate the probability of each one. The intervals can but need not overlap. For example, TradeSports featured a set of contracts used to predict how many votes Judge Samuel Alito would receive on the floor of the Senate to confirm him as a justice of the U.S. Supreme Court. The six contracts specified that they would pay off if Alito received more than forty votes, more than fifty votes, more than sixty votes, more than seventy votes, more than eighty votes, and more than ninety votes. An alternative approach would have included contracts corresponding to the cases in which Alito received forty votes or fewer, from forty-one to fifty votes, from fifty-one to sixty votes, and so on.

These approaches are somewhat clunky, for they do not allow for an easy calculation of the average expected result. For example, on January 10, 2006, just after Alito's confirmation hearings began, the bid-ask midpoint for the "more than sixty" contract was 60.8, and for the "more than seventy" contract the midpoint was 15.2. That suggests that the market estimated a 45.6 percent chance that Alito would receive between sixty and seventy votes but provides little information about what the best estimate actually would be. A partial solution would be to offer additional contracts—more than sixty-two votes, more than sixty-four, and so on—but this, too, becomes cumbersome, in part because there might be few people interested in trading on each of these contracts. The interval approach does have its uses—it is the most straightforward way of determining, for example, the probability that a majority of senators will vote to confirm—but it is less useful when one is seeking a point estimate of the number of votes that Alito is likely to receive.

There is, however, a simple alternative. The prediction markets we have seen so far are binary—for example, paying off ten dollars per contract if the event occurs or not paying at all. But payouts can range depending on a number that is verifiable ex post. For example, TradeSports might have used this approach with Alito, promising to pay nothing if Alito received no votes, ten cents if Alito received one vote, and so on. Of course, it is particularly convenient that the Senate happens to have one hundred members at this time,

making each vote worth a dime. It will similarly be simple to design a prediction market that predicts a percentage. For example, in addition to sponsoring
"winner-take-all" markets, the Iowa Electronic Markets sponsors vote share
markets. Figure 1.7 shows the vote share market for the 2004 U.S. presidential
election. Each penny in closing price corresponds to an anticipated 1 percent
of the vote. Aside from a temporary spike in Kerry shares (to which I return
below), the anticipated outcome was remarkably stable, providing the appearance of an almost boring election cycle. Of course, the election was not boring, because the anticipated Bush and Kerry shares happened to be quite close
at some points in the election cycle. The graph, however, emphasizes that the
real fight was about a relatively small number of swing votes.

A numeric estimate prediction market can also be used to predict numbers
that will fall on a closed interval between numbers other than zero and one
hundred. One possibility, if the interval is a subset of that range, is simply to
use the same approach as the vote share market. For example, TradeSports includes shares that predict the number of games each team in the National
Basketball Association will win in a particular year's regular season. The maximum possible is eighty-two according to the current NBA schedule, but this
simply means that no one will rationally purchase a chance of a $10 payout for
a price above $8.20. Another possibility is to map the range linearly from zero

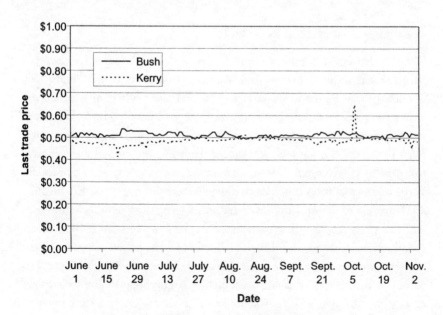

Figure 1.7. Predicted vote shares for the 2004 U.S. presidential election

to one hundred. So, for example, TradeSports might have provided that a tradable contract would pay off 1000/82 cents per win.

More generally, a prediction market can be used to predict *any* number that will become apparent at some later time. A prediction market could be used for a number that might turn out to be positive or negative. Either the interval can be translated to a more familiar one, such as zero to one hundred, or trading at negative prices could be allowed. If I purchased a tradable contract at minus five cents I would receive five cents from the seller. A prediction market also might be used to predict a number on an unbounded interval, say, from zero to infinity. The only problem is that if very high numbers become plausible, then the prediction market sponsor might be unable to pay off the contract, and individual traders might not be able to afford to engage in transactions. Thus, as a general matter, the trick is to translate a plausible range of numbers into a manageable contract size. The rules can always provide that if the actual number exceeds the maximum, then the payoff will be the maximum. For example, a prediction market might be used to predict how many points an NBA team will score in a season, with every hundred points paying off one cent. The rules could stipulate that ten thousand points or more will pay off one dollar. If this outcome is particularly unlikely, it should have little effect on the pricing.

THE ACCURACY OF PREDICTION MARKETS

The experience with the Iowa Electronic Markets for vote share suggests that such markets have relatively strong accuracy. In a paper considering fifteen elections, Joyce Berg and coauthors show that the markets on election eve were more accurate on average than were final preelection polls.[40] The average absolute error of a vote share forecast derived from the market price at midnight before the election was 1.49 percent,[41] whereas the average absolute error from the polls, averaged across all candidates and all polls, was 1.93 percent. Berg and her coauthors conclude that the markets therefore appear to be more accurate than the most widely available set of forecasting tools for elections.[42] Another study suggests that participants in the Iowa Electronic Markets respond rationally to new information.[43] Although the pattern of participants' responses indicates that their original assessments may have been biased, this pattern is insufficient to create a profitable trading opportunity. One might tentatively infer that prediction markets will give reasonably accurate predictions, at least in the election context, though some imperfections may remain.

Robert Erikson and Christopher Wlezien have sought to debunk the claimed superiority of prediction markets to polls, at least well in advance of elections.[44] Although on average the markets beat a naïve reading of polls, a more sophisticated methodology, discounting the favorite's lead on the basis of research indicating that leads tend to shrink, makes polls better than the market. One danger of this conclusion is that it is often possible after the fact to construct a model that produces high levels of accuracy. We cannot be sure that Erikson and Wlezien would have chosen the same methodology if forced to announce a prediction algorithm before the elections they surveyed. Their approach, however, does not appear particularly complicated, and it at least suggests that we should not be confident that market prices are better than any that might be derived using alternative techniques, such as the regression analysis that Erikson and Wlezien provide.

It would be a mistake, however, to conclude from Erikson and Wlezien's analysis that markets did a poor job of aggregating predictions. Their analysis of discounting of leads, after all, had not been performed prior to the election, and if it had been, reasonable observers might have differed about the extent to which past trends would continue into later elections. Erikson and Wlezien point out that given the volume of trading on the Iowa markets, their profit from trading on the strategy would have been quite low. Should they or others make available predictions based on their methodology in future elections, other traders making assessments might take these numbers into account in their own trading. Erikson and Wlezien say that polls "that are properly discounted for the favorite's inflated lead outperform the market," but the properly discounted numbers were not widely available at the time.

Prediction markets cannot necessarily be counted on to beat any other method of aggregating data and predictions. Laboratory experiments involving securities markets show that sometimes these markets do not reflect "rational expectations" by perfectly incorporating information.[45] For instance, Joyce Berg and Thomas Rietz found small inefficiencies in the Iowa Electronic Markets that could serve as the basis of a profitable trading strategy.[46] What makes prediction markets particularly useful for the media is that they are relatively objective while still accurate compared to other approaches to aggregation. Someone with an agenda, for example, promoting a particular candidate, might devise a statistical methodology that makes that candidate appear stronger than previously thought. And usually it is easy to find some basis for defending the methodology on the merits. A journalist is not in a good position to make decisions about whether the creators of a methodology were motivated by a desire to promote particular results or simply by a desire to develop the best predictions possible. And even if a journalist can be confident about objectivity, different objective people might reasonably take different approaches to arrive at different conclusions.

Of course, a prediction market can be seen as just another methodology, but at least it will not be easy to create a prediction market to promote a particular agenda. Robert Forsythe and coauthors have shown that although the participants in an early election market were predominantly Republicans, and though many participants only traded in favor of their preferred candidates, this did not produce a biased prediction.[47] Rather, enough people traded both for and against their preferred candidates that the demographics of the trader community did not have much effect. The traders who were particularly influential were more likely than other traders to place limit orders at prices slightly different from the market price. This suggests that if one opens a prediction market to a modestly large group of traders, one will not be able to affect the market price much by choosing a demographically unrepresentative sample. It will be particularly difficult to skew a prediction market generally available to traders on the Internet.

The great virtue, then, of prediction markets is not that they will always be more accurate than alternative future methodologies or existing ones. Rather, it is that prediction markets are relatively objective. At the same time, there is a strong theoretical reason to believe that prediction market participants will seek to take into account at least easily accessible data such as opinion polls.[48] By citing prediction market forecasts, a journalist can give a concise, consensus prediction, whether about an upcoming election or about any other event being forecast by a prediction market.

THE DANGER OF MANIPULATION

Though the creator of a prediction market cannot, absent fraud, guarantee a preferred result, there is a danger that individual traders in a prediction market might be able to manipulate forecasts. One way to do so would be to disseminate false information. To the extent that this approach is successful, it works because it changes individual probability assessments. Prediction markets sometimes might fail to filter out misinformation, but the more troublesome possibility is that someone might be able to manipulate the market by engaging in trades. Perhaps attempts at manipulation have been relatively uncommon in prediction markets because there is little to be gained from such attempts. A Yankees fan might like to manipulate a game to ensure a Yankees victory, but manipulating a prediction market to predict a Yankees victory seems unlikely to have any real-world consequences. Moreover, buying shares and pushing prices above their fundamental values is costly.

There might be prediction markets, however, that some individuals would like to manipulate.[49] Suppose, for example, that some voters decide whom to vote for in part based on whom they expect to win.[50] Further, suppose that some of these same voters base their predictions of who will win either directly or indirectly on prediction markets. It might then be in the financial or at least the ideological interest of some wealthy individuals to seek to manipulate prediction markets that forecast election returns. A significant investment in prediction markets might have the direct effect of causing financial loss, at least if prices immediately push back in the original direction. Such an investment, however, conceivably could affect the election if the results were readily available to the public. This scenario admittedly seems unlikely today given the lack of attention to prediction market forecasts, but the question remains whether prediction markets will remain effective if intense pressures exist to manipulate them.

There are theoretical and empirical reasons to believe that prediction markets can be manipulated in the short term. The theoretical point is simply that the number of orders on the bid and ask queues at any time is finite. Rational traders will limit their exposure to trading on bid and ask queues, since leaving offers on such queues opens traders to losses in the event that new developments make substantial changes in probability assessments. So, if I buy enough shares, I can buy not only all the shares available at the lowest quoted price but also some shares at the next higher price. At least at the moment the trade is completed, the last traded price will likely be different from the previous price, and the midpoint of the bid-ask spread will also rise. Indeed, for enough money, I should be able temporarily to drive the price to whatever level I please.

The empirical point is that there have been efforts to manipulate prediction markets. Such an attempt presumably explains the early October blip in Kerry shares visible in figure 1.7. Other attempts have been documented. For example, speculators briefly increased the value of Pat Buchanan shares in an Iowa Electronic Markets contest.[51] In addition, Paul Rhode and Koleman Strumpf document and analyze two sustained attempts to manipulate the TradeSports 2004 election markets on September 13 and October 15, 2004, leading to large price changes that do not appear to have been based on any information.[52]

Rhode and Strumpf show that such attempts at manipulation were nothing new. Precursors to modern election markets existed between 1880 and 1940,[53] and Rhode and Strumpf identify apparent attempts at manipulation in these early markets.[54] In all cases, the authors show that the effects of manipulation attempts on prices decreased over time.

Rhode and Strumpf also ran an interesting field experiment on the Iowa Electronic Markets during the 2000 presidential campaign.[55] At predetermined times, they made a total of eleven planned trades, determining at random the side in which to invest. On some occasions, Rhode and Strumpf bet only on one of the election markets (either vote share or winner take all), to determine whether the trade on one market contaminated the other. Such contamination indeed may have occurred in the minutes after the initial trade, though it was not statistically significant. On other occasions, Rhode and Strumpf attacked both election markets simultaneously. That approach might be expected to be more likely to convince other market participants that the trades were based on real information, because someone seeking to profit on new information is likely to bet on both markets. In all cases, Rhode and Strumpf demonstrate significant changes in the short term on the level of other participants' trades, but as hours passed, there was no effect. Planning random trades would appear to have no effect at all on prices twenty-four hours later.

These results are not surprising. There is relatively little "private" information about presidential elections, or at least relatively little that one could keep secret for very long. Someone playing the markets, therefore, would place relatively little emphasis in deciding what to do about trades made twenty-four hours earlier. Over time, the effects of trades should be expected to dissipate. But this is not entirely reassuring for two reasons. The first is John Maynard Keynes's observation that in the long run we will all be dead. The long run in this context is very short, but the short run is still long enough that manipulation conceivably could have some effect. This is particularly true if a market is expected to end at a particular time, so manipulation immediately prior to the market end might go unchecked. The second is that some prediction markets might depend on a relatively small number of traders who have a fair amount of private information or private analysis of public information. In such a market, a trader might put considerable emphasis on preceding trades.

Other experimental evidence, however, suggests that manipulation may be difficult even in a market in which private information exists, at least when market participants are aware of the incentives for manipulation. Robin

Hanson, Ryan Oprea, and David Porter ran an experimental market in which subjects traded an asset and received different information relevant to determining the value of the asset. Some randomly chosen traders were given an incentive to manipulate the market: they were promised that the higher the final market price, the higher the payout. All traders were aware that some traders were given an incentive to manipulate the market and knew whether the incentive was to manipulate prices up or down. Those who were given manipulation incentives in fact submitted higher bids, but this ultimately had no effect on market prices. Individuals who were not given manipulation incentives bid against the manipulators and drove the market prices down.

More generally, to the extent that traders know in advance that certain parties will have incentives to manipulate, they will have incentives to counteract such manipulation by seeking to push prices in the opposite direction. Indeed, Hanson et al. show that attempts to manipulate the market might *increase* market accuracy.[56] In securities markets generally, "noise traders," that is, traders who do not trade according to fundamentals, may increase market accuracy because informed traders can profit by trading against them. (In Chapter 7 we will encounter arguments that noise traders may decrease market accuracy.) Adding unidentifiable noise traders for any particular security may decrease accuracy, but noise traders as a whole should increase accuracy. In a prediction market, the larger the number of people who can be expected to trade in a market for reasons unrelated to fundamentals, the greater the incentives for others to enter the market, and the additional insight provided by these entrants should increase market accuracy. From the perspective of market efficiency, Hanson et al. argue, manipulators can be seen simply as noise traders.

Manipulation is more likely to succeed when market participants are not informed of the incentive of some participants to manipulate a market. An experiment by Martin Strobel confirms this.[57] The experiment used prediction markets to estimate the number of black balls and white balls in an urn. Different participants in the market were able to view different subsets of the balls. In some iterations of the experiment, a robot trader sought to manipulate the market in one direction. The results confirmed that the manipulation attempts did have a statistically significant effect in the expected direction. Market participants in this experiment cannot know whether someone with whom they are trading is trading on the basis of information or on the basis of a manipulation incentive. They thus ascribe some positive probability to the contingency that the trades reflect information, and this changes the assessment of market participants about the number of balls in the urn.

Manipulation seems likely to have a long-term effect on markets only to the extent that market participants misestimate the extent of attempts at such manipulation. For example, if market participants believe that there are probably individuals who are seeking to bid up market prices, these participants will respond by seeking to push prices in the opposite direction. But if in fact there are no manipulators, then this error will cause prices to be too low. On the other hand, if market participants underestimate the extent of market manipulation, that manipulation will be somewhat successful. In order to manipulate a market successfully, one has to attempt manipulation in higher volumes than other parties expect. This analysis suggests that manipulation might affect prediction market prices, but only to the extent that neutral market participants are genuinely fooled into misestimating others' private information. Prediction markets should continue to reflect consensus predictions, but misinformation through trading can have some effect. When the general level of manipulation is known but it is not known which tradable contracts have been targeted and in which direction, manipulation should increase overall average price accuracy while nonetheless succeeding at biasing the particular targeted results.

Manipulation may be the most serious obstacle to widespread adoption of prediction markets, but it will not tend to bias prices when the degree of incentives of participants to manipulate is known. It seems especially unlikely to be a problem where there is little private information and thus little derivatively informed trading, that is, where individuals' price assessments are not greatly affected by the trades of others. If manipulation is nonetheless deemed too serious a problem for some applications of prediction markets, there are two possible solutions. First, where there is a discrete group of potential manipulators, those individuals can be barred from participation. Of course, there is always a danger that these potential manipulators can pay off other market participants, but legal or contractual sanctions can reduce that possibility. Second, prediction markets might be limited to a group of authorized traders who are believed to have no incentive to manipulate the outcome.

NEWS YOU CAN USE

Regarding many topics, private information seems unlikely to be a significant concern, and few players will have sufficient financial incentives to seek to manipulate prediction markets anyway. In those cases, the media might consider publishing forecasts from prediction markets or perhaps sponsoring prediction markets. Media organizations, after all, have a long tradition of being involved in polling, so they can provide their readers and viewers with information that historically was not immediately available to those who view other news organizations' coverage. Legal restrictions might limit the ability of media organizations in the United States to sponsor prediction markets (see Chapter 2), but media organizations in other countries could consider creating such markets, and U.S. media might create prediction markets using play money.

Elections are among the most obvious subjects for media coverage of prediction markets, in part because many such markets already exist and in part because of the intense interest of the public in elections. Sports and entertainment markets (predicting winners of the Grammy Awards, for example) also seem like reasonable candidates. But the media in theory could create prediction markets on virtually any topic of interest to readers. Within the political arena, the media might create innovative new markets. For example, a market might predict what the president's approval rating will be at the end of the term. This would help counteract a tendency for approval ratings to be based largely on recent events. At some times, the purpose of approval ratings is to assess the president's recent performance, but at others, it might make sense to seek a long-term perspective. Or a market might predict whether particular legislation that is of interest to readers is likely to be passed. At the very least, prediction markets could supplement explicitly predictive coverage. For example, the *National Journal* runs a congressional insiders' poll that routinely shows vast discrepancies in predictions between Democrats and Republicans.[58]

Outside the political arena, there are many possibilities for prediction markets that could offer information that journalists ordinarily cannot easily provide with objectivity. For example, instead of simply reporting on what politicians and academics predict will be the number of troops that the United States will have in a particular country in the future, a newspaper might set up a numeric estimate prediction market. Or a probability estimate prediction market might be used to predict whether the United States will have withdrawn entirely from a country by a particular date. A prediction market might be used to forecast inflation or deflation in house sales in a particular geographical market at a particular time; this would at least provide a baseline that would contextualize quotations from alleged experts on the future of the housing market. Prediction markets might even be used to predict traffic patterns, the number of restaurants that will open in particular areas, or future test scores in school districts that are implementing reforms.

Chapter 2 Policy Analysts

The number of prediction markets that media organizations can be expected to sponsor in the future will in all likelihood be limited. Although it is possible to imagine a great number of topics regarding which prediction market predictions might be of interest to readers, a limited number of individuals may wish to bet on prediction markets. This is especially so if prediction markets are zero-sum games, in which sophisticated players systematically earn profits from those who are less sophisticated. At some point, one might expect the latter to wise up, though the number of sports gamblers in this country might suggest otherwise. At least, relatively few seem likely to participate in prediction markets on esoteric topics. Without these unsophisticated bettors to take advantage of, many sophisticated players will have little interest as well. This is unfortunate, because if prediction markets are to have the potential to improve democratic governance, it will not be by revolutionizing predictions about which team will win the World Series.

There are, however, many organizations committed to improving public policy through improved analysis, and some of these do so largely for free. These organizations include think tanks and even universities, particularly those specializing in fields such as economics, international relations, and law. I will refer to the group of scholars and other thinkers who engage in analysis relevant to public policy as "policy analysts." The world of policy analysts is a strange one. The analysis produced might be seen largely as a public good; if a professor publishes a new theory, it will be hard to exclude anyone from finding out about it, despite the availability of copyright protection, and the fact that one person has learned about the theory will in general not make the theory any less valuable to someone else. There is thus a case for governmental funding of some policy analysis, and indeed the government funds some analysis via grant programs and via contracts awarded to organizations such as the Rand Corporation. To a great extent, however, analysis is subsidized by private donors such as the sponsors of think tanks and wealthy alumni after whom chaired professorships are sometimes named. These donors indirectly provide a valuable resource to the public.

But how valuable is this resource really? Even many policy analysts who believe that they are making important scholarly contributions might not be confident in concluding that they are providing sufficient value to the world to justify from a social standpoint the portion of their salaries that might be attributable to research. Some might nonetheless take some satisfaction in the conclusion that their research would make the world a better place, if only others would adopt their suggestions. Others might acknowledge that their individual contributions will not have direct consequences but take pride in working out details of a broader intellectual movement that might have ramifications in the longer term. And still others might point out that a few policy analysts do produce breakthrough findings that produce gains for public policy, but because we cannot figure out who those analysts will be in advance, the system must subsidize a broader policy analysis community that produces mostly work of little value.

There might, however, be another factor that contributes to the nagging suspicion that policy analysts might in the end not contribute much to policy. The problem is that we generally do not have good mechanisms with which to aggregate the views of different policy analysts and to produce consensus recommendations. This is particularly problematic in a world in which disagreement is pervasive. The basis of the humor in many jokes about economists, after all, is that economics is an inexact science. (Consider, for example, the economist who, asked what two plus two equals, answers, "What do you want it to equal?") Indeed, formal surveys of economists identify numerous questions concerning which economists disagree.[1] Yet, presumably, regarding any given economics question, it might be valuable for policy makers to have available to them some numbers aggregating the conventional wisdom, in spite of the reality that the conventional wisdom can be wrong. The policy analysis community might contribute greater value to policy analysis if somewhat less effort were paid to developing policy arguments and somewhat more effort were paid to identifying consensus positions.

The problem, of course, is that we need institutions that can produce consensus positions of policy analysts. Surveys provide one means of identifying specific questions concerning which large numbers of policy analysts agree, but they are much less useful when applied to discrete questions for which only a relatively small number of individuals have done research that equips them to give good answers. There is rarely an objective metric for determining who is qualified to answer a particular question. Even if such a metric existed, the people surveyed might not be a random sample of the broader community of potential analysts. Perhaps liberals or conservatives, or simply people with strong prior beliefs about a particular issue, are more likely to obtain expertise about that issue. Moreover, surveyed policy analysts might not give honest answers, particularly if their answers might have some effect on policy. An analyst might favor a particular policy because it has one effect that he or she believes is beneficial, and he or she might therefore claim that the policy has a different effect that is the subject of the survey.

Prediction markets might help produce estimates of consensus. This chapter considers only the ways in which prediction markets might be used to make predictions about factually verifiable matters, though much of the disagreement among policy analysts presumably reflects differences in values. (In Chapter 6 we will consider whether prediction markets might be useful ways of aggregating normative commitments, but presumably the normative commitments of policy analysts will not be of any special interest.) Policy analysis organizations can play a critical role in this process in two ways. First, they might sponsor prediction markets on objective questions that are of interest to public policy. Second, they might encourage the policy analysts who work for them to participate in prediction markets. It will be a long time before an academic coming up for tenure will boast that she has published four articles and earned a hundred thousand dollars playing prediction markets on the university account. If a goal of policy analysis is not merely to create new knowledge but to aggregate knowledge in an accessible form, then participation in prediction markets should be encouraged, however. This is especially important for some of society's most divisive issues, such as global warming, concerning which objective predictions could be quite useful.

This chapter elaborates the argument that prediction markets can help aggregate information, noting that at times what prediction markets aggregate might more accurately be understood as individual assessments of information. Prediction markets' aggregative powers will be greater if markets are subsidized, and this chapter 1 explains how the market mechanisms described so far might be subsidized. It provides a partial description of the Policy Analysis Market, which was to have been a governmentally subsidized set of prediction markets. The collapse of that program should give caution to those who are optimistic about the short-term possibilities of prediction markets. This chapter also describes current regulatory obstacles and ways they might be avoided. It then discusses an existing application of prediction markets, the Foresight Exchange, which avoids those obstacles by using play money, and then imagines two potential government applications of prediction markets.

THE PROBLEM OF INFORMATION AGGREGATION

Markets are sometimes said to be good at aggregating information,[2] but it may be useful to distinguish two types of information that prediction markets might aggregate. One type is the evidence that someone might use to make a particular prediction. For example, in a prediction market that forecasts election returns, it might include poll data, historical data, economic data, and the like. Secret news from campaign officials would also fall within this category. Another type of information is the predictive assessment that any particular individual makes on the basis of such evidence. For example, after reading data of the first type, you might share with me that you believe that there is a 65 percent chance that a particular candidate will win the election. Suppose that I had consulted the same data and had concluded, before you shared your assessment with me, that there was a 55 percent chance that the candidate would win. Once I hear your assessment, I will probably adjust my prediction to somewhere between 55 percent and 65 percent, depending on my judgment about our relative abilities as predictors.[3]

Ideally, we might hope that prediction markets would aggregate both kinds of information, which we might distinguish with the labels "evidence" and "assessments," respectively. The relative importance of evidence and assessment aggregation might vary across prediction market contexts, but in many, the latter is more important than the former. In an election market, for example, different traders ordinarily have access to the same data, and the primary function of the prediction market is to aggregate different traders' views of those data. To be sure, on occasion, some traders might trade on the basis of data not yet available to the public, such as poll results that have not yet been publicly released. The sponsors of a prediction market might even wish to encourage such insider trading. Nonetheless, in many contexts that are of relevance to public policy, evidence generally is widely available. The primary goal of many prediction markets is to provide a form of assessment aggregation.

The distinction between evidence aggregation and assessment aggregation helps explain a common criticism of prediction markets: they do not seem to tell participants much more than they could figure out themselves by considering the underlying materials. For example, Orin Kerr commented on a Trade-Sports market used to predict the probability that each of various individuals would be chosen by President Bush as his nominee to replace Justice O'Connor. Kerr points out that neither the president nor any of his advisers seems likely to place bets on TradeSports.com, so "the people who are placing bets presumably are outsiders who are getting their predictions from newspaper articles, blogs, horoscopes, etc., and then placing bets." As a result, "a site like TradeSports would seem to just mirror the collective common wisdom of newspapers and blogs on a question like this."[4]

One possible answer to Kerr is that the Supreme Court selection market at least opened up the possibility of accomplishing the task of evidence aggregation. For example, someone might acquire some unique piece of information such as an observation of a particular candidate and his or her family driving into the gates of the White House. Perhaps the better response, however, is that Kerr's observation is correct. The primary purpose of the market is assessment aggregation, but that can be important. For someone who is interested in assessing the probabilities of various candidates, it will probably take less time to look at the TradeSports prices than to read all of the underlying information. And although it will always be possible for someone skilled at reading blogs and tea leaves to beat the market, for the typical observer, the prediction market forecast will on average be more accurate than the prediction that the observer independently could derive, because the market will represent an aggregation of the views of a large number of observers. It might therefore in part cancel out random errors that individuals make in predictions by overweighing or underweighing particular pieces of evidence.

Kerr's critique emphasizes, however, that we should not blithely assume that prediction markets will succeed at perfectly aggregating information, whatever its type, and any claim that the Supreme Court market would incorporate inside information was clearly erroneous. Indeed, on the morning Bush made his announcement, the market followed many news reports' rumors that Judge Edith Clement would be the president's choice. The markets obtained the right answer only once the administration started notifying the press that the president had chosen Judge John Roberts instead.[5] A market that perfectly performed the task of evidence aggregation would have confidently predicted Roberts's selection as soon as the president had decided to pick him, but of course such perfection is impossible. That the trading price followed reports that many independent observers and journalists thought credible might seem to be an indictment of the market if its goal is seen as evidence aggregation. Such a market might have been even more useful, but the market's performance was admirable if its task is seen as assessment aggregation.

Although evidence and assessment are forms of information, aggregation of assessments often is an easier task than aggregation of evidence. Given the same public information, market participants often make similar assessments because they are considering the same underlying data. Individual assessments are not statistically independent, though for difficult estimation problems, individual assessments might vary considerably. Individual pieces of evidence, on the other hand, might be independent. Moreover, it may be very difficult for someone who possesses a piece of evidence to generate an accurate sense of what the broader distribution of pieces of evidence might look like. Suppose, for example, that a prediction market is used to predict the outcome of a criminal trial about which little public information has been released. One trader finds out about a piece of evidence that is not a smoking gun but militates toward guilt. It is very difficult to determine how important the piece of evidence is relative to other pieces of evidence. Even if each piece of information is known to one trader on the market, the prediction market might not do a great job of producing the probability estimate that someone who had all pieces of evidence might reach.

The lines between evidence and assessments sometimes can be blurry, because analysis of data is somewhat like evidence and somewhat like assessments. Different participants in some prediction markets might analyze evidence in a relatively sophisticated way, for example, by using regression analysis. These individuals might take slightly different approaches and produce different results. On one hand, to the extent that each participant's analysis determines that analyst's prediction, the outcome of the analysis functions as a kind of independent assessment. On the other hand, if these participants do not release their analyses, then each analysis might be thought of as a piece of private evidence available only to that participant. The more sophisticated the individual analyses, and the greater the degree to which relatively sophisticated players effectively determine prediction market prices, the more the challenge of a prediction market can be said to be evidence aggregation rather than assessment aggregation and the more we might need to worry about whether the market does as good a job at information aggregation as would alternative possible institutions.

It is difficult to know for sure where existing prediction markets are on the continuum between evidence aggregation and assessment aggregation. We cannot know for sure whether trading prices in the Iowa Electronic Markets or TradeSports are largely determined by sophisticated but secret statistical analyses, which themselves might be seen as representing a type of evidence. The overall level of market sophistication is less than the overall level of academic sophistication, given the academic studies showing profitable trading strategies. But there is some chance that the publicly released academic models, which were built on data that already exist, will ultimately be proved inferior to more sophisticated models being used by private traders. And there is a reasonable chance that this will be true in the future if it is not true today.

Most existing prediction markets focus on questions of fairly general public interest. But it might also be useful to have prediction markets focusing on public policy questions that have policymaking relevance but are only interesting to small communities of people. Yet more arcane prediction markets might produce too few people to provide for a meaningful level of trading; we will see how market design can address this concern in Chapters 3 and 4. If there were a sufficient number of policy analysts who have expertise in the relevant area and engage in trading, however, would these public policy prediction markets primarily perform assessment aggregation, or would they perform evidence aggregation? The greater the extent to which a prediction market for a relatively arcane issue incorporates sophisticated models, presumably, the more accurate it will be. And of course, if the market encourages the creation of sophisticated models for questions of public interest, so much the better. That still leaves the question of how we can improve the market's success at performing evidence aggregation if these models are created, a question I address below. The more immediate question, however, is whether prediction markets could draw in a sufficient number of policy analysts to perform even rudimentary assessment aggregation.

SUBSIDIZED MARKETS

One reason that prediction markets sponsored by TradeSports do not necessarily reflect the predictions that could be made by the most sophisticated models is that TradeSports charges commissions. These commissions, we have seen, are small, but they compound the inherent risk of investing in prediction markets. The best strategy for prediction market investing could go awry in the short term, just as the best card counters in poker might lose money on a bad day or in a bad year. Thus, someone who has created a model and is confident that this model can beat the market by two or three percentage points on average might well decide not to invest in the TradeSports markets. Enough sports fans and gamblers exist to provide ample trading at many of the TradeSports markets anyway, but this is less likely to be the case for markets on esoteric topics aimed at policy analysts. Many policy analysts seem likely to invest only if they can expect to make money. For example, development of an improved account of how clouds work might improve knowledge about global warming, but it could still be risky to invest money in a global warming prediction market.

The first step toward increasing incentives for prediction market participation would be to eliminate commissions. Of course, a for-profit institution such as TradeSports seems unlikely to take this step, though an alternative profit model would be to earn money by collecting interest on invested money.[6] The non-profit Iowa Electronic Markets does not charge commissions, and other non-profit entities might follow suit. Even TradeSports has eliminated the per-transaction commissions charged to a market participant who places an order on the bid and ask queue that another trader later accepts. Presumably, this is because TradeSports recognizes that subsidizing the placement of these orders increases market liquidity and will make others more willing to consider trading. On the other hand, if it turned out that sophisticated players were more likely to place such limit orders, the subsidy of such participation might make rational third parties no more willing to play. So it is not clear how well the TradeSports strategy in general might translate to other contexts.

Ultimately, reducing commissions might not be sufficient to encourage participation. Ideally, prediction markets should be subsidized. Policy analysis institutions might provide such subsidies if the government does not. Admittedly, subsidizing prediction markets would leave the policy analysis institutions with less control over the output than would directly subsidizing position papers and scholarship. But sometimes such an institution might genuinely be interested in a particular question and thus might be willing to fund a prediction market in the area. At other times, it might be confident that the market prediction will support its position regarding a particular public policy issue. Suppose, for example, that some politicians have called for limits on oil drilling because they want to make sure that oil will remain available in the distant future. It might then be in the economic interest of the oil industry trade association to persuade the public that the amount of oil produced twenty years from now will be relatively high, but observers will discount the claims and studies of oil industry executives. If the trade association truly believes its position, it might fund a prediction market to show that its position in fact is widely shared.

The challenge is to devise a means of subsidizing the market that rewards participants who are acting in a way that enhances market accuracy. The danger is that various techniques might be used to obtain a portion of the subsidy at low risk. For example, a sponsor of a prediction market might promise to distribute a fixed amount of money—say, ten thousand dollars—in proportion to the amount individuals win in the market. A problem with this approach is that it might encourage individuals to enter wash transactions. For example, suppose the bid-ask spread is twenty-eight cents to thirty cents. I might simultaneously enter a large volume of buy and sell orders at 29, using separate accounts. Placing aside the subsidy, and in the absence of transactions fees, there would be no economic upside or downside to the transaction, but the subsidy would mean that one of the accounts is likely to make money. Of course, the result is not only that the subsidy might be distributed to parties who have provided no informational benefit but also that many trades would reflect no information and could distort the market. Distributing a subsidy in proportion to winnings is therefore too simplistic an approach.

An alternative approach might be to use some type of market maker. In securities markets, a market maker is a trading firm, often called a specialist. A market maker maintains an inventory of securities of a particular type, posting offers to buy and sell the securities. The bid-ask spread provides the market maker with an opportunity to profit by buying a share at a low price and simultaneously selling a share at a high price. A market maker, however, can lose money on some transactions owing to unexpected changes in prices. In some exchanges, one or more market makers will commit to maintaining a bid-ask spread of no more than a certain size, thus promising to provide liquidity. These market makers receive access to the market as part of the bargain. In many exchanges, traders can execute transactions only with the market maker, rather than with one another, as in a continuous double auction.

Independent market makers generally seek to maximize their own profit. In a laboratory experiment, Jan Krahnen and Martin Weber have shown that when there is a single market maker, it keeps a wide bid-ask spread and earns some monopolistic rents, which come at the expense of profits for informed traders.[7] When there are competing market makers, informed traders can earn considerably greater profits, and the losses of uninformed traders are reduced. This is especially true if the market makers are just as informed as market participants, but often that is not the case in prediction markets. A continuous double auction design can improve the ability of informed traders to profit on their information by allowing them to enter into transactions with uninformed traders. This helps explain why the prediction markets we have considered so far rely on the continuous double auction without market makers.

Uninformed traders may have little interest in some prediction markets, however, especially if they are not generally suitable as investment vehicles. To make it possible for informed traders to profit, the sponsor of the market might wish to add a market maker that is willing to lose money to the continuous double auction, thus subsidizing the market. One approach is for the sponsor of a prediction market to develop an automated market maker, which uses a computer algorithm to offer tradable contracts to buy and sell and provide liquidity to the market. The Hollywood Stock Exchange (HSE) uses such an automated market, and it has received a U.S. patent on its particular approach.[8] Its automated market seeks to enhance liquidity, and it shifts the bid and ask prices it offers in response to changes in bid and ask orders submitted by traders.

A disadvantage of the HSE approach is that it may be difficult for the sponsor of the prediction market to determine the extent of the subsidy that it is providing the market by adding liquidity. The subsidy might end up being higher or lower than intended, particularly when trading volume cannot easily be anticipated. The problem is particularly severe in prediction markets involving a very small number of traders, because slight differences in trading volume and in the dispersion of information might have large effects on the subsidy provided. The subsidy, for example, might turn out to be relatively low if all traders have approximately the same estimates and relatively high if a single trader has unexpected information that allows that trader to push the tradable contract price a great distance in the correct direction. In Chapter 4 we will consider the market scoring rule, which can function as an automated market maker that limits the maximum potential loss associated with the market, but even with this rule, the subsidy is not fixed.

If the market sponsor wishes to offer a fixed, predictable subsidy, it might agree to pay the full amount of the subsidy to an independent firm that agrees to serve as the market maker. It could choose the firm by holding an auction, agreeing to provide the subsidy to the firm that commits to maintaining at all times the shortest bid-ask spread. That firm might in turn use an automated market maker or human specialists, but it would bear the risk. Placing this high level of risk on a single third party might mean, however, that the best offer the exchange receives will not be as generous as it might prefer.

A DECENTRALIZED SUBSIDY APPROACH

A decentralized strategy for dispersing the risk assumed by market makers would borrow from the TradeSports policy of offering lower commissions to traders who make bid or ask offers that are later accepted. One possibility is to distribute a fixed subsidy to traders who offer the most generous bid and ask prices, in proportion to the time and volume of the traders' exposure. (Higher subsidies might be offered for exposure at times of day in which trading is more likely to occur.) For example, suppose that the current bid and ask prices are 28 cents and 30 cents, respectively. If I offer to buy up to 100 shares at a price of twenty-nine cents, and if that offer stays at the front of the bid queue for ten minutes, I would receive 100×10, or 1,000 credits.[9] The same would be true if I offered to sell up to 100 shares at a price of twenty-nine cents, if that offer stayed at the front of the ask queue for the same length of time.

If over the duration of the market 1,000,000 credits were awarded, then 1,000 credits would be worth 0.1 percent of the total fixed subsidy amount. This system would provide traders with incentives to make generous bid and ask offers, allowing those with information to profit on that information. In effect, this system improves the incentives for individuals to serve as market makers willing to buy and sell tradable contracts and for these individuals to maintain a small spread between the prices at which they are willing to buy and sell. The system is not easily manipulated. If, in the above example, I simultaneously offered to buy at twenty-nine cents and to sell at twenty-nine cents, those orders would be fulfilled immediately, and so, having exposed myself to no risk, I would receive no credit.

This might not be the only subsidy system available, but it should help convert what otherwise would be a zero-sum (or, with commissions, negative-sum) game from the perspective of traders into a positive-sum game, and it therefore should help enhance market participation even if the topic is of intrinsic interest to only a few individuals. Someone who feels relatively confident in a prediction, regardless of the extent to which that prediction is the result of private information, may be able to profit in two ways. First, if the trader's prediction is below the bid price or above the ask price, the trader can accept the corresponding offer. The subsidy should result in more favorable terms' being available to that trader than otherwise would exist, thus increasing trading profits. Second, after any such transactions clear, the trader might seek to make more generous offers to buy and sell than those currently in the queue, thus directly earning a portion of the subsidy. This approach provides a reward not only for a trader who finds that a tradable contract is mispriced but potentially also for a trader whose efforts provide additional confidence that a tradable contract is correctly priced.

Will subsidies be sufficient to allow a prediction market effectively to perform the task of information aggregation? The answer depends both on the amount of the subsidy and on the nature of the prediction market. A million-dollar subsidy, after all, would attract interest in virtually any topic, and though the number might seem impossibly large, some policy analysts or philanthropists might think such a subsidy would be well spent. Of course, for some issues, no subsidy at all is necessary, and indeed TradeSports shows that prediction markets can flourish with the opposite of subsidy: commissions. A relatively small subsidy, say, one thousand or one hundred dollars, might be enough to accomplish the task of assessment aggregation on an issue regarding which relatively few people have opinions. Many of these individuals ordinarily might not be interested in participating a game in which they might be as likely to lose as to gain money, but they might participate when making money is the more likely outcome for a skilled participant.

Subsidies will be particularly helpful if a prediction market might aggregate not only assessments but also evidence. If private information is likely to be useful in generating the predictions, then individuals who do not have such information ordinarily might be unwilling to trade. The possibility of evidence aggregation makes it more difficult to aggregate assessments, because individuals who have assessments based on available evidence will be less likely to trade if others can take advantage of the assessors' relative lack of knowledge. Where the goal of a prediction market is simply assessment aggregation, that goal will be more difficult to achieve when some participants might hope to profit from evidence aggregation. In general, the greater the degree of private information in a market, the larger the bid-ask spread in that market. Subsidies will tend to narrow the spread between the bid and ask prices, and thus if few trades occur, the bid-ask midpoint can serve as an effective prediction.

THE POLICY ANALYSIS MARKET

This chapter has imagined that policy analysis organizations might subsidize prediction markets concerning issues relevant to public policy. Private sponsorship is more likely than government sponsorship, because the sole governmental foray into prediction markets ended in a public relations disaster. The plan, called the Policy Analysis Market (PAM), was to use prediction markets to aggregate expert assessments of military and policy instability. It was funded by the Defense Advanced Research Projects Agency (DARPA), but the military cancelled funding in August 2003 after Senators Ron Wyden and Byron Dorgan generated national press coverage by complaining in a press conference that the military's plan was to allow gambling on terrorism.

The program was originally conceived by Michael Foster of the National Science Foundation, who had been familiar with earlier studies of prediction markets.[10] The research sponsored by DARPA concerned many speculative technologies that might have relevance to national defense. It solicited proposals from government contractors to "develop electronic market-based methods and software for decision analysis, to aggregate information and opinions from groups of experts."[11] The solicitation called for proposals that would cover multiple phases. In Phase I, the contractor would select events of interest to the Department of Defense to review and to construct and design an electronic market. In Phase II, the contractor would manage the markets previously developed and analyze their performance. Finally, the department envisioned that the markets developed might have nonmilitary applications, so that in Phase III, the technology could be used "in strategic analysis for business, technology prediction for engineering, and other analyses of decision outcomes." The research program as a whole was named FutureMAP.

The FutureMAP program led to multiple contracts, including one with a company called Net Exchange, which was founded by John Ledyard, an economist at the California Institute of Technology. Net Exchange subcontracted to two professors at George Mason University, including Robin Hanson, who originated the idea of prediction markets in the early 1990s.[12] It was Net

Exchange that designed PAM, which was to predict for each of eight nations various indicators of military activity, economic growth, U.S. military activity, U.S. financial involvement, and political instability, all of which the Intelligence Unit of the *Economist* agreed to assess after the fact. This market also would produce some other predictions, including worldwide U.S. military casualties and western terrorist casualties. (A significant goal of PAM was to allow for prediction of some variables that were conditional on others, an approach that I consider in Chapters 5 and 7.) Initially, the program was to be limited to a preselected group of traders with expertise in the relevant areas, although eventually organizers contemplated a broader group of traders.

Two decisions that might have appeared innocuous at the time contributed to the eventual termination of the FutureMAP program. First, DARPA placed FutureMAP within the Information Awareness Office. This office had already attracted considerable controversy for a plan titled Total Information Awareness that would use a statistical technology called "data mining" to help identify and stop terrorist activity.[13] The office was run by Admiral John Poindexter, a Reagan Administration National Security Advisor who had been implicated in the Iran-Contra Affair.[14] He was convicted of various charges in connection with that earlier controversy, but the convictions were overturned on the basis of a grant of immunity that Poindexter had earlier received.[15] Second, the l PAM Web site included as examples predictions of the assassination of Palestinian leader Yasser Arafat and a missile attack from North Korea, though no decision had been made to make predictions of these possible events.

The two senators who criticized the PAM program, Ron Wyden (D-Ore.) and Byron Dorgan (D-N.D.), described the market incompletely as a market in terrorist attacks. Some of their and others' criticism reflected concern that the market might be inherently repugnant. The theory might be that the market inappropriately commodified human lives and tragedy. There are many other important institutions, however, that do the same. Life insurance companies, for example, in effect make bets on how long individuals will live. Of course, a life insurer hopes that its clients will live long lives, but society also tolerates sellers of annuities and even viatical companies, which provide cash value for future life insurance proceeds.[16] These companies in effect are betting that specific individuals will die, and yet because there are benefits to allowing them (for example, enabling the terminally ill to meet their medical expenses), they are widely tolerated. Presumably, critics of PAM thought the benefits of PAM too small to outweigh any discomfort that it might cause. Senators Wyden and Dorgan also suggested that the funding ($8 million had been requested for future extensions of the markets) would be better spent on more traditional intelligence activities.

Other criticisms were more sophisticated. Consider, for example, the critique of Joseph E. Stiglitz, who won the Nobel Prize in Economics in 2001.[17] Stiglitz offered reasonable concerns that the market might be manipulated, perhaps providing false comfort or unnecessary alarm, though he did not offer any analysis to defend the claim that manipulation might succeed. More central to Stiglitz's analysis were the following rhetorical questions: "Did [Poindexter] believe there is widespread information about terrorist activity not currently being either captured or appropriately analyzed by the 'experts' in the FBI and the CIA? Did he believe that the 1,000 people 'selected' for the new futures program would have this information?" These questions seem to suggest that Stiglitz was unaware that PAM would focus on issues such as economic growth and political instability in addition to terrorism. But the questions also suggest that whatever the context, Stiglitz assumed that assessment aggregation would have relatively little value.

Stiglitz noted that markets might not produce reliable information "where there are large asymmetries of information." He won the Nobel Prize largely for his work on the implications of asymmetric information in markets, and his comment accurately reflects the point made above that private information can lead to very wide bid-ask spreads in prediction markets. Stiglitz's comments, however, also appear to reflect an assumption that the purpose of PAM was to perform the task of *evidence aggregation* by allowing individuals with private information about particular terrorist attacks to profit by trading on that information. Robin Hanson has since argued that it might be possible to design markets to predict specific terrorist attacks based on concrete information,[18] but PAM clearly was not designed to perform this task. These traders might not have had access to specific information available to the FBI and the CIA, but at least the market would have done a reasonable job of assessment aggregation based on public information.

Such assessment aggregation, moreover, might have been useful in this context. Congress and the Department of Defense routinely have to make decisions about resource allocations, and the predictions made by PAM might have been relevant to these decisions. To be sure, government decision makers might rely on official governmental analyses of these questions, but there is always a danger that official analyses will reflect the predictions that the government believes will justify the policies that it prefers. For example, an administration with deep ties to the leadership in Saudi Arabia might tend to minimize the dangers of political instability there, in part because it does not want critics to question whether those ties should continue. A prediction market performing the task of assessment aggregation can provide a prediction that neither the administration nor interested actors will be able easily to manipulate. In a world in which policy analysts and governmental officials might make very different predictions to support their diverse political ends, a tool that can ascertain the degree of confidence that different participants have in their predictions can be quite useful. This was an ambition of PAM, and there was no reason to think that the market would have performed poorly.

REGULATORY IMPEDIMENTS TO
PREDICTION MARKETS

In closing his critique of PAM, Stiglitz asks, "If this is such a good idea, why haven't the markets created it on their own?"[19] The question suggests that those who believe in markets ought to explain why markets have not already created market-based institutions. There might, however, be some straightforward answers. There is no incentive for private firms to create prediction markets for the purpose of selling the data that they produce, because they would be unable to prevent others from obtaining the facts for free. Under U.S. law, copyright protection does not extend to facts,[20] and so anyone would be able to monitor and republish trades in a prediction market. Thus, if prediction markets are to be created, it will likely be done by policy analysis organizations that wish to provide the public with a social benefit. One reason that few such markets have been created might be that it is still early in the intellectual history of prediction markets. A probably more serious obstacle is that prediction markets face considerable regulatory impediments, at least in the United States.

Perhaps the most serious obstacle to prediction markets is gambling law. Almost all of the states strictly regulate gambling, and some states have specifically prohibited gambling over the Internet.[21] The Federal Wire Act of 1961 also prohibits using "wire communications" to place bets and has been used to prosecute U.S. citizens who have created online gambling Web sites.[22] State law does not always define *gambling*, so it is possible that some state courts might find that wagering on prediction markets does not count.

In an analysis of the legality of prediction markets concerning scientific propositions, Tom Bell assesses whether prediction markets would be found to be gambling under the common-law definition.[23] Two of the three elements of

gambling under the common law—the existence of a prize and of consideration (in this case, payment for the right to the prize)—are present, but presence of the third element, chance, is unclear. Bell notes that many legal activities, such as investing in Treasury bonds, produce returns subject to some
degree of chance. Indeed, a California court has explained, "It is the character
of the game rather than a particular player's skill or lack of it that determines
whether the game is one of chance or skill."[24] Courts seem likely to find that
chance predominates in prediction markets devoted to predicting the results
of sports contests, even if one could show that the players with the most
sophisticated models emerge over time as winners.

Nonetheless, there are strong policy arguments that prediction markets, in
particular those dealing with esoteric topics of policy interest, will not generally cause the social ills often attributed to gambling.[25] Bell, commenting
specifically on markets in scientific areas, notes that prediction markets are not
designed for entertainment purposes, that the slow pace of such markets
seems less likely to encourage compulsive gambling, and that markets could
provide social benefits that might more than balance any harm that is
caused.[26] Given the current weakness of gambling enforcement—numerous
Web sites, including TradeSports, operate overseas and serve American customers—it seems doubtful that authorizing prediction markets would do
much harm, even if such trading did cause considerable social ills. A recent
federal statute requires finance companies to block transactions to gambling
Web sites,[27] but it is not clear that this approach will be successful.[28] Taken together, these considerations suggest that governments should clarify that prediction markets, or at least some such markets, do not violate gambling laws.
This is not yet a legislative priority, though, and probably it will not be until
prediction markets establish legitimacy among the general public. In the
meantime, policy analysis organizations located in the United States presumably do not wish to risk incurring legal liability.

The other obstacle is federal regulation of futures exchanges by the Commodity Futures Trading Commission (CFTC). The CFTC regulates markets
such as the Chicago Mercantile Exchange, which allows for trading of securities based on commodities (such as frozen concentrated orange juice) and
on economic variables such as interest rates and foreign exchange rates.[29]
Whether prediction markets are subject to CFTC regulation is a legal question that is not easily resolved. "Commodities" include "all services, rights,
and interests in which contracts for future delivery are presently or in the future dealt in."[30] Bell suggests that prediction markets do not involve "contracts

for future delivery," because the contracts that may or may not pay off are or can be delivered immediately to the traders involved.[31] One might argue, however, that a prediction market contract promises future delivery of money, though the amount of such money (for example, nothing or one dollar) is uncertain. If prediction market contracts are viewed as involving commodities, they might count as "excluded commodities,"[32] although additional ambiguous statutory hurdles would need to be overcome before the prediction markets can escape regulation.[33]

Prediction markets can seek to register with and operate under the authority of the CFTC, and at least one, HedgeStreet, appears to have taken this path.[34] But such regulation is perhaps too cumbersome for relatively low-volume prediction markets. In particular, CFTC regulation currently requires clearance for individual contracts to be traded, including demonstrations that the trading will not be susceptible to price manipulation.[35] An alternative is to register with the CFTC as an "exempt board of trade."[36] The Trade Exchange Network, which owns TradeSports, has registered via this route,[37] but such exempt boards are subject to considerable restrictions; for example, trading is limited to certain types of organizations and individuals with a net worth of more than $10,000,000.[38] A representative of TradeSports reports that Trade-Sports is considering creating markets to allow large entities subject to risk associated with events such as sports contests, for example, sports teams and broadcast networks, to hedge that risk.

The only easily accessible real-money legal prediction market in the United States is the Iowa Electronic Markets. The IEM received a no-action letter from the CFTC in 1993 promising not to prosecute the IEM for violating the Commodity Exchange Act, provided that the IEM restricted its activities in certain ways.[39] The no-action letter, however, emphasized several factors unique to the IEM: "the operation of the [IEM] is limited solely to academic research and experimental purposes," the IEM does not receive a profit, and "the maximum investment by any single participant in any one Submarket is five hundred dollars," among others. So far, the letter does not appear to have served as a precedent leading to other real-money prediction markets. The reference to "experimental purposes" suggests some caution about the possibility of promises not to prosecute for-profit prediction markets for violating federal law. A no-action letter would not provide any protection against state gambling laws,[40] though the fact that there has been no prosecution of the IEM suggests that state attorneys general might not have any interest in stopping similar ventures.

It is possible, of course, that the CFTC will seek to deregulate prediction markets or find some mechanism for providing a less onerous regulatory regime. Economists from the CFTC have attended at least one academic conference concerning prediction markets and appear to be interested in the topic. Robert Hahn and Paul Tetlock have suggested one regulatory approach: encouraging the CFTC to allow all prediction markets that pass an "economic purpose test." For example, the creator of a prediction market could show that the particular contract would "provide significant financial hedging opportunities" or that the "prevailing price of the information market contract is likely to provide valuable information for improving economic decisions."[41] In order to overcome concerns about state gambling regulation, they suggest that the CFTC declare state law to be preempted for prediction markets with such contracts. In addition, they recommend broad exemptions from any regulation for markets that (for example) limit the maximum size of individual investments. If not exempt, prediction markets should be permitted to self-certify contracts, thus avoiding the necessity of obtaining CFTC approval before listing each contract.

Such an approach would be a good start to legitimating prediction markets, but there is a strong case that they could be expanded further. Focusing on economic purposes rather than on a broader range of public purposes could unnecessarily restrict prediction markets. Election markets, after all, do not clearly fit within the scope of the definition. Conceivably, if "significant hedging opportunities" were interpreted broadly, some election markets might be allowed, because certain companies face risk associated with uncertain presidential elections. But this would cover only a few markets of great significance and presumably would not include, for example, election markets focusing on individual congressional elections. Election markets, of course, are not the only markets of public policy significance that have little economic resonance. The Policy Analysis Market itself would have predicted political instability, in addition to economic variables, and ideally the law would tolerate, if not encourage, such markets.

The case for initially restricting legality to economically significant markets is that such markets are the only ones that are likely to be politically feasible. Yet most markets with public policy implications seem likely to incite no more opposition than economic markets. An alternative approach to regulation might be to authorize all prediction markets *except* those fitting within specific classifications. For example, markets for predicting the outcome of sports contests could be excluded, although they might present hedging opportunities, for example, for a broadcaster that stands to lose advertising revenue if the World Series lasts only four or five games. An exempt board of trade restricted to organizations such as hedge funds and sports teams might sponsor such a market, but because opposition to legalized prediction markets is likely to be based on concerns about gambling, individuals might be precluded from trading.

Similarly, prediction markets concerning the entertainment industry (for example, the Oscars) might be excluded, as would those for purely random events (such as the spin of a roulette wheel). Regulations allowing prediction markets also might exclude any markets making predictions about numbers of deaths or terrorist incidents; such markets might well be useful, but the experience with PAM suggests that they are not yet politically feasible.

REGULATORY ARBITRAGE

As long as prediction markets remain illegal in the United States, U.S. policy analysis organizations' options are considerably restricted, but there might still be some means of taking advantage of the information aggregation power of prediction markets. One approach is to enter into a contract with an organization abroad that runs prediction markets. I know of no examples of this type of arrangement, but sufficient demand would presumably bring supply. An organization such as TradeSports, after all, can add markets quite easily and presumably would be willing to host a market for a fee. TradeSports might even be willing to implement subsidized markets, provided the market sponsor pays the subsidy and some fee that would at least cover the hosting services that TradeSports provides.

This approach reflects a form of regulatory arbitrage, taking advantage of the legality of TradeSports in the jurisdiction in which it exists. As long as the sponsor of a prediction market retains no control and no knowledge of who participates in the market, it seems unlikely that U.S. authorities would seek to hold the market sponsor liable for any trading that illegally originates from the United States. It is difficult to know for sure, however, and prosecutors and judges might be more skeptical of this arrangement if the prediction market is used specifically to forecast events in the United States.

The prediction market sponsor could instead provide money to each of a number of selected participants with the stipulation that this money could be used to bet on a prediction market but that no participant would be allowed to bet any more money than initially provided. For example, a trader who receives one hundred dollars might lose that money but could not lose any more than that. Perhaps in part because of legal restrictions, PAM was to have been structured this way. Conceivably, prosecutors might claim that such an arrangement violates gambling laws, though the impossibility of losing any money from the market as a whole would seem to make such a prosecution unlikely. To improve appearances and decrease the chance of such a prosecution, the prediction market might run on the basis of points, with points convertible into dollars only after the market closes. It seems unlikely that the CFTC would seek to prevent such an arrangement, because the individual traders receiving subsidies would not likely be seen as ordinary investors.

A danger in taking this approach to subsidizing a market is that some traders might not participate in evaluation and trading. Instead, they might simply pocket the money provided to them. Sponsors may be tempted to require that funds be traded at least a certain number of times, but there are hazards to this approach. In particular, traders might seek to evade the limitation by executing the same kind of wash transactions that, we saw above, could frustrate a simplistic subsidy design.

A single trader presumably would not be allowed to open multiple accounts, but traders might work together to enter wash transactions. For example, one trader might agree with another to buy a number of shares from the other at a price somewhere in the bid-ask spread, with the traders then immediately executing the same set of transactions in reverse. The market sponsor would need to find some way of policing such transactions, as well as more subtle variations. If it were possible to do so, individual traders might respond to the requirements by executing only the minimum number of trades and hedging risk with offsetting transactions over time.

An alternative approach might be to use the decentralized subsidy system (described in Chapter 2) to provide incentives for individuals to place their money at risk. For example, suppose that a would-be sponsor of a prediction market would like to invest ten thousand dollars to derive probability estimates from one hundred individuals who seem likely to have information or to be able to obtain information about a particular prediction. Instead of simply giving each of these individuals one hundred dollars that they might trade, the prediction market sponsor might give each trader fifty dollars and then offer five thousand dollars as a subsidy, to be distributed among those who place the money provided to them at risk by placing bid or ask orders.

The market sponsor might run a points-only prediction market in which points would not be redeemable for dollars but then distribute the entire ten-thousand-dollar subsidy in proportion to the number of points that participants put at risk. Those who seek a portion of the subsidy by placing points at risk could expect to earn profits, and more knowledgeable participants should expect to earn higher profits than less knowledgeable ones. Although the points in this system have no direct cash value, they are valuable as means of obtaining subsidies, and so market participants will have incentives to be careful about the bid and ask offers that they make. Usually, however, it will be preferable to allow points to be cashed in at some value, in order to provide robust incentives for individuals to accept bid and ask offers when they believe that there has been mispricing.

Although allocating a greater portion of a subsidy to encourage trading reduces the risk that individuals will simply pocket the trading funds, there is a significant drawback if too large a portion of the subsidy is allocated in this way. In a market in which points initially allocated are not redeemable for dollars or are redeemable for only a small portion of the subsidy, someone who does have a better probability estimate might not be able to invest any more than individuals with worse probability estimates. Such a market design is likely to be successful only if the appropriate probability estimate will tend to become more obvious to all participants over time. In that case, an individual who makes a sensible trade will earn points while the market is still operating and will thus have more points to place at risk in order to obtain a higher portion of the subsidy. If predictions are not likely to improve markedly over the life of the market, then someone who has good information will not accumulate points much faster than others and therefore will not receive a particularly large portion of the subsidy. The remedy is to allocate a meaningful portion of the subsidy to initial funds, so that trading can directly lead to profits.

This analysis suggests that careful design can improve traders' incentives in a market in which no participant can lose money. That does not mean that such markets will be just as good as subsidized markets in which traders can put their own money at risk. The markets will be particularly poor at encouraging evidence aggregation. Someone who has a specific piece of information indicating that the market price is off by a significant amount will be able to push the market in the right direction using only whatever dollars or points are initially assigned to the trader's account. Even if the market succeeds in encouraging traders to place large amounts of money at risk in the bid and ask queues, the increased liquidity will not greatly increase the amount of money that someone with information will be able to earn by trading.

Suppose that the total subsidy to a market with one hundred participants is ten thousand dollars. It will be difficult for any participant to earn a significant portion of that amount, and the market will provide only very limited incentives for individuals to conduct complicated and time-consuming analysis. If the goal is simply to obtain a crude form of assessment aggregation, however, the market is likely to be more successful. In this case, though, the market will not weigh individual traders' confidence in their predictions as effectively as a market in which traders can invest their own funds.

One approach to making markets in which participants cannot lose more like real prediction markets is to provide participants with accounts that can be used in each of a variety of prediction markets. Suppose, for example, that a policy analysis organization is interested in sponsoring ten different prediction markets in related topics and that it has identified a group of individuals that it wishes to encourage to trade in these markets. It could provide each individual with ten separate accounts, each assigned to a separate market. But pooling the accounts gives each trader an incentive to decide which market or markets to focus on. A trader, for example, who has private information relevant to only one of the markets might invest all of the funds allotted to trading in that market. Other traders will tend to invest in the markets in which they have information. Thus, each trader is likely to move prices more in markets in which the trader might have information, providing some assurance that market prices will be weighted by the self-confidence each trader has for that market.

THE FORESIGHT EXCHANGE

An alternative means of complying with legal restrictions on prediction markets is to sponsor a play-money market. As discussed in Chapter 1, some such markets, such as the Hollywood Stock Exchange, have shown remarkable predictive capacity. The HSE does not provide any cash subsidy, although market participants can cash in some of their play money for discounts at the HSE's on-line store. (For example, a mere ten million dollars in HSE currency lowers the price of a T-shirt from twelve dollars in real currency to five dollars, perhaps still enough for the Exchange at least to break even on such sales.) It is difficult, however, to design prediction markets with substantial subsidies available to anyone who signs up for free on the Internet, because individuals might open accounts simply to take high-risk gambles.

Given such possibilities for manipulation, absent alternative designs that are responsive to this problem, a market using only play money might produce as much accuracy or perhaps more than a market in which play money is convertible to real money. People may be less likely to try to engage in market manipulation when they are playing only for points than when they are playing for dollars. This is not necessarily true, however, as anyone who has observed cheating in a pick-up basketball game or a game of Monopoly knows. The theory behind a play-money game is that people will seek to earn the recognition associated with play money, and so if cheating is undetectable, people might cheat to obtain such recognition. Participants in multiplayer on-line games often genuinely care about their scores, so much so that there is a robust market in which people exchange their virtual earnings for real cash.[42] Prediction markets, however, seem likely to be less addictive than graphically intense on-line games that allow for greater degrees of virtual interaction, and so play-money markets without any subsidy whatsoever might generate at least roughly reliable predictions.

Indeed, someone interested in creating a play-money market need not host a server running that market, for an existing Web site has hosted play-money prediction markets. The Web site, called the Foresight Exchange,[43] initially provides each participant with fifty dollars in virtual money plus an additional fifty for each week of continued participation. Participants can pay some of the money that they have earned—or, more accurately, been given—to sponsor new claims. A new claim can in effect be a probability estimate or a numeric estimate prediction market. On the Foresight Exchange, the latter are called "scaled claims," paying off somewhere between nothing and one dollar according to a formula decided by the market creator. Both probabilistic and scaled claims have an expiration date, and a judge is assigned to each claim. The judge reports in advance on how he or she plans to address any apparent ambiguities in the claim and resolves the claim as soon as it is possible to do so.

On casual analysis, the Foresight Exchange generally seems to do a reasonably good job of assessment aggregation. In mid-January 2006, for example, the market predicted a 42 percent chance that the United States would attack Iran (for example, in an air strike aimed at eliminating Iran's nuclear facilities) by January 21, 2009. Some predictions, however, seem somewhat implausible. For example, the market predicted an 8 percent chance that Arnold Schwarzenegger would become president of the United States by 2022. Given that the Constitution would need to be amended for this to take place[44] and that he would then need to win the Republican nomination and the general election, that seems implausibly high. More systematic study of 172 completed

Foresight Exchange markets appears to confirm, however, that market prices can indeed be interpreted as probability estimates.[45]

Of course, this analysis emphasizes that objectively ascertaining market accuracy is difficult, given that individuals might have different views of the appropriate probability for a particular tradable contract. Looking at predictions in closed markets might not resolve the mystery, given the absence of an alternative set of predictions to which to compare the Foresight Exchange's predictions. It is troubling, however, that some of the market's predictions seemed to be at variance with those of real-money prediction markets. For example, also as of mid-January 2006, the Foresight Exchange predicted a 63 percent chance that a Democrat would be elected president in 2008, but the corresponding prediction in the TradeSports market was 48 percent. This suggests either that prediction markets generally might be wildly inconsistent or (more plausibly, in my view) that prediction markets that depend on points alone leave considerable room for mispricing that no one bothers to correct.

The Foresight Exchange includes claims in a wide variety of topics. For example, it has a math category with a contract about whether the Poincaré Conjecture will be proved by 2031 (a 97 percent chance), a medicine category including a contract about whether cancer mortality will by 2010 have fallen 90 percent relative to 1994 (a 17 percent chance), and a physics category including a contract concerning whether a power plant will sell nuclear energy produced by fusion by 2045 (a 73 percent chance). Whatever the plausibility of these contract estimates, they cover relatively important issues in the relevant fields. It seems likely that the market would be less accurate if contracts concerned much more esoteric issues, because only a small number of people, who might have very little direct knowledge, would be interested in trading on those issues. Thus, although the Foresight Exchange provides an interesting example of working prediction markets in issues that in some cases have public policy relevance, it seems unlikely that the Exchange would perform well if taxed with much more specific claims.

If the Foresight Exchange's performance is disappointing, it might not require a large subsidy to improve it considerably. Many transactions in the Exchange appear to be due to a relatively small number of active traders, some of whom have amassed substantial virtual wealth (more than thirteen thousand dollars in one case). Some of these traders, however, appear to invest in only a few tradable contracts that are wildly mispriced, and so a subsidy scheme that encouraged these traders to reduce bid-ask spreads might improve market accuracy. A scheme rewarding provision of liquidity might help the market even if points were not redeemable for dollars. Adding a direct subsidy might give a small core of generalist traders an adequate incentive to push the market toward reasonable assessment aggregation. The more difficult question is how to provide such a subsidy in a way that minimizes the danger of manipulation from people who open free accounts and make either random trades or non-random trades designed to benefit other participants.

An imperfect solution is to reward one or more of the top participants in a market or in a group of markets. Such a system, however, provides little incentive for someone unlikely to be among these top participants to take part. Nonetheless, in some contexts, it might be sufficient. NewsFutures, for example, has used this approach with success. According to Emile Servan-Schreiber, by the end of trading in a market in which ten prizes might be awarded, about one hundred people might be competing for these prizes. Servan-Schreiber also reports that massive fraud attempts can generally be detected.[46] There is a danger, however, that as the value of prizes goes up, attempts to mask these schemes could become more sophisticated. In general, a broader prize base (in the extreme, a system that cashes out all points on a per-point basis) encourages more participation but also more gaming of the system.

AGGREGATION OF SECRET INFORMATION

In all of these cases, the information that is relevant to the task is largely public, so the markets would be performing assessment aggregation. Some contexts, however, might lend themselves to sophisticated modeling more than would others, and to the extent that the predictions of sophisticated models count as private information, these markets might perform evidence aggregation as well. It might be possible to create markets specifically designed to aggregate evidence, in particular, evidence that otherwise would be secret.

Prediction markets, for example, might be used to make forecasts that ordinarily would need to be based on information largely unavailable to the public. For such markets to have a chance of reflecting the secret information, individuals with access to that information will need sufficient incentive to participate. Recall the markets that were used to predict whether weapons of mass destruction would be found in Iraq (see Chapter 1). A casual analysis suggests that the markets did a reasonable job of aggregating assessments, reducing its confidence over time that weapons would be found. But with the advantage of hindsight, it seems apparent that the markets did a poor job of aggregating secret information. Subsequent governmental investigations showed that there was evidence that would have substantially reduced an objective analyst's assessment of the probability that such weapons would be found. But the markets presumably did not reflect this information.

Perhaps a heavily subsidized prediction market would have done so. In this context, however, the subsidy would have to be quite high. After all, the secret information was top secret in the legal sense, and individuals with access to such information might have feared the possibility of prosecution for revealing information if they traded on it. An interesting legal question would be whether trading on top-secret information violates laws against spying; more likely, it violates government ethics rules.[47] It could be argued, however, that it ought to be legal. In this case, at least, there was no governmental interest in keeping secret the officials' true estimates of the probability that weapons of mass destruction would be found. Indeed, top governmental officials were working hard to convince the public that they really did perceive a threat.

Conceivably, had the officials with access to the information been able to participate in a prediction market, the market might have established that the officials genuinely believed this. Or it might have shown that the claimed confidence in fact was mere bluster. Prediction markets could have served as a kind of lie detector that either proved the government's good faith or revealed a deception. Either way, by providing objective forecasts, prediction markets could improve democratic governance, but only if officials with the relevant information are allowed to trade.

Given the aftermath of PAM, it is likely to be a long time before the government sponsors prediction markets. But it could do much to spur the development of markets by tolerating governmental officials' trading on such markets, at least where public release of the prediction itself could not jeopardize national security. Admittedly, just as presidents and other officials seek to suppress leaks to the press, so, too, might they seek to suppress or otherwise discourage prediction market trading. But if government policy toward trading remains ambiguous, some government officials might invest anonymously in subsidized markets. This provides an opportunity for policy analysis organizations to sponsor subsidized prediction markets if they believe that the public is being misled.

Prediction markets that encourage individuals to trade on secret information can, of course, be used for good or ill, and sometimes one might argue about which is which. Historically there has been an intense debate about the degree to which government should be open. A free press keeps the government more open than it might like, and a privately sponsored prediction market could be used as another weapon by those who seek more openness.

Prediction markets also might be used to obtain information about corporate plans. Companies often have had difficulty keeping some of their plans secret; Apple Computer is a particularly prominent example of a company that has tried to suppress information release.[48] At least those companies know that there are a sufficient number of false rumors to give the public trouble identifying true ones. Privately sponsored prediction markets in corporate plans, however, might make it easier to distinguish true rumors from false ones.

Policy analysis organizations might sponsor some markets in order to improve their monitoring of corporations. For example, rumors that Wal-Mart was exploring the possibility of investing in robotic research so that it could replace human labor did not receive much traction after a heated denial by the company.[49] It might have, however, if prediction markets had suggested that Wal-Mart in fact would deploy robots within the next twenty years. Independent organizations also might sponsor prediction markets that would track the effects of corporate activity. For example, the Recording Industry Association of America might sponsor a market that would predict the number of copyrighted songs that will be downloaded over some future time span on a particular file-sharing service, thus making clear that particular designs were viewed as likely to foster copyright violations. Conceivably, companies might also sponsor prediction markets to help reveal their competitors' information and plans. Courts in the future might need to decide whether such actions should be seen as violations of laws governing trade secrets.

Prediction markets sponsored by third parties to find information about an organization might not be as successful as those sponsored by the organization itself. One reason, of course, is that loyal employees might worry that they are betraying their employer if they make personal trades based on information obtained at the job or might even worry about legal liability—for example, for insider trading.[50] A less obvious reason is that individuals with information will ordinarily have liquidity constraints and may not push prediction market prices as far in the appropriate direction as their information would justify. If other traders knew that the trades were coming from individuals who might have access to relevant information, then those traders might change their evaluations. But in a large market that does not identify traders, such derivatively informed trading will not occur. As this analysis suggests, if a sponsor of a prediction market wants to encourage such trading, it might sponsor two markets, one for people who might be expected to have private information (perhaps receiving a higher subsidy) and one for anyone. Presumably, trading on the private market would have significant ramifications for the public one.

This strategy, however, might be difficult to accomplish without the cooperation of the organization in which the private information lies.

Of course, policy analysis organizations will only have an interest in subsidizing such prediction markets if in fact they aggregate evidence well enough that the media, government, and public grow to have confidence in them. But public acceptance of prediction markets is unlikely to materialize in the absence of markets that inspire confidence. A particular danger is that unsubsidized prediction markets might not aggregate evidence very effectively, and the public will grow to distrust the markets before the market designs most likely to spur success have been tried. Chicken-and-egg problems, however, have a way of solving themselves eventually. In the short term, it is likely that only a few policy analysis organizations will sponsor prediction markets, and these markets will probably be unsubsidized. At some point, though, some organizations might try offering modest subsidies, and if these subsidies prove successful, prediction markets that provide strong incentives for individuals with information to trade might develop.

LONG-TERM ECONOMIC TRENDS

If subsidized prediction markets are implemented, one of the most useful would be one that forecasts long-term economic trends. Policy debates frequently center around questions of the long-term economic outlook. For example, the political parties may debate the consequences of current spending for the budget deficit and the accumulated debt. Although the Congressional Budget Office estimates the effect of policies on the deficit and has established a reputation for relatively independent analysis, the office necessarily makes its projections on the basis of current law and current policy options, without ordinarily considering how decisions now might lead to legal changes later.[51] A prediction market might better show how changes in policy have affected the outlook for the future.

Moreover, the parties may disagree about how to calculate indirect effects of policies. For example, Republicans are more likely than Democrats to urge that tax cuts will in part pay for themselves by spurring economic growth and thus greater tax collection. Although the Congressional Budget Office can develop an approach to resolve such methodological disputes, there will always be the danger that politics will have affected decision making. And if the office consistently opts for the approach that leaves the least room for subjective decision making (for example, by adopting an assumption that tax cuts will not affect growth), that approach might not be the most accurate. The sponsor of a prediction market making such projections, in contrast, does not need to specify a methodology in advance. Instead, traders will have incentives to make their own assessments of the extent to which tax cuts will finance themselves. Even if privately sponsored, a prediction market projecting the debt in various years in the future could play an important role in public policy debates. For example, the media might come to report on how the prediction market's projections have changed as the president announces new policies.

The national debt, of course, is not the only economic variable of interest. Prediction markets also might be used to assess such variables as economic growth, the unemployment rate, the degree of economic inequality (measured, for example, by the variance of income across the population), and the savings rate. A separate prediction market contract might be used to measure each of these variables for each of a number of years in the future. This would provide a snapshot of the consensus view of how economic conditions are likely to change and make it possible to examine how this consensus view of the future has changed over time. It would also be possible, for one or more years, to use a number of prediction markets to estimate the probability that each of these variables will equal certain values. For example, one contract might estimate the probability that economic growth in 2020 will exceed 0.0 percent, another would estimate the probability that it will exceed 0.1 percent, and so on for a variety of plausible positive and negative values of economic growth. In effect, by expanding the number of prediction market contracts, it is possible to produce not only a point estimate of a future economic indicator but also a probability distribution.

Another useful set of prediction markets might be used to help policy makers and individual investors anticipate the long-term future of Social Security. Advocates of a public social insurance system argue that such a system reduces the risk to future retirees, whose money will not depend on the gyrations of the stock market. Advocates of privatization respond that public social insurance introduces a new kind of risk—political risk—because Congress in theory can change the amount of Social Security payments at any time.[52] It is difficult, however, to obtain a sense of the relative size of these risks.

A set of prediction markets might forecast, again using multiple contracts to create probability distributions, what payments each of a variety of hypothetical individuals can expect from Social Security. At the same time, other prediction markets might produce estimates of the probability of different returns if a set amount of money were placed in some private investment vehicle such as an index fund. Of course, to obtain reasonable probability estimates, such a market would need a substantial subsidy, and still politicians and economists legitimately might offer a range of opinions. But if prediction markets become better understood, if only among policy elites, such markets could become standard reference points in political debates. Studies indicate that market-generated predictions of macroeconomic data releases avoid some anomalies previously found in surveys of professional forecasters.[53]

Markets could be used to predict noneconomic variables as well. There are many noneconomic contexts in which the task of assessment aggregation also might be useful. For example, prediction markets might be used, at least if information is available ex post, to predict the number of abortions that women in the United States will obtain legally in future years. Because the predictions could change over time, such markets could help show the effect of changes in government policy. For example, changes in sex education curricula might or might not have some effect on market predictions. Of course, other factors, such as unexpected demographic shifts or political changes, also might change the numbers. It would also be possible to predict other relevant numbers, such as the number of deaths of women having abortions, the probability of the overruling of *Roe v. Wade*,[54] or the probability that abortion will be illegal in a particular state in the future. Policy analysis organizations sponsoring such markets would be able to place news in context, providing consensus estimates that would help provide objective indicia of the extent to which changes in the world would have policy consequences in the future.

Chapter 3 Businesses

In most of the examples discussed so far, the sponsors of prediction markets have been public-spirited, though perhaps animated by private concerns as well. The media might wish to attract readers and viewers, and policy analysis organizations might hope that markets will make predictions that support policies that they independently favor. In all of these cases, however, the organizations produce prediction markets for consumption primarily by the public at large and by policy makers. Nonetheless, we should expect that the number of such markets will, from the perspective of social welfare, be so low as to be inefficient. It will be difficult to keep secret the predictions of these markets and accordingly difficult to create systems of property rights that allow producers of information to sell the predictions they produce, such as economic forecasts that are of interest to a wide range of customers. Organizations will thus generally sponsor prediction markets only to the extent that they advance the organizations' reputations or policy agendas, although this is also true of other kinds of information that organizations produce, such as restaurant reviews or polling data.

Some organizations, in any event, might sponsor prediction markets that would produce information for their own purposes. Businesses, in particular, might do so to help them make a wide range of forecasts. Of course, businesses will be wary of sponsoring prediction markets when the information will help their competitors. Trade associations, however, might sponsor markets that are useful to a variety of competitors in a particular industry. Businesses, meanwhile, will be hesitant to sponsor prediction markets that would reveal trade secrets to the outside world. But they might seek to create markets consisting solely of company employees, allowing trading by a relatively small number of insiders who have signed confidentiality pledges. Most important, there will be many situations in which some piece of information will be more useful to a business than to its competitors. In these cases, businesses have an incentive to sponsor prediction markets.

Even so, there still might be an undersupply of prediction markets. Today, they remain experimental. Until businesses gain much more experience with prediction markets, they might remain hesitant to rely on their forecasts. Businesses might have particularly limited incentives to adopt novel approaches to structuring markets, such as the proposed subsidy scheme described in Chapter 2, and might also be hesitant in interpreting the results. because of the lack of other experiments validating novel approaches. The value of experimentation accrues largely to the public, not to the individual business, and businesses will be hesitant to subsidize these experiments, especially for prediction markets that might be controversial. Enough experimentation is already taking place so that a wide range of businesses might someday integrate prediction markets into their planning. Some resistance is inevitable, however, as those who run companies may resist prediction markets that make their own expertise less valuable.

The advent of prediction markets also will provide businesses with opportunities for helping others develop market infrastructures. It is not surprising that some, most prominently NewsFutures.com, already do. The NewsFutures Web site features an impressive client list including companies such as Yahoo!, Corning, Abbott Laboratories, and Lilly. NewsFutures and other companies will have some incentive to experiment with new prediction market designs that they can then offer to their clients. Conceivably, if these companies develop improved market designs, they could file for and obtain "business method patents" that will allow them a degree of market exclusivity for twenty years.[1] Individual businesses, however, also might implement unpatented market designs without hiring these companies. At least one open-source product for implementing prediction markets, Zocalo, produced by Chris Hibbert of commerce.net,[2] is available for free.

It is too early to determine whether the use of prediction markets by businesses is just a fad or whether they will prove to have sufficient value. In the long run, though, prediction market services should become inexpensive, so if information aggregation has any value at all, businesses are likely to take advantage of it. Moreover, businesses increasingly have exploited related technologies such as data mining, the use of sophisticated statistical techniques to reveal previously unrecognized relationships in their business decisions. Data mining, for example, allows American Express to recommend products to its customers based on the customers' purchase histories and their past experience with other products and allows Wal-Mart to make decisions about managing local store inventory.[3] Businesses have proved willing to pay a great deal for data mining, and they will also pay for prediction markets if they prove to add value.

It might seem that prediction markets are useless in a world with data mining. Who needs to aggregate opinion when large volumes of data are available for computer number crunchers? What prediction markets provide that data mining technology does not is the ability to aggregate human judgment and assess the extent to which models of the past are likely to continue to be accurate predictors in the future. Suppose, for example, that a gas station has determined through data mining software that it sells more gas around Labor Day and thus is considering placing a bigger gas order. This year, though, there might be some question whether the pattern will continue, for example, because of high gas prices, bad weather, or a pre–Labor Day start date in the local school district. A prediction market could be used to forecast how many cars will pull into the gas station in a specific period. In a hypothetical world in which many businesses run such prediction markets, some individuals will develop expertise at harnessing existing data to make plausible projections. Although statistical models will outperform human judgment, at least in contexts in which there is strong reason to believe that past relationships will hold,[4] there may be other contexts in which there is no substitute for wisdom, which today remains a uniquely human capability.

In this chapter I introduce some possible applications of prediction markets for businesses. One problem that prediction markets might help businesses overcome is "optimism bias," a tendency that people have to overestimate their chances of success at particular projects. Businesses currently have informal ways of overcoming such bias, but prediction markets might provide a new, decentralized technique. I discuss a new means of structuring and subsidizing prediction markets that will be particularly useful where only a very small number of traders might have expertise in a particular question, a context that may be common in business settings, especially if businesses offer a wide range of prediction markets.

I also discuss the experiences of some companies with prediction markets, including the danger that they could encourage sabotage. I then offer a variety of potential applications including prediction markets to assess the success of particular products, to provide information to consumers, and to evaluate employees. All of these markets are designed to provide additional data that businesses might use in their decision-making processes. These markets are not designed to produce bottom-line conclusions regarding whether particular decisions would be advantageous or harmful. That challenge is taken up especially in Chapter 6, which focuses on public corporations but includes discussion of techniques that might be useful for a wide range of organizations.

THE PROBLEM OF OPTIMISM BIAS
AND WISHFUL THINKING

Cognitive psychologists have in a wide range of experiments demonstrated the presence of optimism bias, sometimes called "wishful thinking" or the "valence effect." Research has shown that, excluding the depressed, individuals rate themselves more highly than other people perceive them.[5] People also generally view themselves as less vulnerable to certain risks, such as getting cancer,[6] though individuals are most likely to be excessively optimistic about events over which they have some degree of control.[7] In the legal context, some research suggests that litigants often do not settle because they are excessively optimistic about the strength of their respective positions.[8] It is not only in Garrison Keillor's Lake Wobegon that we are all above average;[9] it is also in all of our brains. Law students (especially men), another study shows, are overly optimistic about their class rank, and the overestimation is not diminished during the first year following feedback about performance on exams.[10]

Unlike the availability heuristic, the optimism bias is not simply a mental shortcut, and it might appear that evolution should have tended to eliminate it. Because one person's optimism can be observed by others, however, optimistic individuals in fact receive higher returns than do pessimists in many strategic interactions, despite biased judgment. Evolution can thus reinforce the bias.[11] Of course, if optimism is advantageous to individuals, it might not be socially optimal. Moreover, the fact that optimism bias has been advantageous over the course of evolutionary history does not mean that it is optimal in all situations today. Especially to the extent that optimism bias affects the behavior of organizations, too, those organizations might be expected to seek ways of countering it.

This bias has particular resonance in the context of business. Managers may tend to overestimate the degree to which they can control outcomes and therefore take risks that might appear unjustified to others. Managers tend to believe that they have an ability to limit risks, and they tend to distinguish sharply "between gambling (where the odds are exogenously determined and uncontrollable) and risk taking (where skill or information can reduce the uncertainty)," believing that the chances they take fit within the latter category.[12] Managers also generally overestimate the success of ventures in which they have invested their own time and effort.[13] To be sure, these cognitive biases might produce certain social advantages, for example, by inducing individuals to work harder and making them more optimistic about their future.

Optimism bias may cause excessive entry into markets. Avishalom Tor notes that economists sometimes argue that cognitive biases are irrelevant in market contexts because market forces tend to weed out those who cannot overcome them.[14] Tor agrees that some market discipline occurs but that a great deal of overconfidence persists. One reason is that the market sometimes rewards those who were overconfident in situations in which ill-advised gambles happen to pay off, and these individuals will continue to take substantial risks.[15] Evolution might lead firms toward efficiency, but evolutionary processes can take eons rather than months. An appreciation of the optimism bias helps explain some observed phenomena, for instance, that startups do not, on average, perform as well when entering a market as do firms with success in other markets that are diversifying.

In addition, optimism bias may help explain decisions that managers in healthy firms make. For example, J. B. Heaton has sought to explain firms' decisions to have "free cash flow," that is, cash above the amount necessary for funding projects likely to produce profits in the long term.[16] Scholars have offered a variety of theories to explain free cash flow: managers might choose this practice when they have information that is unavailable to the market or when it benefits them at the expense of shareholders. Heaton suggests that both of these explanations fit into a broader theory focusing on managerial optimism. Managers tend to believe that markets undervalue their firms and that their own investment opportunities are better than the market believes they are. This leads managers to overestimate the costs of external financing relative to internal financing because managers believe that interest rates offered externally are too high. Free cash flow gives managers the flexibility to fund such projects directly, potentially leading to excessive investment.

Given the existence of optimism bias in business decisions, prediction markets can produce valuable external assessments of probabilities of the success of possible projects. Of course, we should not be overly optimistic about the extent to which prediction market forecasts will succeed at debiasing business decision making. Studies suggest that typical strategies for debiasing, such as emphasizing to decision makers the possibility that things might go wrong, often are not effective.[17] Even if prediction market forecasts are better than centralized predictions, that does not guarantee that decision makers will use them. In a survey of executives, only 4 percent indicated that they accepted risk estimates that were provided to them.[18] Of course, that may be because they have a healthy distrust of the analyses leading to these estimates, but they might have a distrust, healthy or not, of market predictions as well. The mere capacity of information to debias decision makers does not mean that the information will succeed in doing so.

The optimism bias presents both an opportunity and an obstacle for implementation of prediction markets. It presents an opportunity because businesses and other organizations might use prediction markets as standard parts of the decision making process. Even if individuals remain distrustful when prediction markets call their beliefs into question, use of such markets might help people avoid decision-making errors. It presents an obstacle because individuals often believe that their intuitions and analyses are better than the market's. Studies show that only a small percentage of people can consistently beat prediction markets, but a large number of decision makers tend to believe that they are within that small group. Prediction markets will not have a significant effect on decision making until some decision makers come to accept them, but the optimism bias suggests that it might be difficult to win such acceptance.

THE DYNAMIC PARI-MUTUEL MARKET

Prediction markets for business also must overcome a much more practical problem: ensuring that markets have enough liquidity—that is, enough individuals who are willing to trade—to enable those who have or could develop information to trade on that information. It would be hazardous to extrapolate from the success, say, of TradeSports and infer that prediction markets will work well for business decision making. It is conceivable that virtually every business in the country might benefit from prediction markets targeted toward predictions that are of use to them, but few traders will be inherently interested in participating in these markets. As a result, these markets will require subsidies. In Chapter 2, I described one possible approach to subsidization, but that approach would generally still require a reasonable number of individuals who have enough information about a particular problem to trade with individuals with better information. Ideally, a market should produce predictions even when only a very small number of traders studies the relevant issues.

David Pennock has offered a separate proposal for prediction market design that would solve the liquidity problem.[19] (He also filed an application to patent his approach, so anyone wanting to use this approach might need to obtain a license.)[20] A substantial challenge facing prediction markets is that transactions occur only when someone is willing to buy and someone else is willing to sell. In effect, the conflicting predictions of two different traders are required before a single data point can be added. Pennock imagines a system in which individuals could change the prediction market probabilities by making bets that are consistent with their own predictions, without needing to find someone to bet against them. He calls this system a dynamic pari-mutuel market.

Pennock shows that a dynamic pari-mutuel market can be designed in such a way that from the perspective of a trader it appears to be the same as a continuous double auction, the traditional form of a prediction market. A trader can place an order to purchase or to sell shares, and in some cases transactions between traders will be completed, but in other cases a trader will be buying shares from the market sponsor, who in effect always acts as a market maker. Individuals who are familiar with traditionally structured prediction markets and securities trading mechanisms should thus be comfortable with the dynamic pari-mutuel market, although the internal workings are different.

Pari-mutuel betting might seem to be an inappropriate choice for prediction markets that might involve only a small number of individuals, because racetrack betting generally involves very large numbers of individuals. Pari-mutuel betting, however, can work with one or more bettors, given the always lurking possibility that someone else will choose to bet, perhaps at the last possible instant. If I am the only bettor and pick a single outcome though that outcome is far from certain, then someone who restores the pari-mutuel predictions to their appropriate relative levels will generally make money from me. Thus, a pari-mutuel market itself might serve as a useful alternative to prediction markets in some situations. Should only one person participate, that person has an incentive to make an accurate probability estimate by distributing money among different possibilities. When a number of individuals are expected to participate, each bettor will have an incentive to place each dollar bet in a way that restores the market to the correct value.

As we saw in Chapter 1, a problem with pari-mutuel betting markets is that individuals have no incentive to bet early. Pari-mutuel betting might produce accurate predictions eventually, but prediction markets are likely to produce more accurate forecasts over time. A corollary advantage is that someone who buys tradable contracts based on information not generally available can sell those tradable contracts once the market has absorbed and accepted the information, thus saving the trader from any risk associated with the actual probabilistic event being projected. The sequential nature of prediction markets conceivably also might improve final predictions. Especially in prediction markets with small numbers of participants, some individuals might gain reputations for accurate predictions, and thus traders can take reputation into account as another variable that will assist in making predictions. In a pari-mutuel market, anyone with a reputation for accuracy will have an incentive to bet anonymously or at the last minute, because each bettor benefits if the bets in the rest of the market are as far off from the best predictions as possible.

Pennock's paper suggests that with appropriate modifications, a pari-mutuel betting market can also provide accurate probability estimates over time and give incentives for individuals to trade on information as soon as they obtain it. In addition, such a market does not require that there be another trader with whom a particular trader's request is matched, and it can thus overcome the problem of "thin markets" in which little trading takes place. In a standard pari-mutuel market, the cost of a bet on a particular outcome is fixed. In the dynamic pari-mutuel market, by contrast, the price of shares varies over time, with prices changing according to the current probability predictions of the market. Each share in a particular outcome, however, will receive an equal payout if the outcome occurs, regardless of the price at which shares are purchased. The changing prices allow for calculation of the market probability of an outcome at a particular time, using formulas that Pennock develops.

There are a variety of possible approaches to designing a dynamic pari-mutuel market. Two design decisions are particularly critical. The first is whether the winning bets are refunded or simply added to the pool from which the winnings are eventually distributed. An advantage of refunding the winning bets is that it makes it impossible for anyone who has invested in the correct outcome to lose money. If the winning bet is not refunded, then it is possible (though unlikely as a practical matter) that someone who buys a share in the correct outcome at a high price will lose money if the share subsequently falls to a very low price before ultimately winning. There is no inherent reason, however, that this is essential to the market, and refunding bets complicates the mechanism somewhat.

The second design decision is the way the price for a share should be determined at any given time. Assuming that there are two tradable contracts in the market, an attractive approach is for the system to adopt a price function that ensures that the ratio of the prices of the two tradable contracts will be equal to the ratio of the amounts wagered on them at any given time. With this or many other possible price functions, the greater the amount invested in an outcome, the cheaper will be the other outcomes in the market.

Suppose, for example, that the dynamic pari-mutuel market is used to predict the outcome of a race between the turtle and the hare. Let us imagine that so far ten dollars has been invested on the turtle and five dollars has been invested on the hare. The imbalance in the betting indicates that the turtle is the favorite, and accordingly the cost of the turtle share will be twice the cost of the hare share. For various price functions, Pennock offers formulas for determining the price at any time for purchasing an infinitesimal fraction of a share, and he uses these formulas to derive other formulas for calculating the number of shares that can be purchased for a particular sum of money.[21]

Unfortunately, for the price function that equalizes price and investment ratios, Pennock was unable to derive an inverse function—that is, a formula for determining the amount of money that would be necessary for purchasing a particular number of shares. He notes, however, that it would be possible for a computer to calculate an approximation of this inverse function for any degree of precision. Finally, Pennock also offers simple formulas for calculating the market probability of any particular outcome. Of course, all of these numbers easily could be displayed on a computer screen without the user's understanding the mechanics of the market.

Some of Pennock's formulas depend on a simple and probably defensible assumption, albeit one that Pennock concedes he was unable to prove. The assumption is that the expected value of the per share payout for an outcome at a particular time, if that outcome should occur, can be easily calculated as a ratio: the total amount invested in both outcomes divided by the number of shares in the particular outcome.[22] For example, if the $10 invested in the turtle is split among 5 shares, the payout per share would be equal to $3 ($15/5), though the return might vary from share to share depending on initial purchase price.

Pennock shows that this would certainly be true in the instant before the market closes, but the question is whether it is true more generally. In other words, would market prices follow a "random walk," meaning that the current price provides the best prediction of the future price given available information? This is not true in the traditional pari-mutuel market because of the incentive to wait until the last moment to trade. Pennock surmises that this will be true in the dynamic market if traders are rational, though he does not prove it systematically. Empirical analysis of such markets might help determine whether this assumption is in fact true, though Pennock emphasizes that participants can play the game nonetheless,[23] and it seems likely that the market probability estimates will represent true probabilities.

At least one argument suggests that the dynamic market might not follow a random walk, however. In Pennock's prediction market, the amount that is invested can only increase over time, just as in a traditional pari-mutuel betting market. An implication of this is that the market probability prediction will be less sensitive to an investment of a fixed amount of money later than it would have been earlier. The flip side of this is that when one believes that the market prediction diverges from the true value by a particular amount, when more money has been invested it will take a larger investment to correct the market price. One can therefore earn more profit on information that changes consensus predictions by a set amount later in the market.

There might then be some incentive to wait to trade on information until later in the market. This incentive, however, is qualified, because if there is a danger that someone else might trade on the information in the interim, then the market will move closer to the trader's expectation of the true value, and profit potential may be less. Moreover, it might sometimes be possible to move the market price more than once, if other traders do not recognize that the repeat player's original trades are informed. In a traditional prediction market, by contrast, a trader ordinarily always has an incentive to trade on information immediately, unless for some reason the market is expected to provide substantially greater liquidity later on, for example, as traders mistakenly grow increasingly comfortable with a particular estimate. The subsidy method described in Chapter 2 tends to provide roughly equivalent liquidity at all times.

Pennock's prediction market has at least two technical complications. The first is how to deal with markets in which there are three or more outcomes, and the second is how to deal with markets that produce nonprobabilistic numeric estimates. In his patent application Pennock notes, "Some natural extensions . . . would handle more than two outcomes, or a continuous range of outcomes."[24] The key intuition is that purchasing a tradable contract corresponding to one of a number of outcomes amounts to betting against all of those outcomes. The calculations for market price and the market assessed probability therefore must take into account the total money invested and the number of shares in all of the other tradable contracts.

Ideally, the market mechanism should allow someone to bet on two or more items simultaneously. A market with a continuous range of options could work simply by providing proportional payoffs to two tradable contracts. For example, if the number being predicted is between zero and one hundred and turns out to be sixty, then investors in one contract could receive 60 percent of the pool and investors in the other could receive 40 percent. An alternative approach would be to divide the relevant numeric range into a large number of subranges, perhaps one hundred, and allow betting on numerous subranges. This would allow traders to profit by improving the market estimate of the probability distribution.

THE YAHOO! TECH BUZZ MARKET

Pennock is an employee of Yahoo! Laboratories, and so it should not be surprising that Yahoo! has implemented his idea in an experimental play-money market, called the Buzz Game,[25] which is designed to help predict technology trends. The key insight underlying the market is that as technologies become more popular, people are more likely to enter terms describing the technologies in Web search engines. As a result, at any time, one can obtain an approximate sense of the success of different technologies by considering whether users are searching for them more or less frequently. For example, one might track the relative success of Microsoft Office and OpenOffice. The more successful OpenOffice is in achieving its goal of serving as an alternative to Microsoft Office, the higher the percentage of searches for either will be allocated to OpenOffice. Of course, it is interesting to know not only the relative popularity of the two programs today but also to know how their relative popularity might change in the future. The Buzz Game dynamic pari-mutuel market can be used to predict future buzz ratings.

Anyone can sign up, and players initially receive ten thousand fantasy dollars. The game is divided into a variety of markets, each of which pits two or more technologies against one another. For example, a category for "digital video recorders" currently includes various search terms associated with MythTV, ReplayTV, TiVo, and others. Players can buy and sell stock in any of the competing technologies, using the dynamic pari-mutuel mechanism. A trader can specify either the amount of money that the trader would like to spend buying shares of a particular type or the number of shares of a type that the trader owns that the trader would like to sell. Each week, the owner of every stock receives a dividend payment equal to 3 percent of the market capitalization of the stock. The market capitalization depends on the "buzz score." For example, if a total of one hundred thousand dollars has been invested in the digital video recorder market and ReplayTV earns 20 percent of the searches in the category during the week, then ReplayTV stocks pay out a total of 3 percent of twenty thousand dollars, or six hundred dollars, so if six hundred ReplayTV shares are outstanding, each would receive a dividend of one dollar.

Traders have an incentive to care not only about the dividend for the current week but also about dividends in future weeks. They will thus give stocks an approximate value based on discounted anticipated dividends.[26] It is not obvious as a theoretical matter what the discount rate on fantasy dollars is likely to be, so it will be difficult (though perhaps not impossible, with statistical analysis) to convert buzz scores into a discrete prediction about the relative future success of products at any particular time. Nonetheless, the market should indicate over some indeterminate time frame which technologies are likely to receive increased consumer attention and which technologies are likely to receive less.

Alternative dynamic pari-mutuel market designs could easily predict buzz scores at a variety of different times. One set of tradable contracts could correspond to buzz scores at the end of the year, another set to buzz scores at the end of two years, and so on. It is not yet clear how prescient the dynamic market will turn out to be, but more explicit predictions might help establish the effectiveness of the market. Of course, if the dynamic pari-mutuel markets prove to be relatively good predictors, forecasting such variables as sales[27] and profits will turn out to be more important than predicting mere buzz.

The buzz market works somewhat differently than the dynamic pari-mutuel market described in his original paper. In the original design, the market sponsor only bought tradable contracts and did not sell them. But in the Buzz Game, the market sponsor is available to purchase and sell tradable contracts, so there is no need for an aftermarket to sell tradable contracts. (Pennock has not yet disclosed the formulas that the market uses to calculate sales prices, but he has indicated that the price formula for the market follows an approach not discussed in the original paper.[28] This formula ensures that the ratio of prices of two tradable contracts is always equal to the number of shares of the two that are outstanding, instead of the total amount of money invested in the tradable contracts.) One consequence of this arrangement is that a market participant can execute a buy transaction and a sell transaction in rapid succession, and assuming that no one else executes a transaction in between these, the participant will be in the exact same position as he or she was originally, except that the market imposes a disclosed one-penny-per-share transaction fee upon sale. This is important, because the dynamic pari-mutuel mechanism should not allow a player to execute a quick series of transactions that, in the absence of transactions by others, allow the player to emerge with the same portfolio and earn a profit at the same time.

A significant technical obstacle in the buzz market is the danger of cheating. The problem exists only because the buzz market uses play money, and anyone can participate in this market for free. The result is that individuals can open multiple accounts with the goal of executing trades so that money is funneled from throw-away accounts to a permanent one. A simple approach is to use one or more throw-away accounts to bid up the tradable contracts corresponding to a particular outcome and then immediately use the permanent account to purchase tradable contracts corresponding to other outcomes, which will thus be available at lower than the appropriate price.

Yahoo! plainly anticipated the problem, and the rules specifically prohibit opening multiple accounts for any reason or colluding to manipulate the prices or disrupt the game. The penalty for these and other violations is account suspension. Yahoo! has sought to prevent manipulation by monitoring the Internet provider addresses that individuals use to trade, looking for similar logins or identical passwords, and seeking to identify collusive activity. It is hard to know for sure, however, how successful such efforts have been, and presumably some elaborate schemes might be difficult to detect. The possibility of manipulation of this type suggests that it probably would not be practical for the market sponsor to subsidize the market by promising to distribute some subsidy in proportion to points that market participants earn, at least without means of identifying those who open accounts. A substantial subsidy would increase incentives for manipulation.

Despite the potential for manipulation, the Buzz Game could serve as a foundation for broader application of prediction markets in businesses. On its

Web site, Yahoo! indicates some of the reasons why it is sponsoring the project.[29] Obvious goals include providing entertainment for its users and testing the dynamic pari-mutuel mechanism empirically. The project, however, was the result of a collaboration with O'Reilly Media, a computer book publisher, and the site also indicates that a goal of the market was to give O'Reilly a sense of upcoming trends. Another was to provide information about the relation between search engine behavior and events in the real world; perhaps the dynamic pari-mutuel market indirectly may be of assistance in designing better search engines. Of course, if the Buzz Game does prove to be a useful prognosticator of technology trends, many businesses might benefit from the data besides O'Reilly and Yahoo!, and it does not appear that all of the markets were designed with O'Reilly and Yahoo! in mind. (It is difficult to see, for example, why either would care much about the relative buzz received by the Sony Aibo and the iRobot Roomba.)

Many markets akin to the buzz market for other technological fields could be created, and some such markets might target market niches, including relatively rare search terms. One might, for example, imagine a buzz market focusing on particular book titles, and publishers might use such markets to gauge how changes in the publicity plans it makes for books affects the buzz that the books are likely to receive. Such markets would be particularly useful if book publishers are selectively subject to optimism bias and need to recognize when they have succumbed to excessive hype.

Ultimately, however, markets for predicting search terms make up only one possible class of applications, and the potential of the dynamic pari-mutuel market and other prediction market designs lies in the possibility that they might become able to predict a wide variety of phenomena. Once its software is established, after all, it should not be difficult for Yahoo! to scale up its project and allow anyone to become the sponsor of a prediction market in just about anything, as long as the sponsor can determine as individual markets close what the correct values are. Presumably, Yahoo! would charge a fee for such a service, though in the long run competition among different market designs and companies would probably mean that the fees are relatively small.

Although it is likely that larger companies would use such a service before smaller companies do, if such markets become common, they might be useful to small companies as well. Indeed, the greater potential of prediction markets is for relatively small entities, which may lack the in-house professional expertise to make first-rate predictions about variables of interest. It may be impractical today for a small restaurant to hire teams of consultants in all aspects of its business—from trends in décor and food to legal and economic developments that might affect profits and decisions about topics such as expansion. But it might be quite inexpensive to create a few prediction markets in relevant topics, and if these markets offer small subsidies and a large number of similar markets exist, individuals with expertise in particular topics will have an incentive to trade in prediction markets as a means, in effect, of providing consulting services.

Play-money markets may become increasingly common, but they may never seem to be more than a novelty item. Perhaps Yahoo! could obtain the most economic value from its buzz market by licensing its patents and its software to a foreign company beyond the reach of U.S. law but nonetheless able to allow both U.S. and foreign businesses to create prediction markets in topics that are relevant to them, while also permitting real-money betting. My own guess, admittedly, is that prediction markets today would not guess that prediction markets will become an everyday business tool in the near future, but they might gain momentum and become increasingly commonplace.

THE SUBSIDIZED DYNAMIC
PARI-MUTUEL MARKET

An additional technical challenge is the combination of the market with a subsidy mechanism for cases in which a subsidy is desired. Note that simply placing the subsidy in the pool, to be allocated among the winning shares, will not do. That would give individuals an incentive to invest simultaneously in both market outcomes, possibly using separate accounts, a combination of transactions that ordinarily would have no net economic effect but would entitle the trader to a share of the subsidy. In effect, the problem is the same as the one that complicated the design of a subsidy in Chapter 2: traders might enter into wash transactions. One possible solution to this problem would be to charge commissions, which would also be added to the pool. Suppose that $100 total has been invested in a market with a $1 subsidy, and a 5 percent commission is charged. Investing another $100 in direct proportion to the earlier investments just before the market ends would cost the investor $5, though the investor would expect to receive $2.50 of this back when final payouts are issued, plus $0.50 of the subsidy, for a total of $3, a losing proposition. The trick is to identify a commission level that will be high enough given the amount of legitimate trading expected.

An alternative possibility is to build on the subsidy mechanism described in Chapter 2, in which traders receive proportional shares of a fixed subsidy depending on the amount of time that they expose themselves at the front and the back of the bid and ask queue. As Pennock argues, a benefit of the dynamic pari-mutuel market is that it can be presented in a manner similar to a continuous double auction. A complication is that transactions are often fulfilled through the automated market maker rather than by other participants, unless a participant has offered a better deal then the market maker has offered. The subsidy should not be wasted on an offer that is inferior to the market maker's. A solution is for the subsidy to be distributed only to those who have offered third parties better deals than the automated market maker would offer. The result of this subsidy scheme is that prices would move more slowly for traders making purchases on the market, thus allowing greater profits.

A final possibility, which Pennock appears to advocate, requires the market sponsor to place a seed wager, for example, distributing the subsidy randomly over the different possible outcomes or distributing it in accordance with a model of the relevant events developed by the market sponsor. A problem with the seed wager approach is that the exact amount of the subsidy is not fixed in advance. If placed haphazardly, seed wagers will generally be losing propositions, thus providing a subsidy, but sometimes they might produce positive returns for the market sponsor. For example, if the seed wager is distributed unequally to a favorite and a long shot but the long shot wins, then the market sponsor will have made money. The seed wager at least provides an upper limit on the amount of money that the market sponsor will lose, certainly no more than the entire amount of the seed wager. If the market sponsor, meanwhile, distributes the subsidy in accordance with its own model, and that model is relatively good, then the market sponsor may be providing only a very small subsidy to the market. In some cases, of course, this will be exactly what the sponsor intends, because it will be providing higher subsidies when its own model is weaker and it thus needs more help, and yet it does not need to figure out in advance whether its own model is strong or weak.

A separate potential problem with this approach is that most of the benefit of the subsidy will apply at the very beginning of the market. So, for example, the first trader to correct a blatant mispricing at the beginning of the market would receive most of the benefit of the subsidy. This will be a particular danger if the subsidy is distributed randomly or if the market sponsor's model is weak. Of course, the first bettor's investment would provide some additional incentive for others to fix any remaining mispricing, but still much of the subsidy might in effect be wasted on relatively easy fixes, at least unless the seed wager is set in a relatively sophisticated way. To some extent, this mechanism might counteract another problem with the dynamic pari-mutuel market: bettors with relatively good information in the absence of subsidy might have an incentive to wait to trade until there is already some amount invested in the market, in order to get the maximum profit possible from the available investment, at least if no one else is likely to develop the same information. The subsidy counteracts this tendency in an imprecise way, however, so that there might be strong incentives to trade at the very beginning and the very end of the market and less incentive during the bulk of the market.

ORANGE JUICE AND THE WEATHER

The possibility that the predictive power of securities markets might provide information to businesses is in some sense nothing new. Commodity markets have long made it possible for small businesses to purchase commodities for delivery in the future and for speculators to trade these commodities in the hope of making a profit, thus providing market liquidity. The information that these markets provide can help businesses make sensible decisions. If it appears that one commodity seems likely to be expensive at some point in the future, for example, a business might invest in adjustments so that it can use another as a substitute. Indeed, businesses can do this even if they are not investing in the market themselves, because the price of futures contracts facilitates predictions. Businesses, for example, might find out well in advance that heating oil will be more expensive in the coming winter, either by directly consulting the futures markets or by reading or hearing about news reports that rely on them. This information could easily affect business decisions; for example, a business that is losing money might decide on the basis of this information to shut its doors, thus potentially saving it from larger losses.

Studies suggest that commodity market prices do a remarkable job of incorporating information and making relevant predictions about the future. Richard Roll conducted a particularly interesting study, published in 1984, of the market for frozen concentrated orange juice.[30] This commodity market will be familiar to many members of the movie-going public because it played a major role in the plot of the 1983 comedy *Trading Places,* starring Dan

Aykroyd and Eddie Murphy. The premise of the film is that two wealthy commodity traders, played by Don Ameche and Ralph Bellamy, decide to conduct a sociological experiment. They plot to destroy the career of a successful young trader, played by Aykroyd, and have him trade places with a street con artist played by Murphy. The film makes commodity trading appear easy, as Murphy's character proves to be just as shrewd a trader as Aykroyd's, parlaying simple insights about human behavior and tendencies into profits. In the end, the two exact revenge on Ameche's and Bellamy's, selling them a fake Agriculture Department report about farm conditions and leading them to make disastrous trades in the market for frozen concentrated orange juice. The market is thus portrayed as one in which individuals seek to cheat by obtaining insider information, but in which at the same time simple analysis can produce great profits.

It is not surprising that Roll's study shows that the market is somewhat more sophisticated than the movie might suggest. Roll chose orange juice as an object of study because an easily measurable variable, the weather, has significant effects on supply. Orange trees are particularly vulnerable to freezing temperatures, and so falling temperatures should decrease production and raise the price of orange juice futures. At the same time, Roll believed that there were relatively few other factors that would seem likely to produce significant demand and supply shocks. Roll's research verified that weather predictions affected orange juice future prices.

Astonishingly, however, Roll's work demonstrated that the converse was also true: orange juice futures prices could help improve on weather forecasts by the National Weather Service. That is, Roll showed that these prices were statistically significant predictors of the service's forecast error (the number of degrees by which the temperature would diverge from the service's prediction). This suggests that some traders in the market might engage in relatively sophisticated analysis in order to predict price movements, considering not only publicly available data but also their own analyses. Alternatively, perhaps someone managed to transform many casual observations about the weather into a forecast that could improve on the National Weather Service's. To be sure, the market might have been much less accurate if no National Weather Service forecasts existed, but the study suggests that commodity markets take into account both public and private information.

The success of commodity markets at making predictions does not guarantee equal success for predictions generated by prediction markets. The market for frozen concentrated orange juice has substantial liquidity, and so a modestly subsidized prediction market might not perform nearly as well. An advantage of prediction markets, however, is that because they can be designed to predict virtually any variable, they can be customized to the particular needs of businesses. The orange juice market, by contrast, did not produce an explicit prediction of the weather, and it would not have been easy for a casual observer to look at the market price and decide to wear a warm coat. Moreover, a prediction market can provide much more directly targeted incentives to research weather than can an orange juice market, in which other factors may be involved as well. On the other hand, an advantage of the orange juice market is that it already has many investors.

Prediction markets can be designed explicitly to forecast weather phenomena, and indeed there is at least one real-money prediction market devoted to weather, seeking to improve on official projections in tracking the path of hurricanes.[31] Weather prediction markets also might produce up-to-the-second forecasts, showing clear probability distributions that could be useful to businesses that are sensitive to short-term weather fluctuations. That commodity market prices can be translated into predictions about the future is a happy artifact of an institution established for different purposes. Because prediction markets are designed specifically for the purpose of generating predictions, they can be more easily customized to make targeted and detailed predictions.

HEDGING RISK

An important function of commodity markets is to provide a mechanism for reducing risk. Some businesses purchase frozen concentrated orange juice a long time in advance because they can be harmed by price increases, and they do not want to worry about the need to obtain liquidity at the last minute if orange juice prices turn out to be unexpectedly high (and sellers will want to hedge against a drop in prices). The commodity markets thus serve as a kind of insurance mechanism. Even in the absence of any information asymmetries, the cost of bearing risk will differ across businesses. The businesses that can bear the risk associated with pricing uncertainty most cheaply are those that tend to offer to commit to selling orange juice in the future at a fixed price. Trading firms may be better able to diversify the risk of orange juice prices than are businesses that depend heavily on orange juice supplies, and indeed commodity trading firms will typically invest in baskets of large numbers of commodities, so that if some commodities rise in price, others will decrease, and the risk of price changes in the basket as a whole will be small.

Large entities often actively seek to hedge not only risks regarding the price of inputs but also a variety of other risks. For example, many entities are subject to interest rate risks, either making money or losing money as interest rates rise or decline. These companies can invest in securities whose payoffs depend on interest rate changes. Other companies face risk from changing relative currency prices and thus may trade directly in securities whose prices depend on security values. Securities such as these are called *derivatives* because the value at which they pay off, and thus the prices at which they trade, are derivative of the prices of other financial instruments. Of course, because some wish to invest in derivatives in order to hedge risk, others have an incentive to develop mathematical and computer models that predict future changes in securities prices.

In some public policy circles, speculators have a bad name, in part because they might be appearing to seek profits without performing any useful activity. Speculators, however, may well be performing a useful economic function, because accurate predictions of the future will generally improve economic decision making. On the other hand, there is no guarantee that we will have the socially optimal level of speculation. Jack Hirshleifer has argued that there can be excessive investment in securities research because the private gain from securities research can exceed the social gain.[32] But to the extent that firms that do not trade in a particular market might benefit from the predictions that market makes, there could be underinvestment in speculation from a social perspective.[33]

Typically, individuals make relatively few investments, aside from insurance products, with the goal of hedging risk in mind, though individuals often seek to minimize risk by creating a diversified portfolio. I drink quite a bit of orange juice. Conceivably, I could reduce my overall financial risk through careful investing, for example by purchasing contracts for delivery of orange juice next year. Unfortunately, these contracts do not provide for home delivery, but if the price of orange juice goes up, so will the value of the contract, and I can sell it to fund my orange juice habit. I have not, however, made this investment, nor will I. Even with my prodigious consumption, orange juice is too small a risk in my financial portfolio to make it worthwhile to spend the time it would take to figure out just how to go about buying such a contract and calculating how much to spend.

There might, however, be other investments that could help me hedge my risk, and they might be worth my time. For example, I purchased a mortgage to buy a house, and so my overall portfolio is concentrated in real estate. If current housing prices turn out to be a bubble, I will suffer, at least if I need to sell the house and move to an area in which there has been no price decrease. The mortgage itself includes some provisions that reduce my risk—in particular, a fixed interest rate for the first few years of the loan, which reduces my vulnerability to interest rate risk—but because I am risk-averse, it might make sense to purchase some additional securities that would reduce my risk.

For example, I could bet against real estate stocks by selling short. That is, I can borrow real estate securities and sell them, with an agreement to return the securities at a later time, so that I will profit if the price of these securities falls. This is a relatively crude approach to hedging risk. Real estate stocks could perform well nationally even as real estate values decline in my region. Or real estate values might rise in my region but fall in my neighborhood as a result of traffic from a new Wal-Mart.

Increasingly, it is becoming possible for individuals and small businesses to hedge risk. Robert Shiller, in a book titled *The New Financial Order: Risk in the 21st Century,*[34] anticipates and endorses a world in which one can invest in securities that are much more narrowly tailored to one's particular circumstances. For example, one might invest in securities whose payoff will depend on the real estate market in the Washington, D.C., metro area. Some markets, such as Hedgestreet.com, now make it possible to make investments of exactly this type. Or one might invest in securities whose payoff will depend on the overall performance of individuals in a particular sector of the economy. Suppose, for example, that I am a courtroom reporter, and I worry about the possibility that improvements in voice recognition technology will cost me my job in the future. I might buy a tradable contract that will have a higher payoff if, say, the number of help wanted ads for court reporters declines by more than some fixed percentage. That way, I would be able to use the payoff to obtain new training and to maintain my existing standard of living. There are many other possible examples. A pizza business might invest in securities that will pay off if the pizza sector as a whole declines.

There may well be some practical limits to these markets. Some individuals who seek to reduce their risk by purchasing insurance might be hesitant to hedge their risks in this way. Perhaps one reason is that not many people do it, and social norms may explain a lot about individual purchasing decisions. But there are other reasons, too. People may make purchasing decisions in part because they have armchair theories that particular economic sectors will perform well. People who decide to become court reporters, for example, tend to be the people who are least worried about the possibility that technological improvements will put them out of work, and so even if they recognize that it makes sense to hedge risk, they would tend to believe that the cost of the relevant securities is excessively high given their own probability estimates. The problem of optimism bias might compound this problem of self-selection. And if individuals and small businesses were interested in hedging risks, the transactions costs of learning about how to go about it and determining which products to buy and in what amounts might make it not worthwhile.

Another limitation is that these markets tend to allow for trading in risks that are shared by many but not risks that may be unique to individuals. One reason for this is the lemons problem. George Akerlof suggested that people generally are more likely to sell used cars when they have already figured out that those cars are lemons.[35] Because lemons are disproportionately represented in used car lots, someone who sells a good car needs to offer a substantial discount, because others will not be able to verify whether a car is a lemon. The result is that owners of good cars are more likely to keep their cars, making the problem ever more severe. In the insurance context, this problem is known as "adverse selection."[36]

There is a debate about the extent to which adverse selection is in fact a problem in insurance markets, and indeed some evidence suggests that people who buy insurance tend to be relatively low risks.[37] But it would likely be a problem with insurance products that are much more narrowly tailored. If someone indicated an interest in purchasing divorce insurance because of the large financial costs associated with the divorce transaction, for example, I would suspect that the person was having marital problems. As a result, markets in divorce insurance seem unlikely to develop.

Nonetheless, prediction markets might play a role in generally increasing the number of risks that can be hedged relatively cheaply. The technology that companies such as HedgeStreet use is essentially no different from the technology underlying prediction markets. If these products become more popular, the increased liquidity will allow creation of more markets. Conceivably, more innovative prediction market designs might facilitate the creation of markets in which there otherwise would be relatively low liquidity. The information that prediction markets produce also could reduce information asymmetries and thus adverse selection. Someone today who is seeking insurance against a drop in housing prices in a small town might be thought to have some asymmetric information, but as markets develop, it will be more likely that the individual is simply following a sound diversification plan.

The dynamic pari-mutuel market might, meanwhile, be adapted to serve as a vehicle for hedging risk and could function with a very small number of traders. Individuals and small businesses might create particular markets tailored to their own narrow and specific aims. Such individuals might not merely create the market but also provide some initial subsidy to the market to encourage speculators to investigate their particular bet against them. Such a subsidy provides a mechanism by which a sponsor of such a market credibly can provide assurance that the sponsor in fact is interested in trading on the market to reduce risk. Otherwise, third parties might not spend the effort required to investigate particular circumstances and invest in the market.

Such markets would need to focus on topics for which adverse selection seems to be a relatively small danger and for which it will be relatively easy to determine ex post whether tradable contracts should pay out. For example, a business that might be taken by eminent domain might use a prediction market to purchase the equivalent of "takings insurance,"[38] and third parties might be willing to bet that the business will not be subject to eminent domain. Or someone opening a high-end boutique in a gentrifying area might create a subsidized prediction market in the future economic conditions of that area and, as a hedge, place money on gentrification's not occurring.

It might be considerably easier to purchase this kind of protection in a marketplace with many small prediction markets than to individually negotiate the terms of an insurance policy with a specific insurance company. The prediction market would avoid the cost associated with negotiating a complex set of insurance policy terms. Just as auction mechanisms such as eBay reduce the transactions costs of disposing of buying and selling certain goods, so, too, might prediction markets reduce the costs of insuring risk. In effect, prediction markets enable a low-transactions-cost form of peer-to-peer insurance, a modern alternative to customized Lloyd's insurance products.[39]

The possibility that prediction markets will be used to hedge risk leads to an important caveat concerning interpretation of prediction market prices. In a hedging market, probability predictions naïvely derived from market prices might overestimate the probability that the event being hedged against will occur. This is because the only reason why someone or some entity other than the sponsor of such a prediction market will invest in it is that the individual or entity is able to bear the relevant risk more cheaply than the market sponsor, who will take the other side of the bet. But individuals who are taking on risk will demand compensation for this risk by offering prices that are less attractive to the sponsor than pure probability estimates would anticipate. Meanwhile, the market sponsor will be willing to pay a premium to reduce risk and thus should be willing to accept these less attractive prices.

When the two sides of a market seem likely to have systematically different risk exposures, market prices can be biased predictors of the relevant events. Of course, this should produce caution in interpreting the results of any prediction market in which people might invest to achieve hedging, regardless of the purpose for which the market is created. The size of this bias will vary depending on the particular risk. We will see in Chapter 8 how we might use prediction markets to calculate the size of this bias and adjust for it.

INTERNAL MARKETS

So far I have primarily focused on markets with which businesses might aggregate information held by outsiders, although insiders might trade on such markets as well. Markets in which outsiders can participate may be particularly important as a means of combating optimism bias. If one reason for this bias is that optimism can be contagious and that groups of people engaged in a collective enterprise can suffer from "groupthink" that prevents them from seeing another perspective, the discipline of market predictions might force decision makers within the business to reassess priorities. Such markets also can serve as effective means of harnessing information and expertise that might exist somewhere in the world yet is not easily identifiable by the business. A restaurant, for example, might like to hire a consultant who can predict food and dining trends, but it may not have the skills to ascertain which consultants give accurate projections. By using an external market, the restaurant in effect hires the individuals with the highest self-confidence in their ability to make projections.

Nonetheless, to date, the primary use of prediction markets by business has been to create internal markets. In some cases, internal markets may be necessary to prevent the disclosure of trade secrets, but an additional powerful consideration underlying this design choice is that internal markets help overcome regulatory obstacles (see Chapter 2). Even a play-money internal market might work well within the enterprise, if the enterprise implicitly promises to reward those who perform well on such a market, for example, by giving them higher compensation or promotions.

Allowing only authorized individuals to participate in a play-money market reduces the danger of "throw-away" accounts that the designers of the Yahoo!

Buzz Game faced, because there will be a finite number of points for authorized participants to share, and nobody can create a false identity because the company knows the universe of eligible participants. Moreover, social norms within the organization might be successful in discouraging individuals from seeking to manipulate the markets.

The same analysis suggests that internal markets might work relatively well with real money. One approach is to grant each participant a fixed amount of money to bet in the market. This probably succeeds at overcoming the danger of prosecution for gambling, because the employees would be betting only designated funds. Experimental economists have long conducted studies in which individuals in effect have gambled with money granted to them by the experimenters,[40] a practice that appears not to have drawn regulatory scrutiny.

Of course, the sponsors of a prediction market might also seed individuals outside the organization with money, but there are two reasons why seeding accounts for insiders may make a great deal of sense. First, the money in effect serves as a portion of the individual employees' compensation package. An organization can give one hundred dollars in money that can be spent on the prediction market instead of one hundred dollars of alternative compensation. Second, the organization might be able to encourage employees actually to bet the money by, for example, adopting a social norm (with understood financial consequences for the employees) that individuals will not simply pocket the money. An alternative approach to encourage spending would be to grant much of the money in the form of a subsidy for those who place their funds at risk in the market (see the discussion of subsidies in Chapter 2).

There are still reasons to believe that real-money prediction markets may be superior to such markets. The fixed account, we have seen, limits participants' incentives to research the relevant information and prevents the most confident individuals, such as those with the best information, from investing their own funds to move the market a relatively great distance. Nonetheless, businesses might be able to combat this concern by offering very generous grants of money that can be but need not be wagered on the market. For example, a business might give each employee ten thousand dollars that the employee may choose to invest in internal markets, and other compensation might be reduced accordingly. Many employees might not bet much of this money on the market, particularly if the additional subsidies from betting were relatively small, but at least they could do so and therefore could make a substantial impact on the market price if they wished.

Should real-money prediction markets be legalized, a business might still benefit from conducting both an internal prediction market and an external prediction market in the same issue. For example, a business might heavily subsidize the internal prediction market, once again in effect providing a form of employee compensation, while not subsidizing or only lightly subsidizing the external one. The external market could provide better information or assessments than the internal market could. The market could be a useful means of providing a limited opportunity for outsiders to trade even if it turns out that such pairs of markets systematically converge on the same prices. There is good reason to think that they would, given the possibility that employees could arbitrage between the markets, though a business might attempt to prevent employees from participating in the external markets and might seek to prevent information flows from one market to the other, though these restrictions could be difficult to enforce. It would, of course, be interesting if arbitrage could be prevented and two different groups of traders reached substantially different predictions.

An early example of an internal market is one conducted by Hewlett-Packard. Kay-Yut Chen of Hewlett-Packard Laboratories and Charles R. Plott, a leading experimental economist based at the California Institute of Technology, established an internal market, choosing "only a relatively small number of people . . . selected specifically from different parts of the business operation because they were thought to have different patterns of information about the targeted event."[41] Chen and Plott reasoned that with respect to many issues, "small bits and pieces of relevant information exist in the opinions and intuition of individuals who are close to an activity."[42] They included a few engineers in the market, reasoning that they would not have access to the relevant information but might help provide liquidity for other traders.[43]

All participants were given an amount of cash to wager and were paid at the end of each market. Chen and Plott's ambition was that the market would serve not merely as a kind of opinion poll but in fact would succeed at aggregating all of these dispersed pieces of evidence. "Gathering the bits and pieces by traditional means, such as business meetings, is highly inefficient," they reasoned,[44] concluding that a prediction market might economize on transaction costs by aggregating the information efficiently.

Making the experiment particularly interesting, Chen and Plott sought to compare the forecasts of prediction markets with predictions from another source, specifically the official forecasts that Hewlett-Packard routinely made in the course of its business. There are some hazards in such a comparison. It is possible, for example, that one set of comparisons might be based in part on the other, and indeed Chen and Plott report that anecdotal evidence suggested that the market predictions sometimes were used as inputs into the Hewlett-Packard predictions. Evidence traveling in that direction, however, will tend to mean only that the experiment will understate the quality of market predictions, because the official forecasters presumably chose numbers between what would have been their official forecasts and the market-based predictions.

Another caveat is that the comparison depends greatly on the quality of the company's forecasting system. Perhaps Hewlett-Packard was willing to be a laboratory in this area in part because it had problems with its forecasts, or perhaps it simply happens to have worse forecasters than do other businesses. The more general point is that experimental tests comparing prediction markets with other institutions must staff both the prediction markets and those institutions with particular personnel, and the results may depend on the quality of personnel provided to both.

In total, Chen and Plott produced twelve predictions over the course of three years. One concerned the profit-sharing percentage to be announced by upper management, and the other concerned future monthly sales of various products, in some cases a month ahead and in other cases a quarter ahead. Each of the market experiments was conducted between eight and ten times in order to obtain multiple predictions of the same variable. For each market, a number of tradable contracts were issued corresponding to intervals into which the variable eventually might fit, and so the market predicted the probability of different possible ranges of outcomes.

The market prediction was defined as the probability-weighted average of the midpoints of the intervals corresponding to each of the tradable contracts. A complication was that probabilities did not always add up to unity at any given time,[45] and thus the predictions were determined by averaging transaction prices, weighted by volume, toward the end of the market. In addition, the uppermost interval was generally unbounded, although usually it was assigned a very low probability. Chen and Plott thus ran their numbers both by excluding this interval and by averaging in the lower bound of this interval.

The results, Chen and Plott concluded, indicated that the market predictions represented a "considerable improvement over the HP official forecast," a result that was maintained for different specifications of the manner in which probability forecasts were calculated. For six of eight of these prediction problems, the market beat the official forecasts. Whether the difference in performance was statistically significant, however, depended on the forecast method. The results were statistically significant, at the 95 percent confidence level, when predictions were generated by massing predictions for the last interval at the lower bound but were not quite statistically significant when the last interval was simply ignored. Chen and Plott also performed a statistical test suggesting that the probability predictions were "consistent with the underlying distributions that generated the events," that is, that market prices could be interpreted as probabilities.[46]

An interesting fact about the experimental design reveals some potential problems unrelated to accuracy that might beset internal markets: Hewlett-Packard allowed the market to run only at lunch and in the evenings because it did not want employees to be distracted from their ordinary duties. This suggests that the company did not see these market experiments as a priority, but it also points out that internal markets might divert employee energy from more productive pursuits. Of course, given the possibility of other forms of entertainment at work, particularly in the age of the Internet, the effect might be small, especially where active trading on the market is not required or expected. But to the extent that employees' compensation depends on participation, they can be expected at times to substitute market participation for other tasks.

Moreover, the competition created by the market itself could be destructive. There are presumably sound economic reasons why businesses often do not distribute resources, such as office space, through market means. Whatever the theoretical benefits of such commodification of the workplace, individuals might find market transactions less pleasant than nonmarket interactions. Families do not generally allocate chores by conducting internal auctions, and for the same reason. Characterized as a game that employees might play and that might benefit the company, a prediction market might do little harm, but as its importance increases in the organization, some employees might not like the cultural changes that the market could effect. In addition, as market performance becomes viewed increasingly as a more salient indicator of overall performance among employees, some individuals who are good employees but who do not perform well in the market might feel alienated and might leave the firm. A particularly interesting question for future study is whether employees who perform well in the market are good employees more generally. Perhaps market performance serves as a proxy for future employee performance, but if not, then the benefits of any improvement in predictions might be outweighed by the costs.

Ultimately, prediction markets might be used by many companies for tasks such as determining how many units of different products to manufacture and what prices to charge.[47] At least initially, one would expect internal markets to be more common in companies with greater emphasis on individual contributions than on cooperative production. It should thus not be surprising that another company that has proved to be an innovator in the use of prediction markets is Google, the search engine giant.[48] Google offers employees the opportunity to spend 20 percent of their time on projects of their own choice.[49] This is a reflection of a corporate belief in the benefits of decentralized decision making and individual contributions, but it also provided an opportunity for some enterprising employees to establish internal prediction markets.

The Google predictions markets followed the same basic structure as the Iowa Electronic Markets, allowing each employee to spend play money placed into accounts for them in any of various baskets of claims.[50] After paying a fee for all the tradable contracts in a basket, employees could then sell them or buy additional shares from other employees. An interesting twist is that tradable contracts ultimately were cashed out for tickets in a lottery at which prizes were awarded. This had the effect of discouraging employees from using their play money to invest on unlikely outcomes in the hope of becoming a top performer.

The Google market covered more than 146 events in 43 different subject areas.[51] Although it was a pure play-money market, more than one thousand Google employees participated. Because of the relatively large number of predictions generated, the creators of the markets were able to assess the accuracy of prices and determine whether the prices corresponded to probabilities. The prices did correspond quite closely, in much the same way as the predictions of the Iowa Electronic Markets and TradeSports corresponded. The experimenters also assessed the degree to which the market's confidence in its predictions increased over time. Uncertainty, measured by the overall entropy of the relevant distributions, decreased over time, indicating that the market was increasingly confident in its predictions.

THE DANGER OF SABOTAGE

If internal or external markets created by corporations become sufficiently important, they might encourage sabotage, in potentially extreme but more likely mundane forms. Suppose, for example, that Google sponsors a market predicting when a new product will be completed. One strategy would be to take the position that the project will be greatly delayed and then commit an act of destruction to ensure that the prediction comes true. For example, one might delete data from a key computer. Or an employee might simply not work as hard as usual as a result of a particular bet. If the employee has bet that a project will take a long time, and if that employee's efforts will affect the project, then the employee might have a diminished incentive to work. On a large project, this effect will presumably be small, though one justification for giving employees stock options is that this might encourage them to work harder.

A company might reasonably worry that the knowledge that some workers are betting against a particular team might harm morale, though conceivably it also could spur productivity. One possible approach is to create internal markets in which trading is performed only by employees who serve full-time as traders on a wide range of issues. These employees would be encouraged to interview many employees about a wide range of questions and to obtain whatever information they can. The markets themselves might nominally involve only play money, but it would be made clear to employees that their future salary and success would depend on their performance in such markets. A consulting firm also might provide incentives to its consultants in this way, keeping track of their winnings in prediction markets spanning a number of different consulting customers. Relying on full-time or dedicated market traders might yield information as effectively as allowing employees to trade on their own information, yet it largely removes the dangers of low morale and of sabotage.

How great a concern is sabotage in prediction markets generally? Robin Hanson has argued that the concern is small. He notes that after the September 11 terrorist attacks, a theory circulated that individuals, perhaps the terrorists themselves, had bet against airline stocks, perhaps in part as a basis for funding the attacks.[52] A later report concluded that this was not true.[53] Nonetheless, it might seem that the possibility of such sabotage might provide a substantial argument against prediction markets. To the contrary, however, the example suggests that there are much more profitable sabotage opportunities. The financial effects of the September 11 attacks were sufficiently dramatic that the profit potential was probably far higher than anyone could earn by investing in a relatively low-subsidy prediction market. The fact that there are virtually no known examples of sabotage undertaken in order to earn trading profits on the stock market,[54] where it could be relatively profitable, suggests that the sanctions of criminal enforcement are sufficiently robust to deter such activity. At the least, prediction markets seem unlikely to make the danger much higher.

But there might well be more modest forms of sabotage. One rule of the Yahoo! Buzz Game is that individuals cannot seek to manipulate the market by manipulating Web searches (for example, by conducting repeated searches for a particular technology). Presumably, Yahoo! is monitoring searches in order to discount any such repeated behavior not only because it does not want the Buzz Game to give unfair awards but also because it does not want the market to ruin another "product," the contemporaneous buzz scores that searching routinely produces. One might imagine forms of corruption for many prediction markets. For example, it might be profitable for a speculator on orange juice futures to pay off an insider to mispredict the weather in systematic ways each day. Of course, such a scam might be difficult to carry out, given that weather forecasts are produced through complex models, but it might be quite profitable if it were to occur.

THIRD-PARTY ASSURANCE MARKETS

Assuming that problems such as manipulation and sabotage can be overcome, internal and external prediction markets might be useful for predicting future developments and thus influencing decisions that a corporation faces. A separate use of prediction markets might be to aggregate information from within the business and convey it to outsiders. For example, a business seeking outside funding generally wishes to project enthusiasm and confidence about its potential, but venture capitalists and banks recognize that it is in the business's interest to do so, and so it is difficult for outside funding sources to obtain honest assessments of the firm's potential from its employees and managers. If a business has a sufficiently large number of employees that truly anonymous trading would be possible, however, it might report the results of such trading to outside funders as a way of showing that the self-proclaimed confidence is credible. A favorable prediction of future sales or profits from a prediction market signals to a third party the consensus view among those eligible to participate. A prediction market can serve as a lie detector in any context in which information is distributed among a large enough group of people that, even if their collective interest is in suppressing the information, each individual will have an incentive to trade against the group.

A similar strategy might be used to assure customers of a particular company about its ability to deliver promised products. For example, a large supplier of aluminum might use prediction markets to gauge the probability that it will complete deliveries that it has contracted to make. Or a construction firm might use prediction markets to forecast the dates on which particular projects will be completed or particular milestones will be reached. Customers often distrust such predictions, at least in the absence of robust contractual incentives to meet target dates, and this may provide many construction companies with an incentive to be more optimistic than the circumstances warrant. By sponsoring a prediction market in a particular outcome and enabling employees to participate anonymously, a construction company credibly could convey its predictions to customers. Such prediction markets might inspire even greater confidence if the firm permitted outsiders to participate. If such strategies were to become common enough, some individuals might develop expertise in predicting the extent to which a variety of companies will be able to meet their contractual promises and other goals.

Third-party assurance markets might be feasible in virtually any context in which some proxy for performance can be constructed ex post. For example, a market might be used to predict the proportion of customers who will return a particular consumer good. Similarly, a market might be used to predict the amount that customers will need to spend on repair of a good, such as a particular kind of car. A survey at some later time might be used to decide the actual amount that consumers on average spent and thus to resolve the prediction market payouts. Consumers already use sources such as *Consumer Reports* to assess product reliability, but these sources typically report reliability scores averaged over a wide range of products by a particular manufacturer. Thus, even if information is available that might lead informed observers to conclude that a particular product will have a higher or lower reliability rate, that information might not be available to consumers. Prediction markets could provide experts in product design with incentives to ascertain the reliability of individual consumer products. Firms that believe that they have designed relatively reliable products in particular might have incentives to sponsor such markets.

Prediction markets might be especially helpful in assessing products without a long track record. For example, although consumers can look to insurance industry statistics to assess the safety of old cars, this information is not available for new car designs or for new models of any particular design. Consumers must thus consider a bewildering array of information, such as government crash test and private safety ratings, to assess the safety of cars. The result is that automobile manufacturers have an incentive to design cars that do well in such tests, a goal that is largely but not entirely compatible with simply designing the safest possible cars. The noisier the proxies for safety that consumers will rely on, the less manufacturers will focus on safety in design. A prediction market forecasting fatality rates might provide useful information to consumers. Presumably, some experts understand or could develop models to assess the degree to which different tests and different automobile features, such as weight and availability of particular safety features, are reliable indicators of safety. A prediction market could aggregate such information into a single number that consumers easily could understand.

Use of prediction markets for third-party assurance is probably a long way off. It would be necessary for external firms to create such prediction markets and certify that employees at particular companies in fact have been able to trade anonymously on the relevant markets. Equally significant, customers would need to gain confidence in prediction market results. There is no point in creating a market specifically for a customer if that customer has no idea what a prediction market is or distrusts the claim that prediction markets can give relatively accurate predictions. Finally, employees would need to become sufficiently familiar with the mechanics of prediction markets to trade on them. Nonetheless, if such markets could be created, they could become standard elements in many existing and potential contractual relationships. The greatest potential for prediction markets is not for making predictions of a small number of variables that are of interest to a business. Rather, it is that large numbers of markets with small subsidies might be used to make predictions on virtually everything a business does and thus be used regularly in business and consumer decision making.

EMPLOYEE EVALUATION MARKETS

Prediction markets might be used to forecast not only the success of particular projects but also the success of components of a firm, such as employees. Organizations typically rate employees only at set intervals, for example, in quarterly reviews, and the performance ratings are typically private. Although this may aid morale, public ratings could inspire improved employee effort, and continuous ratings could allow employees to correct deficiencies in their work relatively quickly. Prediction markets could make such continuous ratings relatively easy to provide. Anyone might be allowed to bet in a prediction market that will predict an eventual numeric evaluation by each employee's immediate supervisor. Perhaps such markets would do more harm to workplace morale than such a system would be worth, but employees do sometimes complain about not knowing how they are doing in a firm, so these markets could help. An associate at a law firm could not complain of having no information about prospects of joining the partnership if the partners routinely released the results of a market in which they predicted whether the associate would be made a partner. (Of course, this might not be in the interest of law firms if each associate overestimates his or her probability of being made a partner.) The prediction markets might even improve the quality of the ultimate evaluations by giving more information to evaluators.

Perhaps better, a market might predict the result of a future evaluation to be conducted by an outsider after examining the work of all employees, for example, in discussion with the employees and their superiors. External evaluations ordinarily might impose too much risk on employees, who would feel that their livelihood depended on the assessments of an individual who was not generally present in the office, and if different outsiders value different skills, outside evaluation could be akin to a lottery. A market that predicts even noisy evaluation numbers, however, might be relatively reliable, and the firm could use such predictions, rather than the ex post evaluations, to rate employees. The firm might even pay the external reviewer according to the closeness of the reviewer's result to the market prediction, but that would be feasible only if it were possible to keep the prediction from the reviewer. A benefit of outside evaluation in any form is that it could produce a useful check on self-serving behavior and arbitrary favoritism by employees' superiors. It also might be particularly useful for evaluating the performance of independent contractors and other nonemployee contributors to joint projects.

It is possible, of course, that employees will be distracted by employee evaluation markets, checking regularly to determine whether their stock price is going up and down. Employees might also seek to guess who was betting against them in particular trades, producing animosity both when the guess is correct and when it is wrong. One possible solution would be to create an opaque prediction market, in which no participant can see the bid or ask queues or prices at any given time, except that predictions would be released by the business at set intervals.[55] At these times, the business might let all employees know about all other employees or only about the predictions corresponding to themselves. Individual traders would also then find out about their performance on the market. At other times in such a market, a trader would be allowed to place buy or sell orders at any time at any price but would not know whether those orders were fulfilled or how many dollars there were in the trader's account. A trader would be allowed to enter conditional trades. For example, a trader might enter an order to purchase ten shares in a particular employee if and only if the price for that employee is below thirty-two cents and if the trader has at least a certain amount of money still available. Of course, an opaque prediction market might not perform as well as a transparent market, and empirical testing would be needed to assess its reliability.

Chapter 4 Committees

Because prediction markets provide consensus forecasts, their predictions might carry more weight than the assessment of any given individual. A reader of a newspaper who is educated about prediction markets might weight more heavily a prediction of the result of an election than an analysis by an expert, because that expert might be an outlier. A member of a legislative body would do well to be suspicious of the prognostications of a single policy analyst because of the possibility that the analyst might have a policy agenda; rather, the legislator might privilege a prediction market forecast that reflects a consensus of many such analysts. Similarly, businesses might trust prediction markets more than individuals in forecasting the success of particular products, because prediction markets should help overcome the danger of excessive optimism. In all of these examples, prediction markets are useful in part because they reflect the views of large groups of people or at least because the possibility that any number of individuals might trade on prediction markets will tend to discipline the predictions of individuals. This same rationale, however, suggests that a variety of methods for aggregating predictions, such as simple averaging, might also be superior to individual assessments.

Perhaps the challenge that I have presented for prediction markets so far has been too easy. Even if they are more accurate or more objective than individual prognosticators, the real question is whether prediction markets will do better than other means of aggregating the views of a group. Consider, for example, committees. Organizations of many different types use committees to make decisions. Businesses may create committees of employees to explore particular issues, activists may form committees to develop and announce their positions regarding issues of public policy, and legislatures use committees to develop preliminary solutions to particular issues.

The committee is a very useful mechanism for accomplishing work and working out details that most individuals would rather avoid. Organizations might thus assign members to different committees to plan events or prepare reports, spreading work around the organization. On the other hand, committees may be useful when too many people are interested in a particular topic because they allow a few of them to work out disagreements without involving the others. High school prom committees often seem to fit this mold. Nonetheless, the decisions of committees are often merely advisory. Academic departments, for example, commonly use committees to compile lengthy reports about whether junior professors should receive tenure, though typically the entire faculty will eventually vote on the candidacy. The work of a committee focuses subsequent discussion on key issues.

The previous paragraph may well contain the most enthusiastic prose about committees ever written. Indeed, they are frequently objects of derision. The claim is that they are ineffective decision makers, spending too much time considering all of the relevant possibilities. Robert Copeland, for example, has joked, "To get something done, a committee should consist of no more than three men, two of whom are absent."[1] In practice, a decision by a large group to assign an issue to a committee may often be a convenient way of freeing the group from having to worry about it or at least delaying the need for further consideration. By the time the committee report has been received, passions will have cooled, and members of the group may be so disappointed to have to deal with the issue again that they will all quickly vote on a final decision. In part, committees may inspire dread because of the subject matters assigned to them, issues either too boring or too controversial for resolution through other means. Then too, there is the problem that committees typically proceed through meetings, where at least some members inevitably will seek to show their value to the organization by speaking for far longer than others would like. In short, decision making by committee is time-consuming and therefore costly.

Prediction markets as described so far, nonetheless, might be unable to achieve the same benefits as committees, because committees have an ability to engage in deliberation. Although most forms of deliberation are cumbersome and boring, it has certain advantages. Different members of the committee might obtain different pieces of information to share with other members. Individuals might see some arguments on their own but not see others, but in the boredom of a committee meeting, one cannot help but be exposed to alternative perspectives, and the desire to conclude a committee's business will encourage members to be open to accepting others' views.

The fundamental difference between a prediction market as defined so far and a committee is what members do with new or private information. In a prediction market, someone ordinarily trades on the relevant information, whereas in a committee, a member shares the information with others. A committee might, then, be superior to a prediction market whenever decision making would be improved if all decision makers have access to all or at least most of the relevant information. A prediction market in which a dozen people each trade on the basis of separate pieces of information might not make predictions as well as a committee in which all members view all the information. Individual pieces of information might be more easily interpreted in conjunction with other pieces.

The goal of this chapter is to suggest that prediction markets, carefully designed, can serve as an alternative to committees. Once created, prediction markets might allow for more streamlined decision making than committees might, avoiding the necessity of meetings and direct deliberation. At the same time, the profit incentive that prediction markets provide can help overcome some of the pathologies of group decision making. Just as important, it is possible to design a "deliberative prediction market" that gives individual traders incentives to share information with one another, although the possibility of profiting on prediction markets might lead some individuals not to release information that they otherwise would have released unless they can profit by doing so.

Other approaches to encouraging information revelation and reflection already exist, but the decentralized nature of prediction markets might provide for cheaper and even more effective decision making. Because a prediction market can be designed to forecast an expert assessment, prediction markets can be used to make decisions about virtually any topic that committees might address. This chapter concludes by suggesting several possible applications. Deliberative prediction markets might be used as a means of aggregating scientific expertise, for example, in courts or in government agencies responsible for making decisions such as whether to approve particular pharmaceutical drugs. Such markets also might be used to provide incentives for individuals to produce and share legal reasoning about specific controversies.

THE PROMISE AND PROBLEMS
OF DELIBERATION

Although deliberation occurs in a wide range of committees and organizations, it has received the most attention in the political context. Jürgen Habermas, for example, argues that legislation can be legitimate only when citizens assent to it after a deliberative, legally constituted process.[2] Some critics have suggested that Habermas places too much emphasis on the importance of deliberation. Habermas views unanimous agreement as the ultimate goal of deliberation and accepts regimes of majority voting only as a necessary compromise to expedience.[3] Other scholars have placed more emphasis on the instrumental value of democratic deliberation, although it can leave considerable disagreement. Carlos Nino, for example, defended democratic governance on the ground that it fosters the deliberation that provides the best chance of achieving correct answers to moral questions, even if in practice democracy often falls short of producing correct answers, instead tolerating injustice.[4] Nonetheless, these scholars' view of democracy differs from that of political scientists who view democratic processes largely as providing voting protocols that mediate divergent private interests.

One need not accept Habermas's political philosophy, however, to recognize that deliberation at least has the potential to change individuals' views of particular issues and perhaps increase agreement about issues. James Fishkin invented the concept of a "deliberative opinion poll," in which an assembled group of citizens deliberates about particular issues, such as the death penalty, overseen by a moderator.[5] "An ordinary opinion poll models what the public thinks, given how little it knows," Fishkin explains. "A deliberative opinion poll models what the public *would* think, if it had a more adequate chance to think about the questions at issue."[6] To Fishkin this is the next logical step in the evolution of democratic institutions, crystallizing Alexander Hamilton's observation in *Federalist* No. 71 that a democracy should not simply take public opinion in raw form but should instead provide "opportunity for more cool and sedate reflection."[7] Fishkin suggests at least that deliberative opinion polls should bring us closer to the "ideal speech situation" imagined by Habermas, allowing for unlimited and open discussion.[8]

Fishkin is sufficiently optimistic about the possibility that deliberation can improve decision making among the citizenry that he and Bruce Ackerman have argued for a national holiday, called Deliberation Day, two weeks before elections, during which citizens would gather to deliberate about the elections.[9] The holiday in fact would span two days, with employers expected to give one of the days off, so that essential workers such as firefighters could participate. A $150 payment would be made to each participant, and Fishkin and Ackerman estimate that the direct financial cost of the program would be a little more than two billion dollars for approximately seventy million participants,[10] an amount they say would make the holiday "one of the least significant programs" in terms of budgetary impact.[11] The groups would deliberate only after viewing a National Issues Debate, which would follow a town meeting format, with the caveat that the citizens present at the town meeting would be a scientifically selected random sample who themselves would have engaged in a deliberative process before the debate.[12] The deliberation itself would follow a relatively structured format, with citizens meeting in the morning and the afternoon in small groups to develop agendas for larger meetings immediately afterward.[13] Fishkin and Ackerman hope that this holiday would not merely provide an opportunity for deliberation but indeed would revolutionize campaigns more generally, because partisans of various types "would have no choice but to adapt to a more attentive and informed public."[14]

Fishkin shows that deliberation can change some individuals' views, and in some of his experiments, the minority view became the majority view. For example, in one experiment, the percentage of people who believed that sending more offenders to prison is an effective way of fighting crime decreased from 57 percent to 38 percent.[15] Of course, regarding normative political questions, it is difficult to establish objectively whether deliberation led to better or worse judgments by the public. Presumably, the minority of individuals in this experiment who continued to believe that sending offenders to prison is effective must have concluded that the deliberation overall led to worse conclusions. Perhaps the amount of deliberation was not sufficient to allow for truly informed assessments of issues. The results of a deliberative opinion poll might be more meaningful if the relevant group deliberated for several years, allowing members to learn about and exchange information about topics such as economics and political theory, but for most issues such deep reflection is not possible.

Nonetheless, more information generally should produce more informed views than less information, and a deliberative opinion poll of any duration can provide a group of people with an opportunity to obtain more information about a particular topic before making a decision about it. This should be expected to provide some improvement on the status quo for issues of public concern, given the generally dismal state of voter knowledge.[16] Deliberation might be even more valuable when it focuses on a somewhat nondivisive issue and when the deliberators begin their work with a substantial amount of information.

Yet there is also a literature suggesting that group discussion may not always be valuable. A major problem, explored in detail by Cass Sunstein,[17] is the phenomenon of group polarization. Sunstein explains that "group polarization means that members of a deliberating group predictably move toward a more extreme point in the direction indicated by the members' predeliberation tendencies"[18] concerning the issue itself or its underlying normative dimensions. For example, in a group that tends moderately to support the death penalty, deliberation will tend to move the group to support the death penalty further, and in a group that tends moderately to oppose the death penalty, deliberation will move the group toward stronger opposition. In part this may be because a limited group of people who already tend to hold a particular position might not be familiar with the opposing arguments, and when such arguments are not forthcoming, participants may conclude that the arguments do not exist. This strengthens their initial positions. At the same time, the social milieu may help individuals avoid cognitive dissonance by dismissing information that is at variance with their preexisting beliefs.[19] This is because group members generally want other group members to view them favorably.

The potential perils of deliberation suggest that at least two correctives might be useful. First, relatively large, heterogeneous groups might be assembled. The larger the number of people joined for a deliberative task, the smaller the chance that random factors will lead the group to be unrepresentative of the broader populace from which they are chosen. Moreover, if at least a few individuals have well developed views about a minority position, they can act to make these views available, reducing the possibility that group polarization will occur simply as a result of a failure to consider certain arguments. Fishkin and Ackerman argue that the heterogeneity of groups in deliberative polling experiments explains why group polarization has not occurred.[20]

An experiment conducted by Sunstein, David Schkade, and Reid Hastie seems to confirm that deliberative polling has avoided group polarization only because it involved heterogeneous groups.[21] Sunstein and his coauthors convened two Deliberation Day groups to discuss three particularly controversial issues: affirmative action, international responses to global warming, and civil unions for gays. One deliberation occurred in predominantly liberal Boulder, Colorado, the other in predominantly conservative Colorado Springs. The experiment showed significant polarization, with the liberals becoming more liberal and the conservatives becoming more conservative. The experiment suggests that achieving sufficiently heterogeneous groups may be challenging given the constraints of geography.

The second corrective to the polarization problem involves structuring deliberation to involve individuals who are relatively well informed and thus likely to be familiar with or able to derive or obtain the full range of relevant arguments. Moreover, the more informed the members of a group, the less likely that rhetoric will sway views in manners inconsistent with the merits of the issue.

Of course, each of these approaches has a drawback. Often it is not possible to draw large deliberative groups because gathering large numbers of people is expensive, and in such groups, each individual will derive less satisfaction from participation. At the same time, limiting deliberation to experts requires some means of identifying who the experts are and potentially reduces the acceptability of a particular decision. In some circumstances it might be possible to use an initial deliberation among people generally to pick the experts, and another deliberation for the experts themselves, an approach that bears structural similarities to representative government but would provide more deliberation in the selection of experts and may produce specialists rather than generalists for the ultimate decision making.

A tempting additional corrective is to appoint a group leader who can seek to avoid the danger of polarization by encouraging consideration of different views and who is relatively well-informed. This strategy, however, can accentuate a different problem: reflexive following of the leader's views. The result can be that groups may conform to certain views before considering all of the evidence, including evidence that might tend to argue against these views. In 1972 the psychologist Irving Janis gave the label "groupthink" to the unwillingness of members to question views of the group.[22] In an extreme case, the group coalesces around a view with which each member of the group disagrees because each member believes that it is preferable to suspend his or her own view in favor of that of the group.

Janis postulated a number of conditions that would make groupthink particularly likely, including group cohesiveness, homogeneity, and an absence of procedures and norms designed to encourage the presentation of contrary views. Janis's theory purported to identify groupthink as a source of various foreign policy fiascos. Although more rigorous subsequent studies have failed to verify some of the more specific details of the theory,[23] the possibility remains that groupthink may arise. The theory was cited in 2004 as a cause of the U.S. government's mistaken conclusion before its invasion of Iraq that weapons of mass destruction existed there.[24]

An important question is whether a prediction market can serve as a substitute to deliberation, at least when what is being deliberated is not a normative question but a prediction that can be numerically verified ex post. Prediction markets provide a financial incentive for individuals to identify evidence and arguments that other members of a group might have ignored. If individuals seek to conform to group norms in social settings, they may be willing to defy the conventional wisdom if there is some benefit to them from doing so. The potential for profits might thus motivate individuals to try to ascertain their true views, rather than to adjust their views to fit with the social consensus. The anonymity or potential anonymity of prediction markets also might promote accuracy by shielding traders from social censure by those who have different views.

Trading, of course, is not a form of deliberation in which individuals exchange arguments but rather a means of communication through bids and financial transactions. It is possible that traders will adjust their own view of issues in part based on the trading behavior of others, moving closer to a consensus, but they might not always be able to ascertain the reason why the market consensus differs from their own views. Ideally, prediction markets would serve not merely as a substitute to deliberation but as a means by which deliberation might be advanced. We will see how prediction markets might serve as a decentralized mechanism that encourages information exchange and deliberation, but first, it is useful to consider another approach to encouraging deliberation among experts.

THE DELPHI METHOD

The Delphi Method, developed by the Rand Corporation in the 1950s, provides a means of fostering deliberation among dispersed individuals over time. The method involves sending iterated questionnaires to a group of identified experts.[25] After the experts return their questionnaires, a person in charge of running the process, known as a Delphi, analyzes the responses and sends a summary explanation to the group, highlighting areas of consensus and disagreement, while excluding analysis that is judged irrelevant. This summary explanation does not identify particular opinions with the individuals who espoused them. A second questionnaire is enclosed as well, and this process can be repeated any number of times, depending, for example, on whether an adequate degree of expert consensus is achieved. The approach can be used for virtually any decision making context. As Harold Linstone, one of the chief academic researchers of the process, explains, the Delphi technique can be used for issues ranging from "exposing priorities of personal values and social goals" to "evaluating budget allocations."[26] Most experimentation conducted with the Delphi Method occurred within industry, though some governmental organizations also occasionally employed the approach.[27]

Though named after the Greek oracle, the Delphi Method is designed not to produce supernatural predictions but to aggregate expert knowledge and intuition. The designers of the approach believed that it would be a useful way of overcoming some of the problems and pressures of face-to-face group deliberation. In a report on the first known application of the Delphi Method, Norman Dalkey and Olaf Helmer claimed that the method "appears to be more conducive to independent thought on the part of the experts and to aid them in the gradual formation of a considered opinion."[28] They thus expected that, in a Delphi used to estimate a particular number, expert forecasts would converge over time, though "it cannot even ideally be expected that the final responses will coincide, since the uncertainties of the future call for intuitive probability estimates on the part of each respondent."[29]

The particular experiment reported by Dalkey and Helmer involved the use of a Delphi to estimate how many atomic bombs the Soviet Union would need to use to reduce U.S. munitions output in particular industries to no more than 25 percent of their previous level. (Because of the subject matter, the experiment was initially classified.) The second questionnaire, in addition to reporting various numeric estimates, emphasized several factors that experts believed needed to be taken into consideration, such as the "vulnerability of various potential target systems,"[30] and asked participants to identify other relevant factors. In subsequent rounds the distributed reports contained increasingly specific information, in some cases in response to questions from the experts, reporting, for example, the number of factories accounting for various percentages of output in particular industries. In the course of five such iterations, the experts' assessments converged considerably; whereas the range given in the first questionnaire had been 50 to 5,000 bombs, on the last questionnaire it was about 150 to about 350 bombs.[31]

Of course, it is difficult to determine just why this convergence occurred. Even with the anonymous, decentralized nature of deliberation, participants might have felt some social pressure to adjust their estimates in the direction of those of other experts. One incentive to converge might be to encourage the exercise to end sooner rather than later, just as one reason that jurors generally reach unanimous verdicts is that they tire of deliberation and prefer to return to other activities. In an article about the challenge of selecting experts for a Delphi Method exercise, Gordon Welty noted that one question is whether to use genuine experts or merely laypeople, given that "experts require honoraria, *etc.,* which laymen do not."[32] One might question Welty's confidence that nonexperts will be delighted to answer successive rounds of repetitive questions without compensation, though he is correct that experts often insist on some degree of compensation and that a drawback of the Delphi Method is that it can be expensive. Experts face competing time pressures, and they may rapidly grow bored with the impersonal communications from the Delphi organizer, who also presumably will insist on some form of compensation.

Variants of the Delphi Method have emerged in response to these problems. One form eliminates the organizer, using instead a computer program to aggregate responses from participants.[33] A more radical departure is to dispense with the experts. Welty himself suggested that nonexpert groups often might produce answers comparable to those of experts, though presumably whether this is so will depend on the nature of the problem.[34] The 1960s-era experiment Welty discussed involved assessing whether certain categories of values, such as international, character, and humanitarian values, would receive more or less emphasis in the United States in the year 2000.[35] Experts and students achieved similar results, the only significant differences being that student groups predicted increased emphasis on spiritual values and the expert groups predicted increased emphasis on material values. Other experiments suggested greater differences in expert and lay responses. For example, Bell Canada used groups of experts and housewives to assess aspects of different possible services, such as a "shop-from-home" service. The housewives and the experts gave significantly different answers to some questions, such as whether housewives would purchase produce through a shop-at-home service.[36] The experts split evenly on the question, while 75 percent of the housewives believed that there could be an active market in this category.

A significant criticism of the Delphi Method is that it is largely unscientific; studies report results of particular applications but do not establish whether the technique in fact improves decision making.[37] In the studies described above, for example, one might still disagree, even with the benefit of hindsight, about whether the experts or the laypeople made more accurate predictions. Some studies, however, provide grounds for confidence. For example, Roger Best used several different variants on a Delphi to make an assessment aimed at marketing decision making: the prediction of the level of demand for the discontinued *Oregon Business Review* a year after the publication was revived.[38] This number was unknown, but the participants were also asked to estimate some numbers that were known to the experimenters, such as the number of past subscribers who were Oregon businessmen. The study showed that individuals who rated themselves as experts made significantly more accurate judgments, and, perhaps more important, it showed that estimates improved after individuals received feedback.[39] The study indicated, however, that Delphi exercises in which participants were required to provide written explanations of their views were no more successful than those lacking this requirement.

Given the limited number of questions posed, one might question the extent to which these conclusions can be generalized. It is easy to see, however, why the most objective tests of the Delphi Method generally focused only on a few questions, rather than on a large number in a range broad enough to allow for more confident assessments of scientific validity. It is sufficiently cumbersome to run a Delphi that performing such exercises with a very large number of questions is not feasible. Enough studies report positive results with the Delphi Method that it might be fair tentatively to conclude that it produces better results than does consultation of a randomly selected expert.[40] At the least, some analyses of the dynamics of Delphi exercises provide reason for optimism. For example, one study counterintuitively showed that Delphi participants who were rated as relatively dogmatic on a psychometric evaluation were willing to change their predictions, indeed, more so than individuals who were not rated as dogmatic.[41] This indicates that Delphi forecasts are not simply averages of preexisting opinions weighted by the strength of individual personalities. Much remains uncertain, however. Research has not been able to determine whether the Delphi Method works better if the opinions and forecasts of individuals who rate themselves as having greater expertise are given more weight.[42]

Given the cumbersomeness of the method and the lack of conclusive proof that it is superior to ordinary approaches to deliberation, it should not be surprising that interest in the Delphi Method appears to have waned, with fewer academic publications and industry experiments devoted to it.[43] Indeed, it would be easy to dismiss the Delphi Method as a fad, a product of the idealistic 1960s, when it may have seemed to many that it would be possible to design a cooperative decision-making venture that succeeds in setting aside human foibles and cognitive imperfections. But it should not be dismissed entirely, and it likely remains the best method practiced so far for encouraging careful reflection and analysis by individuals interested in cooperating with one another. Prediction markets take a very different approach, seeking to produce consensus forecasts through competitive rather than cooperative processes, though these consensus forecasts will not ordinarily be accompanied by rigorous analysis of the sort that the Delphi Method produces. Perhaps a better approach might combine the information-sharing of the Delphi Method in a competitive context in which financial incentives animate predictors. Before we can see how that can be done, let us consider an old technology for providing financial incentives for accurate prediction, the scoring rule, and a new prediction market variant, the market scoring rule.

SCORING RULES

A *scoring rule* is simply a mathematical function that is used to calculate a reward to be granted to a forecaster based on the accuracy of the forecast. Suppose that a video game software company is deciding whether to produce a game for a new game platform currently in development, the XCubeStation. A key variable in its decision-making process might be how many XCubeStations will be sold in that product's first year, because there is no sense in writing software for a hardware product that does not catch on. Recognizing that it might not be in the best position to evaluate future sales of XCubeStations, the software company finds an industry expert and it asks the expert for a prediction. Because the software company wants the expert to think hard about the problem, and because it wants to make sure that the expert gives an honest answer, the company makes the payment contingent on the quality of the forecast. For example, it might promise to pay $100,000 less $1 for every 10-unit misestimate. If the expert estimates sales of 1,000,000 units and the number turns out to be 900,000 (or 1,100,000), then the expert would receive only $90,000. The payment formula is a form of scoring rule. As the phrase indicates, scoring rules typically produce numeric scores that can then be translated into dollar amounts.

A significant literature in such areas as mathematics, statistics, economics, management, and meteorology examines scoring rules, particularly for contexts in which the prediction is probabilistic in nature. The old joke is that you can never prove the weatherman wrong when he announces a 50 percent chance of rain, but you can rate his performance according to a scoring rule. Such rules provide particularly meaningful assessments when used for large numbers of predictions. Designing a useful scoring rule for probabilistic forecasts turns out to be somewhat complicated, however. Consider, for example, the following: a forecaster who announces a probability p will receive a score of p if the event occurs and $1-p$ if the event does not occur. It might seem that this rule would provide incentives for the forecaster to announce higher numbers as the probability of the event rises. The problem is that the best strategy turns out to be always to announce an extreme value, 0 or 1. For example, if the forecaster believes that the event will occur with probability 0.75, then the expected (or average) score from announcing 1 will be 0.75, but the expected payout from announcing 0.75 will be only 0.625.[44]

Fortunately, it is possible to devise scoring rules that will always give a forecaster an incentive to announce an honest prediction, and any rule that meets this criterion is called a *strictly proper scoring rule*.[45] With a strictly proper scoring rule, the forecaster will always expect a higher payout on average from announcing a genuine probability prediction than from announcing any other number. Perhaps the simplest such proper scoring rule to describe is the logarithmic scoring rule, which provides a reward to a forecaster who estimates the probability of each of a number of mutually exclusive possible events. The payoff can be calculated simply by taking the logarithm (using either the "ln" or the "log" key on most pocket calculators will do the trick) of the forecaster's estimate of the probability of the event that in fact occurred.

So, for example, if the forecaster estimated a 0.25 probability of no rain and a 0.75 probability of rain, and it rained, then the forecaster's score could be $\log(0.75)$, equal to approximately -0.125. The best possible score is 0, and that occurs when the forecaster estimates that a particular event will occur with probability 1 and turns out to be correct. The worst score is negative infinity, earned if an event that the forecaster claimed was impossible in fact occurred. Because the scores produced by the logarithmic scoring rule will never be greater than zero, a score ordinarily would be used to determine how much money to deduct from the maximum payoff available to a forecaster. For example, one might agree to pay one dollar but require the forecaster to pay back the score in dollars, an amount which could be less than or greater than one dollar, depending on how accurate the forecaster is.

Other strictly proper scoring rules include a quadratic scoring rule[46] and a spherical scoring rule.[47] Scoring rules also exist for a variety of particular circumstances. For example, Carl-Axel Staël von Holstein has explored scoring rules that are sensitive to "distance."[48] Suppose, for example, that a forecaster assigns a 0.25 probability that there will be an amount of rain between zero and one inch tomorrow and that turns out to be the case. With a distance-sensitive scoring rule, the forecaster's score also depends on his of her evaluations of nearby rainfall ranges, so he or she will do better to announce a 0.75 probability of between one and two inches of rain than by announcing a 0.25 probability for that range and a 0.50 probability for more than two inches of rain.

Robert Winkler has developed other innovative scoring rules, for example, those for which the expected payoff for a perfectly calibrated forecaster (that is, one whose probability estimates are always correct in the ex ante sense) is maximized for a probability other than 0.5. The 0.5 level would be the maximum payoff point for a forecaster for all the scoring rules discussed so far.[49] Winkler has also developed scoring rules that seek to provide appropriate incentives when forecasters are not risk-neutral, an assumption made by all of the other scoring rules discussed above.[50]

The wide range of possibilities naturally leads to the question of which scoring rule is best and whether it matters. At least some experimental evidence suggests that it might matter. Robert Nelson and David Bessler performed a laboratory experiment in which participants repeatedly made probability assessments, and they demonstrated a learning effect in which participants gradually learned to deviate from their actual probability assessments when using a linear scoring rule that was not strictly proper.[51] Differences among other scoring rules might not be as great, but the marginal benefit from increased forecaster accuracy differs markedly across scoring rules.

Figure 4.1, for example, illustrates for three different scoring rules the increase in payout for correcting a one-percentage-point error in a forecast of a binary event. The assumption reflected in this figure is that the new forecast is the correct one. The payouts are normalized and are expressed as a proportion of the increased payout for an improvement in probability assessment from 0.01 to 0.02. The spherical scoring rule provides the greatest benefit from improving a prediction in the middle of the probability spectrum, and the logarithmic scoring rule provides the lowest benefit from doing so. With

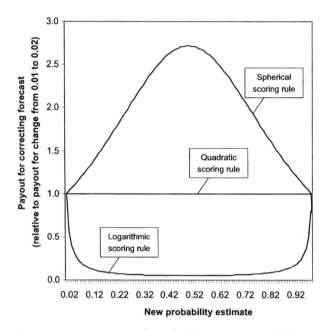

Figure 4.1. Increase in score for probability corrections at different parts of the probability spectrum with three different scoring rules

the quadratic scoring rule, the benefit of prediction improvement is invariant across the probability spectrum.

THE MARKET SCORING RULE

Of course, scoring rules themselves must be compared against other means of eliciting forecasts. Whereas the Delphi Method seeks to maximize information-sharing and collaboration, a scoring rule seeks to elicit the best possible forecast from a single forecaster. Prediction markets, we have seen, generally seek to obtain consensus forecasts rather than simple individual forecasts. Robin Hanson has proposed a prediction market design that builds on the concept of scoring rules. He calls this design the *market scoring rule*.[52]

Hanson's approach is simple. The sponsor of the market scoring rule makes an initial prediction of the relevant probability or probabilities. Others are then permitted to offer replacement predictions, under one condition: any predictor after the first must compensate the prior predictor according to the specific scoring rule, for example, a logarithmic scoring rule. The last predictor is compensated by the market sponsor according to this scoring rule. The insight is that each successive predictor will expect to receive money for improving on the prior prediction (or pay money if the predictor in fact makes a worse prediction). Payouts for marginal improvements in predictions are thus precisely as indicated in figure 4.1. Because it is often desirable to provide constant subsidies across the probability spectrum, the quadratic market scoring rule will be the best choice in many contexts.[53]

One virtue of the market scoring rule is that it can be easily harnessed to make predictions of numbers other than probabilities. Suppose, for example, that a market sponsor is interested in predicting next year's U.S. trade deficit. The market sponsor could select different ranges of plausible outcomes and use either the market scoring rule or one of the other methods for deriving probabilistic forecasts to determine the probability of each range. Sometimes, however, a straight prediction is all that is needed. Indeed, market scoring rules of this sort should be simpler than those used for making probabilistic predictions, because there is less of a need for a strictly proper scoring rule. For example, if the probability distribution of possible values of next year's trade deficit fits roughly on a normal distribution, there would be no incentive for a forecaster facing a simple linear scoring rule to give any number other than the mean of the distribution. Thus, the sponsor of the market might promise to provide the last forecaster with a fixed sum of money, less some amount for each million dollars' worth of inaccuracy in the forecast.

Even when used to assess probabilities, the market scoring rule has significant virtues relative to a probability estimate prediction market. Unlike such a market, the market scoring rule should work well in situations of low liquidity. Like the dynamic pari-mutuel market, the market scoring rule can be presented to a user just as a probability estimate prediction market would be. That is, the user can be presented with bid and ask queues, but the entries on those queues are made by the market sponsor rather than other traders. With this approach, the user can purchase tradable contracts that will pay a set amount if a particular event occurs. The market scoring rule functions as an automated market maker that will always accept buy or sell orders at the price corresponding to current market probabilities. It will buy or sell only an infinitesimally small share at that price, however, and so for any given scoring rule, calculus must be used to derive the equations that can be used to calculate the number of shares that can be purchased for a given amount of money or to move the consensus probability estimate to a particular number.

As Hanson points out, a market scoring rule should provide appropriate incentives when it turns out that only one individual decides to make a prediction.

In that case, the market scoring rule amounts to a scoring rule. Unlike a traditional scoring rule, however, the market scoring rule provides incentives for individuals to make new predictions when they believe that the initial predictor might have made a poor prediction, for example, if there is suspicion that the initial predictor might be trying to manipulate the market. The knowledge that this might occur will decrease the initial predictor's willingness to attempt manipulation.

In order to succeed in manipulating the market scoring rule, a participant would need to be willing to repeatedly revert the prediction against determined challengers back to the value that the participant prefers. In effect, to manipulate the market, one must be willing to take bets against anyone who might challenge the participant and to do so repeatedly. A series of back-and-forth predictions between two competing traders will likely attract interest in the market and independent third-party evaluations. So a manipulator can succeed only if he or she has more money to spend than the rest of the potential market combined or if virtually no one else in the market notices and decides to challenge the manipulator's evaluation.

Because of its particular applicability to low-liquidity environments, a primary competitor of the market scoring rule is the dynamic pari-mutuel market. With both the market scoring rule and a dynamic pari-mutuel market, a participant—it might be inaccurate to call the participant a trader—can profit on information without finding someone with an opposite prediction to enter into a transaction. A significant difference between the two approaches is in incentives related to the timing of trading. We saw in Chapter 3 that with the dynamic pari-mutuel market, a trader with private information sometimes might have an incentive to wait before betting on the information, because a shift in the market will have a bigger payout when more money has been invested in the payout. This is a particular danger if others change their probability evaluations based on the trader's bets. This danger does not occur with the probability estimate prediction market, because there is no inherent trend toward increasing liquidity over the course of the market. With the market scoring rule, meanwhile, there will ordinarily be an incentive to invest on the basis of information as soon as possible, because one earns money only to the extent that one improves on the prior prediction.

Another potential advantage of the market scoring rule is that it provides a relatively straightforward method of subsidizing the market.[54] The market sponsor needs simply to identify a scoring rule that converts the success of the final predictor into dollars. This approach, however, shares two disadvantages of the "seed wager" approach to subsidizing the dynamic pari-mutuel market. First, the subsidy cannot be fixed in advance. Where a market sponsor runs a large number of markets, a solution is for the market sponsor to announce a fixed subsidy for all of the markets. Each individual market would then be run only with points, and the conversion between points and dollars would be determined after the close of all markets, set at the level that will precisely deplete the subsidy. Second, a great proportion of the subsidy might be awarded to the first market participant to make an announcement, especially if the initial estimate offered by the market sponsor is weak. A possible partial solution is to hold an auction for the right to be the initial predictor, with any revenues from the auction added to the amount to be paid to the final predictor in the market. According to this approach, the market sponsor at least will not be wasting a subsidy on information that is publicly available. An alternative approach might be to alter the subsidy level over time.

The market scoring rule might be more appropriate in circumstances in which the underlying events being predicted are highly volatile, and the dynamic pari-mutuel market might be superior where there is relatively little underlying volatility over the course of the market. The dynamic pari-mutuel market will tend to be less sensitive to new predictions relatively late in the betting cycle, but bets that are large enough can always push the prediction any desired distance. High volatility will mean that for each successive probability shift, increasingly large amounts of money will need to be invested in the market to move the market to the new consensus probability, and increasingly large amounts of money can be earned by fixing the probability estimates. A consequence is that the dynamic pari-mutuel market will provide greater liquidity toward the end of the market. With the market scoring rule, by contrast, it will always cost the same amount to move the probability prediction from a particular point to another, regardless of how much has been invested in the market.

The decreased sensitivity of the dynamic pari-mutuel market to bets of a fixed size might be seen as a virtue, however, especially in low-volatility environments. The possibility that a single announcement could dramatically change the market price might be a concern with the market scoring rule. At least participants in a prediction exercise based on the market scoring rule need to establish that they will be able to pay the appropriate amount if a prediction turns out to be a bad one. If participants were not required to pay off the previous predictor in advance or to show evidence of ability to pay through the market sponsor later on, there might be an incentive to change the market prediction arbitrarily.

The final consideration in the comparison between the market scoring rule and other approaches is that the market scoring rule, like scoring rules, may provide differing levels of incentive to gather information and improve the market prediction at different portions of the probability spectrum, as illustrated in figure 4.1. In addition, as figure 4.2 shows, with various versions of the market scoring rule, the reward for moving the probability estimate closer to the correct value decreases as the market value approaches this value. As in figure 4.1, payouts are normalized and expressed as a proportion of the increased payout for an improvement in probability assessment from 0.01 to 0.02. In figure 4.2, however, the correct probability is 0.5, but making the last incremental shift from 0.49 to 0.50 produces almost no profit. These problems might be more of a concern with the market scoring rule than with traditional scoring rules because a major purpose of market scoring rules is to give participants incentives to make small changes in evaluations, but this may be difficult to achieve for many portions of the probability spectrum.

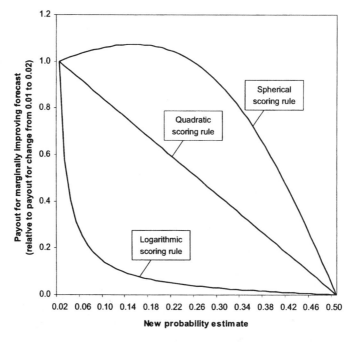

Figure 4.2. Increase in score for improvements at different parts of the probability spectrum with three different scoring rules, when actual probability = 0.5

In many cases, however, there is a potential solution: sequential use of two different market scoring rules. The key insight is that one prediction market can be used to forecast the result of another. As long as the second prediction market is structured in a way that guarantees that forecasters will have an incentive to be honest, the first prediction market can be structured in a way that ensures that the marginal expected profit from improving a probability prediction will remain constant across the probability continuum.

This approach would work as follows: The second process would use the quadratic market scoring rule or one of the other strictly proper scoring rules discussed above, but the first process would use a simple linear scoring rule and would predict the prediction of the second scoring rule, rather than the actual event. Suppose, for example, that what is being predicted is a two-horse race in which the first horse has a 75 percent chance of winning. The race will directly affect profits of participants in the second process, but not in the first. As we have seen, a linear scoring rule ordinarily would give a forecaster an incentive to announce a prediction that the first horse will win with certainty, but in this case a forecaster would recognize that the second market scoring rule will end with a prediction of 0.75, and so it is better to announce a prediction of 0.75 in the first market scoring rule period.

The second market scoring rule could occur over a very short period of time, potentially with quite a modest subsidy, and in general it should not change the prediction of the first market scoring rule by much. The purpose of the second market scoring rule would only be to discipline the first. The technique should work as long as the second market can be completed before the conclusion of the second event becomes obvious. It might not work as well in cases in which an outcome (rather than a probability) becomes increasingly obvious as the relevant event approaches, as for example with predictions of the weather.

DELIBERATIVE PREDICTION MARKETS

When one prediction market is used to predict the outcome of another, participants who have private information in the first prediction market have an incentive to reveal that information to participants in the second. Suppose, for example, that a participant in the two-stage prediction market discussed immediately above were to obtain secret information that the favorite horse had not slept well, lowering his chance of winning from 0.75 to 0.70. Simply entering a prediction of 0.70 in the first prediction market will not be sufficient to profit on the information, because the payoffs in the first prediction market depend on the prediction of the second. The participant might still profit by announcing a prediction in the second prediction market, but if that market has only a small subsidy, the profit from doing that will be small. To maximize profit, the participant will want to reveal the information underlying the prediction to participants in the second market in as credible a way as possible. For example, if the participant can share a video of the horse's restless night, the participants in the second prediction market will lower their own forecasts of the horse's probability of victory. If that market results in a prediction of 0.70, then the holder of the private information will have profited by replacing a prediction of 0.75 with a prediction of 0.70. This approach should work as long as no one has the ability to manipulate the second prediction market.

This structure thus encourages market participants not only to announce predictions or enter into transactions based on their private information but also to share that information with others and to try to convince others that those announcing the predictions have correctly interpreted the information. In other prediction market structures, such as a probability estimate prediction market or a one-stage market scoring rule, such incentives will be much more attenuated. Sometimes a prediction market participant will reveal information to make it possible immediately to capitalize on a prior trade. For example, in a probability estimate prediction market for a horse race, a trader might buy up shares of a horse that is underpriced. The trader could then simply wait for the race to occur, but might wish to cash in on this information before the race, thus avoiding the inherent riskiness of the race itself. So the trader could reveal the evidence or analysis indicating that the horse is underpriced. By changing other traders' evaluations, the trader will be able to sell the shares for a higher price.

There are, however, two reasons why this incentive often is not powerful enough to lead to disclosure of information in some markets. First, in some circumstances, it makes more sense to keep information secret in the hope of buying more cheaply priced shares and earning a higher profit. If, for example, a trader's new information suggests that a share is worth thirty cents, the trader should buy as many shares as possible for less than that price, until no one is willing to sell any more. But there is always the possibility that the market price will fall again, particularly if no one else has access to the trader's information. When that happens, the trader can increase profits by buying up still more shares. Revealing information to the market would block this strategy.

Second, revealing information in a form that succeeds in convincing other traders is not costless. Specific pieces of evidence might need to be documented, by photographs, for example, and distributed. Analysis that a particular trader might have done in her head might need to be explained in a way clear enough for others to understand. Information, moreover, must be conveyed in a way that allows it to be absorbed by other traders easily. Even if revealing information does not cost very much, the benefit associated with making it possible to cash out of a market earlier might not be sufficiently great to justify it. Incentives to reveal information are likely to be particularly low in low-liquidity prediction markets in which very few are expected to participate. In markets with a very small number of traders, the danger that any single trader might have information that the rest of the market lacks is particularly high, and there is little reason voluntarily to give up this advantage.

We can, however, build on the two-stage market scoring rule design to encourage a greater degree of information revelation.[55] That design itself would encourage revelation, but without much hurry. A market participant merely would need to reveal information in time for it to be absorbed by the second prediction market. Participants who hope that their trading will not lead the market implicitly to incorporate the information, thus allowing them to trade further on it, would wait until relatively late to reveal the information. The result is that although the market encourages revelation, the process does not closely resemble a deliberative process, in which participants gradually offer evidence and arguments and respond to those offered by others. Ideally, the prediction market should encourage traders to release evidence and arguments as they become available and to consider the evidence and arguments released by others. A simple way of doing this would be to create a multistage market scoring rule. The profits of predictors in each stage would be determined by the prediction at the end of the next stage. The final stage of the market predicts the event itself, using a strictly proper scoring rule. A possible drawback of this approach is that the market subsidy must be divided among the stages, but it might be difficult to predict in advance which stages will be the most important to subsidize.

An alternative approach is one in which each prediction is evaluated on the basis of the market prediction at some later interval. Suppose, for example, that a prediction market will be run continuously to predict the trade deficit at the end of 2015. The market rules might provide that each prediction shall be evaluated on the basis of the prediction made a week later, except that if the market closes before that time period has expired, the last predictor's profit or loss would be assessed in the usual way. Suppose that the most recent prediction is

$500 billion, but a market participant has developed a complex new economic model that can be used to predict trade deficits and, using the information from that model and other existing information, predicts that the trade deficit in fact will be only $400 billion. At the moment when the participant enters the $400 billion prediction, that is the market prediction. Others, however, might enter new predictions based on the information available to them. Suppose that one week later the market prediction is $430 billion. The trader would then be credited 40 points, where each point corresponds to $1 billion in improved prediction, because the $400 billion prediction was $30 billion away from the $430 billion prediction made a week later, and the preceding $500 billion prediction was $70 billion away.

At the close of the market, points will be converted into dollars at the rate that uses up the market subsidy. In some circumstances, the market sponsor might want to subsidize certain time periods at a higher rate than other time periods. For example, in the trade deficit prediction market, the market sponsor might want to devote half of the market subsidy to the first time interval and split the remainder among the remaining time intervals. This would especially make sense if the task of developing initial predictions requires more work than the task of changing predictions on the basis of new information. There might be other situations, however, in which initial predictions are easy to produce and so the reverse approach should be taken. Accomplishing either would be straightforward. Points could be multiplied by a weighting factor that changes over time in accordance with a plan announced in advance.

In this system the trader will have an incentive to reveal information about his model in an effort to convince others that his prediction was as accurate as possible. Others, meanwhile, will have incentives to scrutinize such information. If a subsequent participant finds that the new prediction was unsubstantiated or that the new information should lead to a different prediction, the participant may enter still another prediction. If someone makes a prediction without any supporting information, other participants will likely assume that there is no such information, and they will move the prediction back to its original level. If the week expires with the prediction at that level, the $430 billion prediction will have produced no profit, even if the model is correct. Of course, someone who does move the prediction back to the original $500 billion level will want to produce analysis supporting that move, because that person will be evaluated based on a prediction yet another week later and will need to convince other market participants of the wisdom of moving the prediction back.

There are at least two potential problems with this system. The first is the danger of manipulation. Someone might announce a prediction and then announce another prediction the instant before a full week has passed, and continue to do this every week. If someone could do this successfully—and it might be difficult, given that many different traders would try to enter the last prediction—that person could make substantial profits. One solution would be to prevent a trader from making repeated predictions, but this still does not eliminate the possibility of collusion among two or more traders. A simple solution is to randomize the exact length of the time interval that will be used to identify the later prediction that disciplines the earlier prediction and to keep such information away from predictors. For example, the interval might be a week plus or minus one day. This will give market participants incentives to identify repeated trades and to enter new predictions pushing in the opposite direction. Of course, the exact length of the time interval might vary from one market to another, although it should be enough time so that market participants will be able to consider information offered in support of that prediction. In some circumstances, the interval might change over the course of the market, with shorter intervals in periods in which more information is available or in which information becomes easier to process, for example, toward the end of the market. A further caveat is that the precise time of the end of the market should also be randomized somewhat to prevent manipulation.

Second, some traders might seek to profit on information without revealing it by developing a reputation for accurate analysis. Suppose, for example, that a market participant has spent a great deal of time and effort developing a sophisticated model that might help make economic predictions useful in a wide variety of market contexts. That participant might announce that such a model exists, and perhaps allow some individuals who sign confidentiality agreements to consider the model, but not release it. If the model in fact is strong, then over time, other traders will come to recognize that this trader's predictions tend to be valid, and the trader will have little incentive to release the model. This result is not altogether lamentable, because this strategy will tend to be useful only when information can improve predictions in many prediction markets deployed at various times, and there are strong reasons to encourage the development of such generally applicable models. When such a model is developed, the information that the model results in a particular prediction itself is a valuable kind of information, even if the inner workings of the model are proprietary.

The real concern is not that an occasional market participant would want to keep some information a trade secret, but rather that large numbers of participants would decide not to reveal information that has little chance of being useful in a later prediction market. For example, a market participant who has developed a reputation for accurate analysis might simply stop releasing analyses, relying instead on his or her reputation for accuracy. Ordinarily, however, this would not be a sound strategy, because some market participants would be worried that the sudden decision not to release analysis might indicate that no such analysis existed. Those participants would thus move predictions in the opposite direction. It would take some amount of experience before the market accepted a participant's claims to have secret analysis that supports predictions, and always some skepticism would remain, preventing the participant from earning as much as he or she could earn by revealing information and analysis. So unless revealing information is expensive, market participants will have incentives to reveal it. At least, participants will have incentives to reveal any analysis that they have already prepared in digital form and that does not contain valuable trade secrets, such as algorithms for making future prediction market forecasts.

If information retention were commonplace, some remedies might be available, though none is probably ideal. One remedy would be to require that predictions and supporting arguments be entered anonymously. Such an approach should be broad enough to preclude market participants from supporting statements by reference to particular models that they have developed. Enforcing this restriction, however, might require effort and would demand some set of penalties. Another approach, which might be used as a complement to the first one, would be to allow market participants falsely to claim to be other market participants. For example, if Model X has produced excellent predictions in the past, anyone would be allowed to claim to be reporting the results of Model X, thus quickly making claims to be announcing results of Model X worthless. This, too, might be difficult to enforce, however, because market participants who have developed models would have incentives to provide ways of verifying to other participants whether particular statements in fact are their own. Yet it might be difficult to do this without obviously flouting the rule requiring anonymous predictions, so conceivably this regime could be effective.

Whether or not it provides perfect incentives to induce revelation of all information, a deliberative prediction market should improve matters, leading to exchange of information and arguments, rather than mere numbers. The approach bridges part of the gap that separates prediction markets from the Delphi Method and its aspiration to structure and facilitate deliberative groups. Deliberative prediction markets will probably do little good where there is a great deal of public information and relatively little private information, such as prediction markets forecasting the outcome of a presidential race; virtually any new piece of evidence in such a market is likely to be a drop in the bucket, and so incentives to release information that is not already publicly available will not be significant. But in prediction markets with few participants in which research and analysis can lead to significant changes in predictions, a deliberative market might help a great deal. The incentive to release information will be greater in this context because any such information will be of greater importance to anyone who might trade subsequently.

Ultimately, the release of information can produce greater prediction market accuracy. The simple reason is that deliberation can improve decision making, particularly where participants have financial incentives to guard against some of the pathologies of deliberation, but the point can be elaborated by considering the relations among the pieces of information exchanged in deliberation. First, participants are better able to judge how much weight to give to the opinions of others. In other prediction market designs, participants assign some weight in their own predictions to the valuations of others, as manifested, for example, by the prices at which transactions clear. These earlier predictions ordinarily reflect some information or at least some analysis that the later predictor cannot observe directly but that presumably has some weight. But it would be very difficult to assess how much weight without the underlying information or analysis.

Second, participants are better able to determine whether information that they possess is truly new private information or is information that others have already traded on. If information in fact is new but a participant estimates that others may have already traded on it, the participant will not move the prediction as far as the new information will warrant.

Third, once information is released, there is no need for other market participants to produce the same information. The result is that the market subsidy will not be wasted on redundant acquisition of information by multiple parties, and it should thus produce more information, leading to greater market accuracy.

Deliberative prediction markets might be particularly useful in contexts in which prediction markets otherwise might affirmatively discourage information release. In the absence of prediction markets, an individual might possess information that has no financial value, and he or she might release that information to advance his or her reputation as someone who has developed and identified important information. With prediction markets, however, that same information suddenly now will have financial value, and so individuals may conceal information that they otherwise would have disclosed to maximize their ability to trade on the information. Once there is a reward for information, what would have been released in the absence of a reward might suddenly be more valuable if kept secret. Prediction markets thus sometimes aggregate information at the expense of nonrelease of analyses that might allow observers better to assess particular problems. Deliberative prediction markets encourage not only information aggregation and production but also information release by providing a reward for convincing others that one is correct.

THE DANGER OF FRAUDULENT INFORMATION

Though they might provide incentives for keeping true information secret, prediction markets also might lead to the opposite problem: announcement of false information. Such announcements can amount to more or less sophisticated frauds. A relatively sophisticated fraud might enlist a wide range of conspirators to try to convince the public that some piece of information is true and might involve the production of falsified photographs or documents. This danger is nothing new; a common securities scam known as "pump and dump" involves revealing information that seems to indicate that a security that one owns is likely to be particularly valuable and then selling that security. Ordinarily, such a scheme seems less likely to be successful in contexts in which there are relatively few traders, many of whom are well informed about the relevant problem.

A danger of the deliberative prediction market, however, is that it might facilitate such frauds, because fraud can be successful as long as it cannot be detected in less than a particular amount of time. If the time interval used to grade predictions is a week, then as long as one can distribute false information whose falsehood will not be detected until after a week, the use of that information can produce profits. For example, one might announce a prediction based on a sophisticated mathematical model, hoping that no one will quickly notice a subtle intentional error buried deep within a complex proof.

One solution to the danger of fraudulent information is to provide a legal regime that imposes civil or criminal penalties on those who commit such frauds. This is the approach taken by the securities laws, and although elaborate frauds sometimes exist, such as the accounting frauds at Enron and WorldCom, the approach at least provides a significant deterrent. The opposite strategy is to provide no regulation and to count on the market to separate fact from fiction. With this approach, people who reveal true information would have incentives to find ways of proving to the market that the information is true, for example by hiring auditors who have earned reputations for identifying the truth of statements.

The empirical question is, what effect would this approach have on the amount of fraud that persists and on the expense associated with disclosing information, either because of legal mandates or because of voluntary market transactions? In the literature about securities law, there is a lively debate about whether the reforms in the Sarbanes-Oxley Act provide enough benefit from fraud reduction to justify the administrative expense that the statute imposes on companies.[56] One argument is that if the expense of new procedures were justified, corporations voluntarily would institute and publicize them.[57] A counterargument is that corporations ordinarily cannot provide criminal sanctions on their own, so there is a useful role for government to play.[58] Another is that uniform standards and procedures imposed by the government make it easier for market participants to process information.[59]

Assuming that current securities law strikes an appropriate balance, the question remains whether the same balance makes sense in the case of prediction markets. It is possible that in spite of the danger of fraud, the option of market enforcement in place of regulation might make more sense with prediction markets, particularly those in which the market capitalization or the subsidy is relatively small. Although the securities laws apply to a wide range of securities, in general the market capitalization for most such securities seems likely to dwarf the typical prediction market. As a result, governmental requirements that might make sense for securities in general will be less advisable in the prediction market context.

For example, the danger of criminal liability might discourage someone from participating in a deliberative prediction market in which the expected profit might amount to a few thousand dollars, even if that individual thought that information was truthful, because it would always be possible that an inadvertent error might lead to an investigation, if not a conviction. At the least, such liability would make market participants more cautious, perhaps excessively so. Some form of regulation may strike an appropriate balance, but the costs associated with the regulatory regime ideally should be relatively small in comparison to the size of the particular market. In many deliberative prediction markets, the simplest form of regulation is to provide a long enough time interval to make it likely that frauds will generally be detected.

THE NOBODY-LOSES PREDICTION MARKET

A variation on the market scoring rule might help with the fraudulent information problem, and more important, with the type of manipulation that we have seen can pose problems for prediction markets that rely entirely on points that can be exchanged for dollars. In this variation, a central computer can limit the amount by which some participants can move the market consensus prediction. For example, if the current prediction of some variable of interest is twenty, and a participant enters a new prediction of forty, the system might announce a new consensus prediction of only thirty. If it turns out that the variable ultimately predicted (with the deliberative market, the market prediction at some later point in time) is forty or higher, the market participant's profit on the transaction will be limited to thirty.

The market would make larger changes in consensus market predictions for traders who have shown themselves to be accurate predictors over time. The system might maintain a statistical model, for example, using regression analysis. Given a new prediction and variables reflecting both the predictor's past success and the current state of the market, the model would calculate a new market consensus prediction. Ordinarily, this would be somewhere between the old consensus prediction and the new one. For the purpose of determining the predictor's profit or loss on the transaction, this new prediction would control. A possible exception would be cases in which the computer's change in the consensus prediction overshoots the change recommended by the predictor, as might happen for predictors who have proved conservative about changing the market consensus.

This system greatly reduces the ability of market participants to enter random predictions in the hope that they might happen to earn significant numbers of points. (An alternative approach is for prediction market designers simply to create an automated trader account that trades immediately after each participant trades, but this does not reduce the incentive to create accounts to make random predictions.) If individuals attempted to do this, then the system would learn not to trust them, and the amount of money that they make initially would be very small. At the same time, traders could earn a good reputation both by winning points and by entering predictions that turn out to be valid. This could happen even within a prediction market if a prediction successfully forecasts a later stage of the market, but it would be more likely across a large number of prediction markets. The system should improve over time; at first, it should be subject to some manipulation, but as it learns which participants are reliable, opportunities for manipulation would decline.

This approach reduces the fraudulent information problem, because market participants' primary incentives are to preserve their reputation. At times a participant with a good reputation might seek to make a killing with fraudulent information, but at least if many future prediction market opportunities exist, this should seldom be a significant problem. At the same time, if the currency is points rather than dollars, the market limits the ability of participants to open phantom accounts from which they make bad predictions, enabling real accounts to take advantage of those predictions. Because the phantom accounts should have only small effects on market predictions, it will be hard to channel points from phantom accounts to real accounts.

The result is that this system can facilitate the creation of a prediction market system in which points can be exchanged for dollars and thus no market participant faces a risk of losing money. In part, this may be useful as a means of attracting risk-averse individuals to the system, but it also is particularly important as a method of avoiding regulatory impediments to prediction markets. Although participants who have established themselves as reliable predictors take a risk with every prediction, courts seem highly unlikely to condemn this system as illegal gambling. After all, anyone who participates in a performance-based reward system faces the risk that a bad performance will lower the eventual reward. At the same time, the market scoring rule is not likely to be subject to securities and commodity futures laws because there are no trades.

An alternative approach that similarly can help aggregate information held by members of a group is to use a prediction market simply to gauge the predictive accuracy of different individuals and their relative tolerance for risk. Then, one can simply ask these individuals for predictions, promising to reward them according to a simple scoring rule, and aggregate the predictions based on the performance in the initial prediction market. Kay-Yut Chen and two coauthors conducted an experiment with this approach,[60] and they found that they achieved greater accuracy than with a prediction market alone. In some settings, particularly where it is feasible to request simultaneous probability assessments from each of a number of participants, this approach therefore might be better than a prediction market alone because it helps isolate prediction market participants whose bad predictions tend to distort market outcomes. If prediction markets are run for long enough, however, underperforming participants may tend to leave the market or correct their errors, so for long-term projects, conventional prediction markets may be superior.

Both of these approaches show that it should be possible to implement prediction markets on a large scale despite existing regulatory limitations. This system, admittedly, might not be as strong as one that allows individuals to place their money at risk. It might not sufficiently take into account the information of genuine predictors, and the need to accrue a good reputation over time might discourage some individuals from participating. Thus, someone who might have information that is relevant to a single short-lived prediction market seems unlikely to participate. The possibility of nobody-loses prediction markets might make policy makers less eager to relax restrictions on prediction markets, though it is also possible that success might lead to a broader appreciation of the possible benefits of prediction markets and thus regulatory relaxation.

PREDICTING DECISIONS

Deliberative prediction markets substitute for the deliberation performed by committees by providing incentives for the production and release of information. Such markets do not by themselves produce decisions (though we will see beginning in Chapter 5 how prediction markets can be designed to make decisions), but they can do much of the work of decision support, providing a range of arguments and counterarguments plus the market's assessment of the persuasiveness of those arguments. Of course, in order to use a market as a substitute for a committee, the market designer must find a suitable number to be predicted that will generate the relevant arguments.

In some cases, this might initially seem quite difficult. Suppose, for example, that a committee is charged with selecting a piece of equipment for a children's playground. It might seem difficult to design a market that would generate arguments about the pros and cons of each piece of equipment, given the absence of an objective correct answer that someday will become available. There is, however, a relatively simple antidote: A prediction market can be used to forecast what a decision will be. For example, one person might be charged with making the decision, and a deliberative prediction market would be used to gauge the probability that each of various pieces of equipment might be chosen. The decision maker could take advantage of the arguments produced by the prediction market. For example, someone might make a prediction based on information that a particular piece of equipment is unsafe, recognizing that the provision of this information ultimately would make the piece of equipment less likely to be chosen.

In principle, a deliberative prediction market can be used to generate information for any decision that can be quantified ex post. That includes not only decisions among two or more choices but also decisions settling on a particular number, such as the number of students who should be admitted in a particular year to an undergraduate institution or the size of a fence that should be placed around company grounds. One aspect of these markets that a decision maker might find particularly attractive is that participants in the markets will seek to provide only information that the decision maker would find relevant. For example, if the decision maker has previously expressed an opinion that the aesthetics of playground equipment should not matter, participants will not have much incentive to produce information about aesthetics. Ordinarily, a decision maker who creates a committee to help with a particular decision takes the risk that the committee will base its recommendations on its own agenda. Even if committee members realized that they should not make arguments about the aesthetics of playground equipment because the ultimate decision maker would not care, they might secretly factor this information into their analyses. In a deliberative prediction market, there would be incentives for participants to identify such hidden agendas.

Not everyone will celebrate the fact that a deliberative prediction market caters to a decision maker's preferences. The decision maker may have idiosyncratic preferences, perhaps preferences that would be inferior to those of a hypothetical average group member. In some organizations, the idiosyncratic preferences might be desirable; perhaps the president of a business is more loyal to the owners than are the employees. In other contexts a more democratic approach to decision making may be appropriate. Where this is the case, however, the deliberative prediction market itself might be used to predict the decision of a more representative committee. There may be danger in allowing those who participate in the decision making also to be on the committee, because decision makers might make decisions in order to boost their profits from prediction rather than on the basis of the best interests of the group. A partial antidote would be to prohibit decision makers from participating only in the final stage of the prediction market, in which a strictly proper scoring rule is used to predict the actual decision. Nonetheless, there is a danger that particular decision makers might gain (and indeed seek) a reputation for making decisions that are consistent with their earlier predictions. Ideally, the decision makers should be separate from the individuals who are predicting their actions.

If this separation is achieved, such prediction markets can help show how unpredictable a particular decision maker is. Suppose, for example, that a decision maker routinely ignores the forecasts of the prediction markets and the information that they produce. That might signal that he or she is not taking into account the considerations that the prediction market thought he or she would take into account. Once arbitrary decision making becomes expected, market participants will hesitate to produce new information and analysis, because they would not think that these considerations were relevant to the decision maker. Unpredictable decision making does not always indicate arbitrariness; perhaps the decision maker simply is smarter than any of the participants in the market and can be expected to produce better analysis than they can.

The information produced in a deliberative prediction market provides a way of assessing what concerns, if any, appear to animate a decision maker. If such a market produces insights about a wide range of considerations, that is a sign that the decision maker has a reputation for taking these considerations into account. If information that might seem irrelevant appears to move the market, that would indicate that market participants, rightly or wrongly, expect the decision maker to take the information into account. It might be disturbing, for example, if the deliberative prediction market used in forecasting the playground equipment choice changed its prediction when a member pointed out that one type of equipment is manufactured by a friend of the ultimate decision maker.

LEGAL REASONING

One context in which a deliberative prediction market for predicting a decision might be useful is in the legal system. In subsequent chapters I consider the use of prediction markets by governmental agencies, trial courts, and legislative bodies to help assess and even make decisions, but another approach is to use such a market to help provide information that might be relevant to a legal decision maker. The considerations used in legal reasoning differ somewhat from those used in other kinds of policy reasoning, but the market process could encourage analysis of these considerations. For example, legal reasoning often depends not only on what the best policy would be if writing on a blank slate but also on the constraints associated with statutory enactments and with judicial decisions. As the length of legal materials such as briefs and administrative agency decisions suggests, legal reasoning often can be complicated. A deliberative prediction market could be used to provide incentives to identify legal arguments of any type and to convince others that these arguments might be important to the eventual decision maker. Ever since the legal realism movement of the first half of the twentieth century, legal scholars have generally agreed that legal decision making often is indeterminate and therefore partly subjective. A legal reasoning prediction market could be expected to assess the degree to which a decision maker is likely to find particular arguments persuasive.

Consider, for example, the possible use of a deliberative prediction market as a substitute for or complement to law clerks. At both the trial court and appellate court levels, law clerks often are assigned the task of writing "bench memos" summarizing the parties' arguments, critiquing them, and making recommendations about how the judge or judges should rule in a particular case. A deliberative prediction market might do much the same thing, providing incentives both to assess the merits of the case on the basis of the parties' arguments and to produce new arguments that judges are likely to find persuasive. The market prediction of how a judge might be expected to rule in effect becomes a recommendation of how the judge should rule, and the information produced in the market serves as an alternative to a bench memo. There are advantages to bench memos, which might tend to be more organized than the information submitted in a prediction market, and to law clerks, who can engage in personal discussion with judges. But the deliberative prediction market approach has its benefits, too. Such a market might provide more powerful incentives to identify arguments that parties might have missed, although the professional values of clerks may already provide powerful incentives. It also might prove particularly useful if there is a concern that law clerks' own political preferences might influence their recommendations, though judges may prefer their clerks' advice for precisely that reason.

A potential drawback of the deliberative prediction market approach to producing legal arguments is that if the identity of the judge or judges making the eventual decision is known, the market might tend to produce only the types of arguments that they tend to find relevant, to the exclusion of arguments that other judges favor. There is, of course, some efficiency in this, and law clerks presumably seek to focus their bench memos on types of analysis that their bosses prefer. But there also is a danger that one-sided presentation of evidence will tend to reinforce the judges' own predispositions, perhaps producing a kind of polarization in which judges tend to become ever more idiosyncratic. Richard Revesz criticized a practice of the U.S. Court of Appeals for the D.C. Circuit, in which the court announced the names of judges before the parties submitted their briefs, on similar grounds.[61]

A simple remedy is to launch the prediction market before judges are selected; this should especially be feasible in the appellate context. This would ensure that market participants have incentives to take into account arguments that appeal to any of the potential judges. If an argument is correct but most judges would reject it, the market will not show the correctness of the argument, but it can at least reflect how judges in general would decide issues and encourage production of a wide variety of arguments. An additional advantage of this approach is that it could allow for an easy measure of how idiosyncratic particular judges are, as viewed by market participants.[62] The greater the changes in the prediction market forecast once the identity of the judge or judges is announced, the more idiosyncratic the decision making is expected to be. Such measures could complement other measures of judicial tendencies that political scientists have developed, for example, measures focusing on whether particular judges are conservative or liberal.[63]

Deliberative prediction markets also might be useful in the context of administrative agency rule making. In general, agencies issue rulemaking decisions using a process of "notice and comment,"[64] in which the agency announces what it is considering doing, accepts comments from the public, and then starts the process over again with a new draft, abandons the rulemaking initiative altogether, or reaches a final decision and includes a statement responding to significant comments. In many contexts, rule making will affect large numbers of individuals and entities, and comments both in favor of and opposed to a rule will be submitted. In some contexts, however, in particular those receiving less attention, very few comments might be submitted, and where many comments are generated, they sometimes may be one-sided.[65] A deliberative prediction market in, say, whether the agency will enact a final rule could serve as an antidote to this tendency, encouraging third parties with little direct interest in a rulemaking to produce information that is unlikely to be duplicative of comments. This might especially be useful when a rule might significantly affect relatively well-organized interests but have smaller effects on a large number of people or entities who do not individually have a sufficient stake to bother organizing. In general, political scientists recognize that law will tend to favor better-organized interests,[66] but deliberative prediction markets might provide a partial corrective.

PREDICTIVE PEER REVIEW

Perhaps one of society's most celebrated deliberative institutions is peer re-view, the process by which experts in a particular field determine whether sci-entific or other papers are accepted by journals or whether particular grant proposals should receive funding. In a typical peer review process, a paper or a grant proposal is sent to one or two referees, who are typically anonymous. They write comments about the papers and may conclude with recommenda-tions about whether the paper or proposal should be accepted. Ultimately, some other decision maker, whether a journal editor or a grant committee, makes the final decision, but social norms ensure that considerable weight is placed on the recommendations of the reviewers, especially in cases in which they agree. The process is often celebrated as central to the dispassionate pro-gression of the scientific method.[67] Like the Delphi Method, peer review relies on experts who are given anonymity, perhaps freeing them to give their gen-uine views, but also involves another party who considers the reviews, provid-ing some incentive for the experts consulted to be rigorous and fair. At the same time, the comments of reviewers can help authors revise and improve their initial submissions.

Peer review, however, has come under sustained attack. Ironically, some of the attacks appear in peer-reviewed publications. A study by Peter Rothwell and Christopher Martyn, for example, reviewed the peer reviews of 295 papers submitted to one of two journals in clinical neuroscience and found that agree-ment between the reviewers about whether to publish particular articles oc-curred no more often than would be expected by chance.[68] Commentators of-fer other criticisms as well. Thomas McGarity argues that peer review in the grant process tends to reinforce scientific consensus, making it difficult to chal-lenge orthodoxy,[69] and David F. Horrobin claims that peer review should seek to accomplish not only the task of quality control but also the challenge of en-couraging innovation.[70] Other critics, though, have worried that peer reviewers might not do a sufficiently good job of blocking works, and in particular too often fail to identify submissions that are the results of scientific fraud.[71] In a well-known hoax, the physicist Alan Sokal was able to publish in the peer-reviewed journal *Social Text* an article about the "hermeneutics of quantum gravity" that he himself thought was rubbish,[72] although this may be more of an indictment of a particular journal than of peer review in general.

These criticisms, not surprisingly, have led to proposals for reform. Some have suggested "open review," in which the reviewers' identities are known.

A randomized trial of open review indicated, however, that it has no significant effect on the quality of reviews as independently rated by third parties and makes it harder to find reviewers.[73] An alternative proposal is "open source review," in which anyone can contribute to a "wiki" (see Chapter 9) assessing whether to accept an article. David Dobbs argues that such review "stands to maintain rigor, turn review processes into productive forums and make publication less a proprietary claim to knowledge than the spark of a fruitful exchange."[74] With this approach, supporters of research and perhaps also competitors would be able to submit assessments, providing more information for both the editor and the authors and limiting the control of the reviewers. There are potential weaknesses, however. First, there might not be many disinterested parties willing to contribute to such a decentralized process. In the existing process, experts may feel obliged to participate as a result of norms demanding such participation and as a result of a desire to maintain good relations with the journal editor. Second, especially where an article is controversial, the process might not produce an objective consensus recommendation.

Predictive peer review would use a deliberative prediction market to forecast the ultimate decision of a journal editor or a panel of experts about whether to accept an article or whether to fund a proposal. The deliberative prediction markets would be subsidized, perhaps in part with fees charged to authors for their consideration. The market should be expected, of course, to work better with relatively large subsidies than with small ones. The subsidy would provide neutral parties with an incentive to review the relevant articles, and the market's estimate of the probability that the submission will be accepted should provide a useful piece of information to the decision maker about the consensus of market participants. At the same time, the market might constrain decision makers somewhat, making them less likely to weigh their own idiosyncratic preferences for articles that reach particular conclusions. Conceivably, reviewers who today note their service as referees on their curriculum vitae instead might advertise their contributions to the review process by reporting how much money they had earned by reviewing. Experts might in such a world be expected not only to publish their own work but also to spend time carefully reviewing the work of others, and money earned in doing so might appear as a useful proxy for their success. Admittedly, predictive peer review would need to become well established as accurate before it could begin to make significant changes in the incentives of scholars.

Chapter 5 Regulatory Bodies

We have seen how private entities can use prediction markets to produce information and predictions that can help them or others make decisions. The media, for example, can use prediction markets to inform their readers, and policy analysts may be able to use prediction markets to separate forecasts that are backed by evidence from unsubstantiated spin. Businesses can use internal or external prediction markets to gather information that might affect their decision making, and deliberative prediction markets might substitute for committees in gathering information for some ultimate decision maker.

In all of these contexts, a prediction market provides one piece of data that decision makers should take into account, but the market does not obviate the need for a decision to be made, nor does it produce an unambiguous recommendation regarding any particular decision. A market might be used to predict the number of individuals who will be convicted of crimes in some year, but that prediction would be only one factor to be taken into account in deciding whether to build a new prison. Other factors might include the financial cost of a new prison or the deterrent effect on crime of new construction.

Beginning with this chapter, I focus on the possibility that prediction markets might make forecasts that could provide almost all of the information needed for some set of decisions. In some cases, prediction markets might be able to replace institutions and individuals assigned to research and make particular decisions.

In particular, this chapter shows how prediction markets might perform decision-making tasks typically assigned to regulatory bodies such as legislatures, administrative agencies, and judges. In subsequent chapters I focus on each of these types of regulatory bodies separately, showing how prediction markets might be structured to perform the tasks that these bodies perform, such as writing legislation, approving new regulations, and issuing verdicts and judgments. The purpose of this chapter is to show prediction markets could make such decision making unnecessary, albeit only for some kinds of problems.

Many governmental decision making tasks are fundamentally predictive in nature, and prediction markets can greatly simplify the task demanded of a regulator. Instead of making predictions of the extent to which some regulated entity will produce some result and then determining whether the entity can proceed to engage in an activity, the regulator merely needs to set some threshold level that the activity must or cannot exceed or produce a set of penalties or bonuses for regulated entities depending on the predictions made. In other words, prediction markets can allow regulators to focus on the normative component of a decision rather than on determining the implications of that component for regulated entities.

Prediction markets are not the only regulatory tools that can simplify the task of regulation. In some regulatory environments, a regime of strict liability (sometimes called "enterprise liability" when applied to business associations) can serve much the same purpose, forcing entities to make their own predictions about the consequences of their actions by requiring them to pay for those consequences ex post.[1] In other contexts, regulatory requirements that specific entities obtain insurance in effect shift the predictive task to insurance companies.[2] Sometimes, however, it might be desirable to generate predictions about the consequence of activities without placing the full cost of those activities on the regulated entities, whether directly (via enterprise liability) or indirectly (via an insurance requirement).

One approach to generating predictions without the legal consequence of full liability is to require that entities insure some portion of the harm that their activities might cause. The price of the insurance, this chapter shows, can be translated into a prediction. A prediction market can serve as an alternative prediction mechanism, and the choice among various prediction mechanisms depends on factors such as whether existing entities already have expertise in making particular kinds of decisions. Another important market-oriented prediction mechanism is a rights trading market, in which regulated entities trade a limited number of rights to engage in some activity, such as pollution. This chapter describes some parallels between these markets and prediction markets but also explains how they differ. A prediction market is but one market-oriented regulatory tool, and this chapter seeks to place prediction markets into a broader context of market-based techniques.

All of these techniques promise to avoid one of the major decisions that regulators face: whether to regulate with a system of rules or with a system of standards. I begin by discussing the venerable jurisprudential debate about the wisdom of these competing approaches. I then explain how the legal system can achieve the flexibility of standards and the certainty of rules by generating predictions that have some effect under a particular legal standard. I call this approach "predictive decision making" and explain how both insurance and prediction markets can serve as the foundation of a predictive decision making regime. Such a regime can provide a previously unrecognized alternative to command-and-control regulation, just as emissions trading systems can save the government from the difficulties associated with defining the particular technologies that regulated entities should use to control pollution. A particularly useful form of market for predictive decision making is the conditional market, which can assess the potential impact of a decision. I discuss some possible applications of predictive decision making and conclude by assessing the danger that predictive decision making in general and prediction markets in particular might not work effectively if markets are relatively inefficient.

RULES VERSUS STANDARDS

Perhaps the most fundamental choice in a legal regime is that between rules and standards. For example, in statistical analysis, a rule might be "reject the null hypothesis if the numbers are not significant at the .05 level"; a standard might be "reject the null hypothesis when the observed event is improbable." A simple legal illustration of the distinction compares a speed limit of fifty-five miles per hour (a rule) with a prohibition on reckless driving (a standard). The rule announces in advance what is required, whereas the standard requires some decision maker, such as a traffic cop or a traffic judge, to make a determination ex post. In practice, the distinction may not always be clear. A speed limit of fifty-five miles per hour might generally be understood to mean that one should not drive any faster than sixty-five or seventy miles per hour, and a rule against reckless driving might be widely understood to apply only to specific kinds of driving behavior.

Nonetheless, there is a genuine conceptual distinction between rules and standards, and there are advantages to both approaches. Rules generally provide the public with a clearer sense than standards do of what is permitted.[3] Rules also economize on enforcement costs, because they reduce the chance that there will be a dispute about whether a particular rule has been violated. Rules, however, also create the possibility of loopholes. In the absence of a reckless driving prohibition, a driver might travel at fifty-five miles per hour on an icy road or in heavy traffic without violating the law. Standards demand more of decision makers, but they can permit them to take into account all relevant circumstances, including ones that the creators of the standards never envisioned.

In his book *Playing by the Rules,* Frederick Schauer offers a comprehensive philosophical account of rules and, by extension, of standards.[4] Rules, Schauer emphasizes, are "entrenched generalizations," meaning that they apply even in situations in which the justification or justifications underlying the rule would seem to dictate a different result. For example, a restaurant door with a sign proclaiming "no dogs allowed" appears to bar "the well-behaved in addition to the troublesome, the clean along with the dirty, and the healthy as well as the diseased."[5] Rules are thus said to be overinclusive and underinclusive,[6] applying in situations where they should not apply (for example, clean dogs) and not applying in situations where they should (poorly behaved, dirty, contagious humans).

A rule is thus not equivalent to its underlying justifications, and indeed some "rule-generating justification" is needed to rationalize having the rule rather than simply having a set of standards to guide decision makers.[7] One such rule-generating justification is the argument from efficiency: the decision maker "is partially freed from the responsibility of scrutinizing every substantively relevant feature of the event."[8] Another is that the ex post decision makers who are applying a standard might make errors, thus introducing the same problems of overinclusion and underinclusion that beset rules.[9]

Prediction markets do not provide a general escape from the choice between rules and standards, but in some contexts prediction markets may make efficient the replacement of a detailed set of rules with a simple standard. Often, a set of rules defines what behavior is permissible based on judgments, implicit or explicit, that the prohibited behavior has negative consequences. The rules, however, may define the category of prohibited behavior in an overinclusive or in an underinclusive way. Prediction markets and other market-oriented approaches may save the government from the task of defining just what behavior will have the negative consequences and therefore must be prohibited.

The government instead can specify that activities will be permitted unless prediction markets forecast that they will have certain negative consequences, in which case they might be taxed or prohibited outright. There are many legal contexts in which the consequences of the regulated entity's actions, such as the injuries that an entity's actions can be expected to produce, will be measurable eventually. Even where the eventual measurement will be imprecise, a prediction of that measurement might provide a reliable policy basis for permitting or prohibiting an entity from engaging in an activity.

The difference between a regulatory regime relying on a prediction market and a regulatory regime relying on a standard is in large part a difference in timing. Standards often must be adjudicated ex post, but prediction markets can provide contemporaneous evaluations of the regulated activity. In some instances, of course, this is impractical. It would be difficult, for example, to replace a standard against reckless driving with a prediction market that continuously estimates the probability that a driver will have an accident in the next few minutes. In other contexts it would be much easier, and contemporaneous assessments might reduce the uncertainty facing regulated entities. Ultimately, a comparison between a standard with traditional ex post adjudication and a rule targeted toward a prediction market depends on which approach will produce more accurate, consistent, and inexpensive assessments.

CONDITIONAL PREDICTION MARKETS:
THE UNWINDING APPROACH

Prediction markets might not seem to be a suitable alternative to standards because they predict what *will* happen, not what will happen *contingent* on some choices or on some other events. A rule of enterprise liability imposed on automobile manufacturers for all automobile accidents will lead those manufacturers to make conditional assessments, considering how many accidents are likely to occur for different possible configurations of safety features. A prediction market can forecast how many accidents will occur for a particular model, and so in theory the government might require a prediction of relatively few accidents before a car could be sold. The prediction market result would be unstable, however. If it anticipates many accidents, then the car cannot be sold, so then there will be few accidents, but then the car can be sold. What we need are conditional prediction markets, in this case assessing how many accidents will occur if a particular model is allowed on the market.

The conceptually simplest approach to implementing conditional prediction markets is to unwind all transactions in the market if the condition does not occur. For example, if A bought a prediction market share in an outcome from the market sponsor for one dollar, then A would be refunded one dollar if the condition were not met. If A later sold the share to B for eighty cents, then A would refund the eighty cents to B. If, for example, a prediction market forecasts the attendance at a baseball game in the event of rain, but it does not rain, then participants will have lost time but not money investing in the market. This approach will not always be simple in practice, especially if the market takes place over a long period of time. The market sponsor will need some mechanism for locating all of the market participants and ensuring that they pay or receive money as appropriate. Refunding money to a party might well be easier than collecting money that a party previously received. One way of accomplishing this is by placing any money received from a market participant in an escrow account, perhaps an interest-bearing one, with amounts to be paid back dependent on whether the condition is met. This approach has, I admit, a significant drawback: the market participant will have no control over funds received in market transactions until the conclusion of the market.

In any event, the unwinding approach has proved commercially feasible, because TradeSports regularly specifies that it will unwind contracts in the event of certain contingencies. For example, for National Basketball Association games, TradeSports notes that games become official after forty-three minutes, and "[g]ames lasting under official time will have all contracts 'unwound.'" Cancellation of basketball games, of course, is relatively rare, and so these rules allow traders to focus on the primary issue of interest, the relative strength of two teams, rather than on factors such as extreme weather that might force a cancellation. If it had preferred to avoid unwinding, TradeSports alternatively could have factored the condition directly into the contract. For example, it might provide that every contract will pay off in the event of a cancellation, but this would make prices harder to interpret. The prices would represent the probability that a team would win or that the game would be canceled, not simply the probability that the team would win if the game were played.

In some contracts, the unwinding condition is of greater significance. For example, when President Bush nominated Harriet Miers to the Supreme Court, TradeSports offered both a contract predicting whether she would be confirmed and a contract predicting whether she would receive at least a specified number of votes in the Senate. Once TradeSports clarified that the latter set of contracts would be unwound if Miers did not receive a Senate floor vote, the trading prices straightforwardly indicated that Miers' probability of receiving fifty votes in the Senate if she received a floor vote was greater than her chance of being confirmed. In the end, Miers withdrew her name from consideration, and so the condition was not met.

A significant drawback of the unwinding approach to conditional markets is that it might encourage relatively little estimation in the case of conditions that are unlikely to hold. Consider, for example, a prediction market forecasting the probability that various potential nominees to the Supreme Court would be confirmed. The incentive to trade shares of someone who only has a small chance of being nominated would be low. A trader's expected profits from improving the probability prediction by a set amount for someone who has only a 1 percent chance of being nominated would be only one-fiftieth the expected profits from doing so for someone who has a 50 percent chance of being nominated. Such a contract could be subsidized, but the potential subsidy, which ordinarily will not be paid, would need to be roughly fifty times higher to compensate for the low probability.

A potential way around this problem is to use a design that rewards market participants for making predictions at a later stage of the market. For example, in the deliberative prediction market proposal described above, each prediction is evaluated on the basis of the degree to which it is consistent with the market prediction at some interval thereafter. With this approach, it would not be necessary to unwind all transactions. Rather, the market sponsor could assign a score of zero (meaning no profit or loss) to any transactions that took place after it became apparent that the condition would not be met or when the probability of its occurrence, as determined by a separate prediction market, fell permanently below some threshold, such as 1 percent. The market sponsor would then also need to assign a score of zero to any earlier predictions that otherwise would have been evaluated on the basis of the market consensus in this time period.

Suppose, for example, that this market were established to determine the probability of confirmation of potential Supreme Court nominees. The market sponsor could create the market well in advance of any expected nomination and provide for a prediction interval of about a month for the conditional probabilities. At the same time, the sponsor would create a market predicting the probability that each of various potential nominees in fact would be nominated by a particular date. If I believed that Judge Jones had only a 5 percent chance of being nominated, I still could trade on information about her confirmation chances. As long as Judge Jones's nomination probability remained above the 1 percent (or other designated) threshold about a month after I entered my prediction, then the fact that the condition might not occur would have no effect on my ability to make money on the basis of my prediction. If Judge Jones were nominated, then the market sponsor would have no need to unwind the market.

The reason that this mechanism would provide appropriate incentives to make predictions is straightforward. Anyone investing in this market would recognize that announcing a conditional prediction can lead to three different possible outcomes when the prediction interval elapses. It might be the case that the condition has become true, that the condition has become false, or that the condition remains uncertain. If the condition becomes true, then market participants will be predicting the unconditional probability of confirmation, and so the original predictor's incentive is to predict this probability. If the condition becomes false, then the prediction will receive of pay nothing, and so that possibility should not affect the prediction. If the condition remains uncertain, future predictors will continue to look toward the possibility of the condition's becoming true, and so once again the best strategy is to announce the unconditional probability of confirmation. Although one could argue about whether the chance of the condition's occurrence provides sufficient discipline in cases of extremely low probabilities (say, one in a billion),[10] it should work for conditions that have some reasonable chance of becoming true.

PREDICTIVE DECISION MAKING

The theory underlying the prediction market approach might be called "predictive decision making,"[11] wherein a legal decision depends on an explicit announced prediction, rather than on a set of detailed rules or on some other normative framework for reaching results in particular cases. A prediction market is only one possible prediction mechanism that might underlie a predictive decision making regime. Such a regime alternatively might depend on some other prediction mechanism, which could be as simple as a requirement that a particular legal decision maker render a decision based on some prediction about the future.

Consider, for example, the role of the federal courts in deciding diversity cases, state law cases that are in federal court only because opposing litigants are from different states. Under the rule of *Erie R.R. v. Tompkins*,[12] a federal court sitting in diversity must decide a case as the relevant state court would resolve it. Where the state rule is unclear, "the job of the federal courts is carefully to predict how the highest court of the forum state would resolve the uncertainty or ambiguity."[13] Predictive decision making in this context is hardly inevitable, and indeed some legal scholars have argued that decision making that follows the *Erie* standard should be less predictive, with federal judges weighing traditional legal arguments as they ordinarily would in a federal case.[14]

In reality, many federal judges in effect may be doing this anyway, in part because the prediction mechanism includes little incentive for a federal judge to make accurate predictions of state law. If prediction rather than normative decision making is desirable in this context, markets predicting how state courts would eventually resolve a particular issue, conditional on its actual resolution, might help. Federal judges might be expected to place some weight on such predictions or, in theory, could be required to abide by them. If a prediction mechanism run by private parties is adequate, there might be little need for publicly appointed legal officials to develop independent predictions. Judges should perhaps devote their time to cases in which they are expected to make normative evaluations, leaving prediction to prediction market participants who have strong incentives to reach correct answers.

I admit that it seems unlikely that judges would defer to prediction markets. In large part, this might be because of the unfamiliarity of prediction markets, the reluctance of judges to yield power to private predictors, and a desire not to call attention to the reality that disagreement about substantive law means that outcomes of cases sometimes depend on the luck of the draw. Inertia, too, can be powerful, and creating binding prediction markets would require some executive or legislative involvement. Decisions would need to be made about precisely what questions should be predicted, how great the market subsidy should be, and later about whether the predictions turned out to be accurate, an inquiry that might be subjective when the content of the state law decision might be contested. It is more plausible, however, that private parties, such as litigants or policy analysis organizations, might establish prediction markets in some cases. This might put some modest reputational pressure on judges inclined to disguise their own normative preferences in predictions, at least if the prediction markets develop a reputation for accuracy.

Erie is not the only context in which we might want judges to make predictions. Professor Einer Elhauge has offered a predictive decision making proposal of his own, though he does not use the term himself.[15] Whenever statutes are ambiguous, Elhauge argues, judges should not use normative frameworks such as economic or philosophical principles to resolve the ambiguities. Instead, judges should predict how the current legislature would resolve the issue. At least, judges should do so when it is possible to guess what choice the legislature is more likely than not to make.[16] Elhauge maintains that this is not only what judges should do but what they already implicitly do, for example, when relying on certain canons of construction.[17]

Elhauge addresses many questions that his proposal invites, such as why statutory interpretation should track the current legislature rather than the legislature that enacted the relevant statute.[18] For our purposes, however, the important question is whether the prediction mechanism—in effect, an instruction to judges to make predictions, along with canons of construction and other rules that will push them to do so—is effective. Elhauge insists on predictions only in cases in which evidence is relatively objective,[19] but he concedes the danger that judges might seek to advance their own "personal preferences in the guise of following current legislative views."[20] Judges might even be biased in determining whether evidence is sufficiently objective to make a prediction.

If Elhauge is right that judges already predict what the current legislature would do if faced with a particular decision, then the choice is not whether judges should engage in predictive decision making but how they should do it. The advantage of the prediction mechanism that courts already use is that it is deeply embedded in judicial tradition; prediction markets are not. But prediction markets might be structured to forecast what the current legislature will end up deciding about a particular issue, if it does confront the issue. The genius of Elhauge's analysis is the observation that intractable normative questions can be reduced to exercises in prediction. If that is desirable, then there is a strong case for eventually using mechanisms such as prediction markets that are well suited to prediction, even if this would represent too great a change for the foreseeable future. Should such markets exist, judges might someday state explicitly why they choose to act in ways that are contrary to legislative intent.

INSURANCE AS A PREDICTIVE TECHNOLOGY

A significant virtue of prediction markets is that they give third parties finan-cial incentives to make accurate predictions. But there are other prediction mechanisms for which this is also true and that can serve as alternatives to pre-diction markets. Perhaps the most familiar is insurance. By requiring insurance for certain events, a government motivates independent insurance companies to calculate the probability that the events will occur and the economic losses that those events will produce. For example, a requirement that business own-ers obtain liability insurance will lead insurance companies to make some as-sessment of the probability that each insurance applicant will face a tort suit and what the damages might be. Bungee jumping tour operators might expect to pay higher insurance premiums than meditation centers, precisely because the insurer has made a prediction that the expected liability is higher for the jumpers.

A full insurance requirement switches the responsibility for making the rel-evant prediction from a regulated entity to a third-party insurer. Ordinarily, entities subject to insurance requirements must show merely that they have obtained insurance, not the price at which they obtained it. But the govern-ment plausibly might sometimes require regulated entities to obtain insurance at no more than a certain price as a condition of operation.[21] Suppose, for ex-ample, that a state decided that it wanted to allow some people between age sixteen and age eighteen to drive, but only those likely to be the safest drivers in that group. The government might doubt its ability to design adequate road tests of driving ability or to determine the criteria that can predict who will drive safely. One possibility, then, would be to allow anyone in the age group to obtain a driver's license if that person is able to obtain or renew insurance for no more than some fixed amount. The state would then be taking advan-tage of the natural incentive that insurance companies have to make predic-tions about driver safety.

The incentive of insurance companies to risk-classify insureds and charge them differential rates, however, is limited. Sometimes, this is because of legal limitations,[22] and a state could make clear that insurance companies would be permitted to charge different rates, except possibly on the basis of prohibited considerations such as race. But it also might be that it is only worthwhile for in-surance companies to spend a small amount assessing driver quality. This may help explain why they do not administer their own road tests. The government could, however, encourage additional care by increasing insurers' exposure, for example, by requiring insurance companies to pay three dollars into a fund for every dollar the insurer pays out as a result of an accident. The fund might then be redistributed to insurers in proportion to the number of insureds under contract with those insurers to minimize the resulting increase in consumer prices. This would provide additional incentives to engage in risk assessment while producing only small increases in the cost of insurance.

The opposite strategy might be useful in contexts in which the government wishes to harness insurance company information without imposing full liability on regulated entities. Suppose, for example, that the government did not want to make automobile manufacturers liable for all damages resulting from automobile accidents but still wanted insurance companies to help provide a prediction of what those damages would be. It is possible to impose a partial insurance requirement on the automobile manufacturers. For example, they might be required to pay for one-hundredth of the damages resulting from vehicle use. The payment might be made to the victims, to the government, or to a fund to be shared among all automobile companies. Regardless, the government could use the price of this insurance as a factor in regulation, for example, by allowing sale of automobiles only if such insurance can be obtained sufficiently cheaply or by imposing additional fines on companies that also have to pay a lot for insurance.

I know of no instances in which government in fact has used a partial insurance requirement to harness information from insurance companies, perhaps indicating that predictive decision making is not an intuitive regulatory strategy. At least one academic proposal, however, has recommended such an insurance requirement. In 1971 professors Kenneth Scott and Thomas Mayer defended mandatory federal deposit insurance but worried that the federal government might not be able to do a good job of pricing such insurance in a way that would predict bank failure.[23] One possible solution would be to require banks to obtain private insurance for a fraction of their deposits. "The resulting demand," Scott and Mayer note, "would bring a new form of private insurance into existence and thereby create a large, independent set of risk judgments."[24]

This suggestion fits the predictive decision making paradigm perfectly. With such a regime, the government would be able to discard the detailed rules that determine when banks can operate, rules that are designed to predict the danger of insolvency. The government also would not need to rely on the discretion of banking officials to determine when a particular institution is in danger.

Instead, any bank might be allowed to operate, as long as it buys the remainder of its insurance from the federal government at actuarially fair rates. Had Scott and Mayer's proposal been accepted, fewer savings and loan institutions might have failed in the 1980s.

This approach can be extended to a wide variety of contexts such as governance of defined benefit pension plans, in which employees are purportedly guaranteed specific benefits. Currently, a complex federal statute, the Employee Retirement Income Security Act of 1974 (ERISA),[25] governs employers' obligations to fund pension plans, and an independent federal agency, the Pension Benefit Guaranty Corp. (PBGC), acts as an insurer of last resort in cases in which an employer demonstrates that it is in severe financial distress. Many commentators have argued that despite these regulatory protections, defined benefit plans are underfunded, and that the PBGC, which collects insurance premiums from employers, will be unable to meet its obligations.[26] A simple market alternative would be to require that employers purchase insurance for some percentage of their pension obligations. The government might then insist that employers purchase additional insurance from the PBGC at the same rates. Or the government might simply permit a business to operate only if the premiums indicate a high probability that employers will be able to meet their obligations. Businesses that are not likely to be able to meet their obligations would need to offer pensions that they would be able to honor.

One advantage of using insurance companies to make predictions is that they have expertise in doing so, but this does not provide a strong argument for using insurance companies rather than prediction markets to make forecasts. After all, insurance companies would be free to deploy their actuaries to make predictions in prediction markets, if they pleased, so prediction markets should be able to harness their skills. The more significant advantage is that insurance is a more familiar and better-tested prediction mechanism, perhaps enabling regulators to put aside concerns about prediction markets, such as whether they might be subject to manipulation by third parties. (On the other hand, a danger of partial insurance requirements is that regulated entities might seek to evade the rules by giving side payments to insurers; although criminal sanctions could reduce this activity, the natural market corrective of prediction markets might be superior.) In theory, partial insurance requirements could be structured to make predictions of just about anything, so insurance might be more feasible as a prediction mechanism in a predictive decision making proposal. Regulators who would feel uncomfortable relying on prediction markets, for reasons both sound and unsound, might be willing to piggyback on insurance company evaluations.

In order for predictive decision making to be effective, the prediction mechanism must be relatively accurate and thus sensitive to factual distinctions between different regulated entities. Suppose, for example, that a partial insurance requirement were used as a way of regulating bank solvency. If insurance companies offered every bank the same rate, regardless of its financial position, that would provide a strong indication that the insurance companies did not find risk classification to be sufficiently profitable to be worthwhile. With some variation in the rates banks are charged, it would be more difficult to determine whether the insurance companies are effective at rate classification. A small variance might indicate some flaw in the insurance companies' approach that might be attributable to poor ability to make differentiated predictions, to legal regulation that discourages differential pricing, or to collusion. But it also might simply indicate that a wide range of banks have quite similar risk profiles.

A simple approach to improving accuracy is to increase stakes. In the insurance context, this might mean increasing the required level of coverage by partial insurance; in the prediction markets context, this would mean a larger subsidy. With larger stakes, participants in the relevant prediction mechanism will have greater incentives to identify and assess smaller pieces of information that might affect the overall prediction. This does not, however, establish that as stakes increase, inaccuracy can be reduced arbitrarily to near zero. One problem is that predictions can be only as good as the best models that are available or that could in theory be developed. Sometimes analysts recognize problems in models that predict whether an event would take place only after the fact. A more serious concern is that it is possible that some systematic errors of which the most informed analysts are aware might persist because of the dynamics of the prediction market itself.

MARKET-BASED SAFETY REGULATION

Perhaps the most obvious potential application of predictive decision making is in the area of government safety regulation. Like many countries, the United States regulates safety in a wide range of contexts. The Occupational Safety and Health Administration (OSHA) regulates workplace safety, and the Federal Aviation Administration (FAA) and Transportation Security Administration (TSA) regulate different aspects of airplane safety. These agencies generally adopt command-and-control approaches, specifying the safety precautions that regulated entities should use in specific contexts. For example, at the end of the Clinton administration, OSHA released "ergonomic regulations," which provided specific rules for employers in order to help avoid musculoskeletal injuries.[27] Opponents of the regulation argued that it would be too expensive,[28] and Congress quickly repealed the rules.[29]

Labor and commercial interests might find more common ground with regard to safety regulatory issues if market-based approaches allowed the government to mandate safety improvements without specifying the precise mechanisms that regulated entities need to follow. Commentators have not previously identified market-based approaches to safety regulation but have focused instead on compromise strategies such as regulations designed to improve the information available to workers.[30] The predictive decision making strategy, however, points to a possible solution. The government could mandate that regulated entities achieve certain safety goals but measure whether the entities have done so only by considering predictions of the likelihood of injuries and accidents.

For example, prediction markets or a partial insurance requirement might be used to predict the number of injuries and deaths for each regulated mine. Government regulations could then specify only targets that particular mines need to achieve, based in part on factors such as the amount of mining and the number of employees in each mine. An alternative, of course, would be simply to provide strict liability for mines, but if that is undesirable or politically infeasible, the predictive decision making strategy allows the government to regulate without imposing detailed regulations or full liability on mine operators. If private predictors can outperform the government in assessing the degree to which particular mining practices invite danger or the cost of implementing various safety precautions, then predictive decision making could allow private entities to achieve any given level of expected safety at a lower cost. Private predictors would reward mine operators for taking relatively low-cost safety precautions and would not punish them excessively for abandoning high-cost precautions that provide little safety benefit.

Market-based safety regulation need not mean less safety. Consider, for example, the nuclear safety context. Because of the Price-Anderson Act,[31] the liability of nuclear power plant operators is limited. The justification for this limitation is that the potential consequences of a nuclear accident are so grave that the insurance industry would not be able to cover it. The liability limitation, however, presumably leads nuclear power plants to invest less in safety, although governmental regulation pushes in the opposite direction. The market approach to safety regulation might insist that each nuclear power plant own-er obtain some small amount of insurance that the insurance industry would be able to handle and then purchase additional insurance from the federal government at actuarially fair rates. Or prediction markets might assess the probability of minor plant accidents and major catastrophes, and the govern-ment might insist that plants achieve at least some level of safety.

PERMIT TRADING SYSTEMS

Market-based safety regulation has much in common with permit trading pro-grams. In emissions trading programs, for example, the government assigns to each regulated entity a pollution allotment for a particular pollutant, often based on past usage.[32] The government then allows each entity to achieve its allotment in whatever way it thinks best and also allows different entities to trade pollution rights with one another. The theory is that allowing such transactions enables the achievement of any desired level of pollution reduc-tion at the lowest possible cost. The flip side, of course, is that it allows maxi-mum pollution reduction for any given cost to be imposed on industry as a whole. As with the market-based safety regulation proposal, emissions trading regimes save the government from the task of making decisions about what technologies are most likely to prevent pollution. The government's role in both approaches is limited to setting goals, facilitating the market, and moni-toring ex post compliance.

A permit-trading system does not count as a prediction market. Its purpose is not simply to produce a prediction but rather to facilitate mutually benefi-cial transactions that impose no net cost on society. The fact that market ac-tivity produces useful information in the form of prices, revealing the least costly means of accomplishing a marginal increment in pollution reduction, is merely a happy artifact of market activity. This information might seem to be in the form of a prediction, because each business is forecasting how much it will cost to achieve a given level of pollution abatement, but this is a relatively straightforward forecasting problem for each firm. Market-based predictive decision making can be helpful when the government cannot easily measure the extent of some social ill that each regulated entity produces in a particular time period, and a permit trading system can be helpful when the government cannot determine which entities are most capable of reducing a social ill.

In some contexts, the two approaches usefully might be combined. For ex-ample, in the safety context, the government may lack good information about the degree of danger posed by various practices, but it also does not have good information about which regulated entities or sectors can improve safety most easily. The market-based safety regulation approach sketched above insists that each firm reaches a specified level of anticipated safety. The government might, however, allow firms to trade rights to pose danger to the public. For example, a firm whose activities are anticipated to cause ten deaths annually but has been allowed a level of twenty predicted deaths by the government could sell its right to pose additional risk to some other firm. This would allow the firms that can increase safety most cheaply to contribute the most to given safety improvements. Trades might be allowed across industrial sectors. It would not be straightforward to allow such trading absent predictions of accidents.

UTILITY REGULATION

Prediction markets sometimes might be useful not only in conjunction with permit trading systems but also in conjunction with other market-oriented devices such as auctions. Consider, for example, Harold Demsetz's proposal to use an auction as an alternative to traditional regulation of utilities such as electricity or cable television providers. Traditionally, utilities have been regulated on the theory that they are natural monopolies, that is, that economies of scale in the industry are so great that inevitably there will be only a single producer. Because prices are higher and quantity is lower in a monopoly than with various forms of competition, the government regulates the prices that natural monopolists can charge and the services that they provide.[33] Demsetz suggested that instead the government might auction the right to serve as the natural monopolist for some period of time.[34] The winner of the auction would be the bidder committing to the best overall deal to society. For example, firms might compete for the right to offer service at the lowest price, with the lowest bid winning the auction.

Demsetzian auctions have not become widespread, and one possible problem is the difficulty in assessing bids.[35] If price were the only variable in bids, then the winning bidder would charge a very low price but offer very low quality. Thus, for the mechanism to work well, there must be some means of assessing the quality of services that bidders will provide. One approach, of course, is simply to rely on the government to assess the proposals. The purpose of the Demsetzian auction, however, is to limit the government's role. One might worry that the government would not do an adequate job of predicting quality and that competing bidders would have incentives to spend a great deal of money to persuade the government that they will offer high-quality service (for example, by wining and dining lawmakers), without necessarily actually providing such service.

An alternative approach is to use a conditional prediction market to gauge how satisfied consumers will be with different proposed service providers. For example, it might be used to predict consumer surplus in future years, and those numbers could then be discounted to present values. The consumer surplus from a transaction is the difference between the maximum that a consumer would pay for the service and the amount that the consumer actually pays. For the firm selected, this might be established ex post by conducting surveys of consumers. Surveys might not produce perfect predictions because consumers might not answer correctly. A consumer might really prefer to pay ten thousand dollars a year rather than not have electricity yet give an answer of two thousand dollars, biased in the direction of the amount that consumers actually pay. Nonetheless, consumers should generally report higher valuations for utilities that succeed in offering higher quality services, and so the relative forecasts from one prediction market to another might be meaningful.

Alternatively, a governmental official might make the evaluation independent of consumer surveys. Because this evaluation would affect only the prediction market participants, the franchisee would have little incentive to try to influence the official making the ex post decision. This is a critical distinction between the predictive decision making proposal and existing approaches to rate regulation. In existing approaches, the regulated entity has every incentive to seek to capture the governmental agency, and short of that, to spend a great deal of money trying to persuade the agency to allow it to charge more to consumers. In the predictive proposal, the eventual decision by the agency would not affect the regulated entity, and so the only parties with a direct incentive to seek to influence the decision would be prediction market participants. At least these participants would have varying interests, however, and the overall stakes would be so much lower that the amount spent would be much less than in the ratemaking context.

It might appear that Demsetz's auction proposal in general and this refinement in particular fail to recognize that a prediction of performance cannot substitute for active monitoring. The government's role, the argument goes, is not merely to select as natural monopolist the company with the best proposal but to ensure that the natural monopolist meets its commitments. Otherwise, the auction winner inevitably would shirk on its promises, and no party would be in a position to enforce them. Yet proposals from prospective utility regulators could include enforcement devices that establish precommitment. For example, one prospective utility operator might authorize consumers to sue to enforce rights that the proposal would specify. Another might promise to pay a third party some set amount of money if quality, as established by independent surveys, falls below a certain level.[36] Yet another might agree to government-conducted (or perhaps third-party-conducted) price regulation. Prediction market participants would have an incentive to anticipate the degree to which such commitments would succeed in improving quality, and prospective utility operators would need to identify the commitment approaches that can achieve quality at the lowest possible price.

REVERSE AUCTIONS

Selection of a natural monopolist is only one possible application of using a prediction market as a means of evaluating different bids in a reverse auction. In a typical reverse auction, a potential buyer of a good or service solicits bids, seeking to pay as little money as possible for the good or service. The buyers, however, care also about quality, and therefore they will generally take various aspects of the different offers into account before entering into a particular transaction. One way of evaluating the offers in any reverse auction would be to use conditional prediction markets. As long as there is some mechanism for evaluating the performance of a bidder whose offer is accepted, for example, by surveying the buyer to assess the buyer's satisfaction level, conditional prediction markets can predict how satisfied the buyer will be with different possibilities.

For some buyers, using conditional prediction markets to assess auction bids will provide little added value. This will be especially true where the buyers have all necessary information about the relevant bids or at least where the buyers' information is much better than third parties' information. Prediction markets will be particularly useful, though, in cases in which third parties may have better information than does the bidder. Some third parties might develop specialized expertise in evaluating offers for particular types of goods and services and developing good information about the reputation of particular sellers. By adopting a predictive decision making approach, the bidder can harness these third parties' information without necessarily doing any independent research. A market subsidy in turn can provide an incentive for these third parties to participate.

As the example of utility regulation suggests, combining prediction markets with reverse auctions might be particularly useful in governmental decision making. The state that selects a natural monopolist is in effect an agent acting on behalf of individuals who may purchase the natural monopolist's services. There is a danger that the agent may not know the interests of those who will be the ultimate purchasers. Prediction markets help overcome this problem by giving those with the best ability to evaluate proposals the incentive to do so. Meanwhile, prediction markets can save the government from the need to draft detailed regulations about the conduct of the individuals who select federal contractors.

Predictive decision making can substitute not only for detailed substantive rules but also for elaborate procedural requirements that are intended to discipline decision making in the face of a standard. A task such as government procurement almost necessarily involves some degree of discretion, at least in contexts in which the quality or reliability of different service providers may be variable. To prevent arbitrariness, government procurement law includes procedural protections that directly protect bidders and indirectly may benefit the public by improving the probability that the government makes good decisions. Conditional prediction markets can serve as a complement to or substitute for such procedural protections. At least, the government could provide lesser procedural protection to bidders whose offers are rated as relatively unattractive, saving resources for the cases in which there is the greatest chance of erroneous or interested governmental decision making.

MERGER ANALYSIS

Because the analysis of planned mergers inherently involves projections into the future, conditional prediction markets that forecast consumer surplus could help. Currently in the United States, the Antitrust Division of the Department of Justice and the Federal Trade Commission (FTC) preclear proposed mergers. One of the agencies, depending on factors such as the industry involved, will evaluate the effect of a merger on competition. It will then decide whether it will challenge the merger in the courts or will promise not to do so. In many cases, the government indicates that it will approve a merger, but only on the condition that certain changes are made, such as sale of specific business units to a third party to avoid the danger of monopoly. Predictably, this system leads to criticism from both sides: from those who believe that the government should be more deferential to prospective merger partners[37] and from those who believe that the government should not be involved at all.[38]

The government's role in merger analysis is predictive; it anticipates the effects of a merger on competition. Because open-ended government decision making might promote considerable uncertainty among businesses considering whether to merge, the Antitrust Division and the FTC have issued joint Horizontal Merger Guidelines.[39] The ultimate goal of the guidelines is to determine whether merged entities would have "market power," that is, "the ability profitably to maintain prices above competitive levels for a significant period of time."[40] The guidelines provide an overview of how the government will define the relevant product and geographical markets that the merger might affect and how the government will calculate the market share of the firms. It also indicates how the government will consider the possibility that competition might be lessened by coordination and the possibility that entry in the future will limit the possibility that a business will operate monopolistically.

In each of these areas, the guidelines provide indications of the approach that the government will take in assessing the issue, not mathematical formulas that potential merger partners can apply to predict the government's approach with certainty. The guidelines thus fall somewhere in the middle of the rules-standards continuum. To the extent that the guidelines indeed constrain the government, they risk leading it to make decisions that it would not make if all factors were considered. To the extent that the guidelines allow open-ended decision making, they risk uncertainty and caprice. An ideal system of merger regulation would provide both more predictability and greater assurance that all relevant factors will be considered.

The predictive decision making approach might use conditional prediction markets to forecast the effect of a merger on consumer surplus in the relevant market. I admit that this specification itself leaves considerable ambiguity by, for example, requiring some assessment of what the relevant product and geographical markets in fact are. But it at least saves the government from the challenge of modeling the effect of the merger on consumer prices. All the government would need to do is to identify a basket of products and promise to conduct consumer surveys or use other economic methodologies to calculate consumer surplus for the basket, whether the merger takes place or not. For example, in a planned merger of office supply stores, the basket might include pens, paper, and so on. The government also would need to provide an appropriate subsidy for the market. Prediction market participants would then have incentives to develop their own models of the merged company's pricing.

The approach might function effectively even without an ex ante identification of the relevant basket of goods. The government could simply provide that in measuring consumer surplus ex post, the agency will attempt to consider a representative basket of goods. Whether the merger takes place or not, years later governmental decision makers would conduct the analysis, focusing perhaps on a few representative products. There is always the danger that the government ex post will pick an unrepresentative basket of goods. The ex post measurement would matter only in disciplining the prediction market payouts, however, not in actually determining whether the merger takes place. So there would be little incentive for ideologically motivated governmental officials to manipulate the decision to advance a particular agenda.

To the extent that manipulation or simply poor measurement might take place, it will be difficult ex ante to predict whether errors are more likely to be made in one direction or in another, especially if the effects of the merger are not to be evaluated for a long period of time. It thus might be the case that any ex post errors or manipulations will generally cancel each other out. This reveals a general point about predictive decision making: even if what is being predicted is only a noisy proxy, the ex ante prediction of it might be relatively stable and predictable. Of course, it is hard to be sure in the absence of experimentation, but it would not necessarily require adoption of this approach to merger analysis. Initial experiments could be purely informational.

If this approach were adopted, prospective merger partners such as utility operators would have incentives to tie their hands in ways that would make the merger appear more attractive to market participants. They might commit to selling off particular divisions, the current practice. An advantage of the market approach, however, is that merger partners might have an incentive to develop other ways of committing not to charge monopoly prices. For example, they might develop a formula, perhaps a very sophisticated one, determining the maximum amount they would charge in the future for particular products. They could specify whether any consumer or only particular groups would be authorized to sue if the merged company arguably ignored the formula. Merging companies might agree to give representatives of consumer groups some role in managing the firm or in making pricing decisions. Prediction market participants once again would have incentives to assess the effectiveness of these various commitments.

INTERIM DECISION-MAKING MARKETS

Predictive decision making can be used to predict not only events that are contingent on a particular decision, but also what a decision might be. We have already seen that prediction markets can forecast decisions (see Chapter 4). The merger analysis example can be viewed as predicting a decision, namely, the ex post measurement of consumer surplus. Often, it might be useful to make a decision based on a prediction of a future decision. For example, sometimes the legal system must establish an interim policy pending a final decision concerning a particular legal issue. In these cases, it often, though not always, will make sense to have the interim policy be the expected final policy. In this case, a prediction market can be used to forecast the final policy decision, and that prediction can serve as the decision during the interim period.

Consider, for example, approval of pharmaceutical drugs by the Food and Drug Administration. Under the current regime, pharmaceuticals cannot be sold until the FDA approves them,[41] and critics complain that the long approval process sometimes leads to unnecessary deaths and hardship.[42] A prediction market could be used to gauge whether each drug ultimately will be approved, and provisional sales of the drug could be allowed pending the FDA decision. For example, the rules might provide that a drug that has at least a 90 percent chance of eventual approval can be sold immediately but would need to be pulled off the market if the probability later fell below 50 percent or if an adverse decision were ultimately reached. There are dangers associated with such a regime: patients and others might stockpile a drug, leaving the FDA powerless to keep the drug away from patients later. But where there is a high probability of eventual FDA approval, and for drugs that are unlikely to be stockpiled, this regime nonetheless might improve on the existing one. One benefit is that the FDA would not need to rush formal approval. An alternative, of course, is simply to allow the FDA to decide case by case whether to allow particular drugs to be sold on an interim basis, but it is difficult to make such decisions without full consideration of the merits of the research studies.

Interim prediction markets also might be used to help courts decide whether preliminary injunctive relief is appropriate in a case in which a permanent injunction is sought. In the current system, a judge who eventually will determine whether a permanent injunction should be granted makes a preliminary assessment. This assessment is based on factors including the danger of irreparable harm from an absence of preliminary relief and the probability that the party seeking the injunction eventually will prevail on the merits.[43] Judges understandably do not want their preliminary injunction decisions to appear lawless, and they thus often consider the factual and legal issues at stake in great detail, despite the preliminary nature of a decision.[44]

To the extent that a preliminary decision requires almost as much effort as a final decision, it might not achieve substantial cost savings. At the same time, there is a danger that judges will be hesitant to change their minds, except perhaps by relying on issues that they did not consider at the preliminary injunction stage, for fear of appearing inconsistent. Using prediction markets to forecast whether a permanent injunction will be issued, on condition that the court ultimately resolves the case, could greatly simplify a court's task. A court would still have to consider issues such as irreparable harm, but in many cases that is far more straightforward. An additional benefit is that prediction markets can take into account not only what will happen at the trial court but also whether that decision will withstand appeal. This would limit the need for appeals of both the preliminary injunction and the eventual decision on the permanent injunction.

Prediction markets also might be used in the criminal context to determine whether a particular defendant should be allowed to remain free pending a verdict. For example, an estimate of the probability that the defendant will be convicted and sentenced to prison might be deemed relevant to a determination of whether the defendant should be allowed to remain free pending trial. Naturally, there are other relevant criteria, such as the risk of flight, and the existing bail system already functions as a kind of predictive decision making regime, with bail bondsmen serving both as predictors and as pursuers when a defendant fails to appear.[45] Moreover, a prediction market might be useful in determining whether a defendant can stay free pending an appeal. In our current system, a defendant's recourse is to the trial court judge, and relying on a prediction market would avoid having a trial court judge assess the probability that his own decision will be reversed on appeal.

Prediction markets might help forecast not only executive or judicial decisions but also legislative decisions. Consider, for example, the problem of states that frequently miss the deadline to complete their annual budgets, leading to predictable disruptions in public services.[46] The legislature could provide that in the absence of agreement, all programs should continue to receive funding at existing levels, but this would provide a bias to the status quo. An alternative approach would be to use prediction markets to assess whether programs will receive funding and to fund them tentatively at the predicted rates. Market participants would have incentives to assess the preferences of existing legislators and monitor decision making concerning specific issues before final decisions are reached. Naturally, this proposal and the others would need considerable refining before they could be implemented. The point, however, is that prediction markets might provide an approach to interim decision making that does not require the ultimate decision making body actually to make decisions, thus overcoming a major problem with interim regimes.

Chapter 6 Administrative Agencies

Predictive decision making offers the promise of saving the government from the need to issue detailed statutes or regulations in areas such as safety and utility regulation. The government's role is limited to establishing goals, running the prediction markets, and enforcing compliance. Though substantial, they are far simpler than tasks such as specifying particular technological requirements and then determining (and litigating) whether those requirements have been met. Prediction markets, however, also might be useful when an administrative agency continues to supervise an administrative regime. The markets might help assess potential decisions about particular issues such as regulations that the agency is considering adopting.

The tools that we have already explored make it straightforward to generate countless proposals for the use of prediction markets to provide information relevant to particular decisions or to assess effects of decisions. Indeed, the Policy Analysis Market (see Chapter 5), as initially envisioned by DARPA, would have harnessed information that was potentially relevant to military and diplomatic decision making. Using the tool of conditional markets would make it straightforward to predict the effects of particular hypothetical decisions on specific variables. For example, the Bureau of Prisons might use conditional markets to predict the effect of opening a proposed prison on variables such as crime rates, unemployment, and housing values. Or the Environmental Protection Agency might predict the effect of a nuclear storage facility on the levels of environmental contaminants in nearby waterways. Or the Securities and Exchange Commission could assess the effect of possible regulations on the market capitalization of regulated firms.

This chapter, however, argues that the application of prediction markets to administrative agency decision making offers the possibility of a distinct benefit. We have seen that prediction markets can be used to aggregate evidence and assessments (see Chapter 2), but they also can be used to aggregate preferences or at least to aggregate expected preferences. Prediction markets can forecast subjective assessments instead of objective facts. If a subjective assessment will be made in the future, then that occurrence is itself an objective fact about a subjective preference. Indeed, some of the prediction markets we have already seen predict assessments of this kind, including the Iowa Electronic Markets' election forecasting markets (see Chapter 1). These prediction markets gauge potential voter sentiment in instances when the voters eventually will make normative assessments in the form of votes. Similarly, prediction markets might gauge the sentiment of potential administrative agency officials without incurring the cost of actually requiring all of these officials to decide an issue in depth.

A major justification for placing reliance on prediction markets to make normative assessments, which we will call normative prediction markets, is that these markets can help constrain ideologically motivated decision making. (Agency officials generally do not want their decision making constrained, however, and this presents a barrier to adoption of these proposals.) I begin by discussing why ideology presents a problem for administrative agency decision making and how normative prediction markets can help. I then focus on two administrative agency tasks that ideology can contaminate: the making of policy decisions and the rendering of statutory interpretation. By predicting what some future decision makers of indeterminate ideology might think, such markets can avoid producing assessments that are affected by the politics of the current administration and thus can help identify decisions that may be ideologically motivated. Predictive cost-benefit analysis, the use of prediction markets to predict retrospective assessments of particular policies, builds on another tool, cost-benefit analysis, which already seeks to limit ideological impact.

Normative prediction markets are promising because they potentially can provide objective guides to policy, but they also may test the limits of whether prediction market forecasts are truly objective. I assess the possibility that the demographics of market participants might have some effects on the results. If this concern can be overcome, prediction markets might be useful not only in evaluating prospective policies but also in making other normative assessments that are critical to agency decision making. For example, they might predict retrospective evaluations of potential administrative officials. In addition, they might predict how different federal judges would be expected to vote on particular regulations, thus helping to expose instances of ideological judging and perhaps providing some incentive to lessen ideological decision making. Prediction markets also might be useful in specific contexts in which administrative agencies might otherwise be excessively politicized, such as in assessing governmental spending decisions or in which "capture" by private interests is a significant danger.

THE PROBLEM OF IDEOLOGY

The presence of ideology in government is so commonplace that we often assume that it is unproblematic, perhaps even a virtue of democratic government. If the people pick a Republican president, then we have administrative agencies with a Republican agenda, and if they vote Democratic, then we have a Democratic agenda. That's democracy. Indeed, but ideological variance across administrations should be seen as an unfortunate by-product of inefficiencies in democratic governance, rather than as a goal of the process. It may be, for example, that a two-party system makes sense in a world in which voters have very little information. The competing presidential candidates may have incentives to push toward the center to appeal to moderate voters in the general election,[1] thus moderating the effects of ideology. The tendency of more committed ideologues to vote in higher numbers in primaries, however, tends to push selected candidates away from the center. Perhaps it is simply impossible to create a system that consistently produces more middle-of-the-road presidents, but if it were, such a system might be better than the existing system.

The case for moderation in decision making is simple. There are many decisions, of course, about which presidents from a wide range of ideologies would agree, but the critical questions are those about which there would be some disagreement. All else being equal, government ideally should produce decisions that more people prefer rather than fewer or at least that more people would prefer if everyone received full information about the relevant question. The appeal of simple majority voting is intuitive, and social choice theorists such as Kenneth May have also demonstrated formally that it has several properties that one might think desirable in a decisional rule.[2] Of course, for any particular binary choice, one might disagree with majority sentiment, and the majority might be wrong. But at least a majority decision making rule seems better than the reverse, in which the minority always wins. Even someone who usually is in the political minority should not like that rule, which might lead to unpleasant resolutions of issues such as whether we should start a nuclear war. At best, someone can reasonably prefer minority rule only in cases in which the minority is substantial.

There are, nonetheless, a few counterarguments to my praise of moderation in decision making. Heather Gerken, for example, celebrates "second-order diversity," in which decision-making bodies sometimes are not representative of the population from which they are drawn.[3] A system that allows dissenters sometimes to decide issues has several benefits because it "contributes to the marketplace of ideas, engages electoral minorities in the project of self-governance, and facilitates self-expression."[4] Allowing dissenters to seek to shift majority sentiment, however, can also engage minority voices, if not as effectively. Those who are dissenters regarding many issues, moreover, still may be in the majority on some; second-order diversity occurs naturally because those in the middle will sometimes agree with one side and sometimes with the other. Gerken and I may disagree not only about the benefits of second-order diversity but also on the magnitude of the costs. When a criminal defendant is convicted only because he happened to receive an unrepresentative pro-prosecution jury, it is no comfort to me that some other defendant will be acquitted only because she happened to receive an unrepresentative pro-defense jury.[5]

Of course, we are unlikely to be able to produce perfectly moderate presidents, let alone perfect moderation in each administration, even if we grant the fantasy of being able to make arbitrary changes to existing electoral processes. Nonetheless, prediction markets might help push decision making in a more moderate direction. A simple use of prediction markets in reducing the role of ideology is to make objective predictions of variables that are used in further decision-making processes. Suppose, for example, that a decision whether to announce a new standard for the amount of fluoride in water depends in part on predictions of the degree to which a change in the standard might affect the incidence of certain kinds of cancer. If this is a controversial issue, then politically motivated officials might produce different estimates, recognizing that the estimates might have some bearing on the ultimate decision. A conditional prediction market, if sufficiently accurate, might produce a more moderate decision.

A conditional market should at least have the benefit of forcing decision makers to explain their views on normative grounds, rather than on the basis of spurious factual claims. It is tempting for someone advancing a particular recommendation to marshal all possible arguments in its defense though that person does not believe that some of the arguments are persuasive. No doubt there are many governmental officials with integrity and an ability to overcome their normative preferences who provide dispassionate analyses of difficult scientific or other factual questions. But at least there is a cognitive process that leads individuals to interpret evidence in a way that generally favors their ultimate conclusions[6] and the possibility of occasional exaggeration. By providing objective assessments regarding some issues, prediction markets might help focus attention on what the divisive issues really are, such as whether a given predicted reduction in cancer rates from a change in the fluoride standard is worth the cost.

Of course, using prediction markets in this way does not preclude second-order diversity. Once we know what the differences in views are regarding the ultimate question, we might still have a decision-making rule that chooses the minority view rather than the majority view or perhaps a rule with a randomization element, for example, making the probability that a view is chosen equal to the proportion of decision makers who would subscribe to that view. Few would endorse such a system if the arbitrariness of second-order diversity were made so explicit. We may, however, tend to reify second-order diversity that occurs over time although we know that for four years, the results of much governmental decision making will depend largely on a handful of voters in Illinois, Florida, or Ohio. To the extent that we can have presidential government but make actual administrative decisions somewhat more consistent and less ideological over time, in the long run we should expect to be better off.

NORMATIVE PREDICTION MARKET

A normative prediction market can provide assessments not tainted by the ideology of current officials concerning questions that are purely normative. Such a market predicts a subjective assessment of an issue to be made at some point in the future. That point could be relatively near if there is some method for identifying a relatively representative group of potential decision makers. For example, if what is most relevant is the view of the hypothetical average informed voter, then one might select at random a single voter, provide the voter with information about the relevant issues, and then ask for that voter's opinion. That voter would not decide the relevant issue—that would be a system that embraces second-order diversity to an extreme—but the voter's conclusion would determine payouts to the participants in the normative prediction market. Such a market would provide an assessment of the way an average member of the population would be expected to treat a particular issue.

This is a relatively populist approach, but for those who believe that administrative agency officials have expertise that voters could not harness, even with a full presentation, an alternative is to select a decision maker from a pool of experts. The challenge is in identifying a suitable pool, given that there may be legitimate disagreement, itself politically charged, about who should count as an expert. Those who are skeptical about environmental issues, for example, will generally not be willing to count any self-proclaimed environmentalist as a neutral expert, and those skeptical about corporate America probably would not accept selecting a random CEO to determine policies governing securities law.

There is, however, a relatively simple solution that anchors the random selection to the political process while avoiding the randomness and variance associated with individual electoral outcomes. That solution is to require that the decision be made by a particular administrative official such as the head of the agency some number of years in the future. The key is for that future point to be far enough away that it will be difficult to forecast who the decision maker might be. Of course, sometimes it is possible to infer that in ten years some anticipated demographic change will shift the country in one direction or another, but in general, the average expected official will be a close approximation of the average current expert opinion about a particular issue. After a decade the political crisis of the moment would be unlikely to provide much guidance about whether a Democrat or a Republican is in the White House, and so a prediction market will weight the possibility of each outcome at roughly 50 percent.

Delay thus serves as a cloaking device, disguising the identities of the eventual decision makers from prediction market participants so that they make their predictions based on some idealized pool. That does not mean, however, that the decision to adopt a normative prediction market itself is politically neutral. Often it will be apparent that adoption of such a market in some context will lead to a predictable deviation from the status quo. Whether one embraces a normative prediction market in a particular context will depend on whether one approves of this expected deviation. This will, of course, make such markets more difficult to enact, because if there is strong support for a particular shift in policy, a majority would not need a prediction market to achieve it, and if there is not, then the majority will not want the prediction market.

Those who oppose adoption of normative prediction markets, moreover, are not necessarily wrong. Individual policies that such markets might produce matter, and it may be legitimate to oppose a procedural device on substantive grounds. Moreover, there might be legitimate grounds for debate about who should constitute the pool of ex post decision makers and for opposing any particular proposal for a normative prediction market on that basis. Ultimately, a normative prediction market is a device for making policy conform more closely to what a specified pool of individuals could be expected to decide if they took the time to study an issue thoroughly. Even as a matter of political theory across a wide range of issues, it may be debatable whether the expected views of any particular defined pool of decision makers should be more legitimate than the actual decisions that emerge from any more traditionally structured democratic process.

An objection to normative prediction markets is that they do not really weigh preferences but instead anticipate preferences. Sure, but so what? Sometimes anticipated preferences might turn out not to forecast actual preferences correctly, for example, because market participants have insufficient information. But this problem can be reduced by greater market subsidy. More important, however, republican government itself is a rather imprecise tool for aggregating preferences. As in all prediction market proposals, the question is how the market-based institution would fare in comparison to the existing institution. It seems plausible that "anticipated preferences" might come closer to meaningfully combining the public's actual preferences or the public's hypothetical informed preferences than does the existing legal system. Agencies' decisions in many cases are quite far from any plausible aggregation of the public's views as a result of ideology.

Perhaps there are many decisions for which the processes of republican government help determine a reasonable aggregation of the public's preferences. With sufficient subsidy, however, prediction market participants might select random decision makers, provide them with information, and measure their reactions. Of course, government could continue to use existing processes for gathering data and arguments, although prediction markets might be designed to accomplish much the same thing. We have seen, for example, that a deliberative prediction market might be used as an alternative to the traditional process of notice-and-comment rule making (see Chapter 4), but predicting the evaluation of a random decision maker rather than of current agency decision makers might further improve the process.

A benefit of the traditional notice-and-comment process is that it forces agency decision makers actually to consider and respond to comments. A designer of a normative prediction market might develop a more formal process by which the randomly selected ex post decision maker would consider the relevant arguments. For example, rules might provide some form of adversarial presentation, both to ensure that all views are presented and that the decision maker actually takes the time to hear them. Advocates might be selected (preferably ex post, so that the anticipated quality of the advocacy does not affect the prediction market) who have some financial incentive to convince the randomly selected decision maker. This would provide market participants with incentives to identify all relevant arguments, not simply those that would be appealing to the current leadership of the administrative agency. It also might be desirable to require or expect that the ex post decision makers would give detailed analysis. They otherwise might shirk, and to the extent that shirking leads to predictable errors, that would harm policy. Granting power to decision makers may be one way of reducing shirking, but it should be possible to develop effective procedural substitutes.

HARD-LOOK REVIEW AND THE PASSIVE RESTRAINTS SAGA

The goal of preventing administrative agencies from making ideological decisions is not a new one. Under the Administrative Procedure Act, a federal court in a proper challenge can strike down a regulation if it is "arbitrary, capricious, an abuse of discretion, or otherwise not in accordance with law."[7] Interpreting that provision, the U.S. Court of Appeals for the District of Columbia Circuit, which hears appeals of many administrative law challenges, has found that the role of the courts is to ensure that the agencies have "genuinely engaged in reasoned decisionmaking."[8] A court is required to intervene if it "becomes aware, especially from a combination of danger signals, that the agency has not really taken a 'hard look' at the salient problems."⁹ This doctrine has come to be known as the "hard-look" doctrine, and although it is technically the agency that must look hard, in practice the courts also carefully consider the administrative record to ensure that the agency has done that.

Although the doctrine is not specifically designed to prevent ideological decision making, as opposed to decision making that is arbitrary because of shortness of time or other factors, it often serves that purpose. The Supreme Court's most famous application of hard-look review occurred in a case involving a politically controversial application of the National Traffic and Motor Vehicle Safety Act of 1966.[10] In 1972 the National Highway Traffic Safety Administration (NHTSA) decided to require, in addition to seat belts, some form of passive protection (air bags or automatic seat belts) for front-seat passengers. Before that decision went into effect, the Secretary of Transportation decided to suspend the requirement in 1976, but his successor disagreed, requiring that either air bags or passive seat belts be installed beginning in 1982. In 1981, however, a new Secretary of Transportation reopened the rulemaking and canceled the previous standard. It was obvious to all that different philosophies of government played a role in the decision, with the Reagan administration more skeptical of such intervention than the Carter administration.

In a review of a lawsuit challenging the Reagan administration's decision,[11] the Supreme Court showed a willingness to scrutinize the particular arguments offered in favor of the change. The NHTSA had observed that manufacturers were complying by introducing passive seat belts rather than air bags, but the passive seat belts could easily be detached and thus were ineffective. The agency, however, never explained why it did not respond to this problem by mandating air bags instead. The effect of the Court's ruling, intended as a guide to how lower courts should make similar assessments, was to vacate the agency's decision. The agency would still have an opportunity to make the same decision, but it would have to provide a better explanation, for example, by showing that an air bag–only rule would be too expensive. Of course, it is not always easy for an agency to convince a court the second time around to approve a decision if the court believes that the arguments in favor of that decision are inherently weak. The hard-look doctrine thus provides some means for the courts to police ideological decision making.

There are, however, at least two problems with this approach. First, in some cases the courts' own ideology will simply replace the administrative agency officials' in determining whether regulations are acceptable. Perhaps having an additional check against aggressive regulatory decisions is useful, but there is no inherent reason to prefer the status quo, and whether the court will serve this role in any event will depend on which judges happen to be selected to hear a particular case. An unfortunate consequence is that judicial review may be unpredictable, and administrative agencies sometimes waste a great deal of time on rulemakings that fail even though they might well have succeeded.

Second, taking the courts' explanations of the doctrine at face value, it leaves a great deal of discretion for administrative agencies. At least in theory, in any case in which reasonable arguments can be developed in support of a position, the courts are supposed to defer to the administrative agencies. The system thus tolerates a relatively high degree of flexibility in decision making. Perhaps this is essential because of the variance in ideological leanings of the judiciary, but it is not inherently desirable.

Normative prediction markets in issues being considered by administrative agencies could become useful data points when the courts consider lawsuits claiming that regulations represent bad policy and should be struck down. If such a market were to forecast that a broadly representative pool of decision makers would generally approve of a particular set of regulations, judges who do not like the policy result might nonetheless approve it. Indeed, agencies sometimes might have incentives to sponsor normative prediction markets if they believe that the markets will tend to support their projects.

In other cases, a normative prediction market might show that most decision makers would be expected to reject particular regulations, and this might help persuade judges to strike down the regulations. Of course, an agency might not have an incentive to sponsor such markets, but private parties might do so as a means of justifying the claim that particular regulations are ideologically motivated. If such markets became commonplace, the courts might be suspicious in cases in which agencies do not create them. Naturally, prediction markets cannot be expected to be considered by judges until they become better accepted as relatively accurate and objective predictors.

Normative prediction markets could help respond to both concerns about the hard look doctrine detailed above. First, such markets might not merely be genuinely useful for judges seeking unbiased assessments of the reasonableness of decisions but also might be effective in unmasking ideological decision making by judges. For example, if two very conservative judges happen to be chosen to review a relatively liberal agency decision, they might hesitate to write an opinion striking down the regulations as poorly reasoned if the prediction market indicated that virtually all agency decision makers would have come to the same conclusion.

Second, normative prediction markets might facilitate more skeptical judicial review of decisions that most agency officials would be expected to reject. Aside from promoting processes that might improve agency decisions, the hard-look doctrine is useful primarily because it can be expected to stop the most egregious agency decisions. It might, however, be useful to block less egregious decisions that most decision makers would nonetheless reject. Normative prediction markets provide a relatively objective assessment of how a wide range of decision makers would view the agency's decision. They could thus facilitate a shift in the hard-look doctrine away from an analysis of the reasoning underlying a decision and toward an analysis of the decision itself. In the absence of such markets, a shift such as this would compromise the relative objectivity of the doctrine.

Normative prediction markets could allow people to focus on what ultimately matters: the decision an agency makes rather than the reasoning of an agency in getting there. Of course, an agency still might explain its reasoning process regarding some questions, because market participants would assess the degree to which these arguments are likely to convince a future decision maker. But the purpose of such explanations would be to persuade, not merely to fill out paperwork that will satisfy a court. Thomas McGarity has complained that the notice-and-comment rulemaking process has produced an "ossification" of the administrative state, preventing agencies from getting much done.[12] To the extent that procedural requirements stop agencies from advancing narrow ideological agendas, they should be embraced. By focusing directly on whether decisions are ideological, normative prediction markets may free agencies from procedural obligations that do not promote substantive goals.

No legislative reform would be needed (as it would be for the vast majority of the proposals advanced in this book) before courts could consider normative prediction markets in conducting hard-look reviews. The review process is already relatively open-ended, and in the air bags case the Supreme Court scrutinized technical studies. All that would be necessary is for a policy analysis organization or other private party to create a normative prediction market, with appropriate specification of how the ultimate decision maker would be chosen. The prediction market might focus on a question related to a particular aspect of the agency's reasoning or on the overall justifiability of the agency's decision. A litigant might then present evidence about the normative prediction market. Only a bold judge would be willing to consider such unconventional data today, but if enough normative prediction markets for assessing agency decisions were created, judges might come to appreciate their virtues.

PREDICTIVE COST-BENEFIT ANALYSIS

A simple approach to deciding on the payouts for a normative prediction market would be to commit to asking the later decision maker whether he or she agrees with or disagrees with the particular decision. Assuming that the ultimate evaluation of the decision occurs a long time after the market has run its course, however, this prediction could be misleading. Suppose that there is a large probability that a particular regulation will on net provide a small social benefit but a small probability that the regulation will cause a very large social harm. If it will become clear before the ultimate evaluation which of these is true, then the prediction market would probably forecast that the decision maker will approve of the regulation. Conceivably, decision makers might be instructed to evaluate the regulation from the ex ante perspective, but the danger of hindsight bias makes this difficult. This normative prediction market design thus forecasts whether a decision will turn out to be justified but not the magnitude of benefit or harm caused by the decision.

A solution to this problem is to require the ex post decision maker to announce not simply whether the decision was desirable, but how beneficial or costly it turned out to be. Although one might devise numerous scales for this assessment, perhaps the most natural is a scale of dollars (or other currency). The ex post decision maker would announce either a positive number, indicating that the decision had net benefits equal to a specified number of dollars, or a negative number, indicating that the decision had net costs. To the extent that the ex post decision might occur at a point before all of the benefits and costs of the decision have been felt, the decision maker would have to consider not only those realized already but also those projected for the future. Ideally, the decision maker should be instructed to aggregate benefits and costs by considering when they occur, using interest rates to discount them to the time at which the decision was made.

This approach builds on a familiar institution of the regulatory state, cost-benefit analysis, and could be called "predictive cost-benefit analysis."[13] Traditional cost-benefit analysis can be subjective, inevitably depending on the assumptions in models of the future.[14] A Democratic administration might find that a particular regulation would have net benefits, while a Republican administration might find that it would have net costs. Partisans of a position might do the cost-benefit analysis in ways that generally support their instinctive views. Though agency officials may conduct cost-benefit analysis in good faith, liberals and conservatives may value some effects of regulations differently. Because predictive cost-benefit analysis would involve a prediction of a cost-benefit analysis to be conducted by someone of indeterminate party membership, it should largely succeed at removing the ideological component or at least averaging a broad spectrum of views.

Predictive cost-benefit analysis is not the only way of seeking to ensure that cost-benefit analysis is relatively objective. An alternative approach is to craft detailed methodological rules for conducting the analysis, in order to ensure that the identity of the practitioner does not have an effect on the result. Indeed, the U.S. government has issued guidelines,[15] although they still leave a great degree of administrative discretion. Even if guidelines could remove all discretion, the predictive approach may be superior. The problem is that guidelines necessarily encode specific value choices, and those choices reflect the ideology of those making them. Lisa Heinzerling has argued, for example, that cost-benefit analysis places excessive weight on the willingness of individuals to pay for environmental goods.[16] Whether she is right or wrong, simply giving a particular administration the right to resolve methodological questions cannot succeed in eliminating the taint of ideology.

With predictive cost-benefit analysis, no guidelines are necessary, but ex post decision makers should be encouraged to provide detailed explanations of their methodologies. Prediction market participants will then need to forecast the proportion of future decision makers who would make particular methodological decisions, and the predictive cost-benefit analysis should reflect a balanced weighting of different methodologies. In traditional cost-benefit analysis, it is often tempting to omit certain considerations altogether, despite their obvious relevance, because there is too much room for debate about how to take the considerations into account. Predictive cost-benefit analysis makes it possible to include all recognized considerations, weighting them as average decision makers would be expected to weight them, without giving the actual decision makers the ability to manipulate the analysis.

Robert Frank and Cass Sunstein have argued, for example, that cost-benefit analysis should take into account that people value some goods in part only because those goods allow them to improve their status relative to other individuals.[17] Because they do not value health care this way, an assessment of the value of life based on willingness to pay for health care will be inaccurate. An employee who is unwilling to pay some amount of money for a health benefit might nonetheless benefit from a law requiring everyone to pay that amount for the benefit. Thomas Kniesner and W. Kip Viscusi, however, have argued that Frank and Sunstein overestimate the effect that they discuss.[18] Given the difficulties of identifying an appropriate methodology for assessing such effects, they are best omitted altogether, according to Kniesner and Viscusi. This might be the best solution in a world in which methodological flexibility introduces the danger of ideological analysis and decision making, but predictive cost-benefit analysis makes this no longer necessary.

Similarly, predictive cost-benefit analysis would permit ex post decision makers to take into account "soft variables" that are difficult to determine through any formal methodology. A recurrent debate about cost-benefit analysis concerns the legitimacy of contingent valuation studies, in which surveys are used to determine individuals' existence values, such as the most that individuals would pay to prevent logging of a forest.[19] Such studies are notoriously vulnerable to framing, with the size of a forest bearing little logical relation to individuals' claimed valuations.[20] The possibility that contingent valuation is a useful methodology means that results of studies would receive some weight in predictive cost-benefit analysis. But prediction market participants would recognize that lack of validity does not mean that existence value should be assumed to be zero. Different decision makers would assign different values based on their own calculations or hunches, and market participants would seek to predict the average of these numbers.

As long as prediction markets are sufficiently well subsidized and thus accurate, predictive cost-benefit analysis should be preferable to cost-benefit analysis even for someone who believes that agencies should be allowed some degree of ideological freedom. The purpose of analysis is to produce a signal about the objective costs and benefits of a particular regulation. Ideology merely adds noise to the signal. Eric Posner, for example, has argued that the purpose of cost-benefit analysis is to offset the informational advantage that agencies have relative to the president and Congress,[21] allowing other branches to determine whether they approve of what the agency is doing. That function, among others, cannot be performed as well if observers must guess the degree to which the agency's decision is the result of idiosyncratic preferences. It would be better to allow administrative officials some flexibility to enact regulations with predicted net costs than to permit them to obfuscate the decision by manipulating a cost-benefit analysis.

AGENCY LEGAL INTERPRETATION
AND THE *CHEVRON* DOCTRINE

The hard-look doctrine represents only one form of judicial review that courts perform in assessing the decisions of administrative agencies. In addition to considering whether the agency's decisions are supportable as a policy matter, a court reviews the agency's factual determinations,[22] as well as whether the agency's decision is legally permissible. This second inquiry is necessary because agencies are constrained by statutes passed by Congress, although statutes often contain a great degree of ambiguity. According to the *Chevron* doctrine,[23] the courts defer to any reasonable construction of an ambiguous statute by the agency that administers it. Courts, however, do not accept an agency's claim that a statute is ambiguous at face value. They use a wide range of legal tools to try to determine whether the statute is ambiguous.

Consider, for example, the Supreme Court case *Babbitt v. Sweet Home Chapter of Communities for a Great Oregon.*[24] The Endangered Species Act made it unlawful for a person to "take" endangered species, and a definitional section of the statute defined *take* as including "harass," "harm," "pursue," "wound," and "kill."[25] The Department of the Interior passed a regulation defining *harm* as including "significant habitat modification or degradation where it actually kills or injures wildlife." The Justices considered a variety of arguments about whether Interior's definition was consistent with the statute, based on the text and structure of the statute, dictionary definitions, canons of construction, the statute's purpose, the legislative history, and subsequent congressional activity. Nonetheless, they split 5–4, with the majority finding the statute sufficiently ambiguous to make the Department of the Interior's definition reasonable.

It is perhaps not surprising that the split was along ideological lines, with the Justices regarded as generally more conservative in the dissent. The task of determining whether a statute is ambiguous is not inherently more objective than the task of determining what the correct meaning of a statute is. Presumably, the resolution of any particular interpretive issue falls on a continuum, with unambiguous resolution one way occupying one end, ambiguity in the middle, and unambiguous resolution the other way occupying the other end. *Chevron* requires the courts to determine whether an issue falls in the amorphous middle of this continuum. De novo review, the approach that the courts used with issues identified as purely legal before *Chevron*,[26] required the courts simply to determine on which side of the continuum a particular issue fell. It is not obvious that the *Chevron* approach reduces the number of cases in which interpreters will disagree. Even if it does, there will remain some cases in which interpreters will generally agree that X is the better interpretation but defer to the agency's choice of Y based on a conclusion that there is sufficient ambiguity in the statute.

Because statutory interpretation is in part subjective, a normative prediction market may be a useful way of gauging how decision makers, on average, would approach a particular question of statutory interpretation. In such a market, the ex post decision maker might be asked to determine whether the statute is somewhat ambiguous. A superior approach, however, might be simply to ask the decision maker which interpretation is the better one.[27] Though it is the job of courts to determine whether a statute is ambiguous, this approach should provide a sound guide, identifying cases in which there is significant disagreement. In existing *Chevron* cases, judges are effectively predicting whether different interpreters of the statute would agree sufficiently often to justify a conclusion that the statute is clear. A normative prediction market can make this type of prediction in a more rigorous way.

Of course, prediction markets might help not only when judges are assessing agency statutory interpretations but also when agencies are initially engaging in interpretation. Ideally, agencies routinely would create normative prediction markets when faced with legal ambiguity. The primary incentive of agencies to do this would be to persuade the courts that they are not engaging in excessively creative statutory interpretation. There is at least one body that generally could benefit from statutory interpretation markets: the legislature. Individual legislators sometimes might prefer creative to plausible interpretations of particular statutory issues, but in general the legislature will prefer that agencies and courts not usurp its power in cases in which it did not intend to delegate that power. If normative prediction markets develop a reputation for accuracy, the legislature someday might require them.

The closer the ex post decision makers are to the original drafters in outlook, the better normative prediction markets will reflect the interpretations that the original drafters would offer. If, for example, the normative prediction market will forecast the future assessment of the administrator of the Environmental Protection Agency, and it is predictable that the administrator will on average be more liberal than the legislature, then the market predictions will not generally reflect what the legislature intended. One possibility is to structure the market so that it predicts an assessment by a randomly selected member of the legislative body. Despite change over time, a legislature might wish prediction markets to forecast its own decisions rather than those of administrative officials or judges.

Such a proposal might seem to duplicate one that we have already seen: the variation I suggested to Einer Elhauge's proposal that courts seek to resolve statutory ambiguities according to current legislative preferences (see Chapter 5). There are, however, two key differences. First, instead of predicting what the entire legislature will do, conditional on the legislature's making a decision, this proposal is to predict what a single randomly selected member of the legislature will do. At least in a unicameral, majoritarian legislature, this should amount to the same thing, given the assumption that the legislature's output will reflect the views of its median member, but it may demand less legislative time. Second, the market would not simply be predicting the current legislature's general political preferences. Rather, it would be predicting how legislators would engage in interpretation of the earlier legislature's views. This approach therefore might be more palatable to someone who believes that statutory ambiguities should be resolved with reference to the enacting and not the current legislature.

The possibility of using prediction markets to discipline statutory interpretation emphasizes that normative prediction markets need not assess open-ended policy reasoning. Statutory interpretation involves normative concerns that differ from those of the hard-look doctrine, and separate prediction markets could be used to perform the two tasks in the same case. Central to statutory interpretation is the premise that adherence to legislative intent ultimately advances rule-of-law values, but there is always a danger in a particular case that it will be more appealing for an administrative agency or a judge to advance a salient policy objective at some very small cost to the rule of law. This is less of a danger with normative prediction markets, because the ultimate decision being predicted has no direct effect on policy; it affects only the payouts of market participants. Making an ideological decision would be an empty gesture, but attempting genuine interpretation would improve overall confidence in the system. Even if ideological decision making still occurs, there will generally be little reason ex ante to think that it will be biased in one direction rather than in another.

THE DANGER OF MARKET UNREPRESENTATIVENESS

The primary virtue of normative prediction markets is that they provide a new approach to ensuring that decisions are representative of the preferences of the population at large. In democratic governments, complex systems of checks and balances determine who has decision-making power. Under the Appointments Clause of the U.S. Constitution, for example, the president nominates and the Senate confirms "principal officers" of the United States such as top agency officials, and the same procedure is used to select federal judges who review, among other cases, administrative agency determinations. At best, however, this process provides only an imperfect assurance that any particular decision will represent what the people would decide, if the people had the relevant information. By predicting the decisions of a randomly selected future agency official or of a random member of the population, normative prediction markets can provide more representative decision making.

This proposal, however, continues to assume that prediction markets are accurate. Any imperfections in prediction markets may be inherently problematic regardless of their source, but one potential source of inaccuracy seems especially troubling. Suppose the demographics and political views of those who participate in prediction markets differ from those of the population at large. If these differences translate into predictions that differ from those of some other group of market participants, then prediction markets are not merely noisy but also biased. This bias would be particularly troubling if it tended to advance the interests of the market participants. In that case, they might appear in effect to have more votes than do other citizens. It would also be troubling if normative markets generally overestimated the extent to which ex post decision makers would agree with the consensus views of traders.

There are two major theoretical reasons to believe that, in general, the views of traders should have virtually no effect on outcomes. The first is that traders have financial incentives to make honest predictions. Perhaps if traders could somehow collude, they might all agree to enter disingenuous predictions and advance their own interests, but as a practical matter such collusion is generally impossible. Each trader is best off predicting as accurately as possible whatever the market is predicting, such as the decision of an ex post decision maker in a normative prediction market. The second is that this favoring of their collective interests would present opportunities for arbitrage. If, for example, traders simply cannot overcome cognitive problems such as a self-serving bias, others may seek specifically to identify situations in which this bias might be operative and make appropriate predictions as a result. Sometimes these arbitrageurs might not compensate enough and at other times they might compensate too much, but on the whole they should at least push markets in the right direction.

Early experimental data also suggest that self-interest will not play a role. As we have seen, in early experiments in the Iowa Electronic Markets, many traders did act in accordance with their political preferences, but a small number of relatively dispassionate traders were able to ensure that the market was relatively accurate (see Chapter 1). One might argue, however, that predicting the outcome of an election may be fundamentally different from predicting the result of a possible government policy. Democrats and Republicans, after all, generally do not have systematic disagreements with one another about the methodologies of election forecasting. They do, however, have fundamental disagreements about the consequences of public policy. So, for example, even after close study, Republicans might be genuinely more optimistic than Democrats about the effect of a school voucher program on test scores. And to the extent that the unfolding of events over time can be expected to affect the decisions of an ex post decision maker in a normative prediction market, Democratic and Republican traders might be mutually optimistic that opinion will move in their direction. Despite the existence of some arbitrageurs, if the vast majority of traders are Republican, predictions might be tilted in a manner consistent with a more conservative worldview.

More experimental work needs to be done on the extent to which the composition of a group of traders affects the predictions of that group. For example, two sets of prediction markets might be created for each of a large number of predictions of the effect of governmental policies. Traders would be assigned to one member of each pair of prediction markets in a way that depends in part on political preferences. The selection process could ensure that for some pairs, all of the conservatives participated on one market and all of the liberals participated on another. Other pairs would feature mixed groups. The question would be the extent to which predictions diverge owing to the identity of the traders. Additional research questions would focus on the extent to which increased subsidies help reduce the divergence, whether informing each trader of the political affiliations of the traders affects market forecasts, and the extent to which the subject matter of the markets affected divergence.

This experiment would not provide a replication of actual market conditions because ordinarily, someone observing a homogeneous trader population can choose to enter the market and correct mispricing. Nonetheless, it might help gauge the extent to which the problem could occur. It is possible that relatively small degrees of heterogeneity are sufficient to overcome any demographic imbalance. In that case, free market entry should help greatly. Yet it is possible that some degree of bias might remain. The question then becomes whether this bias is of sufficient concern to outweigh any advantages of the market approach, and if so, whether there are any approaches that could elim- inate the bias.

One might argue that some small degree of bias should not be fatal to a policy making institution, at least if that institution offers other significant ad- vantages. If the bias is truly small, it will probably make a difference only with respect to relatively close issues. From a public policy perspective, it is gener- ally much more important to ensure that democratic institutions produce the correct answer concerning issues that are not close than for issues that are. Normative prediction markets can limit the danger of highly ideological deci- sion making, so the possibility that it might introduce a small amount of slightly ideological decision making regarding issues that are close anyway is not very disturbing.

If bias attributable to trader demographics is a concern, then one might alter the demographics of traders. For example, participation by Democrats might be subsidized to ensure a more representative pool of participants. This might be accomplished with a variation to the subsidy mechanism described in Chapter 2. Participants would be allowed to place offers that can be accepted only by Democrats, only by Republicans, or by both, and two different subsi- dies would be distributed in proportion to the period of time that these offers were open. Admittedly, there is a danger that market participants could game the Democratic-Republican distinction, for example changing their party affil- iation, so ideally the system would look to past party affiliation, but that can- not be a permanent solution. Another problem is that the liberal-conservative spectrum is not necessarily the only source of disagreement. Inevitably, for ex- ample, traders will be more educated than the population at large, and levels of education may help determine policy views.

Of course, the uneducated already receive less representation given the greater education of government officials than average citizens. This point suggests a more general one about proposals involving prediction markets. There is a natural tendency whenever one considers a new institution to as- sume that any flaws of that institution are inherently fatal and to forget about the flaws of the existing institution. Using a prediction market to make a pre- diction in a very controversial area, such as the effects of global warming, seems likely to be less susceptible to ideological influences than selecting any given governmental official or presidential administration. Normative prediction mar- kets seem likely to make concerns about market unrepresentativeness even smaller. If the ex post decision maker can be chosen in a way that ensures a roughly equal probability of selecting people from different parts of the political continuum, a market for predicting that decision is likely to be far more representative than a decision made by whoever happens to be in office. It is not very hard for a liberal to predict how a conservative will look at a problem or vice-versa, even if slight imperfections arise.

EVALUATION OF ADMINISTRATIVE OFFICIALS

Normative prediction markets help neutralize ideology by making recommendations that are ideologically balanced and independent of incumbent officials. An alternative strategy for reducing the impact of ideology on administrative decisions would focus on inputs rather than outputs, on the personnel who make decisions rather than the decisions those personnel make. A reasonable goal of an appointment process should be to produce officials who are moderates rather than ideologues and who have a high degree of technical competence in the relevant fields. Existing approaches for the selection of administrative and judicial officials, however, might not adequately seek to advance these goals.

Consider, for example, the U.S. Constitution's Appointments Clause. The Senate's confirmation power places a check on the president, although when the president's ideology is aligned with the Senate's, this check seems unlikely to lead to many appointments of officials in the middle of the political spectrum. Many legislators, meanwhile, believe that there should be some degree of deference to the president, absent an appointee who is unqualified or "out of the mainstream."[28] This attitude often reflects a view that it is normatively beneficial for the president to be able to choose officials of the same ideology, even for nominally independent agencies and for independent judges. This view confuses the inevitability of large ideological shifts based on small shifts in the electorate's preferences with the desirability of such shifts. If no one held this view, the system still would not be conducive to appointment of genuine moderates. One reason to grant substantial deference to the president is that positions need to be filled and stalemate can be destructive.

Appointments in the United States thus depend on the degree to which a prospective nominee's views match the president's and the prospective nominee's qualifications. And the old joke about a judge being someone who knows a senator suggests that connections matter, too. Alternative appointment systems seek to focus on merit and thus minimize ideological criteria and connections. One approach, used by countries including Germany to select judges, is to base appointment in large part on an examination that seeks to identify the most legally knowledgeable test-takers.[29] A plausible objection to this approach, however, is that even if an exam is unbiased, it may not be the only relevant variable. Other factors such as experience, demeanor, and judgment might also be relevant, and some of these cannot be assessed entirely mechanically. The intellectual challenge is to develop a system that can take such considerations into account in a truly nonideological way.

Some institutions appear to be relatively successful at nonideological personnel selection. For example, in the United States, the Office of Personnel Management administers the system for the selection of administrative law judges (ALJs).[30] Although the system is called an "examination," the score depends not only on a written test but also on qualifications, a panel interview, and a check of references. The absence of complaints from politicians about this system suggests that it has not become greatly politicized. Nonetheless, there are two reasons to think that the model is not easily transferred to other contexts. First, if ALJs were more important—as important, say, as federal appellate judges or administrative agency heads—it seems likely that the system would be politicized, and the president would seek to install OPM officials with an ideological agenda. Second, although focusing only on the merits tends to reduce ideology, a system that focused directly on ideology might in theory be able to produce more mainstream applicants.

Prediction markets could provide an alternative approach to rating prospective administrative officials or ALJs. A normative prediction market could be used to forecast two evaluations by ex post decision makers, again perhaps a decade away, of the overall quality of a particular candidate, conditional on the candidate's appointment. The ex post decision makers in one market would consist only of Republican members of the legislature (or their designees or some other pool of relatively conservative individuals). The parallel market would consist of Democrats. The greater the degree of divergence in expected evaluations between Democrats and Republicans, the more ideological the candidate.

Meanwhile, the two predictions could be combined to provide an assessment of overall quality independent of ideology. They might simply be averaged, or they might be combined with weights based on a prediction market forecast of the future Democratic-Republican balance in Congress or perhaps in the population at large. A somewhat more elaborate system would use simple statistical methodologies to untangle ideology from assessments of merit. For example, a regression model could be used to predict a particular nominee's average rating by the Democrats and Republicans as a function of the candidate's predicted ideology. The error term for each observation of the regression would identify the corresponding candidate's score controlling for ideology, so more qualified candidates should receive higher scores.

It is true that similar approaches might be used without the benefit of prediction markets and perhaps could represent an improvement. Members of the legislature could simply be asked to rate individual candidates, and the above-mentioned techniques could be used. Indeed, political scientists sometimes look at the difference between the votes of the two political parties to produce a proxy for the ideology of nominees.[31] There are, however, at least two advantages to the use of prediction markets. First, they provide incentives for third parties to gauge the performance of potential candidates and thus to provide information to the legislature. Second, ex post evaluations that have no function other than to resolve the prediction market payouts are likely to be less politicized than evaluations that determine who is selected. With contemporaneous evaluations, actual quality might factor very little into the evaluations, and so numbers produced using the regression method would be very noisy.

The weight ultimately placed on the ideology measure (with more neutral candidates more likely to be selected) and the weight placed on the quality measure could be disputed. But assuming the continued use of existing appointments systems, prediction markets along these lines at least might provide information that could help influence the political debate, once the relative accuracy of such markets is established. It will be difficult to defend someone as being within the mainstream if prediction markets say that the person is not or to claim that someone is unqualified if prediction markets forecast high quality ratings. Of course, prediction markets also could be used if being ideological were viewed as a positive attribute. For example, it may be better in a multi-member decision-making body such as the Federal Communications Commission to ensure that the median member is relatively moderate but that there are also more ideological members to ensure viewpoint diversity.

Normative prediction markets for gauging prospective appointees might be useful not only in selecting people for positions in administrative agencies but also in selecting people who might serve as ex post decision makers in other such markets. The premise of the normative prediction market proposals offered so far is that because the identity of the decision maker is unknown, the market will tend to produce relatively average decisions. This approach increases the risk cost borne by market participants, raising the cost of the market subsidy needed to obtain any given level of accuracy. The alternative is to commit to appointing the decision makers through a normative prediction market designed to select relatively moderate ones. Quality should matter, too, but not as much since nonsystematic analytical errors they make will tend to cancel each other out in expected value terms. Selecting ex post decision makers in this way might be particularly beneficial if it is impractical to wait a decade or so before resolving a normative prediction market.

THE PROBLEM OF SPECIAL INTERESTS

These markets might also be used to constrain not only ideological decision making but also interested decision making. The claim that special interests receive undue benefits from government is as old as government itself. Solutions, however, are elusive. The most frequently mentioned approaches to solving the problem are campaign contribution limits and disclosure requirements. Contribution limits, however, can be evaded by the creation of seemingly independent organizations that do not formally coordinate their actions with those of political parties and campaigns.[32] Cracking down on these organizations is difficult in a country committed to permitting free speech. Disclosure requirements, meanwhile, accomplish little. Studies suggest that few voters go to the trouble of analyzing campaign disclosures,[33] even as those voters complain about the influence of special interests.

Several other strategies show more promise but still have serious problems. One approach is to invest important decisions in independent agencies. But the officials at independent agencies must be selected somehow, and this gives special interests a chance to influence their decisions. Another approach, representing the opposite of the solution suggested by disclosure rules, seeks to make it impossible for contributors and politicians to enter into quid pro quo or implicit deals. Ian Ayres and Jeremy Bulow, for example, have suggested a "donation booth" that would prevent politicians from finding out who has donated to their campaigns.[34] Contributions might be completely anonymous or contributors might be allowed to request refunds of donations. One might instead place the cloak of secrecy over the politicians, for example by using secret ballots in the legislature. But this raises its own problems of self-interested behavior, at least in cases in which legislation might have some direct effect on the legislators.

Normative prediction markets similarly can help provide independent decision making and sever the ability of contributors to buy off politicians, although the strategy is fundamentally different. In order to buy influence, a private party has to somehow publicly commit to spending money to influence the ex post decision makers at some later point in time. It is difficult to make this commitment credibly since at the later point the issue will no longer be important; at most, the interest in following through will be solely to make future commitments of this type more credible. But there is only a small chance that any particular ex post decision maker will be chosen, making contributions more difficult to target. Of course, buying off some decision makers can increase the probability of a favorable result, but at least it will be difficult to pinpoint a single official or small group of officials with the power to negotiate a particular legislative accomplishment.

Careful design of the normative prediction market institution can make it still less likely that special interests can have a disproportionate impact on decision making, though they could always submit arguments that the ex post decision makers could take into account. One approach is to make them relatively independent, for example, by appointing them to nonrenewable terms. The terms can be long, too, though ideally not so long that any ideological bias in the pool of decision makers becomes anticipatable during the normative prediction markets. Providing a diverse portfolio of issues for such market issues can also help; relatively few special interests seek to influence judicial appointments in part because of the small probability that any particular decision maker will be in a position to help any specific third party. A more radical step is to provide anonymity for the ex post decision makers, who would consider arguments submitted to them but not reveal their own identities. Anonymity has drawbacks such as decreased incentive to study any issue in depth, but accountability should be less of a concern when the decision resolves only the prediction market payouts.

Some people may take the position that special interests generally improve policy on the theory that decision makers otherwise might not place enough emphasis on, for example, the welfare of businesses and indirectly on their shareholders and employees. In contexts in which the government seeks to reduce special interest influence, however, normative prediction markets could help. Consider the "line item veto." In *Clinton v. City of New York*[35] the U.S. Supreme Court struck down a line item veto enacted by Congress, but only on technical constitutional grounds.[36] Some commentators believe that Congress could still delegate to the president or to an agency the power to decide not to spend some money tentatively appropriated by Congress.[37] Some, however, might fear that this approach simply means that the special interests favored by the president or by members of Congress who can work out deals with the president will be favored.[38]

A normative prediction market might be used to determine which spending should be cancelled. Congress might provide a general standard for the ex post decision makers to consider, for example, whether a particular appropriation benefits private or concentrated interests at the expense of the general public interest, and the prediction market would forecast the probability that the selected person would find that the spending would be found undesirable. A modest reform, short of using normative prediction markets in an independent agency, would be to enact a congressional rule providing a "fast track" to a bill following the recommendations of the normative prediction markets, with no allowance for floor amendments. Congress has similarly granted fast track authority for international trade agreements in order to prevent individual members from undermining hard-to-negotiate treaties with special pleading.[39] The markets themselves would have no direct power, but a single annual vote on whether to accept prediction market recommendations would test each member of Congress's commitment to avoiding pork.

Nothing in the structure of normative prediction markets means that they can be used only as a one-way ratchet to reduce spending. They just as easily could be used to increase spending. Any member of Congress could be permitted to propose an additional line item, and a normative prediction market would forecast an ex post decision about whether this line item would be in the public interest. Congress could then vote on a package of such line items, and members could tell their constituents that the package was pork-free. Of course, such markets could be used for any number of other goals, for instance, to eliminate discrete tax breaks catering to special interests, determine which military bases should be closed, or choose which states will receive federal money to build new highways. Normative prediction markets can produce assessments that are both representative and relatively independent of attempts at improper influence.

THE TIME INCONSISTENCY PROBLEM

In addition to guarding against the temptation to provide benefits to private interests, normative prediction markets also can be useful in guarding against the temptation to deviate from commitments. In 2004, Finn Kydland and Edward Prescott won the Nobel Prize in Economics in large part because of their work on what is known as the "time inconsistency problem."[40] The problem is that sometimes it makes sense for policy makers to "tie their hands." The metaphor alludes to Ulysses' tying himself to the mast to avoid the Sirens, and in many public policy contexts a decision maker can improve social welfare if he can prevent himself from making the optimal decision at a later time. A policy is said to be "time-inconsistent" when it might make sense to commit to the policy now though, in the absence of commitment, it might make sense to deviate from the policy later. For example, it might be optimal for a government not to offer flood insurance in the hope that individuals will obtain their own but nonetheless to provide disaster relief if a flood occurs. The government can only achieve the time-inconsistent no-insurance policy if it can find some way of tying its hands.

Kydland and Prescott's pathbreaking article dealt in part with the problem of inflation.[41] Sometimes central banks have an incentive to engineer a "surprise inflation,"[42] providing a momentary boost in output. But when inflation is anticipated, the only way to achieve surprise is with greater levels of inflation. Expectations of inflation themselves fuel inflation. Policy makers can achieve lower inflation if they can commit to choosing in the future a lower level of inflation than they otherwise would choose at that time. Inflation policy is thus time-inconsistent, and mechanisms that allow policy makers to tie their hands can achieve considerable benefits. Granting independence to the central bank is one way that the legislature can tie its hands. Similarly, the literature has shown that it will generally be in the interest of the executive to select a central banker who is more of an inflation hawk than is the executive.[43]

The central banker, however, also faces the time consistency problem, and so the banker may seek to commit in advance to a particular approach to monetary policy. This provides at least one argument in support of formulaic approaches to monetary policy, such as a rule that would produce a constant rate of growth of the money supply.[44] But tying one's hands can have the severe drawback of inhibiting the ability of policy makers to respond to unexpected developments. The domestic and world economies are in constant flux, and there is always a danger that a perfect model describing how to perform monetary policy today will no longer be valid in tomorrow's different economic environment. What would be useful would be a mechanism by which the central bank could commit to being hawkish on inflation while still taking all unexpected circumstances into account. In a changing environment, that cannot be done ex ante.

Prediction markets can help in two ways. First, policy makers can commit to actions that are contingent on prediction market forecasts that themselves take into account the changing economic environment.[45] Suppose, for example, that interest rate policy has two potentially conflicting goals: to produce economic growth and to limit inflation. A central bank could establish markets that will predict the effect of different possible changes in interest rates on growth and inflation. The government could then announce some weighting of these two variables and commit in advance to a policy of choosing the interest rate that maximizes social welfare according to this weighting.

A possible change in interest rate policy would be accepted whenever the conditional prediction markets anticipate that this change would improve social welfare. The central bank's incentive will be to announce a weighting that privileges inflation more than it would like to at any particular time, so that it can seize the benefits of precommitment. Indeed, a separate prediction market might be used at the beginning of the program to choose the optimal weight to commit to based on the actual weights assigned by policy makers. By committing to follow the recommendations of these prediction markets, officials could precommit to low inflation while still allowing for policy to adjust with changing circumstances.

Second, policy makers can rely on normative prediction markets that themselves will have no direct effect on policy. Such a market might be set up that will predict at any time what the chairman of the Federal Reserve twenty years hence will conclude would have been an appropriate interest rate for today. The catch is that the chairman will be instructed to announce the interest rate that would have been best to commit to when the market was initially created if it had been possible then to anticipate the state of the economy in the future. The prediction of the retrospective assessment at any given time should reflect a policy that is time-inconsistent yet takes into account all considerations about the economy at the time the assessment is made.

In making the retrospective assessment, the chairman will have no incentive to announce an interest rate that would have produced more inflation than one would have liked to have committed to in advance if all information had been available. Rather, the chairman's incentive will be to announce an interest rate consistent with the optimal ex ante policy, because that will increase the public's estimation of the probability that future such decision makers will also announce retrospective evaluations that accord with the optimal ex ante policy. In effect, because the decision being predicted has no direct effect, the policy maker has no incentive to cheat.

Inflation is a unique policy context, but there are many other areas in which time inconsistency can be a problem. For example, it might be optimal for a nation to commit to the use of military force in more instances than it would be in the nation's interest to use force. In theory, a nation or an international military body could commit to engaging in military action whenever a normative prediction market recommends it. Or it might be optimal for a nation to commit to granting amnesty to future illegal immigrants only if a normative prediction market recommends such amnesty. These scenarios, however, highlight one difficulty of using prediction markets to overcome the time inconsistency problem: the chance that the relevant decision makers will decide to ignore the prediction market. Even if Congress were to pass a statute requiring the Federal Reserve Board to follow a prediction market for interest rate policy, there would remain a chance that Congress would later renege when faced with economic hardship. Nonetheless, because it takes effort to overturn statutes, prediction markets can help.

Normative prediction markets' ability to overcome the time inconsistency problem by producing time-inconsistent yet context-sensitive policies also means that they can help promote the rule of law. Consider again the use of normative prediction markets in the context of statutory interpretation. When an agency is considering a regulation that appears sensible but inconsistent with a statute, the agency may have some incentive to pass the regulation nonetheless. Similarly, a court will have some incentive to use disingenuous reasoning to approve of the regulation. The independence of the courts reduces the possibility, but judges surely recognize that their decisions have policy effects. Judges, too, thus have some incentive to "cheat" via disingenuous readings of statutes.

As a general matter, administrative officials and judges will follow higher-order legal principles when they conflict with preferred results in particular cases than they would like to commit to in advance if such precommitment were possible. Ex post decision makers in the normative prediction market can adhere more easily to the higher-order legal principles. Of course, it may not be optimal to precommit to always following higher-order legal principles, and ex post decision makers might sometimes use disingenuous reasoning or candidly acknowledge that the law should have been ignored. But at least they will have incentives to ascertain whether time-inconsistent policy, where higher-order legal principles trump expedient decision making, is desirable all in all. Normative prediction markets of this sort might be particularly useful for improving administrative decisions in countries that have not developed strong cultural norms supporting the rule of law.[46]

EMERGENCY GOVERNANCE

Whereas prediction markets might help assist administrative agencies in their day-to-day operations, they might be particularly useful in emergencies. Consider, for example, the federal and state governments' response to Hurricane Katrina. Critics generally complained that the governments had engaged in poor planning.[47] Moreover, some governmental decisions, such as those that prevented the Red Cross from providing immediate relief, seemed counterproductive.[48] Whatever the merits of these critiques, it often becomes apparent in a crisis that planning has been inadequate and that improvisation and new approaches are needed.

Simply giving an agency extraordinary powers may help, but there are problems with this approach. First, an agency may not have sufficient information about the facts on the ground to make good decisions. Second, in a time of crisis, an agency might not have sufficient time to consider adequately all policy options. Indeed, reports from Hurricane Katrina indicate both that decision makers in Washington were not aware of the facts on the ground[49] and that a number of decisions made in the immediate wake of the storm, such as the expensive rental of cruise ships to provide temporary housing, were wasteful.[50]

The simplest use of prediction markets would be to provide information about the facts on the ground. Prediction markets might, for example, estimate the number of deaths and the amount of property destruction in particular areas, as well as the number of law enforcement personnel present in particular locations. These markets should be heavily subsidized. Those who have access to scarce communications resources in a crisis, such as satellite phones, will then have an incentive to use these phones to send information to other people through the markets. It might seem implausible to imagine people worrying about trading during a crisis, but if there is enough publicity and subsidies are sufficiently high, individuals will have an incentive to communicate information using whatever means they can and, more important, others will have incentives to piece together all emerging data. Deliberative prediction markets might be particularly useful, giving incentives to share data as well as incentives to aggregate existing data. Absent a national security need for confidentiality, government should share its information in real time. Overall, these decentralized methods for information-gathering should improve on whatever the government can provide by itself.

A possible objection to this scheme is that the government would need to commit in advance to providing such markets, but it might be difficult to anticipate what markets are needed and how much they should be subsidized. Certainly precommitment would be useful, in part because it would give incentives for private parties to acquire technology that might allow them to profit on information in the event of a disaster. But as long as there is a commitment to using prediction markets, not much advanced planning of the particular subjects that the markets should cover would be needed. Indeed, the best solution may be to use conditional normative prediction markets to determine what other prediction markets should be created and at what level they should be subsidized. These proposal markets could anticipate the future assessment of a decision maker of whether the proposed prediction markets, if created, were useful. The proposals could come from members of the public. A simple regime might require someone proposing a prediction market to pay the fee to subsidize a corresponding proposal market, with the promise of receiving a bonus if the agency creates the proposed market.

A similar mechanism could be used to determine what prediction markets should be created to assess particular decisions that the administrative agency might make. For example, private contractors might be permitted to post offers to provide goods or services in exchange for payments from the government. One prediction market would be used to determine whether to create and how much to subsidize another prediction market that would evaluate a particular private contractor's proposal. The latter market, if created, would be a conditional normative prediction market. It would assess the net benefits of the spending proposal. Another set of prediction markets might be used to evaluate policy decisions, such as whether particular areas should be evacuated or whether martial law should be declared. Presumably, agency officials will focus a great deal of their attention on some of the more vital proposals. Stressed and strained for time, however, agency officials would have stronger incentives than usual to abide by many of the proposal market's recommendations.

Prediction markets for assessing decisions may be particularly useful in the emergency context because emergencies necessarily demand the relaxation of procedural regularities. When time is of the essence, public pressure cannot promptly be brought to bear when there is a risk of poor or interested decision making. To be sure, prediction markets will not eliminate the need for some individual decision making, particularly in contexts in which individual officials on the ground must make decisions without the ability or the time to consult with superiors. It will not be practical for a police officer who sees looting to consult the prediction market to determine whether she should arrest the looters or allocate scarce time to helping people in need. Prediction markets, however, at least can have a substantial role for decisions that can be made over the course of a few hours or days rather than instantaneously.

Perhaps the more fundamental justification for prediction markets in this context, however, is that they provide an easy means of scaling decision making. Especially if they are well subsidized, many capable individuals who would not otherwise have participated in information and strategy analysis will do so. An emergency agency may be able, with appropriate legal authorization, to take advantage of certain resources, such as the military, to keep order. Borrowing additional decision makers and deliberators, however, ordinarily will be difficult, though the number of decisions that must be made during a disaster will probably dwarf the number that are made before a disaster. Even if the head of the emergency agency makes a sensible allocation of time and delegates to available subordinates, each individual decision will have received far less attention than it deserves. Prediction markets can potentially ensure that each of thousands of decisions receives a great deal of attention. And although some market participants might have limited ability to make assessments, large numbers should be able to steer the agency in the right direction and considerably improve decision making.

Chapter 7 Public Corporations

The approaches developed in Chapters 5 and 6 allow the government to make decisions based on private parties' predictions about the effects of both private and potential governmental actions. Nongovernmental decision makers, however, also might be interested in harnessing the power of prediction markets to assess the effects of their decisions. We have seen that businesses might use prediction markets to gather specific information that might be relevant to their work. A more intensive use of prediction markets would generate conditional predictions about the effects of particular decisions on the business.

It is useful for a company to be able to predict demand for an existing product so that, for example, the company can better manage inventory and assign personnel. But it is more useful for a company to be able to predict demand for a product that it is considering creating. Indeed, making assessments of the effects of particular business decisions lies at the heart of business management. Should a business build another factory? Lay off or hire workers? Adopt a new organizational structure? Prediction markets can make forecasts about all of these decisions, providing at least a presumption about the best course in a particular situation.

Conditional prediction markets of this type seem particularly promising for public corporations because the stock market already provides a kind of prediction of corporations' future success. The existence of stock markets is relevant for two reasons. First, they already serve a critical role in guiding corporate decision making. Chief executive officers are sometimes said to be obsessed with increasing stock price, and in the absence of that indicator, CEOs might try less vigorously to increase shareholder wealth. They have incentives to try to understand the dynamics of stock prices and to identify strategies that might lead to improvements in stock price. The fact that many corporations are already run with an eye on maintaining a high and rising stock price should make reliance on corporate prediction markets much less of a change than it would be in government. Although there are risks in relying on uncertain new decision making technologies, the competitive pressures affecting public corporations probably mean that prediction markets will play a significant role in the corporate sector well before they play a significant role in the public sector.

Second, because the stock price of a corporation provides a barometer of the corporation's performance, it can serve as an excellent variable to predict. One challenge in designing prediction markets is determining just what should be predicted. Regardless of whether maximizing shareholder wealth is the exclusive goal of a particular corporation, it is surely an important goal. Prediction markets can be used to assess the effect of particular possible decisions on stock price. A prediction market forecast that one decision would lead to a higher stock price than another at least provides a strong basis for the corporation to make that decision. A corporation might further seek to provide strong incentives for managers to follow such recommendations, and corporate law might provide somewhat less deference to managerial decisions when they flout prediction market forecasts.

This chapter explores ways in which public corporations might harness the benefits of prediction markets. A major challenge addressed by corporate law scholarship is that agency costs sometimes might lead managers to make decisions that advance their own interests rather than those of the shareholders. A prediction market can be seen as a mechanism that can help counter these agency costs, and it may be more effective than some alternative mechanisms, such as shareholder voting. I explore a range of potential applications of prediction markets. A more powerful Hollywood Stock Exchange might not merely predict movie success but also be used to determine which movies would be made. Market mechanisms might be used to select a CEO or members of the board of directors or to decide which shareholder proposals should be enacted.

In addition, prediction markets might promote the flow of information, both to managers and to actual and potential shareholders. Indeed, prediction markets can serve as a weak form of insider trading. Corporate law scholarship has long recognized that insider trading has benefits as well as costs, and prediction markets can help provide a reasonable compromise between the extremes of entirely prohibiting the practice and allowing all forms of it. Prediction markets might mislead, however, by failing to take into account some insider information or by taking into account that potential decisions might be the result of insider information. A broader concern is that prediction markets, like securities markets in general, might be inefficient, subject to investment pathologies that lead to bubbles and undermine accurate predictions. These problems, however, may be manageable, and at least corporate experimentation with prediction markets should help identify the best ways to use them in large enterprises.

AGENCY COSTS

Thomas Malone, in his book *The Future of Work,* has identified the prediction market as one of a number of mechanisms that allow managers to take advantage of decentralized decision making rather than relying solely on their own normative lights.[1] If the predictions that are of interest to businesses are useful bases on which to make decisions, then managers who choose to rely on them will be successful and should be more likely to be promoted to more important positions, within and outside an organization. It is possible, however, that prediction markets might become influential not merely because managers defer to them but also because owners of businesses might pressure the managers to take them into account. The more effective and accurate prediction markets prove to be, the greater will be the importance that shareholders will place on the degree to which managers follow their recommendations.

One of the most significant considerations in the optimal design of a corporation is the existence of a divergence between the interests of its shareholders and the interests of its management, including executives and members of the board of directors. Managers are the agents of the shareholders, but agents often do not do just what their principals would prefer. In a famous article,

Michael Jensen and William Meckling defined the social loss from this divergence as "agency costs."[2] These costs have three components: monitoring costs, bonding costs, and the residual loss.[3]

These costs are perhaps most easily seen in a simple business such as a restaurant. The owner might install video cameras to make sure that the servers are working hard, a monitoring cost. The employees might agree to have their income be dependent on tips rather than on a salary although ordinarily the owner would be in a better position to assume risk, a bonding cost. And because each employee still sometimes might not work as hard as if the employee owned the restaurant, the restaurant might lose some customers, a residual loss.

A major goal of corporate law is to create corporate structures that minimize agency costs. For example, different corporate law structures can involve different levels of monitoring of managers. The board of directors helps monitor executives, though it can do so more or less intensively. For example, a board composed largely of independent directors might be expected to oversee executives more intensively, though the empirical evidence of whether independent boards lead to better performance is mixed.[4] The monitors sometimes need monitoring. Various corporate law rules governing conflicts of interest help in monitoring board members and prevent them from facilitating self-interested transactions.[5] Just as important, board members are overseen by shareholders, who have the power to select them and in some circumstances to replace them, as well as the power to advance proposals concerning the governance of the corporation. Because the time of shareholders is scarce, however, this form of monitoring can be expensive, and because each shareholder has only a limited incentive to acquire information relevant to voting, shareholder monitoring may not always benefit the corporation.

Board members and executives, meanwhile, may bond themselves to perform well by agreeing to accept compensation in forms such as stock options. Such approaches might not always be effective bonding devices, because they may give managers incentives to manipulate financial results to maximize their option payouts, potentially causing further losses to the firm's shareholders. Also serving as a potential bonding mechanism is a regime subjecting managers or board members to liability for bad decisions. The business judgment rule in corporate law generally sharply limits such liability, deferring to business judgment even where it turns out to be poor. This suggests that the bonding costs of more robust damages regimes might be substantial or else that liability can be counterproductive, leading decision makers to act too conservatively. These examples show that sometimes it is not clear whether bonding mechanisms will work as intended.

To the extent that monitoring and bonding mechanisms lead agents to act more as the principals would act, they should be adopted as long as their marginal benefits exceed their marginal costs. The benefits of these mechanisms are that they reduce the residual loss from the divergence in incentives of principals and agents. The costs are that monitoring and bonding are expensive, in part because they increase the amount of compensation that decision makers will require to leave them equally well off. Managers might dislike criticism and scrutiny, for example, and they therefore might be less attracted to firms in which they will be monitored more intensively, all else being equal. Managers also might not work as hard if they perceive that they do not have real decision-making authority.[6] In addition, managers are risk-averse and prefer relatively safe jobs to ones in which they stand a good chance of being fired as a result of their decisions. Finally, managers might inherently value power, including the power to execute their view of what is best for the firm, and they therefore might dislike monitoring technologies that directly or indirectly limit their power.

Prediction markets might serve not only as tools that managers can use to improve their own decision making but also as means to improve monitoring and bonding. To the extent that prediction markets provide direct assessments of issues facing managers, they can make it easier for individual shareholders to determine whether managers appear to be acting in their own interests. Shareholders might be suspicious of a manager who repeatedly acts in a way that prediction markets forecast will not succeed. Of course, shareholders can also and more easily monitor stock price, but a comparison of prediction market forecasts and the decisions of a CEO could allow for more fine-grained assessments of the reasons for declines in stock prices. Managers, meanwhile, might respond to the presence of prediction markets by agreeing, explicitly or implicitly, to follow their recommendations, at least when those recommendations are relatively unequivocal. A manager who announces a managerial philosophy of generally deferring to prediction markets has accepted a bonding mechanism that reduces individual discretion. Although the manager still might ignore the recommendation of a market, doing so would exact some reputational cost.

In theory, the forecasts of prediction markets might be enforced not only by pressure from shareholders but also by pressure from the courts. Under the law of Delaware, the home of most major American corporations, the business decisions of a board of directors will not be second-guessed by a court unless the court finds that the directors have breached their duty of loyalty by, for example, entering into a contract in which there is a conflict of interest, or their duty of care, by conducting insufficient investigation or deliberation to form the basis of a business judgment.[7] One reason why courts are so reluctant to second-guess business decisions of managers is the danger of hindsight bias. Prediction markets, however, have the potential to provide contemporaneous assessments of decisions, thus reducing this danger. Ex post judicial monitoring may be more effective when it can rely on ex ante prediction market monitoring.

There is thus an argument that when managers make decisions that the markets have predicted would be mistakes, the courts should be more willing to find that the directors have breached their fiduciary duties. That does not mean that a prediction market forecast should be the only relevant consideration. Courts, for example, might also consider whether there is any reason to believe that a divergence between the interests of directors and shareholders exists as to a particular issue, even if this divergence does not amount to a full-fledged conflict. The degree to which courts should seek ex post to punish misguided deviations from prediction market recommendations would depend also on the accuracy of the predictions and the degree to which managers might have information that was unavailable to the market. Of course, if increased reliance on prediction markets is desirable, firms might create mechanisms to advance prediction markets, for example, by insisting on contracts that expose managers to greater liability. The case for forcing prediction markets on unwilling firms is weak, unless an agency cost prevents firms from adopting a superior monitoring technology.

CONDITIONAL PREDICTION MARKETS: THE COMBINATORIAL APPROACH

So far, businesses that have taken advantage of prediction markets have made direct predictions of events relevant to their decision making, but as the above discussion implies, it may be far more useful to have prediction markets make forecasts that are contingent on the outcomes of particular decisions. We have already seen that conditional prediction markets can be implemented by unwinding transactions in the event that a condition is not met. In the corporate context, a prediction market contract might be used to forecast the corporation's stock price at some point in the future, but only if the corporation decides to build a particular factory. If the corporation ends up not building the factory, all transactions in the market are refunded. Another market might predict the corporation's stock price in the event that the corporation does not make a particular decision. Even with conditional markets structured in this way, reaching meaningful decisions requires comparing the two (or more) conditional predictions.

An alternative approach to conditional markets is to combine mathematically the prices of two or more tradable contracts to generate a single prediction. An early use of conditional markets takes this approach. Joyce Berg and Thomas Rietz, who help run the Iowa Electronic Markets, decided in the 1996 U.S. presidential election to make conditional predictions of the success of different possible Republican candidates against Bill Clinton, the Democratic incumbent. For each candidate, the IEM included a contract that would pay off one cent for each percentage of the popular vote the candidate would win in the general election but would pay nothing if the candidate were not the Republican nominee. At the same time, the IEM ran a probability estimate prediction market to gauge who the Republican nominee would be. Dividing the first number by the second number would produce an estimate of the percentage of votes the candidate would receive against Clinton if nominated.

A problem with this approach to conditional markets is that to the extent that the price of any individual tradable contract has some amount of noise, the division of the prices of two separate tradable contracts has the potential to aggravate the noise. Consider, for example, figure 7.1, which uses tradable IEM contracts to calculate Bush's conditional vote share a year before the 2004 election, during the first week of November 2003. Not much happened that week, but the conditional vote shares as calculated by this method changed considerably and in different ways for different candidates. It seems implausible, for example, that Hillary Clinton's expected performance against Bush, had she run and won, would have fallen from 68 percent of the electorate one day to 53 percent the next day, a massive shift by political standards. These numbers seem hard to reconcile with reality and with the relative stability of political campaigns generally as illustrated by market predictions of their results.

The high volatility of the shares shown in figure 7.1 is probably in part a result of relatively low market liquidity, and indeed conditional probabilities stabilized somewhat later in the election season. Given relatively large bid-ask spreads and the possibility of asymmetric information, there often will be little incentive for market participants to correct slight mispricings in

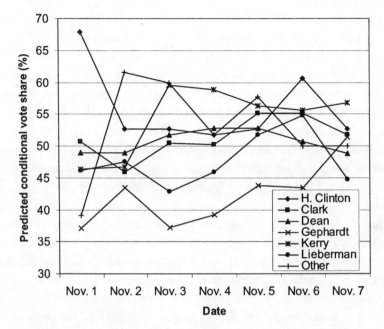

Figure 7.1. Early conditional market predictions in the Iowa Electronic Markets

a prediction market tradable contract. Small mispricings in each of two trad-able contracts can combine to create greater deviations when the two tradable contracts are combined mathematically. The problem, of course, becomes greater when the prices of three or more tradable contracts must be considered. For example, in order to determine how much better one candidate can be ex-pected to fare than another in the general election, one would need to subtract the derived conditional estimate for one from that of another.

It seems likely that other market designs might alleviate the problem to some degree. For example, with the market scoring rule, it will more often be in the interest of a market participant to correct a slight mispricing in a tradable con-tract, putting aside the time cost of entering into a transaction, because some-one making such a correction would not be accepting the underlying risk as-sociated with the contract as a whole. Similarly, market subsidies would give greater incentives to correct mispricing, so market participants will have strong incentives to identify situations in which the relationship between two or more tradable contract prices does not correspond with perceived reality and correct the mispricings.

Research has also focused on the development of market designs for contexts in which market participants might want to make predictions about complex combinations of large numbers of variables. Robin Hanson, for example, has described how to create a market maker that would allow anyone to bet in a "state space" representing relationships among a number of variables, and he argues that in theory it should cost no more to fund an automated market maker to allow trades in the entire state space than to fund automated market makers limited to each variable.[8] Lance Fortnow and coauthors have similarly described a prediction market design that allows participants to trade in tradable contracts based on logical formulas expressed in propositional logic.[9] For example, if A and B represent events that might or might not occur, one could bet not only on A or on B but on "A and B" and "if A then B," as well as more complex combinations.

An advantage of these approaches is that the market maker would automatically ensure coherence among the variables, because it would not create an additional tradable contract for every combination. For example, someone betting on "if A then B" might automatically be given shares on "A and B" and shares on "not A." In the appropriate proportions, this combination is equivalent to the conditional bet, as long as there are just enough "not A" shares so that the nonoccurrence of condition A leads to an exact refund of the total investment. From a user interface perspective, users would not need to know the difference. The principal difficulty with these approaches is that the necessary calculations would increase exponentially in the number of variables, making a market allowing bets about any relationships among a large number of variables potentially infeasible with today's computers. These systems, however, may work well if limited to a dozen binary variables or so, enough for many practical applications.

At least until better systems for allowing conditional betting and betting on other relationships between variables are fully developed, it may be hazardous to place too much emphasis on the difference between the price of two conditional tradable contracts. This is true even if the unwinding approach to conditional markets is used. The danger is especially high in cases in which the price difference is relatively small in comparison to the prices of the two tradable contracts. Suppose, for example, that a conditional prediction market of any type is used to gauge the price of Apple Computer stock at some point in the future if an additional water cooler is installed on the third floor of 1 Infinite Loop, and another such market is used to predict the price if the water cooler is not installed. The connection between the water cooler and the price of Apple stock is likely to be so attenuated that market participants will have little incentive to take it into account in their models. Any difference between the price of the two tradable contracts is likely to represent random noise.

Assessing alternative decisions using conditional markets will thus likely work best when the condition seems likely to have a significant effect on the variable of interest. At the very least, any subsidy the market sponsor has provided will be better spent, because the more important the variable of interest, the greater the effort market participants will make to model its effect. There may, however, be some techniques that could be used to make conditional market predictions more reliable. For example, a prediction market might be used to assess the difference in the assessments of two other markets making conditional forecasts based on two different possible decisions. At least with this prediction market, participants would focus directly on the effect of the decision. Though a large amount of market noise might make the difference in predictions an unreliable indicator of market sentiment at any one time, because noise is largely unpredictable, a prediction of the difference between two tradable contracts' prices might be a reliable indicator of the effect of the relevant decision.

A similar approach would be to use conditional prediction markets to forecast the change in stock price in the five minutes after an official decision was announced. If the relevant decision merely involved a water cooler, then, because the stock price would be unaffected, both prediction markets would anticipate zero effect on Apple stock or both might reflect a very small stock price increase attributable to the general tendency of shares to rise, but there would be virtually no difference between these markets. If, however, the decision reflected an issue that might have an effect of a few cents on stock price, such as whether to cancel a particular computer line, then the conditional prediction markets might make slightly different decisions. Market participants would not need to worry much about the overall health of Apple but instead would focus on the extent to which the decision might change Apple's profitability. The result is that the market subsidy would be better targeted.

This system does introduce the danger of a new kind of manipulation: a person who credibly commits to buying or selling stock whenever the decision happens to be made. It might not be difficult for someone with modest capital to commit to buying or selling enough shares at a particular point in time to change the market price for a short period of time. One solution is to add some uncertainty to the length of time that determines the measurement of stock price change that is used to resolve the prediction market payouts. The average interval would need to be long enough that manipulating the market in this way would be prohibitively expensive. Even a wealthy investor cannot change stock price over a long period of time without losing a great deal of money.

A somewhat more complex alternative would be for the conditional prediction markets to be forecasting the change in another prediction market anticipating the future stock price in the minutes after the announcement. This second prediction market could be structured as a deliberative market in which the time frame used to assess predictions is short, though somewhat uncertain (see Chapter 4). The advantage of this approach is that manipulation of this second market would be much easier to counter, because arbitrage would not require purchase or sale of equity interests in the firm as a whole. In addition, the second market might predict change in the actual stock market over a longer period of time, with greater uncertainty about the exact measurement point, making it difficult to commit credibly to manipulating this market.

IMPROVING THE HOLLYWOOD STOCK EXCHANGE

To see how conditional prediction markets might be used by corporations, consider again the Hollywood Stock Exchange (see Chapter 1), which has been shown to be a relatively accurate predictor of the success of movies at the box office. The exchange allows purchase of stocks representing individual movies well before the movies' release, indeed, in the concept stage. If the movies are never made or released, the corresponding stocks are cashed out at zero. This means, however, that especially at early stages, prices involve at least two different considerations: the probability that a movie in fact will be made and how well it will do if made. The low prices for the movie *Action Abramowitz,* which was to have starred Ray Romano as an accountant turned action hero, may have been due to an expectation that the movie would not really be made or to a view that characters with names similar to Abramowicz don't make good action heroes.

Movie studios and television stations currently rely on their own employees' ability to determine which concepts are most likely to be successful. It is quite possible, though not certain, that prediction markets might perform as well as or better than existing decision makers. It would be straightforward for a studio to make subsidized prediction markets that conditionally predicted the success of different possible productions. The Hollywood Stock Exchange also might create such tradable contracts, although it might have less incentive to provide a significant subsidy. Different tradable contracts might be used to predict how well a movie would perform at different possible funding levels or if particular directors or performers could be lured to participate. Studios might need to enter into contracts that would prevent authors of highly rated scripts from using the information to enter into contracts with other studios, but these should not be difficult to draft.

How might we expect such prediction markets to change decision making at studios? At first, probably not much, although market predictions might lead executives to take a second look at some proposals. Over time, however, it would become clear how markets compared to executives at making forecasts. If, for example, movies that prediction markets forecast as duds in fact crashed at the box office, that would at least indicate that prediction markets should be relied on to block some projects. It might turn out that the market consistently appears to beat the executives. One might then expect the studios to spend less money on those executives, substituting cheaper and more mechanical decision makers, while perhaps increasing subsidies to the prediction market.

Suppose, however, that it turned out that at least some studios had executives who consistently could beat the market. That would not necessarily mean that the market was useless. Indeed, one would expect that if the executives were fired and their salaries were added to the market subsidy, they might well decide to invest in the prediction markets themselves. If they keep their jobs, participants in the prediction markets should learn to take their ratings into account. These executives might announce their evaluations of different proposals, and these evaluations presumably would have an effect not only on the market estimation of the probability that a movie would be made but also on its estimation of the success of the movie if made.

This provides a counterargument to at least one plausible argument against greater reliance on prediction markets: that executives might have better information or better judgment than prediction market participants. If that is so, market participants ought to take that ability into account, much as a novice chess player would assume that a grandmaster's move was wise even if it made no sense to the novice. Someone who insists that prediction markets would not take publicly announced positions of experts sufficiently into account in effect is stating not only that the experts are better than market participants, but also that he or she knows better than the market participants know about how much to take experts' views into account. That position would demand some further justification and explanation.

THE DANGER OF PRIVATE DECISION
MAKER INFORMATION

When private decision makers can convey their information to the market, even in summary form, there is no reason to expect that prediction markets should fail to give it adequate weight. Until they convey their views, however, their private information presents another danger: that participants in conditional prediction markets will evaluate possible decisions in part by assessing the circumstances that might lead a decision maker to make them. Suppose, for example, that *Action Abramowitz* seems likely to be a bad movie if it stars Ray Romano but a successful movie if it stars Ben Stiller. Prediction market participants might then reason that the movie studio will make the movie only if the studio finds that it can sign Stiller. The prediction of the movie's success will then reflect its success only if it stars Stiller.

In this case there might be a straightforward solution: creating separate conditional markets for the cases in which the movie stars Romano and Stiller. At times, however, private information might not be so easily identified. In general, this should lead prediction markets to be biased in favor of being optimistic about every decision. If knowledgeable decision makers choose to make *Action Abramowitz,* that would indicate that the project is a bit better than market participants would have thought, but the same will be true for every other concept. Market participants will think not about their intrinsic views of particular concepts but about how each concept would likely fare in a world in which someone actually chose to produce it. This should not produce biased evaluations of the movies that are selected for production, but it should mean that the market will be overvaluing the movies that are not selected.

In the movie context this should not generally be a serious problem, because what is most important is the relative evaluation of the success of different possible projects, though it does suggest that decision makers should not necessarily produce every concept that is forecast to have positive value. There might, however, be situations in which the amount of private information is expected to be different for different decisions. If, for example, a particular studio executive seems to have an uncanny ability to pick the best comedies but not much skill at picking dramas, the market should rate all comedies relatively highly. A higher price for a comedy than a drama would not necessarily reflect a market prediction that the comedy would be more successful than the drama.

A related problem is the danger of future information. Suppose, for example, that conditional markets are used to predict a corporation's stock price, contingent on decisions to build or not build a particular production facility. If that decision will not be made for another year, participants in the market now will anticipate that the eventual decision maker will have information not available to them. For example, it might be the case that the corporation will choose to build another production facility only if other unrelated projects are quite successful. The conditional market prediction might then seem to indicate that the production facility will raise the corporate stock price, when really the prediction simply means that if the corporation builds the facility, that might be because the corporation performed well in the intervening year.

These considerations suggest that care is needed in assessing predictions of conditional prediction markets in cases in which private information will likely be significant. There may also be some ways of reducing the risk of problems. For example, conditional prediction markets might be established relatively near in time to when a decision will be reached. Another promising, if counterintuitive, approach may be to remove decision-making power from the individuals most likely to have inside information. Individuals with private information can contribute to a decision by announcing their views of how the decision should be made or perhaps by trading directly on the market. The decision maker would then be someone without inside information who would consider the market predictions along with the content of the experts' stated opinions. Using less well-informed but still prudent decision makers may make the conditional prediction markets work better and thus perhaps improve the overall quality of decision making.

MARKETS FOR INSIDER TRADING

An alternative approach to improving corporate decision making is to seek to reduce information asymmetries using prediction markets. There are circumstances, of course, in which corporations want to keep certain information secret and therefore do not want to use prediction markets that might reveal the information. For example, a company might not want to have a market predicting the sales of a possible product if there is a significant chance that other firms will copy the idea and steal market share. In these cases, a possible solution is to use internal prediction markets, though there is always the danger that such markets might increase the probability that information about secret projects will leak. Nonetheless, there are many situations in which prediction markets would not reveal trade secrets, and in those cases prediction markets might usefully give private parties incentives to reveal, at least in the form of predictions, whatever information they know. A conditional deliberative prediction market, moreover, might give participants the incentive to reveal concrete information and analysis about issues, thus reducing the possibility that the ultimate decision maker will have much of an informational advantage relative to other market participants.

Prediction markets are useful not only for disseminating information that the top decision makers already have but also for giving them better information. Prediction markets might provide a useful way of revealing the consensus views of individuals in particular departments about the prospects of that department as a whole, for example, by predicting the release date of a particular software product or the number of bug reports that users can be expected to generate about it. Ordinarily, corporate information is filtered up the corporate hierarchy through managers. Employees, however, may sometimes have incentives to be excessively optimistic with their managers, and managers in turn may have incentives to be excessively optimistic with their superiors. To be sure, some are excessively cautious, but in any case this adds to the noise that makes it difficult for decision makers to make prudent decisions.

A possible objection to these markets is that they in effect allow for a type of insider trading. Yet they do not allow for insider trading in the stock of the firm. The trades on these markets presumably would not legally constitute insider trading, at least as long as the prediction markets are not subject to the regulatory authority that governs insider trading, such as the Securities and Exchange Commission in the United States. Superficially, some theories of insider trading liability might seem to apply if the prediction markets were regulated. For example, it might appear that employees who make the predictions are misappropriating knowledge that is corporate property. Misappropriation, however, depends on lack of consent, so although this concern might be applicable to employee forecasts in prediction markets established by third parties, it would not appear relevant to prediction markets created by the corporation itself.

A more powerful response to the objection is to argue that to the extent that prediction markets do constitute insider trading, such insider trading should be embraced. Henry Manne famously argued that the practice should be permitted, largely because it promotes market efficiency by ensuring that market prices incorporate privately held information.[10] He also pointed out that profits from insider trading could serve as a form of managerial compensation, and so uninformed shareholders should not conclude that they have been unfairly treated. More recently, Manne has argued that the advent of prediction markets in corporations supports his thesis that insider trading more generally should be permitted.[11] He states that investors did not appear to care about insider trading before it was prohibited and that the preliminary successes of prediction markets show one reason that this might have been so: insider trading improved market efficiency and thus the information available to investors.

Whatever the merits of insider trading regulation, prediction markets potentially can produce many of the benefits of insider trading without the costs. On the benefits side, if prediction market forecasts are made public, then buyers and sellers of stock will have more information with which to make assessments of the value of stock. Because prediction markets can focus on specific questions, they can provide better information to buyers and sellers, as well as to shareholders who wish to monitor management. On the costs side, insider trading should not decrease confidence in stock markets or the willingness of outsiders to invest in the firm, because prohibitions on trading on inside information in the stock of the company itself would still remain. Conceivably, internal prediction markets that are not made public might worsen the insider trading problem by providing insiders with access to better information than is available to outsiders. But even in this case, as long as insider trading on the company's stock is prohibited, an employee might be criminally liable for buying or selling stock on the basis of prediction market forecasts, at least where those predictions amounted to material information.

It is much more likely that prediction markets, in particular those made publicly available, will reduce information asymmetries rather than increase them. Even simple prediction markets forecasting the corporate stock price in the future may be quite useful, providing outsiders with a sense of insider views about the corporation's overall health. It might make sense to limit participation to individuals within the corporation or at least to provide some way of identifying predictions made by insiders. Such markets could be subsidized, and different markets might be used for different groups of employees, including upper management. Ideally, for such markets to have the potential to serve a whistleblower function that would alert management and shareholders to problems before they become too serious, anonymous trading on these markets should be permitted. A series of bets coming from within a particular division could help sound an alert that problems were expected.

Members of the board of directors might be entitled to trade on their own anonymous market, and their trades could help reveal to the public whether the board truly is optimistic about the future of the corporation. Of course, initially, the boards most likely to adopt such markets would be those that genuinely believe that the markets have undervalued their companies' stocks.

A similar strategy could be used to induce information revelation by corporate auditors. The auditing scandal involving Arthur Andersen and Enron helped expose the fact that auditors have incentives to bless aggressive accounting by their client firms. The scandal also revealed that such aggressive accounting might have serious repercussions, such as potential criminal liability.[12] A wide variety of reforms have been implemented or proposed to ensure that auditors act appropriately. For example, the Sarbanes-Oxley Act has required that auditors be independent and thus that audits not be rewards for other work that corporations steer to accounting firms. The act also established the Public Company Accounting Oversight Board to provide accounting standards. As long as auditors are paid by corporations, however, there will always be some incentive for auditors to please their clients, and the only question is whether counterincentives are adequate, insufficient, or excessive. More innovative proposals have taken a predictive decision making approach to monitoring auditors by, for example, requiring auditors to obtain insurance and disclose the price of that insurance.[13]

A different approach would seek to provide the auditors with appropriate incentives, rather than creating a gatekeeper to monitor the auditors. One might create prediction markets on which the auditors would be permitted to gauge variables such as future corporate stock price, earnings, and the probability that a particular financial statement issued by the corporation eventually will have to be revised. If enough members of the auditing firm participate in the audit, it would be difficult for the members to collude not to participate in the prediction market or to make unjustified predictions, particularly if trading is anonymous. Regulation would still be needed to assure that auditors have access to corporate information and that a sufficient number of members of the auditing team have access to information collected, but such regulation is far simpler than alternative regimes. Whatever incentives the auditors have in releasing formal reports and in certifying financial statements, the individual incentives of the auditors would be to relay their true information. Indeed, with prediction markets, the need for more formal means of disclosure, including those imposed on auditors and the corporations themselves, becomes considerably smaller.

Ideally, such a market should be subsidized to give auditors strong incentives to participate. Indeed, one regulatory approach might require that at least some percentage of the auditors' compensation, perhaps a high percentage, come in the form of such prediction market subsidies, making participation all the more irresistible. It might be desirable to allow the public generally to make predictions on the same markets, especially to counter any perceived collusion among the auditors. But it may be important to target the subsidy to the auditors rather than for the general public. This can be accomplished easily using the decentralized strategy for subsidizing markets discussed in Chapter 2. The individuals who make the most attractive bid and ask offers would receive a subsidy, because these offers increase the amount by which auditors can profit on their inside information. The individuals making these offers, however, could specify that only users identified as auditors would be allowed to accept them.

SELF-DECIDING PREDICTION MARKETS

Although reducing information asymmetries provides a partial solution to the problem of private decision maker information discussed above, an admittedly more radical alternative solution can essentially eliminate the problem altogether. That solution is to use prediction markets not merely as a means of providing information to decision makers or assessing decisions that they might make but instead as a means of making decisions.[14] A corporation might commit to deciding an issue in the way that a prediction market forecasts would be best. Corporate officials, such as the CEO, might still provide information to the prediction markets about the course of action that they believe best, and market participants would take such information into account to the extent that they believe it is relevant to predicting the outcome of decisions. Participants, however, would be predicting the consequence of a particular decision, not necessarily whether the decision maker will choose that decision, and thus they will not have to take into account the decision maker's own reasoning.

The self-deciding prediction market design also addresses another possible danger associated with using prediction markets to forecast the outcome of a decision: the possibility that some outcomes might be so improbable that market participants will not have an incentive adequately to investigate them. Suppose, for example, that a prediction market were used to assess the consequences of opening a particular factory. If it already were clear that the corporation was going to open the factory, then market participants would have virtually no incentive to research or correct mispricings on the conditional prediction market corresponding to the possibility that the factory would not be opened. The market might then make a highly unreliable prediction. The overall costs of this error are low, since the corporation would not open the factory anyway. Nonetheless, the error would tend to make conditional market predictions less useful to shareholders who are interested in monitoring the decisions of management.

In a self-deciding prediction market, it is still possible that some decisions will seem so bad that market participants will spend little time researching them and the predictions will still be quite noisy. Often, however, this will be a sensible allocation of participants' time. At least, there should not be situations in which the market prediction of an obviously bad decision is that the decision would be a good one. If the prediction indicated that a decision in fact would be good, then in a self-deciding prediction market, that decision might be adopted. Then, participants would have incentives to research the contingency that the decision might be adopted and given a small possibility that the decision might be enacted, participants will have an incentive to make accurate predictions about the effects of the decision. Because those predictions will be that the decision would be bad, the self-deciding prediction market will provide a natural corrective. In such a market, for any decision that plausibly might emerge as the best decision, participants will make their predictions on the assumption that this decision will be made. Only when a decision seems sure not to be recommended even after research will predictions be noisy, but the noise will not be so great as to make these decisions appear attractive.

Of course, empirical research is needed to verify just how well self-deciding prediction markets would function, and this presents an unfortunate chicken-and-egg problem. Corporate officials seem unlikely to trust conditional prediction markets until they have proved themselves to be accurate predictors, but as a result of the private decision maker information problem, the conditional prediction markets might make bad predictions. Self-deciding prediction markets might resolve the problem, but corporations certainly will not take this dramatic step until conditional prediction markets that are merely used to advise decision makers have proved themselves. This does not mean that conditional and self-deciding prediction markets are doomed. Chicken-and-egg problems often work themselves out; we do have both chickens and eggs. Perhaps conditional markets initially will be limited to questions about which there will be little private decision maker information. But this problem is one reason to suspect that prediction markets will not control corporate decision making for a long while.

REPLACING OR IMPROVING
SHAREHOLDER VOTING

The primary means by which shareholders today can influence a corporation is through occasional votes. For example, shareholders have the right to vote on directors, and shareholders have the right to issue proposals. These powers, however, are generally quite limited, at least in the United States. For example, shareholders generally do not have the power to propose a change in the state of incorporation or to alter the corporate charter.[15] Nor do shareholders have the power to make specific business decisions on behalf of the corporation. According to SEC rules, a company can exclude a shareholder proposal on any of a number of grounds, including the ground that the proposal is not a proper action for shareholders under state law.[16] Because state law generally gives the board of directors the power to act on behalf of the corporation, shareholders generally may not mandate specific approaches to business strategy, although they can recommend, for example, that the board establish a committee to explore a particular issue.[17]

One possible reason why shareholders have so little direct control over corporations is that shareholders may have relatively little information, and each shareholder has only a small incentive to become educated about particular issues. As Lucian Bebchuk points out, this does not provide a strong argument against giving shareholders more power. There are at least some issues, such as issues concerning general governance structure, about which management might be expected to have little inside information, and where management does have such information, it can convey it to shareholders by making recommendations about particular shareholder proposals or about particular candidates for directorships.[18]

Bebchuk argues that even if shareholders generally would defer to the views of management, the benefits of broader shareholder voting power would be relatively high because of the indirect effect of robust shareholder voting on manager incentives,[19] and he maintains that the costs of nuisance proposals would be relatively low.[20] Whether or not Bebchuk is right about these issues, individual shareholders and institutional investors might spend less time than would be optimal for full consideration of the relevant issues, and yet the total amount of time spent by all shareholders on consideration of issues might be more than is necessary. Shareholder voting places light demands on many instead of heavy demands on a few who would be best able to make assessments.

One simple alternative to shareholder voting would be to use a normative prediction market. The market would predict whether a randomly selected shareholder would vote for or against a particular proposal; those owning more shares would have a greater chance of being selected. The randomly selected shareholder's decision would itself receive little weight, but the assurance that it would occur would help discipline the prediction market forecasts. This system economizes on shareholder time by lowering the probability that any particular shareholder will have to consider an issue. A potential problem, however, is that the randomly selected shareholder might not have much incentive to consider the issue in detail, though perhaps the novelty of being selected might increase the shareholder's attention to the issue. A prediction market forecast of a superficial decision might itself be superficial if a particular issue demands subtle analysis.

Self-deciding prediction markets also could be better than shareholder voting, because they could improve the quality of analysis of difficult governance issues. An appropriately designed conditional prediction market can give a relatively small number of parties strong incentives to conduct research and analysis to determine the effect of a possible decision on the share price. At least with prediction market structures that overcome the danger of low liquidity, such as the market scoring rule, the number of participants and the amount of research that they conduct can be expected to adjust to a roughly optimal level. For example, regarding a question for which analysis is easy but opinion may differ greatly, one can expect more participants in the market. Given a much harder question, however, a relatively small number of parties are likely to conduct research and aggressively back the predictions that they develop.

Normative prediction markets or self-deciding prediction markets with sufficiently large subsidies could thus prove superior to shareholder voting. That does not mean, however, that prediction markets cannot improve shareholder voting unless they are self-deciding. Conditional prediction markets and shareholder voting regimes can serve complementary functions. Prediction markets can provide information to shareholders, who then could set corporate policy with a vote, taking into account their own independent views, as well as the recommendations of both the prediction markets and management. Although Bebchuk might be right that the possibility of management recommendations provides a strong argument for empowering shareholders, better information for shareholders can't hurt, at least if it is cheap enough to produce. The better the information available to shareholders, the more seriously management might take their recommendations, and the more shareholders might legitimately object to management decisions to ignore their recommendations.

Whether prediction markets make or recommend policies, additional prediction markets might be used to make decisions about the establishment of conditional prediction markets. For example, prediction markets might be used to sort through initial shareholder proposals to determine which seem promising enough to be subject to a vote. Under current rules in the United States, shareholders holding a sufficient number of votes generally can force a vote, but only on a narrow range of issues.[21] As a result, many shareholder proposals, whatever their merits for society at large, are nuisance proposals that stand relatively little chance of passage. One use of prediction markets would be to gauge the probability that particular proposals would pass if placed on the ballot. All prediction market proposals exceeding some threshold could be presented to shareholders.

Prediction markets also might be used to determine the amount by which a particular prediction market ought to be subsidized. In theory, a prediction market should be subsidized to the point where the marginal increment in subsidy produces an equal marginal benefit, but this can be a difficult calculation in practice. A simple approach might be to use a conditional prediction market to forecast a corporate stock price provided that different subsidy levels are used for a particular prediction market. This seems likely to work only for shareholder proposals that plausibly might have significant effects on the stock price. An alternative approach would be to use a prediction market to assess the expected total volatility of a conditional prediction market, contingent on the subsidy level. Higher subsidies should generally produce greater research and thus greater price changes, but beyond a certain point, the effects might be small. Such a prediction market could be used to ensure that subsidies are at least high enough to allow research that seems reasonably likely to affect predictions.

THE DANGER OF INEFFICIENT MARKETS

An important argument against increasing reliance on prediction markets in the corporate context is that if prediction markets are inaccurate, then their

misleading forecasts might lead to bad decision making. Of course, all proposals to use prediction markets depend at least implicitly on the proposition that
the markets are accurate, at least relative to plausible alternatives. Ultimately,
empirical work is needed to establish how accurate prediction markets are. The
evidence that we have seen so far is encouraging. It is hard to look, for example,
at the trading patterns in the Iowa Electronic Markets and detect significant
shifts in prices that seem unrelated to the underlying dynamics of the various
election races. Nonetheless, accuracy is a matter of degree, and further experiments may help to show the degree to which increases in market subsidies improve accuracy. Skeptics, moreover, might claim that a consideration of only
evidence of the accuracy of prediction markets is too narrow, for our broader
experience with the accuracy of market pricing is relevant to the issue of prediction markets. Indeed, these skeptics are likely to argue that evidence suggests
that there are inefficiencies in securities markets generally and in the stock market in particular, and that prediction markets might inherit these inefficiencies.

Not so long ago, claims that securities markets could be inefficient seemed to
many observers to be unfounded. One reason is that there seemed to be a
strong theoretical case that markets would be self-correcting. In 1953 Milton
Friedman, arguing for flexible rather than fixed exchange rates, offered two
simple reasons why "noise traders" acting on the basis of pet theories rather
than evidence would not influence securities prices.[22] First, other traders would
have incentives to function as arbitrageurs and bet against the noise traders. Indeed, the presence of noise traders should increase the overall incentives to participate in the market because they make it possible to make money by trading.
This rationale is, of course, similar to the simple theoretical case for prediction
markets: that they give incentives for people with relatively good information
to profit from that information by in effect betting against those with worse
information. Second, the noise traders should tend to lose money and thus
disappear from the market over time. By the same token, this Darwinian theory suggests that the most successful traders will tend to increase the money
they have available to invest.

In addition to this simple theoretical argument, until recently it seemed that
at least some versions of the Efficient Capital Markets Hypothesis had a robust
empirical foundation, for example, in studies indicating that it was not possible
to predict the future direction of stock prices from past prices.[23] In its
strongest form, the hypothesis states that markets incorporate all information,
both public and private. That view long ago proved untenable for at least two
reasons. First, there are instances in which insider trading laws do succeed at

preventing private information from being incorporated into securities prices. This will not always be so, and there is substantial evidence that insider trading occurs; one interesting study shows that members of Congress earn significantly higher returns than one would ordinarily expect, suggesting that they have inside information.[24] But sometimes, public release of information previously known to private parties has an effect on market prices. Second, it is often expensive to find and analyze information. Thus, defenders of the hypothesis acknowledge that information will be incorporated into market prices only to the extent that it is cost-effective to trade on the information.[25]

In spite of these caveats, acceptance of the Efficient Capital Markets Hypothesis would tend to limit concerns about inaccuracy in prediction markets to concerns that there might be too little incentive in some contexts to find and analyze information. Recent developments in the finance literature, however, suggest that even this weaker version of the hypothesis might be vulnerable. In particular, a large literature has developed concerning "behavioral finance," elaborating how human cognitive heuristics and biases might lead to systematic distortions in market pricing. Models suggest that in some circumstances well-informed traders might recognize that a market is in disequilibrium yet not have adequate incentive to engage in arbitrage to correct the disequilibrium. If such effects are sufficiently large, then markets sometimes might produce predictions that are not equivalent to what the best-informed individuals believe. The behavioral finance literature seeks to explain phenomena including "bubbles" such as the alleged technology bubble of the late 1990s that peaked in early 2000. If asset markets in general can be subject to bubbles, or for that matter to panics leading to depressions, then perhaps the same psychological factors can influence prediction markets as well.

The behavioral finance literature provides an important qualification to optimism about the power of markets to make predictions, but from a practical standpoint, the concerns do not seem to be of sufficiently high magnitude to bring into question most prediction market proposals. The ultimate question, after all, is not whether a prediction market is a perfect predictive tool but whether it is the best available predictor. Virtually no one suggests that the literature would justify replacement of our securities markets with a radically different institution. Although there are some who advocate consolidating investment decisions in a centralized government decision maker,[26] it is generally thought that the incentives of government officials to make decisions about which business ventures are likely to succeed would be inadequate. Private markets, whatever their flaws, seem likely to allocate scarce social resources more efficiently. Similarly, though prediction markets have imperfections, for some but not all predictive decision making proposals, these imperfections may be small relative to the flaws of the governmental decision-making approach that they seek to replace. Occasional gross mispricing, if such a phenomenon could be identified with confidence, would not necessarily justify abandonment of the technique.

It would be a mistake, moreover, to infer that any market inefficiencies in securities markets generally will necessarily carry over to prediction markets. The concept of a prediction market, we have seen, does not refer to any single implementation but rather to a class of approaches that give financial incentives to individuals who sequentially make predictions about an event of interest. The probability estimate prediction market and numeric estimate prediction market introduced in Chapter 1 seem akin to classic securities markets, but even with these market designs, investors might behave differently. Prediction markets would not ordinarily be useful vehicles for retirement, because investments in them do not have a systematic upward trend, and so the investors choosing to place money into prediction markets on the whole might be a more sophisticated group. The systematic upward trend in the stock market means that many foolish investors will make some money, but it might be much harder for noise traders to make money on prediction markets. Even with subsidized prediction markets, potential noise traders should recognize at least that they should focus on prediction markets in which they might have some insight about the variable being predicted.

Unsophisticated investors who choose to invest in prediction markets might be more sophisticated about their predictions than they are about their decisions whether to move funds into the stock market. Some people, for example, might try to "time" the stock market. An empirical study analyzing ninety-one thousand investors in an index fund shows that investors can be grouped into two rough categories: those who generally seek to follow trends and those who generally act against trends.[27] Individuals who blindly follow stock market trends, potentially providing a feedback effect that can lead to a bubble, might not follow prediction market trends. Someone might mistakenly believe that if the stock market is going up it will keep going up but not believe that because George W. Bush's probability of winning has risen from 50 percent to 60 percent in the past week in the Iowa Electronic Markets that inevitably his price will keep rising. For one thing, it will be obvious to participants that the trend is not sustainable, that Bush will never have a 110 percent chance of winning.

Indeed, those who are most skeptical about the efficiency of the stock market might not be skeptical of the accuracy of individual prediction markets. For example, Robert Shiller, a leading behavioral finance theorist, has emphasized that "no one should conclude from any of my or others' research on financial markets that these markets are totally crazy."[28] Rather, he believes that "the *aggregate stock market* in the United States in the last century has been driven primarily by psychology and fads."[29] Even if psychological factors determine whether many Americans put their money in the stock market or under their mattresses, the ratio among the prices of individual securities may still be meaningful. Participants in prediction markets do not simply put their money "in the market," causing occasional bouts of systematic irrational exuberance, but must make specific predictions in one direction or another. Given the heterogeneity of markets, there seems to be no reason to suspect that investors would conclude that as a general matter it makes sense to push all predictions up or all predictions down.

Prediction market forecasts in many cases also might be simpler to make than stock market predictions. Shiller points out that "investing for the long term means judging the distant future, judging how history will be made, how society will change, how the world economy will change. . . . With such a confusion of factors, it is hard for anyone to make objective judgments without being influenced by the recent success behavior of the market and the recent success of investments."[30] Modeling the result of a presidential race might also involve many imponderables, and the most sophisticated prediction market participants will do a better job of assessing these than will others. But because these imponderables will have largely marginal effects, with basics such as poll numbers largely determining prices, investors are less likely to throw up their hands and focus solely on immediate past trends. Of course, some prediction markets might involve forecasts that are just as difficult as anticipating the future success of the stock market, and with those markets, psychological factors might have more of an effect.

Another reason that anomalies in the stock market might not appear in prediction markets is that the mechanisms by which the markets operate might be different. Would anomalies observed in traditional stock markets also occur in the dynamic pari-mutuel market? In the market scoring rule, which seems more like a series of bets than a market in any meaningful sense? Some behavioral finance anomalies might persist in a wide variety of market designs, but in other cases, market design might make bubbles and other observable deviations from rationality less sustainable. Of course, prediction markets might introduce anomalies and imperfections of their own, but the literature identifying specific anomalies in stock market investing, such as the closed-end fund anomaly,[31] might not be helpful in anticipating particular reasons that prediction markets might be inaccurate. It is possible that some pathologies of the stock market will have analogues in prediction markets, but prediction market design might limit or exacerbate these pathologies.

One possible source of volatility in markets is people's overreaction to the information of others. Kenneth French and Richard Roll point out, for example, that if the first ten trades on a particular stock all happen to be sell orders one morning, other traders "might draw the reasonable conclusion that something bad has happened to the company," and their sales might induce others to sell as well.[32] Colin Camerer and Keith Weigelt conducted a laboratory experiment in which they sought to identify such "information mirages."[33] The experimental design spanned a number of periods, and in each period all experimental subjects shared certain public information about the price of an experimental asset. In some cases, however, some randomly chosen subjects also received additional inside information about the price. Of a total of forty-seven periods in which no such information existed, in a total of four periods a mirage occurred in which traders acted as if some information did exist. "Sustained mirages do occur," Camerer and Weigelt conclude, "but they are not common."[34]

Something similar could occur in a prediction market. Suppose that different predictors in a market have different levels of information, with some predictors functioning as "noise traders" who have no information at all making predictions based on crackpot theories that well-informed traders would discount. Because each predictor has only a limited amount of information available, predictors should discount their own views to some extent and give weight to the predictions of other traders. Occasionally a predictor might misestimate the quality of information possessed by other predictors. Sometimes this might mean that the market insufficiently reflects good information, but at other times this might mean that the market places too much weight on a meaningless prediction. The eventual market prediction might thus be a mirage, a result of misinterpretation of activity in the market itself. In the situations in which a mirage occurs, other prediction mechanisms might have outperformed the market.

There are at least two reasons that this type of flawed derivatively informed trading does not provide a strong argument against prediction markets. First, the reason that predictors pay attention to others' predictions is rational, and so given a set of predictions in the market, predictors in settings outside the market would have an incentive to take the trades into account. Sometimes information signals that are valuable as a general matter will lead predictors astray. For example, I might decide to bet against a horse only because I find out that the horse did not eat well that morning. I conclude that the horse might be ill, and yet he just might not have liked his oats, and he might win the race. That does not mean that information about horses' eating habits reduces my predictive accuracy or the overall market's. Presumably, the overall accuracy of the markets that Camerer and Weigelt studied would have been reduced if there were no way for traders to divine other traders' information. Relying on others' predictions, like relying on information about a horse's eating, will tend to make one's own predictions and the market's consensus predictions more rather than less accurate, though in some cases the information will lead to mistaken inferences.

Second, many of the prediction markets imagined in this book would involve a relatively small number of participants with relatively high amounts of private information or private analysis about the event being predicted. This will not be true of all prediction markets; the presidential election prediction markets, for example, attract a large number of participants, and there is relatively little private information. When it is true, however, market participants will not simply look for oddball trading patterns but might also consider the reputation and track record of other predictors. Especially in contexts in which some outsiders will have incentives to manipulate the market, prediction market participants will be hesitant to place much weight on the actions of traders without strong track records. Moreover, with a deliberative prediction market design, market participants will have incentives to reveal their underlying reasoning, and others will have incentives to scrutinize that reasoning, so errors and arbitrary decision making might more easily be exposed.

A more difficult scenario is one in which the noise traders, instead of posting arbitrary bets, make systematic errors. Perhaps the most prominent explanation of inefficient markets, developed by J. Bradford De Long, Andrei Shleifer, Lawrence Summers, and Robert Waldmann, relies on such a scenario.[35] Suppose, for example, that a large number of noise traders irrationally think that technology stocks are worth much more than well-informed traders think they are likely to be worth. Rational arbitrageurs will bet against these noise traders by, for example, selling technology stocks short (that is, borrowing shares and selling them in the hope of making profit if the price goes down). But they might not do so sufficiently aggressively to counter the noise traders.

One reason is that there might be some underlying fundamental risk in the securities being traded. The rational parties do not want to assume the risk that technology stocks will appreciate for reasons having nothing to do with the noise traders' predictions.

An additional reason is that the noise traders' actions directly create some additional risk. The rational arbitrageurs may care not only about their long-term profits but also about their medium-term profits. For example, if they have borrowed stocks and then sold them in the hope that the price of the stocks will fall, a strategy known as "short selling," at some point they will have to return those stocks. If the noise traders continue to overvalue technology stocks at that time, then the rational arbitrageurs will lose money. It is not enough to know that a market is in a bubble to profit from that bubble; one must also be able to guess when the bubble will pop, and that must occur sufficiently soon that it will be profitable to bet against the noise traders. They, meanwhile, can be expected to survive in the market, potentially for a long time. Indeed, their willingness to take on risk that the rational arbitrageurs seek to avoid, De Long and his coauthors point out, means that for long periods of time, they may earn higher returns than will the rational parties. This, of course, will encourage even more traders to follow the irrational theory.

Similar dynamics could affect prediction markets, too. Suppose, for example, that a group of Green Party voters have deluded themselves into thinking that their candidate will win the presidency. Sensing a profit opportunity, they buy up TradeSports shares in the Green Party candidate. There might be some limit to the willingness of other market participants to seek to counter this activity (for example, by shorting shares, if TradeSports permitted this). There might be a small risk that the Green Party candidate would surge to victory and a larger risk that the price level could fail to fall for a sufficiently long period of time that arbitrageurs could lose money in the short term. The scenario might be more plausible if the Green Party candidate had some chance of winning, but that chance was considerably smaller than the deluded voters thought.

This scenario seems much less likely than the bubble story that De Long and his coauthors tell, even putting aside the fact that there is no reason to suspect that there would be a group of voters with such an odd prediction. The presidential election will necessarily occur at a particular point in time, whereas stocks generally represent income streams flowing into the indefinite future. This reduces the danger that a bubble will be prolonged and increases the ability of arbitrageurs confidently to combat the foolish trading. Support for this theory comes from a study finding that noise trader sentiment does not affect market price in futures markets that clear at some specific point in the future.[36] Of course, some prediction markets might last for a very long period of time, so in these markets, the danger is somewhat greater. Also, deliberative prediction markets might make the problem worse, because participants would be betting on the price in the next time period rather than on the closing price. In these situations, however, the knowledge that the bubble will necessarily pop by a certain date might lead the bubble to pop well before that date. Arbitrageurs, for example, can seek to obtain loans to be repaid after that date.

Another explanation for bubbles is that in some cases, it might be infeasible for arbitrageurs to short overpriced securities because there might be an insufficient number of such shares to sell. Robert Shiller points out that as arbitrageurs sought to attack the shares of Palm, Inc., they created so much demand for the shares that "the interest cost of borrowing Palm shares reached 35 percent by July 2000, putting a damper on the advantage to exploiting the mispricing."[37] Eli Ofek and Matthew Richardson have argued that restrictions on selling short played a significant role more generally in the alleged technology bubble.[38] This thesis is controversial. Robert Battalio and Paul Schultz argue that more complete data suggest that options prices tracked stock prices so closely during the alleged bubble that possibilities for arbitrage existed for anyone who recognized the existence of the bubble.[39] Nonetheless, if the thesis is correct, the bubble was largely an artifact of the mechanism (short selling) through which traders can profit on a belief that securities are overpriced.

Market mechanisms that save arbitrageurs from the formalities associated with short selling might be able to help. For example, the Iowa Electronic Markets allows any trader to pay one dollar to receive a share in each candidate. An arbitrageur thus does not need directly to short shares or to pay interest charges in doing so but can simply buy shares in all candidates and then sell shares in an overvalued candidate or buy shares in an undervalued candidate. Similarly, the market scoring rule simply allows an arbitrageur to enter a new prediction, and if that prediction is better than the last one, the arbitrageur can expect to make money. With the market scoring rule, the ultimate question becomes which group—the noise traders or the fundamental values traders—will give up first, no longer willing in effect to take bets from the other group. It seems unlikely that there would be many contexts in which the noise traders with a bad theory would have more financial strength than all other traders combined.

Arbitrageurs also tend to have more luck correcting mispricing in prediction markets when there are many prediction markets and the varieties of mispricing differ from one market to another. Andrei Shleifer and Robert Vishny note that one source of systematic deviations from underlying value in markets is that investors "rationally allocate money based on past returns of arbitrageurs," and so arbitrageurs have some incentive to seek to ride a market bubble for some period of time.[40] Survey evidence suggests that investors attempt to do precisely this.[41] The problem is more serious when the mispriced securities form a large portion of the arbitrageurs' portfolio. When mispricing occurs in a single prediction market, the risk from a sustained bubble is not great for arbitrageurs who make predictions in a variety of prediction markets. In such cases, arbitrageurs recognize that they may need to wait out some bubbles longer than others, but the happenstance of an occasional long wait will not prevent them from taking advantage of mispricing.

Some of the problems that can beset stock markets, however, could be at least as serious with many prediction markets. De Long and his coauthors suggest that one underlying psychological mechanism leading to bubbles is that people suffer from a "tendency to underestimate variances and to be overconfident" about their predictions.[42] Experts are vulnerable to this tendency, and prediction markets might tend to attract individuals who are particularly confident, perhaps overconfident, with respect to the particular question posed by the prediction market. This might seem likely to produce systematic errors in probability estimation prediction markets, with too few predictions in the middle of the probability spectrum. This claim is empirically testable, however, indeed more easily testable with prediction markets than in the stock market, because the former eventually end. The preliminary evidence appears to suggest that large errors of this kind do not seem to occur in the prediction markets for which data are available so far (see Chapter 1). Whatever subsequent evidence reveals, analysis of this sort seems more likely to help assess the accuracy of prediction markets than does theorizing about inefficient securities markets in general.

Nonetheless, if securities markets are inefficient, prediction markets that forecast stock prices might be inefficient even if prediction market mechanisms do not inherit the problems of securities markets directly. For example, if a prediction market is gauging the stock price of Google one year hence, and participants believe that Google is in a bubble that is unlikely to pop within a year, then the prediction market will reflect the bubble price. The market price itself would not be a bubble, but an accurate prediction would reflect the bubble in the underlying market. If bubbles are a sufficient concern, it might make sense for prediction markets to take a longer-term perspective. For example, they might forecast the effect of different possible decisions about stock price (controlling, of course, for possible stock splits and dividend payments) five years into the future. As long as a prediction market takes a sufficiently long-term perspective, then the only bubbles that we need to worry about are those within the prediction market itself.

SELECTION, DISMISSAL, AND COMPENSATION OF CEOS

Even if prediction markets are efficient, they cannot easily be used for all decisions. Consider, for example, one of the most significant decisions that a corporation faces, the selection of its CEO. The need for secrecy probably makes self-deciding prediction markets to pick a CEO infeasible, unless they are limited to a small group of people who can be trusted to keep the market activity confidential. This would not be a problem for conditional markets concerning CEO dismissal, a use of conditional markets originally suggested by Robin Hanson.[43] Such markets might be used to predict corporate performance on the condition that the CEO remains with the firm for various lengths of time. Such conditional markets might be biased in favor of CEOs, because if a CEO does stay for a long time, that may be a result of, rather than a cause of, strong performance. A self-deciding prediction market making a decision about whether to dismiss the CEO over a brief period of time would not suffer from this problem, however.

An argument against using prediction markets to forecast the effects of dismissal or at least against relying too heavily on such markets, is that an optimal compensation contract might include some explicit or implicit assurances that a particular official will be able to retain a job if things are going somewhat badly. More generally, managers might be hesitant to work at companies in which they expected frequently to be second-guessed by prediction markets. Although monitoring technologies can reduce agency costs, they might reduce employee morale. This surely explains why few employers have installed video cameras that allow them to monitor employees. Of course, prediction markets might be used to determine whether prediction markets should be used to assess whether a CEO should be dismissed or, indeed, to assess the wisdom of any other application of prediction markets. Especially in the early history of prediction markets, when the effects are unknown and the markets are relatively untested, it is plausible that prediction markets would conclude that using prediction markets to monitor the CEO or individual employees would be inefficient.

Prediction markets might be used with less objection to assess explicit terms of compensation contracts. This is particularly useful because of the difficulty in finding truly independent (rather than merely nominally independent) decision makers to make compensation decisions. Suppose, for example, that a salary increase or other change in compensation is proposed for the CEO. A conditional prediction market, self-deciding or not, could be used to predict whether the stock price would be higher or lower with the compensation change. Prediction market participants would have an incentive to consider that the lower salary, although it would save the corporation a direct expenditure, might increase the possibility that the CEO will leave the company. At the same time, participants would have incentives to assess the degree to which different compensation packages might motivate the CEO or directors to improve stock performance. A similar approach might be used to evaluate specific potential offers to be made to any particular CEO candidate, and conditional markets also might be applied to set the terms of director compensation.

Chapter 8 Courts

We have already considered several proposals for providing information and predictions to judges to help them improve their decision making. In Chapter 4, for example, we saw that subsidized deliberative prediction markets might be used to give participants incentives to offer legal arguments that are relevant to particular cases. These prediction markets would both predict judicial decisions and provide analysis that judges deciding particular cases might wish to take into account. In Chapter 5 I suggested that to the extent that federal judges are making predictions when deciding questions of state law or when resolving ambiguities in statutory interpretation, prediction markets might provide a better basis for decision making. Also in that chapter, I noted that courts might rely on prediction markets in making interim decisions, such as whether to impose temporary restraining orders or injunctions. Finally, in Chapter 6, we saw that prediction markets might be useful not only because they could help judges who are interested in their predictions but also because they might constrain judges by increasing in some cases the reputational cost a judge suffers from pursuing an idiosyncratic policy agenda under the guise of hard-look review.

All of these proposals can be considered only speculative possibilities, at least until sufficient experimentation and attention lead judges and observers of the judiciary to accept prediction markets as something more than a curiosity. This chapter considers a yet more speculative possibility: that prediction markets might be used not merely to assist jurists but to perform their work. It might seem at first that a prediction market could not perform the task of adjudication because adjudication tends to be retrospective, whereas prediction is inherently a forward-looking task. We have seen, however, that prediction markets can be used to aggregate preferences. Moreover, these preferences can concern relatively abstract issues such as the weight to give to different types of evidence in statutory interpretation (see Chapter 6), not simply ultimate policy reasoning. Just as a prediction market can be used to produce a cost-benefit analysis that incorporates all considerations that ex post decision makers might be expected to view as relevant, so, too, can one be used to produce a legal analysis incorporating all relevant factors, including the importance of honoring legislative intent. It would be possible, in short, to use prediction markets to anticipate how judges on average would resolve issues in cases and to make the predictions rather than the judicial assessments determinative.

That prediction markets can be used to accomplish a decision-making task does not mean that they should be used in that way. A significant factor that might counsel against widespread adoption of prediction markets in legal markets is that the public may attach a majesty to judicial decision making and perhaps more to jury decision making. Charles Nesson, for example, has argued that the criminal law seeks to instill public confidence by minimizing the intrusion of probabilistic reasoning into the process.[1] Although I am skeptical that his description is accurate,[2] it remains possible that widespread use of market mechanisms might lead the public to be more skeptical of judicial decisions. My own view is that this would probably be for the best and that greater public awareness of the inherent difficulties of adjudication would not increase public unrest. There may, however, be an even stronger case in the judicial than in other contexts for postponing adoption of prediction market mechanisms until the public generally becomes more comfortable with them.

In some contexts—those involving money and not greatly affecting individual rights—concerns about public confidence seem minimal. Moreover, I argue, there are potential benefits of adjudication through prediction markets instead of more traditional adjudication. These benefits are the same that we have seen in other prediction market contexts. Adjudication is a process that involves the aggregation of information, and prediction markets provide incentives for participants to take all relevant information into account and, with sufficient subsidies, to seek out new evidence and analysis regarding particular questions. In addition, the adjudicative process presents a risk analogous to that of ideology in the context of administrative agencies: that judges might have idiosyncratic preferences about issues, adding substantial randomness to case resolution. Prediction markets can smooth out idiosyncrasies and potentially result in more consistent adjudication. The judicial process seeks to apply our collective preferences about the law (including preferences about high-level principles such as the importance of following precedent) to the facts of particular cases. Prediction markets can perform both tasks effectively.

Perhaps the most obvious advantage of prediction markets compared to conventional forms of adjudication is that they present the opportunity for simplified judicial procedure. I thus begin this chapter by explaining how procedural rules can increase litigation expense. I then describe probabilistic prediction markets, a form of conditional prediction market in which the event being forecast is used to resolve prediction market payouts only on occasion. This is useful when it is expensive to conduct the event being predicted or to come up with an ex post measurement used to discipline a prediction market. In a probabilistic prediction market for adjudication, some percentage of cases would be selected for traditional adjudication, and the remaining cases would be resolved by the market prediction, thus saving much of the expense of traditional adjudication. I then discuss the ways prediction markets might be used to conduct small claims cases and argue that market-based adjudication might share some of the virtues of the common law.

A drawback of probabilistic prediction markets, indeed, a drawback of conditional markets more generally, is that they can increase the risk associated with market participation. I explain how the cost of that risk can be reduced. I also consider a variety of other applications of prediction markets in the judicial context and suggest that market-based adjudication might be most useful for causes of action that are simply infeasible under existing procedural constraints. In particular, normative probabilistic prediction markets could be used to allow for relatively efficient adjudication under a vague standard, even when standards would lead to excessive disparities and litigation costs in more traditional adjudication. Such markets might be used to implement legislation adjustment assistance, with which individuals adversely affected by specified legislation could seek a tailored redress, or a system of penalizing excessive spending in litigation itself. Prediction markets also might be used as alternatives to existing mechanisms that seek to encourage whistle-blowing, for example, against companies that have defrauded the government. Finally, I consider the possibilities that prediction markets might be used to supervise the discovery process and might have a role in the criminal justice process.

THE PROBLEM OF PROCEDURAL EXPENSE

Litigation is expensive. But is it too expensive? Charles Silver has argued that it might not be.[3] Silver points out that in assessing litigation expense, one cannot consider only matters that are tried because many cases are settled out of court, and what is relevant is how much is spent on average, not how much is spent in the cases that prove resistant to private agreement.[4] Indeed, it may be arbitrary to consider only cases in which a complaint is filed, because many disputes are settled without any formal resort to legal process.[5] Settlement occurs in the "shadow of the law,"[6] and so if the legal system is successful at generating settlements, it may not be too expensive overall. Moreover, Silver argues, litigants will rationally reduce their own expenses when possible, and they may cooperate to resolve many procedural issues without judicial intervention.[7] In short, Silver suggests, the reason that litigation costs as much as it does is that it is expensive to figure out how much lawsuits are worth and to negotiate agreements.

There is a strong theoretical reason, however, to suspect that the amount spent on litigation is generally socially excessive. The reason is that in deciding how much to spend on each phase of litigation, a litigant considers the personal benefit and costs rather than the social ones. These diverge, because additional spending at least has an expected negative effect on the adverse party, either by reducing the probability that the other party will win (always an intended effect) or by increasing the amount that the other party must spend in response (often an intended effect, if a prohibited one).[8]

It is possible to imagine a spare litigation process in which each side spends only a few dollars gathering the essential evidence needed to make its case and the judge spends a few minutes on a decision. This is probably suboptimal, because increased spending will increase the accuracy of adjudication, producing benefits such as increasing the reliability of contracting and deterrence of tortfeasors. But litigants have incentives to spend more than the social optimum at each stage of the litigation. From a private perspective, a litigant should spend until the marginal dollar spent produces a marginal dollar in private return, but from the social perspective, optimal spending should generally be lower than this.[9]

If judges could be made to work for free, and courthouses could be constructed at no cost, the problem of excessive litigation expense would persist. The central problem is that clients spend too much on lawyers who gather information and advocate for them. To some extent, however, the structure of the litigation process itself increases client spending. This is especially so for the relatively few cases that go to trial. Trials are expensive in part because all of the participants, including the lawyers and witnesses, must come together in a common location, which may well be far from where some of them live. Much of the direct and cross examination is repetitive for the parties, at least whenever the questioning repeats exchanges from prior depositions and interrogatories. In an era before videotaping became inexpensive, these expenses could perhaps be justified by the theory that it is difficult to evaluate witnesses from reading deposition transcripts. This might not be true; there is some psychological evidence that people perform better at truth-telling when reading than when watching testimony.[10] The justification, however, seems even more limited today. In the vast majority of cases, any improvement in adjudicative accuracy gained from in-person presentation seems unlikely to be worth the cost.

The civil trial is an anachronism. Perhaps there are cases in which the common presence of the litigants and the decision maker bears an important social meaning. There are, however, many cases in which the most important process values are accuracy and economy. Paul Carrington has argued that improvements in digital communications technology will lead to "virtual trials."[11] "A trial," Carrington predicts, "will normally be a movie presentation."[12] He leaves open the possibility that courts sometimes might insist on the presentation of a particular witness where demeanor evidence is critical, though given the ability to view recorded testimony, he believes that this could be rare.[13] The virtual trial could also allow fact-finders access to recordings of physical evidence, in particular documents, though again there might be some situations in which there will be no substitute for the original.

Virtual trials could spare jurors from having to wait during legal sparring over objections and sidebar conferences, and lawyers might further be encouraged to edit out irrelevant questioning.[14] Carrington even suggests that appeals can occur in advance of trials, so that the legal system can settle on the appropriate presentation to the fact-finder before the fact-finder is summoned.[15] This would eliminate the need for the "harmless error doctrine," under which courts conclude that fact-finders would not have been affected by trial mistakes.

Carrington's virtual legal system would help reduce the cost of trial, although he recognizes that "[n]either the profession, nor the courts, nor the litigants . . . are ready for it."[16] The legal system evolves so slowly that neither Carrington's proposal nor most of the proposals given in this book can be seen as imminent. If we are imagining potential improvements to our legal system that theoretically could be made, however, we might take a step beyond what Carrington has suggested. He imagines that the fundamental structure of the legal system and of the trial would remain the same, with judges and juries assuming their usual duties in the resolution of questions of law and fact. But if prediction markets were commonplace, centralized decision making could become as anachronistic as centralized presentation of testimony and evidence.

Using a single, randomly selected judge or jury adds randomness to the judicial process. Why not instead use a prediction market to anticipate what decision makers on average would decide if a case were taken to trial? Assuming that prediction markets in fact are effective vehicles for analyzing facts, they can reach verdicts more consistently than can the committee that we call the civil jury. And if prediction markets excel at aggregating normative views, they can resolve legal issues with more consistency than can individual judges or appellate panels.

These proposals can be justified both as measures to improve the consistency of the adjudicative process and as measures to reduce cost. Given the rarity of trial, it might seem that the cost savings would be relatively insignificant, especially in comparison to the subsidies that would be needed to give prediction market participants incentives to evaluate evidence. Indeed, whereas decentralized information processing may be better than centralized information processing, reducing individual variations and errors, there is no inherent reason why it should be cheaper. If we hope for more decision makers to assess the relevant evidence, decentralized evaluation can be more expensive. In the judicial context, however, there is a strong reason to believe that decentralized evaluation can reduce cost: prediction markets decrease the need for formality. The ability to eliminate the formality of the trial is but one manifestation of this. Much of the formality of legal systems in general is attributable to the centralized nature of decision making.

Why don't we allow judges to resolve cases in whatever way they deem most efficient? One might imagine a world in which judges, after receiving a complaint, could take whatever approach to the resolution of the case they thought best. They might pick up the phone to call a few witnesses or the lawyers and might allow the parties to submit evidence in whatever form they thought most convenient. The judges might then ask for additional evidence where needed. At some point, they could simply declare a winner of the trial. Even when the judge is fact-finder, we do not take this approach, and for good reason. The system presents the danger that judges would shirk, resolving boring cases prematurely. Forcing judges to hear all of the evidence that adversaries legitimately may introduce can ultimately improve decision making. Moreover, the formal nature of evidentiary presentation allows for judicial review, limiting the extent to which a judge's biases can influence the outcome. And so our legal system allows judges to resolve disputes prior to trial only when they can show that there is no legal claim or no disputed issue of material fact, not when they believe that one party will surely emerge as the winner.[17]

With prediction market adjudication, little formality would be necessary. Evidence could be uploaded to a central server at any time, and the market would continuously evaluate the strength of the evidence. Prediction market adjudication eliminates the concern that the decision maker will not have adequate incentives to consider all of the evidence. As long as the market is sufficiently subsidized, market participants will have incentives to evaluate whether the evidence is consistent with the current consensus prediction, because mispredictions present profit opportunities. At the same time, prediction market adjudication eliminates the concern that a particular judge's bias will lead to a poor decision. Market participants will have incentives to anticipate how judges on average will resolve cases. That means that one of the major justifications for appellate review, preventing idiosyncratic or biased decision making, is eliminated, too, and there is less of a need to maintain a formal record of the proceedings. To the extent that procedural rules are vehicles for constraining decision makers and limiting error, prediction market adjudication should make them less necessary.

Litigants would still have some incentive to cast evidence that they informally present to market participants in the best possible light. Instead of trying to convince a judge, they would need to convince the market. Nonetheless, it seems likely that litigants would not work as hard on polishing their presentation of evidence. Prediction market participants would have incentives to anticipate how persuasive evidence would be *if* a case were taken to trial and the lawyers made the best arguments that they could about that evidence. Litigants would offer detailed arguments about evidence only if they worried that no prediction market participants would call attention to important facts or arguments. In many cases it is not hard to extrapolate from a sample of the evidence the approximate probability that a case will be decided in favor of the plaintiff but in which the process of formally presenting the evidence, as each side tries to shift this probability slightly, can be time-consuming. Because prediction market adjudication is less dependent on any one decision maker, litigants might see less of a need to perfect their presentation.

PROBABILISTIC PREDICTION MARKETS

One way of implementing prediction markets that conduct adjudication is to use a probabilistic prediction market. In a simple version of a probabilistic prediction market, a random number is drawn at the conclusion of the prediction market to determine whether what the market was forecasting will in fact be measured.[18] Consider again, for example, the proposal for predictive cost-benefit analysis. Actually conducting an ex post cost-benefit analysis might be expensive, and so it might be desirable to have such analyses discipline prediction market decision making only some percentage of the time, say, 10 percent. A probabilistic prediction market can simply be a conditional prediction market in which the condition depends on the random number. Most straightforward, the unwinding approach (discussed in Chapter 5) could be used to cancel all of the transactions in the conditional market unless a random number drawn from 0 to 1 were less than 0.10. Market participants would then operate on the assumption that the condition will be met, anticipating the result of an ex post cost-benefit analysis although one might not be performed. The same approach can be used with litigation because the random number generator would lead to a trial only some of the time.

This approach might, however, make participation in the conditional market quite risky. A market participant might spend a great deal of time on a particular case, apparently earning a great deal of money based on market movements, only to have the case not be selected for adjudication. A possible result is that market participants would organize themselves into partnerships or other groups to pool this risk, even if such organization were not otherwise efficient. We have already seen, however, that conditional markets can be designed to reduce participation risk by using a two-stage structure (see Chapter 5). An initial prediction market would not be conditional, but it would be predicting the consensus prediction emerging from a second prediction market.

This second market would be a conditional market of the form described above, and the second market would conclude just before the random number generation.

The vast bulk of the market subsidy would be devoted to the first market, because the purpose of the second market would simply be to discipline the first, not to generate any new information. The second market could occur very quickly, and its modest subsidy would be sufficient to generate predictions that ordinarily would be approximately equal to the predictions of the first market. In most cases this second market would be unwound, but in a few cases (10 percent in the above example) payouts in the market would be resolved on the basis of the actual event being predicted, such as the predictive cost-benefit analysis. Given this approach, the probability in the second market might be made very low, perhaps just one in one hundred or one in one thousand, although it must be high enough that there remains some incentive to participate. With a low probability, the market would be predicting an event that is almost certain not to happen. Multiple stages could be used, with the second stage functioning as a conditional market predicting another conditional market in a third stage, so the probability of actual adjudication can be made arbitrarily low.

An important question in the design of a probabilistic prediction market is what the effect of a decision should be in the few cases in which an ex post decision actually is made. The decision must at least discipline the prediction market or, more precisely, the last-stage prediction market. But it need not necessarily do more. The occasional predictive cost-benefit analysis presumably would not have a direct effect on policy, except perhaps indirectly by slightly affecting what people think others might decide in future predictive cost-benefit analyses. With probabilistic adjudication, the adjudication need not have any direct effect on the original litigants. Because the prediction market process produces a virtual docket, there is relatively little need for further adversarial presentation. The ex post decision maker can simply consider the arguments and evidence previously logged by litigants and predictors on the Web site. It is possible that this would change his or her approach. Perhaps he or she will spend a little less time on the case, and that might be problematic when deeper analysis would tend to favor one side or the other. The caliber of individuals willing to be judges might decline, too. On the other hand, the ex post decision maker might be more inclined to decide on the basis of the law rather than personal sympathy, potentially providing for better decision making in that case and in others.

TRIAL BY MARKET

Robert Frost once wrote, "Modern poets talk against business, poor things, but all of us write for money. Beginners are subjected to trial by market."[19] Frost, of course, was not claiming that beginning poets literally were put on trial but that market forces would provide a metaphorical trial of their work. The quotation emphasizes that though we try to avoid market forces, they are inescapable. And so it is also with civil litigation. The civil litigation process is market-driven, with litigants generally trying to gain or keep as much money as possible and lawyers seeking to make money, too. It is a cardinal principal of judicial ethics, however, that the judge cannot have any direct financial interest in a litigation over which he or she presides.[20] Judicial income is largely independent of the quality of a judge's decisions, although some lower court judges might hope that writing good decisions (whatever those are) might lead to a promotion.[21] Perhaps removing financial incentives from judging frees judges to decide according to the rule of law.

And yet the reverse may also occur. Because there is no financial sanction for a bad decision, judges are free to ignore the rule of law in favor of their own policy preferences. Indeed, one might wonder whether providing direct financial incentives would improve judicial performance.[22] A relatively simple (albeit radical) means of accomplishing that aim would be to select randomly a subset of a judge's decisions, assign them to another judge selected at random (perhaps from an appellate pool), and give the initial judge a bonus if the second judge agrees with the first judge's conclusion. Judges' identities might be kept from one another to reduce the danger of collusion. This system would tend to discourage judges from being idiosyncratic by, for example, allowing their personal ideology to influence their decision making. Some might argue that idiosyncratic decision making is beneficial (see Chapter 6), but in my view the judicial system ordinarily should prefer to adopt a view that most judges would hold to than a view that only a few would hold. Of course, the second-level judges might still decide idiosyncratically, but the first-level judges would not know in advance if a second judge would evaluate the case, and if so who would be chosen.

Prediction market adjudication takes the logic a step farther. Nudging judges in the direction of deciding cases as other judges would is pushing them to make predictive decisions. Prediction markets can do this as well, and they can provide more than a nudge. Market participants may or may not care about how the case is resolved, but the provision of financial incentives will ensure that individual sympathies have little to no effect on market predictions. Even in a system that provides judges with financial incentives, a judge could decide that achieving a certain result is more valuable than the lost financial remuneration. With prediction markets, anyone trying to manipulate the market to achieve a particular result will need to overcome other market participants seeking to identify and bet against such attempts at manipulation. Attempts at manipulation not only may be expensive but also in general may not succeed. This does not necessarily mean that the prediction market's outcomes will be heartless. The market, for better or for worse, will still be forecasting the result of traditional adjudication, involving trial judges, juries, and appellate judges. But the market should help to avoid idiosyncratic outcomes.

And thus would "trial by market" become more than a metaphor. We could, of course, imagine making some modifications to trial by market. For example, we might limit participation to individuals selected through some sort of political process, such as that currently used to select judges. Further, we might allow only a small group of individuals to participate, perhaps one for trial proceedings or three for appellate proceedings. We might decide to ensure that each of these individuals has the same amount of money with which to bet on each case, prohibiting market participants from investing more in cases in which they have greater confidence. And we might require that all bets be placed at a single time, with the outcome simply the one that receives the most bets. Then we might decide not to use real money but to use play money instead, giving each of the authorized participants a play dollar to put on a particular outcome. Finally, we might call the play dollar a "vote" and the participants "judges," and we might recognize that we are left with something akin to the existing judicial system.

In each stage of this hypothetical transition from trial by market back to our current adjudicative world, a step is made that seems likely to reduce the incentives of the market participants individually and collectively to put aside their own views. Prediction markets may provide the most reliable available means of gauging how judges on average would apply the law to a particular set of facts. Arguments against trial by market thus seem likely to fall primarily into three groups: first, that prediction markets are not in fact sufficiently accurate; second, that idiosyncratic decision making is beneficial; and third, that market-based adjudication would undermine public confidence in law. All of these arguments might have merit given existing knowledge about and acceptance of prediction markets, at least for some kinds of cases. But the benefits of increasing consistency and information aggregation are sufficiently great that trial by market might prove viable in some collection of cases.

There are other benefits of trial by market. One follows directly from consistency: The practice might greatly reduce frivolous lawsuits. Suppose that a plaintiff believes that there is a 10 percent chance that a lawsuit would be successful in generating a particular level of damages. Despite concerns about litigation cost, a defendant would have an incentive to settle this suit at about 10 percent of the damages. Some have an intuition that this seems like a fair result, but there is a strong argument that this is not socially desirable. The percentages reflect the fact that the vast majority of decision makers believe that the plaintiff should not recover anything. If we adopt the assumption that the majority is more likely to be correct than the minority, at least more often than not, a legal system that insists on zero damages in such cases should be judged as more accurate than a legal system that allows ten percent damages. The system of trial by market could impose no damages when the legal system determines that less than 50 percent of cases would result in liability for the defendant and full damages when more than 50 percent of cases would result in liability. The result of this arrangement would be that there would be little incentive, placing litigation costs aside, for defendants to settle nuisance suits or for plaintiffs in meritorious suits to accept less than full damages.

The argument is borrowed from John Coons, who sought to justify our legal system's preponderance-of-the-evidence standard.[23] This standard results in imposition of full damages when a defendant is more likely than not responsible for a plaintiff's injuries and no damages when a defendant is less than 50 percent likely. An alternative regime would provide damages in proportion to the probability of liability. In a case in which the probability of liability is 90 percent, the choice between the preponderance regime and proportional damages is a choice about whether, given that a plaintiff will be awarded 90 percent of damages, the plaintiff will receive also the additional 10 percent of damages. There is a 90 percent chance that the plaintiff in fact should receive that 10 percent, too, and so the preponderance regime is superior to proportional damages. The argument is symmetric on the opposite side of the probability spectrum, and it can apply not just to the question of what damages should be awarded at trial but also to the question of whether the legal system should seek to discourage settlement of nuisance cases. Of course, trial by market could insist on proportional damages, and perhaps it should near the middle of the probability spectrum,[24] but a significant advantage of the system is that it could facilitate reduction of proportional settlements.

Trial by market itself would require a substantial subsidy in order to be successful, but there are several means by which it could reduce litigation costs. The continuous evaluation of evidence presented to a prediction market would facilitate negotiation. Ordinarily, litigants must anticipate how the decision makers (judge, jury, and appellate judges) will rule once all of the evidence has been provided. With a prediction market serving as adjudicator, litigants would be able to assess the adjudicator's current evaluation of all available evidence. There might still be situations in which litigants will not be able to agree on the value of a legal claim because, for example, they disagree about the effect that subsequent evidence might have on the prediction. Such inherent disagreement is likely, however, to be considerably rarer. The continuous prediction, meanwhile, would make it harder for litigants to bluff about their views of the claim's value in an effort to keep as much of the surplus from settlement as possible. The prediction market approach to adjudication thus can help eliminate two primary causes of failed settlement negotiations: asymmetric claim valuation and strategic bargaining.

The continuous evaluation of evidence also might limit costs by helping reduce excessive investment in litigation preparation. For example, a rule might provide for the automatic end of the case when the probability that a particular party would win fell below some threshold, such as 10 percent. Somewhat more elaborately, a conditional prediction market might be used to assess the probability, conditional on the allowing of further evidence, that the market's probability assessment will cross the 50 percent threshold. If there is only a low probability that any future evidence could change the market's prediction of what a majority of decision makers would decide, then that suggests that further presentation will not do any good. Such a prediction market might lead litigants voluntarily to give up losing causes, although a rule automatically ending a case past some level of futility could still be useful, because litigants generally wish to pursue a cause longer than would be socially optimal.

As a less radical example, the initial prediction market assessment might be used as a means of allocating fee-shifting. On the basis of the market assessment at some early point, the party that is expected to lose might be allowed to proceed only if the party agrees to assume the adversary's costs. To prevent this arrangement from leading the nonpaying party to generate excessive costs, the rule could limit fee-shifting to the amount spent by the paying party on its own costs.[25] This approach would alleviate a significant drawback of fee-shifting rules, namely, that they may tend to decrease settlement.[26] Because trial will occur anyway only where litigants are mutually optimistic, fee-shifting makes trial seem more attractive to both sets of litigants in cases in which trial is possible. A regime of ex ante fee shifting does not produce this problem, because the trial outcome has no effect on who pays the fees.[27] Ex ante fee-shifting based on prediction markets thus may be a more promising approach to eliminating both the filing of frivolous lawsuits and frivolous defenses of meritorious lawsuits.

Finally, trial by market also could alleviate jurisdictional wrangling. If the prediction market is anticipating the outcome of traditional adjudication, then it can simply weigh the probabilities that this traditional adjudication might be held in various fora, such as particular state, federal, or international courts. In the existing system of adjudication, the location where the lawsuit occurs must be decided early in the litigation process, so that a judge can be selected to supervise the remainder of the adjudication. Even in cases that are likely eventually to settle, the adjudication of the jurisdictional questions may occur while negotiations are in progress and can be expensive. With trial by market, the probability that a case might end up in different jurisdictions would simply be priced into the market's ultimate assessment of the probability of victory. The same holds for disputes about which substantive law should apply. Of course, there might still be considerable disputes about whether individual cases should be tried by market or by courts in the first place.

SMALL CLAIMS COURT ADJUDICATION

Whatever the merits of using prediction markets to accomplish adjudication, no legislature seems likely to adopt it even for a subset of cases, at least unless it has already proved to be a cheap and accurate means of resolving disputes. The best chance for application of the approach would be in the private sector. Participants in alternative dispute resolution, however, seem unlikely to be willing to try an untested technique if significant amounts of money are at stake. But the method might be used to resolve very small disputes. For example, one or more on-line multiplayer games might seek to deploy some virtual system of dispute resolution, thus implementing Carrington's vision for resolving disputes in virtual space,[28] and perhaps later could integrate prediction markets. Such games increasingly bring the potential for resolving disputes over property rights, and although commentators have speculated that such disputes will spill over into real-world courts,[29] game designers may prefer an internal system of dispute resolution.

If prediction markets work in cyberspace, then perhaps they will someday be adopted for disputes about commercial transactions so small that resolution in a court is impractical. SquareTrade currently performs dispute resolution for many disputes arising on the on-line auction site eBay.[30] If initial information exchange fails to lead to a settlement, SquareTrade appoints a mediator. This mediator, however, does not have an arbitrator's power to make binding decisions. Some users might prefer a system in which an arbitrator does have such power, and yet there might be concern that such arbitrators could exercise power arbitrarily. An on-line service that is already taking advantage of market mechanisms might be more open to the possibility of market-based adjudication than other services. The market-based system might require one of the parties to pay money to the other, and failing that, the system could expel the other from the service.[31]

If market-based adjudication is to have a place in public courts, the first application might similarly be for the adjudication of small claims disputes. Small claims courts currently require a relatively high degree of effort relative to what is at stake because litigants and witnesses must show up at court, often waiting a long time for their case to be called. Thus there is, as a practical matter, no public adjudication system for very small disputes, such as disputes over a few dollars. Presumably, the theory of small claims courts is that they encourage parties to follow through on contractual promises and discourage small torts. These goals could be advanced more effectively if small claims adjudication were cheaper, making adjudication more feasible for claims of, say, a hundred dollars. The mere existence of a cheaper small claims mechanism should lead to fairer resolution of many disputes without any trial at all. And the system would provide an outlet for customers who feel that they have been cheated by large corporations that pass them from one customer service agent to another without resolving or understanding their problems.

Jurisdictions could create a simple Web-based system to operate as a small claims court. Litigants would be able to submit statements, either in writing or with audio and video, as well as statements of witnesses, as in Carrington's proposal. Just as adverse decisions in small claims court often can be appealed to a state's trial courts for an entirely new trial,[32] so, too, might disputes in this small claims court be appealable to a more traditional one. In reality, the stakes will rarely be sufficiently great to justify elevating a dispute to the next level. In initial versions of this system, small claims judges might be responsible for resolving all of the on-line disputes, giving short explanations. A useful addendum to this system could be prediction markets that anticipate how these judges or the judges immediately above them would resolve the cases. These prediction markets could gauge the probability of a verdict for the plaintiff, and conditional on such a verdict, the expected amount of damages. If the prediction markets work well, it would then be a relatively small step for a jurisdiction to eliminate the judges from most cases, substituting trial by market while still granting a full right of appeal.

THE COMMON LAW AND DECENTRALIZED DECISION MAKING

Some might object that trial by market might inhibit the creation of precedent. Some cases still might be appealed, but possibly far fewer than before, and the cases selected would only by coincidence be those that raise the most interesting legal issues. The result could be increased legal uncertainty. Moreover, it might seem that trial by market would impoverish the common law, itself a remarkable product of decentralized decision making. William Landes and Judge Richard Posner have argued that the common law tends over time to economic efficiency as decision makers faced with particular factual scenarios modify legal principles in ways that accommodate the relevant difficulties.[33] Like trial by market, the common law can limit idiosyncratic decision making, but the constraints come from the past rather than from the future. Of course, many areas of law are codified. Nonetheless, common law helps resolve legal ambiguity over time.

Trial by market, however, might achieve the virtues of the common law without precedent. Let us suppose that trial by market is accomplished with a deliberative information market, so that market participants will have an incentive to explain their views of the outcome of each case. They will be encouraged to consider all legal issues that might affect the result and to develop relevant legal arguments. If such discussions were held in public fora, then prediction market participants might cite discussions from previous cases about particular issues, in much the same way as authors of blogs cite and debate one another. These past discussions, of course, would count only as what lawyers would call "persuasive authority" and would not bind future decision makers. But the process would produce a body of analysis of difficult problems in much the same way as the common law. Over time, market participants would recognize some arguments as more persuasive than others to the eventual decision makers, and these arguments would increase in importance in much the same way as thoughtful judicial opinions gradually win influence.

The decision makers, of course, could still be bound by legal precedent of the traditional sort. As legal precedents change, the prediction market participants would respond accordingly. For each issue resolved only in a prediction market, however, there would be a body of analysis and a common practice from the market that would approximate the wisdom of the common law. Indeed, with trial by market, perhaps the ultimate decision makers should not set precedents and then be constrained by them. According to this view, judges would still make decisions, but those decisions would be used only to discipline the prediction markets, not to set binding precedents. This would help avoid the danger that by virtue of path dependence and the random selection of judges, a poor legal decision will be reached. Prediction markets do not need precedent to achieve two principal benefits of the common law: generating wisdom and preventing idiosyncratic preference from influencing cases. Because participants in a deliberative prediction market are always engaged in collective decision making, and because they are concerned with what decision makers will decide on average, there is no longer a need to have rules that constrain them.

Nonetheless, it might seem that a role for precedent remains, because precedent promotes legal certainty. When 75 percent of judges would adopt a particular position, it might be better for that position to be formally adopted than for the issue to simply be priced out at 75 percent. One solution might be to use prediction markets to accomplish the task of lawmaking, as described in Chapter 9. But this might not be necessary. If following precedent ordinarily is important, than decision makers ex post should be expected to place some weight on this consideration. Thus, when 75 percent of judges would adopt a particular position, the issue might be priced out at almost 100 percent.

Judges ex post who would take the minority position if writing on a clean slate might generally agree that the majority position should be accepted given the results of prior market adjudications. Indeed, they should be less resistant to the force of precedent in cases in which they disagree with the result, because the ex post decisions do not have any direct effect. There would still be room for the law to change in cases in which other considerations overwhelmed the force of precedent. The difference is that precedents would be set and undone along a continuum rather than in a binary fashion, as in the present legal system. Trial by market can be a system that cares about the past, while predicting how decisions will be made in the future.

NORMATIVE PROBABILISTIC
PREDICTION MARKETS

The above argument about precedent echoes an earlier theme: that predictive decision making strengthens the case for standards as compared to rules (see Chapter 5). One reason why our legal system has a rule-based approach to precedent is that we wish to reduce the effect of idiosyncratic decision making, to force decision makers to decide cases as others have in the past. The rule-based approach also reduces litigation expense because there is less argument about what the law requires. This approach has its deficiencies, among them that it can perpetuate idiosyncratic views if those views happen to appear in the first judicial opinions to address an issue.

Once prediction markets are used to decide cases, the case for a standard-based approach to precedent becomes stronger. Because no single person will decide the current case, there is less of a need for constraint. In addition, because prediction markets price out anticipated disagreement, the entire case will not turn on a single judge's views of a contentious legal issue. A standard-based approach therefore will limit increases in litigation costs when prediction markets are used, and there will be less risk associated with uncertainty about how particular issues will be resolved.

This general argument applies not only to the issue of precedent but also to any issue that might be adjudicated by probabilistic prediction markets. Such a market might be used to predict a future decision based solely on a standard. Indeed, it often will make sense to combine such markets with normative prediction markets to create normative probabilistic prediction markets. Predictive cost-benefit analysis is one possible use of a normative market, although there is no inherent need for the factors in a normative market to be reducible to dollar values.

A normative prediction market can be used not merely as a replacement for more rule-based approaches to legal decision making but also in contexts in which it simply is infeasible to devise rules with sufficient precision to enable any decision making at all. There is a natural tendency in thinking about the choice between rules and standards to consider existing legal applications. If prediction markets enable more efficient utilization of standards, however, then they may allow entirely new applications.

Suppose, for example, that a government thought that it wanted to encourage nice and pleasant personal behavior. It may be that the right to be mean is central to liberty and that we would not want the government to try to steer us to act artificially nicely. But let us imagine that we believed that in principle, subsidies given to nice people would increase social welfare by providing incentives for niceness. Using current legal technology, however, it would still probably be infeasible to reward niceness because it would require a centralized governmental determination of how nice each of us was.

Probabilistic normative prediction markets could make implementation of a niceness program straightforward. Everyone would have an incentive to assess the niceness of people they knew by participating in individualized prediction markets, and the government would discipline the market by having some niceness judges investigate the niceness of a few randomly selected individuals. My own view is that this system would create a level of anxiety and discomfort that would outweigh the benefits of any increased niceness. The technical point remains, however, that such markets would be feasible. An assessment project that otherwise would be monstrously complex could probably be accomplished with just a few dollars' worth of subsidy per person.

Normative probabilistic prediction markets might be used to compensate for limitations of other prediction market mechanisms. For example, such markets might be used to adjust other market predictions for biases. Recall the concern that hedging activity might bias the results of prediction markets (Chapter 3), with shares that serve an insurance function being more expensive than probabilities alone would justify. It is not easy to determine just how much to compensate for this in making probability estimates, in part because it depends on the risk profiles of traders on both sides of the transactions. Nonetheless, there is a case for making an adjustment. A normative probabilistic prediction market could be used, for example, to anticipate what an average statistician or econometrician would conclude should be added or subtracted from the market prices to produce unbiased probability estimates.

Such markets might similarly be used as alternatives to deliberative prediction markets to encourage release of information and analysis relevant to a prediction market. Normative probabilistic prediction markets could be used to determine how much to reward individuals who provide information and analysis. An ex post decision maker would rate the input of each contributor with some probability, and the prediction market would anticipate each contributor's rating. A fixed subsidy could then be distributed in proportion to these predictions. In the absence of probabilistic prediction markets, an approach like this would likely be infeasible. With traditional adjudicative mechanisms, it could be too costly to assess each individual's contributions, too risky to contribute if a single individual would determine the value of one's contributions, and too difficult to craft rules that could measure the quality of contributions objectively.

Before considering two possible applications of normative prediction markets beyond correcting problems with other prediction market designs, I should anticipate one objection. Suppose that a very small number of ex post decision makers have extraordinarily idiosyncratic views, so idiosyncratic that these views would end up having a disproportionate effect on the initial predictions. For example, imagine that Mary announced to the world that if she were selected as ex post decision maker in the information release subsidy market described above, she would rate John's contribution at a billion trillion dollars. Though Mary's selection is highly unlikely, in expected value terms it might have a significant effect on John's return.

There is, however, a simple solution to this technical problem. If the ex post decision maker's assessment deviates sufficiently far from the prediction, two additional ex post decision makers (or more) could be chosen, and the median prediction could control. Depending on how far is sufficiently far, this system could be used to make a prediction approximate a median more closely than it would an average, because it will tend to reduce the effect of extreme views. Another approach to accomplishing the same goal is to provide that where the number used to resolve the market payouts deviates from the prediction by more than a certain amount, a number that deviates less will be used. This will lead market participants to discount extreme outcomes. Whether the views of something like the median or the average ex post decision maker should control might depend on the particular application.

LEGISLATION ADJUSTMENT ASSISTANCE

Prediction markets could be used to provide social insurance against privately harmful legal change. Such a program could mute opposition to socially beneficial change, making it easier to enact. In at least one context the U.S. government has attempted to do this: by providing trade adjustment assistance.[34] The theory is that free trade generally increases social welfare by allowing each nation to exercise its comparative advantage, but the losses associated with free trade are concentrated, for example, on a particular industry and the employees in that industry. A trade bill can thus provide benefits, in the form of cash or job training or other programs, to those who will suffer from passage of a trade bill. Economists use the phrase "Kaldor-Hicks improvement" to describe a change when the winners in theory could compensate the losers, though they are not required to do so.[35] Trade adjustment assistance in theory can transform a policy that qualifies as a Kaldor-Hicks improvement into one that counts as a Pareto improvement, one in which at least one person is better off and nobody is worse off.

Legislation adjustment assistance can increase social welfare both by performing a social insurance function and by facilitating beneficial legal changes. That does not necessarily mean that it is always justified. For example, it may be desirable to encourage private actors to anticipate possible changes in the law. One would not want someone to build a large plant in the United States knowing that it will not be profitable because of an impending change in trade rules but believing that trade adjustment assistance will make it worthwhile.[36] Such behavior would be an example of "moral hazard," in which an insured engages in risky or socially undesirable behavior because the insurance will cover part of the losses from that behavior. Even if the moral hazard problem is not severe, legislative adjustment assistance may be difficult to implement. Trade adjustment assistance provides a relatively strong case because the losers are relatively easy to identify, but it may be difficult to create rules that allow straightforward computation of each individual's loss.

Normative probabilistic prediction markets could eliminate the need for detailed rules and thus make otherwise infeasible legislative adjustment assistance programs feasible. One approach would be for a statute enacting some legal change to create a fund consisting of a fixed amount of money. Any person or entity adversely affected by the legislation would be permitted to apply on-line for a portion of this fixed fund. A normative probabilistic prediction market would then be used to calculate the optimal payment to each applicant, predicting ex post evaluations of each individual's case. To ensure that the total payments exactly exhaust the fund, each applicant would receive a share in the fund for each dollar of optimal payment predicted immediately after the adjudication of that applicant's case. An applicant could cash out by selling shares right away, but the fund itself would be distributed only after the deadline for applications had passed and all claims had been adjudicated by the market.

Ex post decision makers estimating the optimal payment presumably would start by estimating the amount that a particular person stands to lose as a result of a particular piece of legislation. Suppose, for example, that the legislation imposes a large gas tax. The decision makers might take into account factors such as how far an applicant lived from a place of work, whether the applicant generally drove to work, what kind of car the applicant owns, and what method the applicant uses to heat a home. It would be difficult for a legislature to figure out how much to weigh each of these considerations, but prediction market participants will have incentives to assess how much weight ex post decision makers would be expected to give. Presumably, market participants would also consider the degree to which individuals can mitigate the loss. How difficult would it be for someone to move closer to the workplace or move the workplace closer to home? Could this person switch to mass transit, and if so, at what cost? These questions alone are sufficiently fact-intensive to elude a coherent rule-based legislative scheme.

If the total market subsidy were only a few dollars per applicant, the total subsidy for such a market could be sufficiently large to generate robust incentives to participate. Participants, perhaps combining together in firms to take advantage of diverse skills, would have incentives to devise methods of assessing large numbers of claims. This task would involve resolution of questions at different levels of generality. Participants would need to develop ways of anticipating how much weight ex post decision makers could be expected to give to different types of considerations, such as the nature of the applicant's job. Then, for each anticipated consideration, they might consider various classes of fact scenarios, for example, classifying jobs based on how much individuals in those jobs will lose on the basis of a gas tax.

Finally, participants might consider details of particular applications, using some combination of artificial and human intelligence, both to categorize these applications generally and to identify unique factual scenarios, while also assessing the quality of the evidence submitted. Presumably, participants also would seek to understand the models being used by rivals and to consider whether to adjust their own models accordingly. And they would have incentives to seek to identify manipulation, for example, by flagging cases in which market participants have made predictions about only a small number of individuals.

Prediction markets assessing a hundred million applications or so would be extraordinarily demanding, and there is no way of knowing in advance just how accurate such markets would be. A legislature undoubtedly would want experience with some smaller markets before enacting a plan of this type, although it is possible that economies of scale would improve the quality of results. Experience could establish the degree of variability in ex post decision makers' assessments and clarify the extent to which the market succeeds at treating similarly situated individuals similarly.

THE LITIGIOUSNESS PUNISHMENT MARKET

The use of prediction markets to set subsidies for other prediction markets is one example of a general strategy: when a particular prediction market design seems to have some problem or to leave open some question, use another prediction market to solve the problem. Infinite recursion, of course, is impossible. We would need to determine how much to subsidize the markets used to determine the subsidy for other markets, and we could use another set of markets to do that, but eventually we would need to have some market in which the subsidy is set in advance. It might then seem that problems associated with prediction markets cannot be escaped. Often, however, problems become simpler with each additional level of regression. It is extraordinarily difficult for a legislature to develop a set of rules determining the optimal compensation from a gas tax, pretty difficult to create rules specifying how great the subsidy should be for prediction markets determining this optimal compensation, and less difficult to set a subsidy for a market that sets the subsidy for another market.

Normative probabilistic prediction markets also might be used to address some problems that occur in both traditional and market institutions. Consider again the problem this chapter first addressed: excessive spending on litigation costs. I argued above that trial by market might reduce litigation costs, but it does not address the fundamental problem that at each stage of the process, individuals spend too much on their own cases. This would be true for virtually any normative probabilistic prediction market, such as the legislative adjustment assistance market described above. Each person's incentive is to spend money collecting and organizing evidence until the marginal benefit of evidence collection exceeds the marginal cost, a level that might be far above the social optimum. Meanwhile, trial by market saves on judicial costs, but the subsidies needed to induce market estimation might need to be at least as great, so further refinements are needed if trial by market is to reduce costs substantially.

With both traditional adjudication and various kinds of normative probabilistic prediction markets, the problem is that it may be impossible to develop tailored ex ante rules that limit what affected individuals such as litigants can spend. There are so many factors that are legitimately related to litigation expense that crafting tables precisely calculating how much litigants could spend would be a hopelessly complex task. And yet sometimes it will not be too hard to reach a judgment about whether someone has spent a lot or a little and to make a subjective assessment of whether the amount spent is too much.

Currently, the law largely avoids subjective approaches to determining whether litigants have engaged in socially wasteful litigation spending. Those who file frivolous lawsuits can be subject to sanction,[37] but courts rarely impose such penalties, and when they do, they use relatively objective legal standards to assess frivolousness by, for example, determining whether the court has previously resolved the issue.[38] But there may be many gradations of weak cases, and even individuals with strong cases might, from a social perspective, spend too much on those cases. Fee-shifting rules take a rule-based approach to discouraging frivolous litigation. These rules therefore are necessarily over-inclusive and underinclusive. One problem is that the ultimate decision that determines fee-shifting might be the opposite of what most judges or juries would have done, and so fee-shifting rules can magnify injustice. The law also discourages excessive litigation in other brute force ways, such as imposing page limits on briefs, but this does not present a general strategy for discouraging litigation expense.

The litigiousness punishment market would predict an ex post evaluation of a fine that litigants would receive for engaging in excessive litigation. Of course, excessiveness is extraordinarily hard to measure, but this is more of an argument for than against the market, because the market would aggregate diverse views. The fines that it would produce might not be perfectly scientific, but participants would have incentives to make the approach to fines fairly consistent across cases. At least, the market could incorporate relatively important factors such as how much a party's lawyer charged, how many hours the lawyer billed, and the complexity of the case. The market also might penalize parties for refusing reasonable settlements. Even if the market predictions are not perfectly scientific, they may provide a sufficiently reliable assessment of excessiveness that imposing these fines could improve on the status quo. The approach would impose some degree of risk and uncertainty on litigants, but the continuous nature of the prediction markets would provide litigants feedback about whether their spending level might lead to fines.

A plausible objection is that virtually everyone would have to pay some fine no matter what, because some portion of ex post decision makers would find spending to be excessive. There are, however, various possible solutions. First, one might use an approach that comes closer to making a prediction of median assessments than of average assessments (see Chapter 8). Second, the market might provide bonuses to litigants who spend too little. A market could be designed to be self-funding, so that across some group of cases, the total fines imposed would always be equal to the total bonuses distributed. Third, two normative probabilistic prediction markets might be used for each litigant. One would resolve the threshold issue of whether any fine should be imposed. Only if most decision makers would impose some fine would the second prediction market's determined fine actually be imposed.

As this last approach shows, adoption of the litigiousness punishment market would not necessarily produce a drastic immediate change in practice. Rather, at first, decision makers probably would be expected to impose fines only in egregious cases, so that the market would more closely resemble a market alternative to current means of fining litigants for frivolous claims and defenses. Over time, as ex post decision makers' confidence in the mechanism increased, they might be expected to use the mechanism more liberally.

This is, of course, a version of another general strategy that can be used to defend proposals involving normative probabilistic prediction markets. The ex post decision makers should be encouraged to take the problems that these markets might produce into account to the optimal extent. Indeed, it is expected that ex post decision makers will seek to make adjustments to overcome potential problems that make normative prediction markets more flexible than rule-based alternatives. Here, ex post decision makers should be expected to take into account the costs of abrupt regime changes.

MARKET-BASED DISCOVERY

There is at least one more objection to using prediction markets for adjudicative tasks that can easily be answered with the creation of more prediction markets. The objection is that a major function of the litigation system is to oversee the discovery process. Prediction markets will not reach accurate outcomes if they do not have access to the relevant information. But one could easily imagine the creation of a discovery market. As in the current system, litigants initially would seek to resolve any discovery disputes themselves, but failing that, a litigant could file a discovery complaint. That complaint would be adjudicated in a normative probabilistic prediction market of its own that forecasts the decision of an ex post decision maker who would determine whether discovery should have been compelled or whether other discovery violations have occurred. These predictions themselves would control the resolution of discovery disputes. In theory, normative probabilistic prediction markets could enforce the judgments by finding parties to be in contempt of court and imposing fines, though it would also be possible to leave these functions to a more traditional court.

One objection is that market consideration of evidence sometimes might itself produce the revelation of information that some litigants wish to oppose. Market-based discovery, however, could even work in cases in which information needs to be examined secretly. Under existing rules, a judge will sometimes examine evidence secretly, or *in camera,* and make a decision based on that assessment.[39] Similarly, a party might provide evidence secretly to a third party, either for a fee or in exchange for the right to make a prediction on the market in response to this secret evidence. The evidence could then be considered *in camera* by the ex post decision maker if the discovery dispute were randomly selected for more traditional resolution. Other prediction market participants would have incentives to assess the reputation of the third party that assessed the evidence secretly, and litigants might choose to provide information secretly to several third parties in order to convey information even more clearly to the market. The incentives of these third parties might be at least as strong as the incentives of judges, who know that no one will ordinarily be able to scrutinize decisions that they make *in camera.*

That prediction markets could perform the task of discovery does not mean that they would be indispensable to market-based adjudication. It is possible that many adjudicative markets could work efficiently enough if there were no means of compelling discovery. George Shepherd has argued that the social costs of discovery exceed the benefits.[40] Although some plaintiffs might lose cases as a result of an inability to access defendants' internal documents if discovery were abolished, Shepherd asserts that this is less than the number who currently abandon cases because they cannot handle burdensome discovery requests. Shepherd prefers a system that, like other countries,' relies on burdens of proof to stimulate release of information.

Prediction markets could take into account whatever information parties have produced and how open parties have been without formal discovery rules or burdens of proof. Economic models show that parties often have broad incentives voluntarily to release even damaging information, lest others conclude that the information is worse than it is.[41] Resolution of whether these models are applicable, however, is not necessary to an assessment of market-based adjudication, because all issues, including discovery disputes, could be adjudicated by markets if deemed desirable. Use of prediction markets to conduct discovery, however, could be used not only as a supplement to trial by market but alternatively in conjunction with traditional adjudication. This system would free judges to focus on issues other than discovery.

PREDICTION MARKETS FOR CRIMINAL JUSTICE

Prediction markets seem less likely to be justified for criminal adjudication than for civil adjudication. In the criminal context it may be more important to have individuals judged by juries of their peers, because a criminal jury verdict achieves some expressive or educative function. As long as prediction market verdicts appear less legitimate than traditional jury verdicts, there would be a cost to using prediction markets to accomplish the task of criminal trials. On the other hand, there might still be benefits, for example, a reduced need for plea bargaining if the cost of litigation is reduced and decreased risk of an idiosyncratic result attributable to the natures of jurors or attributable to the group dynamics of the jury's decision making. At least in theory, trial by market could be accommodated to the criminal context, with markets predicting the probability that a jury acting as ex post decision maker would find the defendant to be guilty beyond a reasonable doubt. A probability greater than 50 percent might translate into a conviction, though higher thresholds might be used if it were desirable to reduce the risk of erroneous convictions still further.

That criminal trial by market seems especially unlikely, at least unless the public comes to see prediction market decision making as more legitimate than alternative approaches, does not mean that prediction markets have no place in criminal justice. One limitation of our current system is that it is very stingy about granting new trials, reserving grants of habeas corpus to situations in which individuals' constitutional rights have been found to be violated. This is unfortunate, because there may be cases in which doubt is cast on particular testimony after a trial, yet there is no real constitutional violation.

Consider, for example, cases in which individuals long ago were convicted of child molestation based on repressed memory testimony or memories that surfaced after extended adult questioning, techniques that have recently received substantial criticism.[42] In some such cases, it might be useful to have a new trial so that the jury could consider expert testimony based on improvements in the underlying social science. But a rule stipulating that defendants are entitled to a retrial whenever a judge felt that the outcome might be different would be susceptible to too much abuse, and so we have a strong principle of finality.

A prediction market alternative would be straightforward. It would provide a continuous rather than a one-time assessment of the defendant's guilt. Conditional prediction markets could be used to predict the probability that a convicted defendant, if granted a new trial, would be acquitted. This system could still reflect the principle of finality, if that were desirable. In a case in which there is a 50 percent chance of acquittal on retrial, that might not be deemed sufficient. Such a probability, after all, would reflect the chance of a conviction with the beyond-a-reasonable-doubt standard, and there is no inherent reason to grant repeated new trials to everyone whose case is near that threshold. Perhaps a defendant should need to show an 80 percent or a 90 percent probability to win a new trial.

It also might be desirable for the retrial to operate under special rules. For example, all testimony from the original trial might be read into the record, and then the prosecution and the defense would be allowed to present new testimony. This could reduce the cost of repeated proceedings while still giving defendants who genuinely have new evidence another chance. In a system without a rule against double jeopardy, one might also imagine using prediction markets to determine whether prosecutors could bring a case anew against an acquitted defendant. That might make sense in cases in which prosecutors botched the government presentation or in which the trial court inappropriately excluded evidence.

This proposal imagines that the prediction market would automatically determine whether a retrial should be granted, but this need not be and indeed is unlikely to be the case. Conditional prediction markets could be established to determine the probability of conviction if a new trial is granted for any reason, such as a constitutional violation. Such prediction markets might be subsidized by private parties eager to show that a particular defendant has been wrongfully convicted or perhaps that the defendant would surely be convicted all over again. Criminal cases are often sufficiently complex that it is difficult for casual observers to assess the strength of the evidence, and even judges often may not have time to review every exhibit and page of testimony. In death penalty cases, the state sometimes argues that many judges have rejected a convicted defendant's claims of innocence,[43] but in reality, only the original jury directly faced the question of whether the defendant was guilty beyond a reasonable doubt. In death penalty cases as well as others, subsidized prediction markets could provide government officials and the public with an informed basis for assessing claims of innocence. In the absence of prediction markets, it may be impossible for the well-informed credibly to convey to the public the sincerity of their views.

Chapter 9 Legislative Bodies

The preceding few chapters have shown that prediction markets can substitute for voting regimes of many kinds. Instead of using a vote of administrative agency commissioners to decide whether to enact particular regulations, we could use predictive cost-benefit analysis, according to Chapter 6. Instead of relying on a board to defend the interests of shareholders or on shareholders to defend their own interests, we could use self-deciding conditional prediction markets that would force corporations to adopt policies that would maximize share price, according to Chapter 7. And instead of having appellate judges vote in reviewing the decisions of trial judges and juries, we could use prediction markets to accomplish the task of adjudication, according to Chapter 8.

If these proposals indeed make the relevant institutions more attractive, there might be somewhat less for a legislature to do. Predictive decision making in general, we saw in Chapter 5, can allow replacement of rules with standards. Prediction markets can enable a legislature to focus more on high-level issues than on the details of implementation. If predictive cost-benefit analysis is a good means of deciding whether particular regulations should be enacted, authorizing legislation for particular agencies could be short. Just as prediction markets could allow corporations to consider the interests of constituencies other than shareholders (see Chapter 7), so, too, could widespread adoption by corporations facilitate legislative efforts to force corporations to consider various public interests, saving the legislature the trouble of developing carrots and sticks via its own decision making. And if normative probabilistic prediction markets for performing adjudication can really take into account values such as the importance of consistency (see Chapter 8), there may be much less need for a legislature to provide advance notice to the public in detailed rules.

Nonetheless, we have assumed that the legislature continues to play a critical role in the background. Prediction markets as described so far might be used to assess whether particular regulations accord with legislative intent (see Chapter 6) but not to supplant it. Corporations would still be bound by applicable legislation, and prediction market adjudication would anticipate the results of traditional adjudication that would take laws into account in the usual way. And yet some of the reasons why prediction markets might usefully perform regulatory tasks suggest also that they might usefully perform legislative ones. Because legislatures are relatively large, they may not be susceptible to quite the same extent of ideological shifts as are administrative agencies (see Chapter 5), but still party discipline means that relatively small shifts in the electorate can have outsized consequences for policy. Prediction markets can ensure more consistently moderate decision making. We have also seen that prediction markets can limit the impact of special interests on decisions, a benefit that may be great for legislative decision making.

Naturally, the possibility that prediction markets would replace legislatures is still more fanciful than the schemes discussed above. For one thing, there is little need for the change, aside from saving a small amount of legislators' salaries, given that legislatures simply could delegate more to administrative agencies that employ prediction markets. And if we were designing a new government for a country recovering from totalitarian rule, there are sound reasons to adopt structures that have been tried before. But considering the possibility of a market-based legislature nonetheless serves an important analytical purpose. Much of this book is intended less as a policy recommendation than as an existence theorem, and the task of designing a market-based legislature is more complicated than those that have come before. A legislature produces outputs not in the form of probabilities or binary decisions but in the form of texts. In order to construct a market-based legislature, we must find a way to take the building blocks of prediction markets that can make binary decisions or produce linear predictions and make them into an author. Given the full expressiveness of the human language, a prediction market that can write texts can make decisions about just about anything.

Indeed, while considering the possibility of market-based legislatures, a major purpose of this chapter is to develop the idea of text-authoring prediction markets that might be used to produce consensus "texts" of various types for a variety of purposes. After describing how such a market could work, I discuss "chain novels"—those that actually exist and those that are mere metaphors for legal philosophers. Whether or not prediction markets could write high-quality chain novels, they almost surely could write encyclopedias, and I consider whether prediction markets might facilitate improvements on Wikipedia, the decentralized encyclopedia, or help organize open-source software projects. In order to assess the theoretical potential of prediction markets, I then consider the more adventurous application of a market-based legislature, a model that also could be easily applied to tasks such as market-based drafting of administrative regulations. I also consider what some of the limitations might be of a text-authoring market as a reflection of collective choice and the possibility of modifying the market to take into account intensity of preference. Finally, I consider a less radical possibility: the use of prediction markets to create restatements of the laws.

THE TEXT-AUTHORING MARKET

We have already seen that a prediction market can be used to approve a text. Predictive cost-benefit analysis, after all, predicts whether a regulation will have more benefits than costs, a condition that might count as constituting approval. This approach can be easily generalized. Given a requirement to approve a text for a particular purpose, anyone might be allowed to propose a text. A prediction market could then be used to anticipate the evaluation of an ex post decision maker who will decide whether the text should have been approved or disapproved. If the prediction market anticipates that the text should be approved, then it is approved. Otherwise, other participants can propose alternative texts, perhaps with the requirement that the individuals pay the subsidy for the market. Eventually, this market might well approve a text. A publisher might use it, for example, to decide whether to publish novels submitted to it. Although one or more humans will have written each proposed novel, the market acts to approve texts, and so we might count it as a text-authoring market.

This approach, however, leaves much to be desired. Ideally, there should be an opportunity for multiple human authors to coordinate their activities and produce a jointly written text. What is needed, in short, is a means for individuals to make edits to the texts of others. This modification is relatively easily accomplished. Initially, the market's text is blank, but anyone can propose amendments to it. Whether an amendment to the text is accepted would be determined by a prediction market anticipating the evaluation (which might occur only with some positive probability) of an ex post decision maker. In effect, each amendment replaces the proposed text with another text. Amendments also might be proposed to amendments. Once the text has been fully amended, a prediction market can be used to determine whether to accept the text as a whole. This approach assures that the creation of the text is a collaborative effort of all market participants. And yet it need not be they whose taste determines what is included. Rather, it is the participants' prediction of the taste of the ex post decision maker. And so, by altering the pool of ex post decision makers, one can alter the incentives of the authors.

The principal complication concerns timing. If we allow anyone to offer an amendment to any text and provide a set time for the market to consider it, then the market might never get around to approving a text, especially if there are some market participants who would benefit from such delay. We thus need some mechanism for ending prediction market deliberation about individual amendments and about the text as a whole. Prediction markets, of course, can be used to make this assessment. At any time, someone might call for resolution of a decision on a particular amendment, and a prediction market would be used to assess this call for a decision. If that market predicted that an ex post decision maker would agree that it was time for a decision, then the amendment would be accepted or rejected in its current form, and all undecided proposed amendments to the amendment would be rejected. The same approach could be applied to the text as a whole.

There are, of course, possible variations on this system. Instead of relying on repeated separate markets for assessing whether the market should end at a particular time, a single continuous market might be used. For example, the market might predict an ex post decision maker's assessment of the optimal ending time for the market. The market would then end once its prediction of the optimal time exceeded the actual time—if that prediction continued to hold for some period of time. That period of time would ideally be partly randomized and would need to be long enough to allow participants to discipline any attempts at manipulation by those who have an interest in the market's ending, so that no participant could unilaterally force an end to a market by effecting a transient change in price.

Once the market ended, the ex post decision maker would assess when the market optimally should have ended. Anticipating this decision, market participants would try to determine what amount of time made sense for a particular market, updating assessments based on new developments. Market participants presumably also would consider the relations among proposed amendments. For example, ordinarily they would decide that an amendment to an amendment should be resolved before the underlying amendment, though sometimes they might conclude that it makes sense to resolve an amendment without considering an amendment to it.

The only important remaining issue is how to subsidize the text-authoring market. It may be important to subsidize both those who make predictions and those who suggest text and amendments. First, both the main prediction markets and the timing markets would receive some subsidy. The level of the subsidy might be determined by yet more prediction markets, which could forecast an ex post decision maker's assessment of the importance of each of the main prediction markets and the timing prediction markets.

Each text-authoring market as a whole might be given a single fixed subsidy. This fixed subsidy could be distributed to market participants and amendment proposers in proportion to the assessments of the subsidy prediction markets. Of course, the market designer would also need to subsidize each of the subsidy prediction markets. It would be possible to use prediction markets to perform that task, too, leaving the market designer the task of setting a subsidy for the markets that determine the subsidy of the main and the timing markets.

Second, each text proposal could receive a subsidy, too, perhaps a portion of the single fixed subsidy, with the exact portion to be determined by a normative prediction market. The subsidy for a particular text proposal also could be determined by a subsidy prediction market to gauge the assessments of ex post decision makers. They presumably would recommend higher subsidies for successful amendments, although they might find that some unsuccessful ones deserve a subsidy as well, for example, if they inspire some other amendments.

Chain Novels

The text-authoring market can produce texts of any type, for any purpose. That does not necessarily mean, however, that the market is always the best way to produce texts. Perhaps the ultimate challenge would be producing a novel. It is not inherently difficult for groups to produce novels collaboratively. A group could agree, for example, to produce a chain novel. One person writes the first chapter, someone else writes the second chapter, and so forth, until the end of the book. Indeed, some chain novels exist. In a recent twist on the concept, rights to author each page of a chain novel were successively auctioned on eBay.[1] But no good chain novels exist.

It is easy to write a chain novel collaboratively, but extraordinarily hard to write a good one collaboratively. Ordinarily, the writing style of a novel should be roughly the same from chapter to chapter, and themes should recur throughout the book. Of course, it is possible that chain novels are bad because the writers who have created them are not very good. But good writers might have difficulty completing a chain novel that another good writer has started, because different writers might have different views of the aims of a book.

How can we improve on the chain novel? One useful improvement, already adopted on the Internet,[2] is for collaborators to exchange general ideas about plots, characters, and themes before any chapters are produced. Better still would be a system that allowed collaborators to reach tentative agreement about these and other issues, including questions of style, before writing. A text-authoring market could easily allow this. At the early stages of the creation of a text, market participants might accept amendments that they would never ultimately want included in the eventual text of the book.

The text produced by these amendments might consist of outlines, stubs, or general statements of principle. This approach would reduce the danger that different authors later would seek to pull the book in different directions, and if that happened, subsequent amendments could resolve disagreements relatively early, before too much inconsistent writing has been done. Over time, outline text would be replaced with plausible final text. Meanwhile, some contributors might make numerous small changes, ensuring consistency of writing style and other elements. The text-authoring market encourages specialization, allowing different writers to contribute at different stages of development.

The market might thus produce novels that are considerably better than the typical chain novel. Quality undoubtedly would depend at least in part on the level of the market subsidy. But could a high subsidy—say, ten million dollars—produce a great novel? Perhaps writing is so inherently personal that group collaboration will inevitably detract from rather than enhance the product. But even great writers can benefit from great editors.[3] At first the market might tentatively adopt an entire book written by a single individual, and only relatively minor amendments would be accepted because participants would realize that drastic amendments, however well-intentioned, would detract from the quality. An advantage of the text-authoring market is that market participants will have incentives to determine the optimal size of individual contributions, and participants might adopt an approach that incorporates one individual's contributions far more than others'.

It is also possible, however, that with enough financial incentive, many writers could collaborate effectively and that larger numbers of writers would enhance rather than detract from the end product. If not true for a novel, that might be true for a television show. Television shows, after all, are already generally collaborative projects involving several writers. The text-authoring market increases the number of potential collaborators in each stage of a television show's development, including identifying an overall concept, choosing a plot arc for a season, mapping out individual episodes, and writing dialogue.

It may be optimal for only a small group of writers to create a particular television show, but that may be in part because of the lack of effective tools for group decision making. It may be that adding more writers will improve the overall quality, even if each additional writer adds less than the preceding one. And if not, the text-authoring market should be successful in identifying a small number of contributors whose work should be allowed and ignoring the ideas of others. The group decision making apparatus might slow progress, but one cannot be sure unless the project is attempted.

Today, chain novels have little place in the real world, but the metaphor of the chain novel has earned an important place in legal theory. The legal philosopher Ronald Dworkin has likened the process of judicial interpretation to the task of adding a new chapter to a chain novel. The task of Hercules, the mythical judge who adds a new chapter, is to make the law and the chain novel the best that they can be, a task that requires some attention to what has come before. Dworkin's metaphor has received a number of criticisms. One is that the task that he places before Hercules is indeed Herculean. Dworkin believes that there is a "right answer," but critics respond that cognitively limited judges may not be able to find that answer.[4] Moreover, the longer the chain novel, the less it constrains. An empirical study suggests that the more precedents that arise, the more likely a judge will be to resolve a case in accordance with his or her political preferences.[5]

In theory, a text-authoring market could replace individual judges as the authors of judicial opinions. In Chapter 8 we imagined that prediction markets might resolve cases without the need for judicial opinions as the pricing of factual distinctions replaced judicial opinions in providing reasoning such as the common law. But the text-authoring market also could enable market crafting of judicial opinions.

This market might respond in part to the two criticisms of Dworkin's theory. The collective wisdom of such a market might produce opinions that are better integrated into past case law, because market participants would have incentives to identify inconsistencies. They might correct minor inconsistencies with small changes, although sometimes recognition of small problems might lead market participants to change their initial view about the appropriate holding of a case. At the same time, such a text-authoring market could produce a chain novel that is consistently ideologically moderate, rather than conservative in one chapter and liberal in another.

Perhaps the output of such a market would lack the verve of a Benjamin Cardozo or a Richard Posner, but the greatest jurists could contribute to the most important cases, even if not formally appointed to the courts. And the lesser jurists, working on lesser cases, at least could correct many mistakes that individual judges otherwise might make.

AN IMPROVED WIKIPEDIA

Although such a text-authoring market does not yet exist, there is another approach to creating collaborative texts that is thriving. A *wiki* is a page on the Internet that anyone can edit, and the most fully developed wiki is the Wikipedia,[6] an on-line encyclopedia created entirely from voluntary contributions. It might appear that the project would be doomed to fail because anyone can vandalize a page, for example, by deleting it or by adding false material. But Wikipedia allows users to undo the changes of other users, and there are more people on Wikipedia who are interested in maintaining it than there are who are interested in destroying it. Indeed, in this sense, Wikipedia bears some resemblance to a prediction market. It is difficult to manipulate a prediction market, because an attempt to push price artificially in one direction will be countered by others pushing it back. Remarkably, Wikipedia has developed elaborate norms, such as a rule that no one should revert any particular change more than three times in a day, and dispute resolution procedures.[7]

Much of Wikipedia's content is produced by a relatively small percentage of users,[8] though the absolute number is growing over time. Today, Wikipedia is larger than the privately produced *Encyclopedia Britannica*. And yet Wikipedia could be better. First, critics claim that it is inaccurate. This is disputed, and a study by *Nature* concluded that Wikipedia's coverage of scientific topics was as accurate as *Britannica*'s,[9] a claim that the *Britannica* editors reject.[10] Whatever the relative merits of the two, everyone agrees that Wikipedia has some errors and that errors are more common on relatively more obscure pages. Second, even if errors are corrected rapidly, there is always a risk that a Wikipedia user will read a page at a moment when an error exists. It might be preferable if the main text of Wikipedia consisted only of text that community members already concluded was of sufficiently high quality to be included. Another benefit of this approach is that readers would not encounter commentary sometimes mixed in with pages recommending particular edits.

Wikipedia might be improved by subsidizing its production. Current proposals would allow individuals to subsidize work on individual topics, although those proposals are hotly disputed.[11] It is possible that introducing some monetary compensation into the Wikipedia system would alienate many volunteers and reduce the quality of the product.[12] Nonetheless, there is surely some level of compensation that would lead to an improved Wikipedia. It is remarkable that a volunteer project has been able to exceed the leading private project, at least in scope, but that does not mean that it is impossible to develop models that provide incentives that could stimulate higher-quality peer production. There is at least one private project under way that may seek to compete with Wikipedia by paying some editors who would supervise particular sections of the encyclopedia.[13] Perhaps a better means of competing with Wikipedia would be to provide decentralized incentives by, for example, using prediction market subsidies to calculate payments to be made to individual contributors.

It may be, of course, that Wikipedia has such a big head start that it would cost more to compete credibly with Wikipedia than could be recovered. Wikipedia itself, however, often considers reforms, and perhaps it eventually will consider using subsidies to compensate individual contributors. The text-authoring market itself might also be a useful reform. Wikipedia could implement subsidization using prediction markets based on points. A significant advantage of the text-authoring market is that it would allow Wikipedia to ensure that there would always be a relatively clean official version of the encyclopedia.

Wikipedia already goes to some lengths to disguise some of its internal workings, providing a discussion page corresponding to but separate from each encyclopedia page, but changes can still be made to the main pages without being officially approved. Of course, users would still be able to look at the proposed amendments in pages devoted to the text-authoring market, but readers who need greater confidence in the accuracy of information could restrict themselves to the officially approved pages.

Another benefit of the text-authoring approach is that it might allow development of collaborative texts that would express the consensus about particular issues. That may not be appropriate for an encyclopedia, and Wikipedia's norms strongly favor neutrality. But in other contexts, it may be useful to generate text indicating the consensus of a community. The *Los Angeles Times* briefly experimented with creating some editorials via wikis, but the experiment was a disaster.[14] Part of the problem was that pages were vandalized with inappropriate content such as pornography, a danger that the text-authoring market would solve by rejecting changes amounting to vandalism before they appeared on the main page. But perhaps the more significant problem was that the wiki approach does not seem to work well when the goal is to present a consensus rather than reporting on all sides of an issue. The text-authoring market can solve this problem by requiring only that the authors designate a pool from which ex post decision makers will occasionally be chosen to judge whether particular changes were good or bad. A newspaper, for example, might make volunteer readers its official judges.

Indeed, the text-authoring market could easily be adapted to produce not simply an on-line site but also a hard-copy daily newspaper. The market has three distinct advantages over the wiki format for generating a decentralized newspaper. First, it provides a straightforward means for subsidizing content, which is probably essential if the aspiration is to produce a full newspaper. In theory, the text-authoring market can rely on a fully decentralized news staff, potentially spending less than a newspaper that must provide salaries and facilities to its reporters. Second, the approach provides a way of mediating ideological and other disagreements about both editorial and news content that could lead to content instability, especially in the moments before the paper must be finalized and sent to the printer. Third, the text-authoring approach can greatly limit the danger that last-minute vandalism and incomplete work will make it into the final product. It may be acceptable for the Wikipedia to note that some articles should be improved on later, but that might not be suitable for a newspaper.

Application of the text-authoring market to create a newspaper might involve some distinct challenges. The market produces a string of text, not two-dimensional pages complete with headlines, photos, and captions. But the market can be used to assign the task of laying out particular pages (or entire sections or only portions of pages) to individual market participants, and a computer program could translate the current state of that text-authoring market into permission to work on particular parts of the newspaper. Such markets also might be used to make long-term and short-term story assignments and to decide which combination of stories, perhaps including some borrowed from the wires, to use on any particular day. Just as a regular newspaper scrambles to compensate when someone does not perform as expected, so could the decentralized newspaper, which could punish those who have not performed well by giving them fewer assignments.

OPEN-SOURCE SOFTWARE

Prediction markets might be used to enhance other forms of peer production as well. Consider, for example, open-source software. Such software obviously cannot work in the same way as Wikipedia because of the much higher cost of errors. If anyone could change a zero to a one or a one to a zero in an open-source program's binary code, then at any given time there would be bugs as a result of vandalism. And because a computer processes code much faster than individuals can read it, computers running open-source software would crash often. It is not surprising that open-source software projects use centralized means of determining what should be included in each release of the software. Only fully tested software is included, although sometimes there is debate about when particular proposed new features indeed would improve or detract from an open-source program as a whole.

A text-authoring market might provide for a more democratic means of determining what should be included in open-source software packages. Software programs are generated from source code spread out over a number of files. A text-authoring market could be used to generate the next version of an open-source software package. The timing prediction market would anticipate when the next release would be generated, and decisions would be made along the way about what changes from the previous version to allow and what changes to reject. Just as with existing software packages, sometimes initial deadlines would be met, perhaps with some features dropped, and sometimes not.

The markets might also include many files devoted to comments consisting of discussion about what proposed software to include and not include, as well as files devoted to official documentation. Different text-authoring markets might exist simultaneously for minor releases of software such as a version 1.0.1 consisting of bug fixes, major releases, and a version 1.1 or 2.0 with the next significant release, as well as "alpha" and "beta" releases of software at times in which many bugs are still present. Participants in the markets would recognize that ex post decision makers would have different standards for different versions of the software. Once the text-authoring market approved a particular text, the relevant software would be compiled and officially released.

Once again, subsidies could greatly increase the quality of open-source software. Indeed, production of such software is already heavily subsidized by companies such as IBM, which makes money by servicing open-source customers. Prediction markets could provide decentralized and possibly more efficient means of stimulating production of open-source software that they believe would help their businesses. One possible inefficiency of decentralized production is the danger of duplicative effort as competing programmers seek to capture bounties offered by a single provider. Just as there are benefits but also costs to patent races,[15] there might be benefits and costs to decentralized competition.

A market sponsor, however, could create a text-authoring market that could tentatively assign projects to particular programmers or that could decide in some cases that it would be better to allow limited or full competition. Programmers might even offer to accept reduced compensation, for example, two-thirds of what they ordinarily would receive from the ex post decision maker. That person in turn would have an incentive to take into account such concessions in making decisions determining subsidies, as well as the initial assignments. In effect, the text-authoring market could itself evolve an informal system of intellectual property rights and contracting auctions.

One might argue that governments, too, should subsidize open-source software. The argument can find an analogy in proposals for governments to subsidize scientific research, either with grants or with prizes, rather than relying entirely on the patent system.[16] A social cost of patents is that some who value patented products such as pharmaceuticals at more than the cost to produce them will nonetheless not purchase them at the prices charged, resulting in what economists call "deadweight loss." Similarly, a cost of private production of software is that many who value software at more than the trivial cost of reproducing it will not be able to afford it, for example, because they would use the software rarely. Research whose results are placed in the public domain and open-source software largely solve this problem. That alone does not mean that subsidies are justified. If the government does not spend research money efficiently, then government spending on public-domain intellectual property can reduce social welfare. Perhaps the chief virtue of the patent and copyright systems is that the incentives they provide to produce goods are roughly proportional to the level at which private parties value them.

Prediction markets at least make the case for government subsidy stronger. Ordinarily, a significant danger of governmental subsidies is that they simply lead to "rent-seeking" behavior as private parties lobby the government in order to get a piece of the pie. We have seen, though, that prediction market–based decision making can greatly reduce the impact of special interests (see Chapter 6), and so the best way for private parties to obtain a portion of the subsidies may be to make useful contributions rather than to lobby. Apart from rent-seeking, the government may make poor decisions about where to allocate research funds. Yet prediction markets might do a relatively good job of evaluating the importance of various contributions to open-source software, in part because no one person would have much ability to influence the development of software to fit idiosyncratic agendas. Government subsidy of vastly improved free software might on the whole be a better deal for the average citizen, who would pay more in taxes but would pay less for more software. Whether this is true, of course, is a difficult empirical question, but at least a case can be made for limited experimentation.

HANSON'S FUTARCHY

Using text-authoring markets to write encyclopedias or to determine the final content of open-source software packages are relatively plausible applications of prediction markets, though these may not exist in the next few decades. Let us now turn to the least plausible proposals, those that could fundamentally remake the legislative core of democratic governance but seem exceedingly unlikely to happen, at least in our lifetimes. In part, my desire to consider such possibilities is similar to the desire that leads some to write science fiction, to imagine worlds yet unknown but that perhaps might someday come to be. There is, however, a more immediate reason. If prediction markets indeed have many of the useful attributes that I have identified—efficiently aggregating information, lowering the cost of decision making, providing for the possibility of consistently moderate decision making, avoiding excessive influence by special interests—then it should be possible to create a market-based legislature that would produce better results than do existing alternatives.

If I were to concede that prediction markets could not do that, then I would need to identify a more fundamental problem with prediction markets. While recognizing the possibility that any number of hurdles, such as the danger of manipulation (see Chapter 1), could prove insuperable, I see no technical reason why market-based legislatures would necessarily fail, if in fact prediction markets turn out to be a robust means of aggregating information. Therefore, I will make a theoretical case for using prediction markets at the core of government, temporarily setting aside problems of transition, democratic legitimacy, and democratic participation, all of which admittedly are decisive in favor of the status quo in the short term and even in the fairly long term.

Before considering my own proposal, however, I will consider another. Robin Hanson, the originator of prediction markets, has sketched out a vision that he calls "futarchy," imagining that this might arise in some country after successful experiments with prediction markets for corporate and administrative agency decision making have been conducted.[17] At the heart of Hanson's proposal is the use of conditional markets to estimate the effect of proposed policies on a measure of national welfare. Initially, Hanson suggests, futarchy might depend on an existing imperfect measure of national welfare, such as gross domestic product (GDP).[18]

The existing legislature, however, could pass legislation to change the welfare measure, producing what he calls GDP+, a measure that "could include measures of lifespan, leisure, environmental assets, cultural prowess, and happiness."[19] Any policy that, according to a prediction market, would clearly improve GDP+ would be automatically adopted, at least unless another prediction market produced an opposite forecast. The legislature would continue to have a role in determining the ends that the state should seek, but prediction markets would determine how we would get there. Hanson thus appropriately titles his paper "Shall We Vote on Values, But Bet on Beliefs?"

Hanson's vision is not very different from mine, and he offers cogent responses to thirty criticisms of his proposal. Many small decisions, however, will have such a minor impact on welfare that the market will never "clearly" recommend them.[20] As discussed in Chapter 7, conditional prediction markets may each have enough noise that comparison of the market prices is meaningless. This may be an even greater problem than Hanson allows, because probably only a relatively small percentage of policy proposals would be big enough to have a significant impact on GDP+. Suppose, for example, that the level of precision of each conditional prediction market would be within 0.1 percent. That would mean an error of approximately eleven billion dollars based on current values, so proposals whose impact would be in the millions or low billions of dollars could not be clearly evaluated. Greater accuracy might be achieved, and the errors in the two prediction markets assessing the worlds in which the condition is and is not met might be highly correlated, but still there will be some range of policies that are simply too inconsequential to be assessed with conditional markets (see Chapter 7).

Hanson offers two general solutions. First, he notes that many small changes, individually too minor to make a marked difference in welfare, might be added together into a single proposal. But one might then want some type of system for determining how to decide which policies should be aggregated. Otherwise, some bad proposals could be bundled with good ones. Sometimes the market might reject a proposal that on balance would be good because it would recognize that rejection of the proposal would lead to a better proposal that subsequently would be adopted, but some pretty good yet far-from-perfect proposals might still be adopted because any additional improvements would not have measurable effects on welfare.

An optimistic response is that later prediction markets might reverse this problem. Someone who is eager to advance a good proposal will have an incentive to bundle it with other good proposals, including those that undo previous bad proposals. At least in some cases, however, the initial approval of the bad proposal will have had some immediate effect, such as government expenditures, and so bad policy choices will not always be easily reversible. It might take a long time before all of the good proposals are exhausted and cannot be used as cover for bad ones, and there might be many unnecessary policy shifts in the interim.

Second, Hanson suggests that his policy could be applied recursively to approve other prediction market schemes. For example, legislation might approve widespread use of prediction markets based on more narrow criteria. A bill, Hanson suggests, might create a new general policy that sports stadiums should be built "whenever markets estimated that it would increase some measure of regional welfare, or of stadium profitability."[21] A general stadium bill, however, might have only a negligible impact on GDP+. Moreover, there might be little incentive to identify the appropriate more localized criterion. A general policy relying on a weak proxy might improve social welfare to some extent and thus be approved, though another hypothetical policy relying on a better proxy might improve social welfare more. For example, the localized stadium regime might not take into account all relevant effects on the environment or the community. Once again, that could be fixed in later bundles of market proposals, but a mechanism that can make small improvements to already good proposals before they are enacted might be superior to one that counts on future proposals to fix imperfections.

Having a perfect measurement of GDP+ would not guarantee optimal policies if the prediction market would endorse localized prediction markets relying on simpler measures. Futarchy might well overemphasize easily measurable variables compared to less easily measurable ones. Hanson anticipates this objection, illustrating with the example that it might not be good to reward teachers based on test scores if other important outcomes of teaching are difficult to measure.[22] Hanson's response is that there may be proxies besides test scores for other outcomes of teaching. It might not make sense to reward teachers on the basis of those proxies, because teachers (like nonteachers) are risk-averse. But decisions about whether to enact particular policies could be based on these proxies, because any risk aversion of market speculators should have only de minimis effects on predictions. Indeed, we have noted already that noisy ex post measures do not doom prediction markets (see Chapter 3). Both the measure of GDP+ and the measures to be applied to localized prediction markets could rely on these relatively noisy proxies.

But what are these noisy proxies? In the teacher reward context, perhaps one might use a measure of how many students decide to transfer from public to private school, or, to gauge generalized learning, one might assess how well students performed on tests for other courses. Such proxies, however, not only might be noisy but also might not in an expected value sense capture the underlying issue of interest, namely, the extent to which a teacher is effective in ways that cannot be captured by test scores. Ultimately, the best proxy will often be a subjective judgment. In the teacher reward context, that subjective judgment might be a measure of student satisfaction or an outside evaluation of teaching. In the policy context, a subjective judgment would take into account all of the soft variables for which objective proxies cannot easily be developed. Perhaps recognizing the benefit of subjective judgment, Hanson suggests that futarchy sometimes might adopt my proposal for predictive cost-benefit analysis in particular settings.[23] In my view, Hanson has it backward. Aggregating subjective judgment should be the core task of a hypothetical prediction market government, which in many cases might then decide to create localized prediction markets to forecast objective measurements.

THE MARKET-BASED LEGISLATURE

The market-based legislature would be a text-authoring market charged with the task of drafting bills. The bills, if enacted, would be legislative acts, and these in turn might amend a codified text, much as in the United States public laws typically amend the U.S. Code. The central question is, who would constitute the pool of ex post decision makers, whose assessments of amendments would be predicted? A simple solution would be to use an institution similar to the existing legislature to serve that function. Unlike Hanson's legislature, individuals in this legislature might be asked to vote not on values that others would then seek to achieve but instead on concrete statutory proposals, as existing legislatures do today. These legislators' decisions, however, would have no immediate effect but would serve only to discipline the text-authoring market, whose decisions would determine whether particular amendments were allowed and particular bills were enacted. Legislators also might have the responsibility of originating bills, though in principle there is no reason why prediction markets could not be used to assess bills originating from the broader public, perhaps on payment of some or all of the subsidy.

There might be alternative approaches to creating the group of ex post decision makers. A more populist version might require selection of a random citizen to serve that function. That citizen could read arguments on both sides of a particular issue and then make a decision that resolves the prediction market payouts. A weakness of this approach is that to the extent that citizens might systematically fail to appreciate certain subtleties, the market will tend to disregard those elements of an issue. A slightly less populist proposal would require a citizen to select a member of the legislature (perhaps from among a randomly selected group) who would make the decision. There are still less populist variations as well. We could select a decision maker from the judiciary or from a new judiciary created explicitly for this purpose. This might help ensure that the ultimate decision makers have the expertise needed to analyze proposals effectively. Or one could go a bit further and have members of the judiciary select the ex post decision maker, in much the same way as federal judges in the United States are constitutionally authorized to choose inferior officers.[24] Or one could go less far and have a randomly selected member of the legislature choose a member of the judiciary to make an ex post decision.

As these possibilities suggest, the choice of how populist to make the market-based legislature presents a tradeoff. On one hand, less populist approaches can result in a more expert decision-making body. On the other, more populist approaches will increase the chance that policy corresponds with what a majority of the population would prefer. There might be a danger that elites may tend to prefer policies that will benefit them at the expense of the people as a whole. At least initially, the first proposal described above, in which a randomly selected legislator would make a decision, would represent the least dramatic change from the status quo. This institution would be the most similar to the existing legislature, except that it would serve as an ex post decision maker rather than an ex ante one. The legislature itself sometimes might decide to delegate some of its power as ex post decision maker, either in a more or less populist dimension. Perhaps delegation in one direction or another would improve results, but there is little need to resolve this issue in sketching out the market-based legislature.

The market-based legislature also might dictate changes that would make the market more like the regime of predictive cost-benefit analysis while still producing integrated texts rather than dollar figures. First, the proposal described above imagines that there would be no delay before ex post decision makers reach their decisions. We have seen, however, that adding some delay can reduce ideological variability. Because a legislature is large, its median voter should not change as often as the leadership of an administrative agency, but delay could still provide some benefit. Delay has costs, too, in particular the risk that the nation will be ruled by its future rather than its present demographics. Second, the proposal imagines that ex post decision makers would vote for or against proposals, making binary decisions. It would also be possible, however, to have them produce a figure that reflects net costs or benefits. The result of this change would be that a relatively small number of strong views among the pool of ex post decision makers could have an increased effect. Intermediate regimes can limit the possibility that a very small number of such decision makers could control results with wild estimates (see Chapter 8).

The market-based legislature also might decide to resolve some issues using prediction markets that anticipate objective numbers rather than opinions. The key difference between Hanson's proposal and mine, which might well amount to little difference in practice, is that I would have the central prediction market decision-making mechanism be a form of a normative prediction market. The primary reasons for this preference are technical. Normative prediction markets can evaluate small as well as large decisions. Perhaps the most important legislative changes would be those that would have a large anticipatable impact on the measure of national welfare, but a legislature ought to be able to make smaller changes as well. At the same time, the market-based legislature would not need to rely on proxies for the national welfare but could directly forecast ex post decision makers' assessments of whether particular proposals would increase or reduce welfare. Those decision makers, one might hope, in turn would consult prediction markets that are making assessments of objectively verifiable variables, but they also would apply their own intuitions and judgment about issues that elude easy measurement.

There is also a more philosophical reason to prefer a normative prediction market to Hanson's futarchy. If the public does have preferences about means as well as ends, there is no inherent reason why these preferences should be disregarded. It might be possible for Hanson's legislature to factor into the measurement of national welfare an assessment of the degree to which the public is benefited or harmed by having its preferences as to means followed or disregarded, but this seems like a rather indirect way to honor these preferences. Ultimately, accepting the legitimacy of preferences concerning means rather than ends is one reason that my envisioned market-based legislature should not exist for the foreseeable future; people would not want it, no matter how wonderful it might be. I, too, would not adopt the market-based legislature today, though if prediction markets continue to prove effective, I might prefer it at some time in the future, probably before the population at large does. But I count as a benefit of my proposal that it would not recommend itself for a long time and suggest that the day it would recommend itself in some country, should that day ever come, is the day it should be adopted.

THE PROBLEM OF SOCIAL CHOICE

I do not claim that the market-based legislature is an objectively ideal instrument of democracy. Indeed, social choice theory teaches that there can be no ideal, no means of translating personal preferences into collective decisions that will not suffer from some weakness. The most famous result in social choice theory is Arrow's Theorem, developed by Kenneth Arrow, who ultimately won the Nobel Prize in Economics.[25] Arrow's Theorem postulates four conditions, each seemingly modest, to which any system of collective choice might aspire: universality (the system should consistently select an outcome for any set of individual rankings of possible alternatives); unanimity (if everyone prefers one possibility to another, then the system must prefer that possibility); nondictatorship (the system must take into account more than the preferences of a single voter); and independence of irrelevant alternatives (the system should produce the same ranking among a set of choices regardless of whether other choices are also included). Arrow's proof showed that no system can meet all four of these criteria. This result applies to market-based legislatures with the substitution of expected votes (among the ex post decision makers) for actual votes.

That does not mean, however, that one should not care about which of these conditions is violated for a particular institution. Different institutional arrangements may relax different conditions, depending on their needs. Maxwell Stearns, for example, has argued that the Supreme Court relaxes the unanimity requirement, whereas Congress relaxes the independence-of-irrelevant-alternatives requirement instead.[26] Because norms require Supreme Court Justices to explain their opinions in writing, they cannot ordinarily trade votes across cases. It is therefore possible that across a number of cases a different set of outcomes would make all Justices happier. In Congress, vote trading (sometimes called "logrolling") is possible, making it more likely that Congress will meet the unanimity requirement. Members of Congress, however, routinely vote strategically, anticipating how the failure or success of a motion or bill might affect later bills, so the alternatives are not irrelevant.

Arrow's Theorem might seem to imply that policy results will "cycle," meaning that different alternatives will be chosen at different times, a violation of the universality requirement. The possibility of cycling had been observed by the Marquis de Condorcet in the late eighteenth century, using a simple example. Suppose that Voter 1 prefers A to B to C, Voter 2 prefers B to C to A, and Voter 3 prefers C to A to B. In a vote between A and B, A will win with the support of Voters 1 and 3, but Voters 2 and 3 will then have an incentive to call for a new vote between A and C, which C will win. Finally, Voters 1 and 2 will call for another vote so that B can defeat C, and so on ad infinitum. No choice is stable, because there will always be some coalition that would benefit from changing to another option. Preferences will not always be structured in this way. When policy results can be placed along a continuum (for example, from "liberal" to "conservative"), and each voter has an ideal point along this continuum, votes will not cycle. Some theorists, however, have suggested that the potential for preferences that would produce cycling in never-ending votes is significant.[27]

In practice, cycling appears to be relatively rare. Some theorists suggest that this is a result of "structure-induced equilibrium."[28] That is, democratic institutions make sacrifices along other dimensions of Arrow's Theorem to prevent cycling. For example, Stearns has shown that in courts, the doctrine of stare decisis helps prevent cycling,[29] although it has the disadvantage of making the evolution of doctrine path-dependent. In turn, the doctrine of standing limits the ability of private parties to take advantage of stare decisis by manipulating the path of precedent.[30] Similarly, in legislatures, committee voting and rules preventing reconsideration of rejected alternatives can prevent cycling. The power to set the voting agenda, often possessed by the majority party, can be critical in determining the final outcome. These conventions, Saul Levmore has noted, can mean that majority voting "can fairly be described as arbitrary, in the sense that some undemocratic or unappealing means must be used to settle things down."[31]

A possible critique of the market-based legislature is that it might induce cycling. After all, it lacks the institutional checks that legislatures use to prevent it. The resulting cycling might make it difficult for private parties to rely on legislative decisions and to make investments in light of them. The prospect of this result, however, helps suggest that cycling is unlikely, as a practical matter, to occur. Ex post decision makers can factor reliance interests into their evaluations, so eventually market participants are likely to anticipate that ex post decision makers will believe that additional changes will be too costly, and further changes will be disallowed. If only a few seconds have passed since a decision has been made, some ex post decision makers will disfavor a change because they view cycling as inherently undesirable. Thus, without formal mechanisms, informal norms against reconsideration of rejected alternatives can limit cycling.

The market-based legislature then must make a sacrifice of one of the other conditions in Arrow's Theorem. One condition likely to be sacrificed, as it is in existing legislatures, is independence of irrelevant alternatives. But this sacrifice might be less detrimental to social welfare than in existing legislatures. What differentiates the market from existing legislatures is that the agenda setter, consisting of the markets that determine the times at which different votes will be held, is decentralized. The agenda setter is thus more likely to be a relatively moderate decision maker. Market participants will anticipate that individual ex post decision makers might assess whether a decision should be made about an amendment based in part on how doing so will affect the path of decision making. When averaged through prediction, however, these decisions will not generally be motivated by a desire to manipulate the path of precedent in a way that would produce results that appeal to any extremist group. Irrelevant alternatives will affect decisions, but not necessarily in a way that seems particularly troubling.

Indeed, in general, irrelevant alternatives may end up mattering in a benign way because the market will consider such alternatives as a means of ensuring that the market comes as close as possible to achieving the goal of unanimity. Some ex post decision makers seem likely, in deciding on the timing of different amendments, to privilege outcomes that would increase overall satisfaction, even when these outcomes do not accord with their own preferences. Suppose, for example, that there are three options—A, B, and C—and that the anticipated preferences of the ex post decision makers suggest that the Condorcet paradox is operative, that A is preferred by a majority to B, which is preferred by a majority to C, which is preferred by a majority to A. Suppose, however, that a few voters, those who prefer A to B, feel particularly strongly about that issue. Some ex post decision makers are likely to resolve timing decisions in a way that would result in the ultimate adoption of policy A, because they believe as a general matter that cycles should be resolved in a way that maximizes overall political satisfaction.

To some extent, this may happen in existing legislatures, too. Arrow considers only ordinal (relative) preferences, but other scholars have argued that the reality of cardinal (absolute) preferences suggests that Arrow's Theorem is not troubling for democratic government.[32] Specifically, if technically irrelevant alternatives affect existing decisions only in the sense that they lead to decisions that maximize some aggregation of cardinal preferences, then the alternatives are not irrelevant in a practical sense.[33] Timing decisions, however, may be more likely to cardinalize preferences in the market-based legislature than in existing legislatures. The basis for this is the unique position of the ex post decision maker. In an existing legislature, an agenda setter facing a limited set of options seems likely to seek to steer decision making in a way that will maximize the agenda setter's own utility. An ex post decision maker, however, has much less incentive to be strategic, because the actual decision already has been reached. As a result, timing decisions in the market-based legislature might be based more on abstract principles, such as maximizing overall preferences or ensuring optimal deliberation, than primarily on individual preferences.

INCORPORATING INTENSITY OF PREFERENCE

The above argument suggests that when policy options otherwise might cycle, the market-based legislature might choose among them in part on the basis of intensity of preference. It is plausible, however, that intensity of preference still will not matter as much in the market-based legislature as in existing legislatures. In the latter, committees and informal bargaining among major constituencies facilitate vote trading. One committee member who cares a great deal about one goal can agree to compromise on two other goals to win the vote of another committee member. Permitting amendments that could undo individual elements of these deals might inhibit such compromises and therefore prevent intensity of preference from having an effect on policy.

That does not mean that intensity of preference would not matter at all in the market-based legislature as described so far. The market spontaneously might package together various proposals for reasons relating to intensity of preference. Whether that would happen, of course, depends on the antici-pated decisions of the ex post decision makers. Suppose, for example, that a bill would not have enough support on its own but that an amendment is pro-posed that would intensely appeal to a small group of ex post decision makers, thus securing enough anticipated votes for passage of the overall bill. The amendment might fail if most ex post decision makers opposed it. It is pos-sible, however, that some of them would recognize that the amendment was necessary for the passage of the overall bill and thus endorse it, implicitly crediting the intense preferences of others.

Nonetheless, it may be possible to improve on the market-based legislature to allow intensity of preference to play a larger role. One approach would be to alter the amendment process so that each amendment would be judged on the basis of its potential to increase support for the overall bill. That is, conditional markets would assess the probability that the overall bill would pass if an amendment were approved (or that an amendment would pass if an amend-ment to the amendment were approved). Amendments that would improve the prospects of bills (or amendments to which they are in turn amended) would be passed. Only the bill itself would be assessed by a normative predic-tion market. This approach would give market participants incentives to as-semble collections of proposals that in combination would secure majority support.

One interesting aspect of this proposal is that it is not clear that majority support should be the appropriate threshold for assessing whether a bill passes. In theory, if there were zero transactions costs, vote trading could permit truly Pareto optimal legislation that leaves everyone better off.[34] In the real world, there are transactions costs, and requiring unanimity would mean that no bill ever passes. But providing for a higher threshold than a majority for passage of legislation would mean that majorities would need to find ways of compen-sating some of those who would be harmed by bills that only a bare minor-ity would favor. Of course, this is true in existing legislatures, too, and yet we require only that bills have majority support. A supermajority requirement, however, might make somewhat more sense with a market-based legislature, if that legislature reduces the transactions costs associated with combining proposals into compromises that will yield sufficiently large coalitions.

In a traditional legislature, strategic bargaining over how to split the surplus from cooperation can prevent a supermajority (or even a majority) from agreeing to legislation. When there is some hypothetical legislative package that would benefit each of various groups that might together produce the necessary votes, each group has an incentive to seek an even better deal for itself at the expense of the others. The problem may be particularly severe when one political party stands to earn credit for passage of useful legislation, making it difficult to identify deals that will leave minority legislators better off than they would have been. The market-based legislature largely eliminates strategic bargaining. The market predicts ex post assessments, and ex post decision makers have little if any incentive to claim that legislation they would find beneficial is actually harmful.

A very different approach to incorporating intensity of preference would be to maintain normative prediction markets for assessing amendments, but allow ex post decision makers directly to indicate the strength of their preference. One way to accomplish this without allowing easy gaming of the system would be to allow them to allocate votes across the issues that they are considering.[35] For example, an ex post decision maker addressing the wisdom of five amendments might decide to allocate four votes to voting yes on one amendment and one-quarter vote to voting either yes or no on each of the remaining four. He or she would have to allocate at least some fractional vote to each amendment being considered.

Market participants would then anticipate whether some portion of ex post decision makers would feel particularly strongly about, and thus concentrate their votes on, particular issues. For example, suppose that only one-third of them are expected to vote yes on an amendment but that this one-third cares about the issue more than twice as much as the other decision makers. Then the market would approve the amendment. To the extent that some portion of the ex post decision makers are expected to concentrate votes on particular issues, it will decrease their influence on all other issues. Thus they have an incentive to be honest in making their evaluations.

My claim is not that such changes are necessarily desirable. Intensity of preference, after all, helps explain practices that seem deplorable, such as pork-barrel spending, in which each legislator gets a particular project by agreeing to many other projects. These negative consequences, however, might be less likely with ex post decision makers than with ex ante decision makers anyway. An ex post decision maker seems unlikely to allocate the maximum number of votes for highway spending in his or her own district for two reasons. First, he or she ordinarily confronts only a very small percentage of issues and only by remarkable coincidence encounters an issue of intense local interest to himself or herself. Second, he or she does not actually influence policy. There is little incentive to allocate all one's influence to highway funding for one's district when that vote has no effect on whether the district receives the funding.

Nonetheless, there are possible dangers associated with allowing unrestricted application of this intensity-of-preferences approach. Some interest groups might urge ex post decision makers to allocate all of their votes to their issue. If it seems likely that a few of them will make vastly disproportionate allocations of their votes, that could have enormous consequences. It is possible to imagine more limited versions of this system, however. For example, one might allow ex post decision makers to assign no more than two or no more than three of their votes to any one issue. The greater the freedom that they have to allocate their votes, the more the system takes into account intensity of preference, but also the more minorities can exercise their will over contrary majorities. One advantage of the market-based legislature in any event is that this design should make it considerably easier than in a traditional legislature to vary the degree to which preference intensities matter.

RESTATEMENTS OF THE LAW

The market-based legislature, then, appears to illustrate that prediction markets pass the test that I stipulated: they provide a theoretical substitute for some of our most important institutions. The mechanism might provide some advantages over existing institutions, though I make no claims about the relative magnitude of advantages and disadvantages. Admittedly, the market-based legislature does not meet the test of being a plausible proposal in the foreseeable future. An alternative test is whether the text-authoring market might serve a more practical purpose, involving government in a way that the Wikipedia proposal does not but without actually enacting statutes or regulations. One possibility is that private parties might create shadow legislatures or shadow administrative agencies to draft recommended statutes. This section considers an additional private alternative, the possibility that text-authoring markets might be used to create a shadow judiciary, telling the judiciary how it should decide cases.

What makes this endeavor relatively plausible is that there is already an organization that effectively does this: the American Law Institute (ALI). The ALI produces restatements of the law in a variety of areas such as torts, contracts, and agency.[36] In theory, these publications restate, saying what the law is. That task, however, inevitably involves normative judgment, because some judicial decisions conflict with one another. Therefore, the restatements are to some extent aspirational. A benefit of the restatements is that they are developed via intense group consultation involving numerous lawyers, professors, and judges, so they have a greater claim to authority than a treatise written by any single expert. Nonetheless, there is also always a risk that however many people participate in the process, their views will lead the restatement away from the task of restating.

A text-authoring market easily could be used to craft restatements. The market might predict whether randomly selected judges would agree to particular amendments to the text. Amendments would be approved only when most judges would be expected to agree to them. An alternative to using randomly selected judges would be to use actual cases, for example, to determine whether cases citing the restatement followed or rejected its approach to particular issues. Because the restatement itself presumably influences judges, amendments might be passed only when a supermajority of judges would be expected to follow rather than reject the particular principles of law reflected in the amendment. However designed, this market can increase the chance that the restatements will represent the current state of the law. At the same time, the dynamic nature of the text-authoring market could allow regular updates at far shorter intervals than the decades that sometimes separate successive versions of existing restatements. Even without binding force, such a text-authoring market might gradually become more influential than the formal restatements.

If such a project were a success, it might make sense to create a parallel set of restatements, indicating not the present state of the law but where the law should be in the future. For some of those who hoped that the restatements would fill this role, they have been a disappointment. Alan Schwartz and Robert Scott have analogized the ALI and similar groups to private legislatures.[37] Noting that these groups, like public legislatures, are subject to Arrow's Theorem, they generate predictions about how a structure-induced equilibrium might affect the output of these private legislatures. They conclude that these groups are likely to have a strong bias toward the status quo and to prefer abstract standards except in cases in which dominant interest groups influence the process.[38] A text-authoring market that anticipates decisions to be made retrospectively several decades hence might avoid these problems. And if it does, the law reform recommendations produced by these parallel markets might be influential both in courts and in legislatures.

Chapter 10 Predictocracy

The first nine chapters of this book have developed two arguments: first, that prediction markets can serve as a general-purpose tool for prediction, and second, that prediction in turn can serve as a general-purpose tool for aggregation of information, beliefs, and preferences. Underlying both arguments is the observation that prediction markets give incentives to be honest in making evaluations and to take into account all possible information. This observation explains why election markets should provide more accurate forecasts on average than polling data, why markets projecting long-term economic trends should be more objective than official prognosticators, why predictive peer review can provide less idiosyncratic evaluations of articles than ordinary peer review, why predictive cost-benefit analysis can be less ideological than the traditional alternative, why corporate prediction markets can reduce agency costs, why a legislation adjustment assistance program could consistently take into account the facts of individual cases, and why market-authored legal restatements can provide a more reliable account of the state of the law than do current procedures.

Voting regimes can also aggregate information, beliefs, and preferences to some extent, but prediction markets offer two advantages. First, for voting to be effective, there must be a large number of informed voters. With a small number, there is a danger that decisions might be idiosyncratic, and with uninformed voters, there is a danger that decisions will not take into account all relevant considerations. Prediction markets, on the other hand, can function effectively with a small number of participants, each of whom has an independent incentive to be informed. Second, voting increases the danger that individuals pursuing their own interest or their ideological short-term interest will expediently disregard broader principles. When prediction markets forecast ex post decisions, the ex post decision makers will have no direct effect on policy, and they therefore will be more likely to vindicate higher principles, at least to the extent that they believe that these principles ought to be consistently followed. It is hard to follow principle when one knows that this will have immediate effects that one will not like, but easy when the only consequence is that predictors might be more likely to expect principled decision making in the future.

These are the points that help explain the more adventurous proposals in this book, the possibilities that prediction markets could perform the functions of our most important political institutions: administrative agencies, courts, and legislatures. Even these proposals, however, imagine that these institutions would exist within some broader democratic context, for example, one in which a market-based legislature predicts ex post decisions that might be made by a real legislature. The question remains whether prediction markets can constitute an integrated, autonomous government. By *integrated* I mean that prediction markets could perform all tasks, including ones that today might be considered to be executive. By *autonomous* I mean that prediction markets would require no other governmental structure to provide a foundation for their own functioning.

My answer is that prediction markets could indeed not merely serve as instruments within a broader government but rather could constitute all the machinery that is needed for the government to function. I name a government that could function this way a *predictocracy*. That predictocracy is conceptually plausible and might combine the advantages of various market-based institutions does not mean that it will exist or that it should. Most of the thought experiments in this book have placed aside the issue of path-dependence, but the optimal government for the future depends a great deal on the government that we have had and have today. This chapter thus begins by emphasizing that institutions evolve slowly and that although they may evolve too slowly, this does not justify radical change.

I then consider two further new prediction market designs: first, the market web, which could integrate and relate various prediction markets to one another, and second, self-resolving prediction markets, which forecast only their own predictions. I also consider John Maynard Keynes's famous comparison of markets to a beauty pageant to explain why self-resolving prediction markets could produce reasonable decisions. I make a relatively modest proposal, use of prediction markets for collaborative social science modeling, before considering the possibility of predictocracy.

After cautioning that the case for self-government may argue against predictocracy, I note that prediction markets could be used not only for democratic purposes but also for dictatorial ones. Prediction markets, however, also could help dictatorial regimes become more democratic ones, providing for the possibility of slowly increasing democracy without undermining stability. I then explain how predictocracy could honor the need for secrecy in certain governmental decision making contexts and perform the functions of executive power. I explain how predictocracy could accommodate regional preferences and facilitate international cooperation. Finally, I consider how predictocracy could one day evolve from existing institutions while providing some additional reasons why this day might never come.

THE PROBLEM OF INSTITUTIONAL EVOLUTION

The institutions of governance evolve extraordinarily slowly. The broad outlines of the current form of government in the United States would be easily recognizable to our nation's founders, although most specific legislative and administrative programs would be alien. Other institutions, such as corporations and the courts, also have the same structure today that they had many years ago. And yet change does occur. Many scholars have suggested that the framers of the U.S. Constitution would not have imagined the rise of the modern administrative state. Modern corporate and securities law includes many doctrines that are quite different from norms of a hundred years ago,[1] and judicial rules of pleading and joinder bear little resemblance to their historical antecedents.[2] If history is a reliable guide, then the legal system hundreds of years from now will remain familiar in broad outline but will differ in many minor details.

This history guides my cautious prediction about prediction markets: they will play an increasing role in governance of all types over the very long term but not displace our core democratic institutions. Already we have seen other market mechanisms assume increasing importance in governance. The notion of pollution trading markets at one time must have seemed bizarre, in part because such markets were so different from previous models of governmental regulation. Environmentalists originally largely opposed such markets, but today pollution trading lies at the heart of many of the most important environmental initiatives, including the Kyoto accords on global warming.[3] When Ronald Coase proposed that the Federal Communications Commission auction rights to the electromagnetic spectrum,[4] the idea was generally dismissed as clever but fanciful. But with two steps forward and one back, we are far closer to Coase's vision than one would have imagined. When an idea can really improve efficiency, it is not implausible that government will eventually move toward it. An advantage of prediction markets is that they can be adopted gradually: private before public implementation, advisory before dispositive decision making, unsubsidized markets before subsidized ones.

Prediction markets should be adopted gradually. Most members of the public would probably find market-based decision making illegitimate or distasteful, and even if this reflects ignorance about market mechanisms, the public's view matters. Our knowledge of prediction markets, moreover, remains limited. We can expect more experimentation with various prediction market mechanisms, and our knowledge accordingly will grow. Perhaps some of the mechanisms that I have suggested in this book will be tried and prove not to work as I have hoped, and perhaps some of the policy proposals that I have identified will prove to be misguided for reasons that I have or have not anticipated. The core idea that people will make better predictions when they have financial incentives is sufficiently powerful that it seems unlikely to me that prediction markets broadly conceived will turn out to be just a fad. Before making radical changes to our social institutions, though, we will want to have gained greater knowledge about how prediction markets work, so that we can decide what the limitations of existing proposals are and whether there are effective means of working around them. The future of prediction depends on the power of prediction mechanisms.

I have thus forecast that prediction markets will be adopted gradually and argued that they should be adopted gradually. That does not mean, however, that adoption will take place at an optimal pace. To the contrary, prediction markets will probably be adopted so slowly as to be inefficient, because innovators cannot capture the full benefit of their innovations. Consider, for example, a corporation in the position of deciding whether to use conditional prediction markets to help make internal decisions. Corporate decision makers might be unsure whether these prediction markets will raise or lower returns. If the innovation proves valuable, others will copy it; if it is counterproductive, the corporation will fall behind its peers. Given these skewed incentives, corporations will proceed cautiously with modest uses of prediction markets, and even more so with more adventurous uses, such as self-deciding prediction markets. Agency costs make the problem still more severe. Individual managers might be hesitant to approve of prediction technologies that threaten to replace their own discretionary decision making power.

The same effects are present in public decision making. Any particular jurisdiction can adopt a prediction market proposal, but it cannot stop other jurisdictions from free-riding on its experience, and so prediction markets will be underprovided. Meanwhile, agency costs may be more severe. Individual public officials will probably gain little from supporting prediction market projects that turn out to be successful; future politicians tempted to brag about supporting prediction markets might well remember the criticism presidential candidate Al Gore received when he was accused of claiming to have invented the Internet.[5] And yet if prediction market projects are unsuccessful, the officials will receive considerable criticism.

Indeed, as the FutureMAP debacle reveals, merely proposing prediction markets can lead to ridicule. More elite commentators supported the program,[6] but there can be no doubt which side won the public debate at the time. This seems likely to change only once prediction markets become standard operating procedure in the business world. And then individual public officials may still be hesitant to adopt proposals that effectively might outsource their jobs.

These considerations do not suggest that innovation will not proceed at all. Prediction market technology is likely to become less expensive to implement. Already there are open-source software packages that corporations can use easily to run prediction markets. Milestones can be imagined but not yet precisely dated. One milestone has already arrived: an Internet site that allows users to create prediction markets in virtually anything, selecting whether to open such markets only to a group of traders or to a wider audience.[7] Another milestone will be reached when these Web sites offer more innovative prediction market designs, allowing subsidization of markets and providing cash to successful participants. Yet another one will be reached when some Web sites located in market-friendly jurisdictions allow for the creation of real-money markets in which individuals can both make and lose money.

Individual decision makers who are aware of prediction markets will find some modestly innovative applications for the markets to assist them. Prediction markets will become sufficiently familiar that participants in public policy debates will cite prediction market forecasts with little accompanying explanation. Beyond that, the future becomes hazier, but perhaps a government somewhere will mandate for some legal application that the forecasts of a prediction market be accepted as inputs into some administrative decision. A corporation whose work lends itself to decentralized decision making will decide to adopt self-resolving prediction markets. And it will become commonplace to think about how prediction markets can be integrated into decision making procedures.

THE MARKET WEB

If prediction markets were to become commonplace, decision makers might link to them in their own analyses. For example, suppose that a corporation is deciding whether to build a new factory in a particular area. That decision might depend on such variables as future interest rates and geographic patterns. And so a decision maker might build a spreadsheet containing live links to prediction markets that are assessing these issues. That way, as the market predictions change, the spreadsheet's bottom line would change as well. Forecasts in many prediction markets may be interrelated, and so participants in one prediction market will often have incentives to take into account developments in others. Prediction markets thus can affect one another indirectly.

Sometimes, however, it might be desirable to construct links among prediction markets so that changes in one automatically lead to changes in another. Consider, for example, the possibility of a market-based alternative to class-action litigation. In Chapter 8, each adjudicated case represented a separate prediction market, but often different cases have issues in common. Many thousands of cases may depend in part on some common factual issues, as well as on some distinct issues. Legal issues also may be the same or different across cases. Someone who improves the analysis of any common factual or legal issue can thus profit on that only by changing predictions in a very large number of cases. A better system might allow someone to make a change across a single market and have that change take effect automatically in individual cases.

The critical step needed to facilitate creation of the market web is to allow a market participant to propose a mathematical formula to be used for some particular prediction market. Some of the variables in that formula could be references to other prediction markets, sometimes new ones. For example, in a market for determining the level of damages the plaintiff should receive, a participant might propose a formula that is dependent on variables such as the probability that the plaintiff states a cause of action, the probability that the plaintiff was in fact injured, the probability given injury that the defendant caused the injury, the probability given a cause of action that the defendant is subject to strict liability, the probability (given no strict liability) that the defendant was negligent, and the damages that the plaintiff should be awarded if liability is proved. This formula, for example, presumably would allow for no damages where the plaintiff probably does not state a cause of action. Each of the components of this formula might be assessed with a separate prediction market.

We can easily build the market web by combining three tools that have already been described. The first is a text-authoring market. The relevant text would be the formula itself, including specifications of other prediction markets that would be used to calculate specific variables. As with any text-authoring market, a timing market would determine when a proposal to change the text should be resolved. Other markets might become live only once proposals to take them into account were approved. Ex post decision makers would assess the wisdom of these markets' recommendations in some fraction of cases in order to discipline the market's functioning.

The second tool would be a simple normative prediction market corresponding to the text-authoring market. It might also be possible to have computer software that automatically parses the formula and consults various sources, but the market sponsor need not build this tool. Rather, ex post decision makers will assess the appropriate value for the normative prediction market using the formula. An advantage of this approach is that it would make it easy to use complicated formulas, as well as formulas that depend in part on numbers from sources other than prediction markets or from prediction markets of other types. In addition, this approach makes it easy to collapse a formula into a single prediction market, if that should prove desirable. The formula text simply would be changed to a description of the market to be created, such as "adjudication of plaintiff's liability in a particular case."

The third tool is a mechanism for determining the market subsidy. A separate subsidy would be needed for the text-authoring market and the normative prediction market. Each of these subsidies could be determined by additional normative prediction markets, perhaps with fixed subsidies. The subsidy for the text-authoring market would be distributed by that market to individuals who have proposed particular amendments and to individuals who have participated in the assessment of particular amendments. This also could allocate a subsidy to the first individual who creates the market and proposes some text for it. When the text-authoring market produces a new formula reflecting additional prediction markets, the subsidy for the main prediction market would fall (since calculating a formula based on other prediction markets will often be relatively easy).

A single node in the market web would thus consist of a text-authoring market describing the node and providing a formula for calculating it, a normative prediction market, and a set of additional prediction markets for determining how to distribute a subsidy to contributors to the different components of the node. The nodes collectively create a web because the formulas link to other nodes; software, of course, could easily make these links clickable. At the same time, a mechanism is needed to determine what portion of the market subsidy each node should receive. A prediction market could simply be used for every link to determine the portion of the subsidy for each node that should be allocated to each node linked to it. The total should add up to a figure less than one so that a portion of the subsidy is left for the node itself.

Once these markets are established, software could easily distribute a single subsidy for the market as a whole to market participants who have traded on individual nodes when the market closes. Market participants working on one portion of the web, meanwhile, would not have to assess the relative importance of one node to nodes that are only distantly related. It would also be straightforward to have a continuously open market, periodically collecting and distributing money in accordance with individual participants' success on the market.

This assumes that the market web would be arranged on a single server. It is possible, though, that a node on one market web might link to a node on another market web. Allowing such links could promote competition among prediction market providers. It also answers in part one potential criticism of using prediction markets for decision making: that a software engineer might hijack the government by falsifying some prediction market results. Market participants at least will have incentives to identify false prediction markets and not link to them. In principle, it is possible to have government decisions based entirely on decentralized prediction markets, although the government might want to subsidize individual market web providers, and it might use centralized prediction markets to do so.

Whether or not the markets are decentralized, they would allow participants to make it easier to assess the basis for market predictions. Indeed, the
market web is in some ways a substitute for deliberative prediction markets,
because both provide means of helping observers understand the basis for the
market's predictions. An observer could look at any individual node of the market web and understand how it has been calculated, though inevitably there
must be some "leaf" nodes that themselves do not contain any formulas. At
the same time, software might allow an observer to find all of the nodes that
link to a particular node. So a market participant addressing a factual issue
that is relevant to many cases could link to all of the cases represented by that
factual issue. As a particular issue becomes increasingly important, the subsidy
for that node should rise, and market participants can profit on their analysis
of the issues relevant to that node without worrying about details of individual cases.

SELF-RESOLVING PREDICTION MARKETS

Normative prediction markets can be used to make virtually any type of decision, but so far they are not autonomous. They can function only by predicting some normative decision to be made in the future or at least one that
might be made. We have seen that prediction markets can forecast the outcomes of other prediction markets, but in the models discussed so far, eventually some prediction market must be forecasting a number to be determined
in a way that is external to the market. We have even seen that a prediction
market can give participants incentives to anticipate what the same prediction
market's forecast will be at some later point (see Chapter 4), but in this case
also we assume that eventually one or more predictors may be affected by
external assessments.

It is possible, however, to have a prediction market that is entirely self-
resolving, that is, in which there will never be a need for the sponsor to resolve
the market payouts by reference to a number derived outside the prediction
market itself. A simple change to the deliberative prediction market accom-
plishes the trick. As described above, if the market ends when a prediction has
not been resolved by a later prediction, then the payouts for the unresolved
prediction are determined on the basis of the actual event being predicted. An
alternative is to resolve payouts for any unresolved predictions at the close of
the market based on the market-closing consensus forecast. Recall that the exact time at which the market ends will not be known, so it will not be possible

to ensure profits by promising to make a particular prediction just before the market closes. This market is self-resolving in the sense that the payout for each prediction is resolved on the basis of the market consensus prediction at some time.

That it is possible to create a self-resolving market does not mean that it would be useful to do so. At first glance, it might appear that the market would not produce useful information. After all, the market is entirely circular. In effect, the market rewards market participants for predicting numbers that other participants might predict still other participants might predict, and so on. The instructions for the market might provide that participants should forecast interest rates, but participants might decide that they would rather forecast the results of a baseball game. Or different market participants might forecast different things. Perhaps many market participants would in effect enter random numbers, and the prediction market would produce nothing but random noise.

There are reasons, however, that this might not happen. Suppose that you stopped a stranger on the road and asked the stranger to forecast the high temperature for the next day and promised to compensate the stranger for making the forecast. Because you might not ever see the stranger again, you told this stranger that you would then ask another stranger to make the same forecast, and the closer the first stranger's forecast was to the second stranger's, the more you would pay the first. You promised that you would continue this process recursively until someone refused to make a forecast, in which case the prior forecaster would receive no compensation. Perhaps the stranger will be smart enough to recognize the recursive nature of the problem, but the stranger will still be better off making a prediction of the next day's weather than announcing an effectively random number. The reason is that if the second stranger announces a number, there is some chance that it will be a temperature forecast and some chance that it will be effectively random. The first stranger's incentive, like the incentive of every subsequent stranger, is thus to announce a temperature forecast.

In the language of game theory, the participants in the self-resolving prediction market and in the weather poll are playing a "tacit coordination game." Thomas Schelling described a game of this type in *The Strategy of Conflict:* "You are to meet somebody in New York City. You have not been instructed where to meet; you have no prior understanding with the person on where to meet; and you cannot communicate with each other."[8] In an empirical test, a majority of respondents, residents of the New York metropolitan area, picked the same place and time, Grand Central Terminal's information booth at noon. Both the time and place serve as "focal points," and someone trying to coordinate with someone else will choose a focal point.

The game would produce more successful coordination if Schelling had told participants where to go. For example, if he told each of two people that they would win large sums of money if they met the next day and that he would recommend the top of the Empire State Building as a meeting place at noon, it seems almost inevitable that they would meet there. Even if Schelling had referred less directly to the place where Tom Hanks would find love in *Sleepless in Seattle,* the participants, perhaps after asking friends or doing research, would succeed in meeting each other atop the Empire State Building. It seems highly unlikely that one of the two would decide instead to go to a random intersection instead of the Empire State Building. The person might recognize that the tacit coordination game is circular, yet there is some reason to go to the Empire State Building and no reason to go to a random intersection.

The prediction market is much like the version of the Schelling game in which the participants are instructed where to go. The instruction for the prediction market serves as a very strong focal point, and each market participant seems likely to act on the assumption that the next market participant will be seeking to improve on an estimate of whatever the prediction market specified. It is possible that on occasion there will be alternative focal points, such as the number 0 (or, for a probability estimate, 0.5). But market participants are unlikely to pay attention to them, for the same reason that market participants who receive the recommendation to go to the Empire State Building seem unlikely to choose the Grand Central Terminal information booth instead. The instruction makes the original focal point far more inviting.

This analysis admittedly does not guarantee that some other focal point will not occasionally dominate. Imagine, for example, that Schelling gave each of the two players an extremely difficult math puzzle that could be used to derive the longitude, latitude, and altitude at which to meet the other player, but that each player can provide only an imprecise answer to the puzzle, so imprecise that he or she cannot deduce that the answer is the Empire State Building. One or both players might then decide to go to the information booth. Or, alternatively, each player might calculate the location with a very generous round-off. It seems unlikely, however, that the instructions for prediction markets will often be so arbitrary or subjective that participants look for alternative focal points.

Perhaps on rare occasions someone other than the market sponsor could somehow change the problem and thus the focal point. As a general matter, however, this strategy seems unlikely to work. If a market participant could make money by announcing a new instruction and seeing the focal point change accordingly, then market participants would do this repeatedly, and only the original instruction from the market sponsor would differentiate itself. It is possible, however, that market participants might find a particular alternative instruction attractive for some reason. For example, some might argue that participants should not make the prediction requested by the market sponsor but instead should make the prediction that will lead to the most good for the world. This might create an alternative focal point.

The challenge of the self-resolving prediction market is that some criterion other than that recommended by the market sponsor will somehow become focal. General moral and economic reasoning may provide shared modes of analysis and thus provide alternative focal points. Where this is not what the market sponsor intended, however, it is difficult to see why these alternative focal points should defeat the intended one. There will often be many alternative focal points, based on different methodologies that might be used to resolve the market payouts (philosophy, economics, theology, and so on) and different groups whose interests might be relevant to these analyses (the predictors themselves, the citizens of a particular nation, everyone in the world). The one focal point that ordinarily will stand out most prominently will be the one corresponding to the instruction of the market sponsor.

That does not mean that self-resolving prediction markets should not be used to make moral or economic assessments. Perhaps we would be better off if prediction markets did sometimes deviate from their sponsors' intent for the greater good. The question is simply one of fidelity, and ultimately, if self-resolving prediction markets are faithful, they can be harnessed to engage in moral or economic reasoning. The sponsor of the market, after all, might specify a relevant principle for evaluating a particular question: What should be the minimum income the government should guarantee under a Rawlsian theory of justice? Or what should be the optimal toll price for the George Washington Bridge under general economic theory? Similarly, the sponsor could specify whose interests the market participants should and should not take into account or whose ideology should be the basis of reasoning.

Any question, of course, will involve some degree of ambiguity. Market participants can be expected to look to focal points for resolution of particular ambiguities. Suppose, for example, that the market sponsor did not specify whose interests should be taken into account. Then market participants might seek to identify focal weights for the interests of different groups, including the market sponsor. Or, if there are competing interpretations of a specified theory of justice, then market participants would presumably seek to determine the relative strength of different theories. In the end, this may not be very different from what market participants would do in a normative prediction market. In that case, they would anticipate what proportion of individuals would subscribe to particular approaches, whereas in the self-resolving market, participants would seek to identify the approaches' inherent appeal.

THE KEYNESIAN BEAUTY CONTEST

The dynamics of tacit coordination games are worth exploring in part because some have worried that even ordinary capital markets may be susceptible to similar breakdowns. John Maynard Keynes once compared stock markets to "those newspaper competitions in which the competitors have to pick out the six prettiest faces from a hundred photographs, the prize being awarded to the competitor whose choice most nearly corresponds to the average preferences of the competitors as a whole."[9] Keynes worried that each competitor would consider only what other competitors would think, and they in turn would think only about what others would think. Markets, Keynes observed, can have this property too. Some, he suggested, "have reached the third degree where we devote our intelligences to anticipating what average opinion expects the average opinion to be."[10]

Keynes's argument provides a basis for behavioral finance theories (see Chapter 7). Even recognized market bubbles might not pop right away, because everyone would like to ride the bubble and jump off just before everyone else does. We have seen, however, that behavioral finance theories do not suggest that prediction markets will be worse than other methods of prediction. Ironically, though, Keynes's argument does not provide the best basis for a critique of market behavior, because the problem may be less serious in the beauty pageants he describes. Markets can have bubbles because decisions are made over time. In the beauty contest, each market participant should want to choose the same faces that others choose, and so there is no reason to believe that the second or third degrees will be any different from the first degree of analysis.

It is only when contest participants will be rewarded if they can choose the pageant contestants who are the not-quite-most-popular that the dynamics of participants' incentives become interesting. A group of economists experimentally tested games having this property, which they called "p-Beauty Contests."[11]

Each person was asked to submit a number from a range, such as zero to one hundred, and the winner of the contest was the player whose guess was closest to p multiplied by the average response, where p was between zero and one and was announced in advance. Predictably, the mean response was lower than the midpoint of the range. In subsequent rounds of the same game, learning occurred, and the means gradually approached zero. When p is equal to one, however, there is no reason to expect this result. Perhaps some participants would randomize their answers somewhat, not wanting to have the same number as everyone else. This would not be a problem, though, if, instead of competing for a single prize, each person received a continuous payoff, and the closer the participant was to the mean, the higher the payoff.

The self-resolving prediction market is like a p-Beauty Contest with a p of one. The only reasonable concern in most cases is that the market might incorporate new information slowly. The current market price, after all, itself produces a competing focal point, and although market participants will expect the price to move toward the price that would reflect the new information, it may not be clear how fast that will occur. The self-resolving prediction market may be better on this score than are traditional markets. This type of market provides no mechanism for "riding" a bubble because participants in prediction markets that are based ultimately on the market scoring rule do not ordinarily sell their positions. Each participant is rewarded solely for predicting the price at some point in the future, and so prices should converge quickly to the expected end point. As long as this end point is the intended focal point, the market should work well.

A prediction market will have an even better chance of working as intended if it both provides incentives to predict market prices at later times and grounds market dynamics in fundamentals. Sometimes, however, the only fundamentals that can be used to resolve a prediction market ex post might be expected to deviate slightly from what the market sponsor would like. Even with normative markets, there is a danger that the ex post decision maker will be expected to be lazy and that the market therefore will ignore some subtleties. This might be less of a danger with self-resolving prediction markets, because there is no ex post decision maker being predicted. On the other hand, it is possible that self-resolving prediction markets might be worse because participants might see a "rounded-off" answer—one that ignores some details—as more focal than an attempt at better precision.

One can devise prediction markets that are only self-resolving in part. The analysis of the self-resolving prediction market suggests that the market might work as intended even if there is no chance that the hypothetical event that is supposed to be predicted will actually occur and be used to resolve the market. A small possibility of ex post resolution, however, could go far to solidify the intended focal point. Using a deliberative prediction market, the market sponsor could promise to resolve a prediction market 1 percent of the time with the event that is being predicted and 99 percent of the time with the final market price. In effect, this approach allows construction of a probabilistic prediction market but without the second-stage conditional market that gives participants in the first stage a fully internalized incentive to anticipate the result of the event ultimately being forecast (see Chapter 5).

At the least, the dynamics of the self-resolving prediction market should allay concerns about the deliberative prediction market when the market is fully grounded on fundamentals. One might imagine an argument that the deliberative prediction market would not work, because if there are one hundred market periods, then the market will be like the beauty contest one hundred degrees removed. But the above analysis suggests that the beauty contest should work reasonably well even if it is one hundred degrees removed, because the instruction to identify beauty provides contestants with a focal point. If that is so, then there should be less concern about market anomalies in cases in which the market is finally resolved by some objective measure or ex post normative assessment.

MARKET-BASED PRODUCT EVALUATION

Some preliminary experimental data indicate that self-resolving prediction markets in fact will produce meaningful results. A group of computer scientists and business school professors created a prediction market using a conventional double auction design.[12] Each participant in the experiment was given access to on-line information about a number of products; bicycle pumps were used in one experiment and crossover vehicles in another. In addition, each participant received ten thousand dollars in virtual currency and one hundred tradable contracts corresponding to fictitious companies that have produced each of the products. (The price of one tradable contract was fixed at a specific value and not traded.) Participants were permitted to buy and sell the tradable contracts in these virtual companies, and the shares would be redeemed at the end of the market based on the final trading prices. The market was thus circular in the same way as the self-resolving prediction market is. The three participants with the highest portfolio values at the end of the experiment were awarded gift certificates.

The study produced at least two reasons to conclude that the results were meaningful. First, across two iterations of the experiment, the results were highly and statistically significantly correlated. For example, the most popular Silver Bullet bicycle pump received 37.9 percent and 32.9 percent of the total market value in the two experiments, and the Cyclone pump received 19.3 percent and 23.3 percent. Second, the results were correlated with results based on more traditional means of product evaluation, such as testing conducted by allowing individuals physically to inspect samples of the particular products. Admittedly, it is difficult to assess how meaningful these results were and whether they were better or worse than the alternative methods. Because the experiment is purely hypothetical, there is no correct answer that can serve as a benchmark. If there were, it would be necessary to run many different markets before reaching conclusions about relative accuracy. Nonetheless, the studies suggest that these markets can serve reasonably well as alternatives to focus groups and other methods of product evaluation.

At least, the markets did not break down. Although prices moved, they did not swing wildly from one moment to the next. It may be difficult, however, to extrapolate confidently from this result to self-resolving prediction markets. The task presented to the participants in these experiments was relatively well-defined. The product information that they received consisted of evaluations of the relative quality of the product against several set dimensions, as in the magazine *Consumer Reports.* The principal focal point challenge was thus to decide the relative importance of several different sets of features; this is potentially far simpler than some uses to which self-resolving prediction markets might be put. Moreover, it is not clear whether market participants appreciated the circularity of the market and tried to exploit it. We cannot rule out the possibility that aggressive efforts to change a market focal point might succeed. It is too early to conclude that focal point analysis is a perfect substitute for market fundamentals, though the study at least gives some reason for confidence that self-resolving prediction markets can produce potentially useful results.

Self-resolving prediction markets might be most useful in conjunction with the market web. A potential disadvantage of the market web is that a single node might spawn many markets, including the timing and subsidy markets for the text-authoring component market. Even if only a small percentage of these decisions are to be flagged for ex post decisions, the need to arrange for such resolution might be cumbersome in many contexts. The sponsor of a market web would need to arrange, screen, and compensate a pool of ex post decision makers, and although prediction markets could facilitate these tasks, doing so would still add a level of complexity. In addition, those evaluating the markets will need to assess the representativeness of the pool of ex post decision makers to assess the reliability of the market. Once the software for the market web exists, many prediction market sponsors might prefer simply to pay the market subsidy and obtain results, even if these results inspire less confidence than a perfectly executed market web based on market fundamentals.

COLLABORATIVE ECONOMIC MODELING

The market web, with or without self-resolving prediction markets, will be useful in any context in which there are many interrelated components of a predictive problem. A market sponsor in effect subsidizes the creation of a model of some analytical problem. For example, a corporation might create a market web forecasting its future stock price. This could be more useful than a single prediction market making such a forecast because market participants have an incentive to structure the prediction. Deliberative prediction markets can provide incentives for individual participants to reveal their analyses, but the market web is unique in creating an environment for producing consensus modeling. Participants would have incentives to create distinct nodes related to important aspects of the problem. For example, there might be a node that predicts the future sales of a particular product, and that node in turn might depend on other nodes that assess the possibility of particular supplier delays, the appeal of the product to specific niche markets, the pricing of competitive products, and so forth.

Presumably, corporations already seek to take all of these factors into account in making decisions, and many corporations attempt to perform this task with analytical precision. But any given consultant preparing an analysis might miss important aspects of a problem or make a faulty decision about a particular factor. Informal consultation can be successful in reducing this problem, but the information aggregation capabilities of prediction markets may be superior. A corporation could choose to create specific prediction markets relevant to a particular problem, but the market web allows not only decentralized decision making about what markets to create but also decentralized assessment of the ways all of the created markets relate to the overall stock price prediction problem. The only decisions that the corporation would need to make would be whether to create a single market to forecast stock price and how much to subsidize the market. The larger the subsidy, the greater the accuracy and detail of the model that market participants would create.

In addition, the market web might have applications to economics and governance. For example, a market (sponsored either by the government or by the private sector) might predict a gross macroeconomic variable in future years providing an overall summary of the nation's economic condition. Market participants would seek to determine how much weight should be allocated in this measure to considerations such as environmental conditions and economic inequality and also to make time-series projections about these and less controversial variables. Inevitably, the prediction would to some extent be based on macroeconomic modeling, but other forms of modeling would likely also prove relevant at the margins. For example, demographic models could predict population trends. Models of specific economic sectors (such as health care) and specific government programs (such as Social Security) also would have some relevance for assessing overall economic health.

The market web could produce an overall model of virtually everything that is of interest to the economy, and it could help show links among many different types of decisions. In principle, with sufficient subsidy, such a market web might incorporate models relevant to the decision making of many individual corporations. Although a specific product design decision has virtually no effect on the overall economy, it has some effect on the corporation's welfare, which indirectly may affect a specific economic sector, and so forth. One might imagine microscopic levels, considering, for example, the ability of specific managers and employees to perform necessary parts of the overall project. The greater the subsidy, the larger and more reliable the web could be. Market participants, meanwhile, would have incentives to consider tradeoffs between size and reliability.

The purpose of such a project, of course, would not be simply to project future economic performance but to provide a consensus model of the economy that could be useful in many different applications. Internet blogs already provide a similar kind of web, with individual bloggers explaining their arguments in part by linking to the arguments of others. Blogs, however, do not generally provide cohesive integrated mathematical models of the world. Moreover, they do not lead toward consensus. A significant aim of the broad prediction market project is to enable discrete consensus estimates, to help citizens and policy makers sort through the cacophony of conflicting claims. The market web promises to do this on a much more pervasive basis if successfully implemented and gradually accepted as reliable.

Economists and other social scientists already cite one another, but the market web could facilitate greater cooperation. Economists learn from one another by reading articles and improving on earlier ideas. But a single economic model is limited by both math (given the difficulty of reaching closed form solutions of equations with too many variables) and human intelligence (given the difficulty of understanding all related developments). In many contexts, different articles point to different conclusions, and policy analysts would need to closely study the articles to assess which one has more reasonable assumptions and conclusions. The market web would provide a means for social scientists to benefit from one another's models without necessarily understanding all of their details. With the publication of new empirical and theoretical research, market participants (presumably in many cases social scientists themselves, eager to have their own contributions reflected) would have incentives to improve on the relevant portion of the model.

The market web would not supplant social science literature. To the contrary, the market web might link directly to computerized versions of mathematical or simulation models created with Mathematica software or the C++ computer language, for example, and these models in turn might base parameter values on nodes from the market web. In this way, the market web could harness distributed computational power, as well as the benefit of models so complex that they cannot easily be implemented via the mechanism of the market web itself. Both the market web and these models might not only model the existing world but also hypothetical worlds. We have seen that many interesting policy questions are conditional in nature; they assess the consequences of particular hypothetical decisions. Software might enable one to calculate how a change in one variable or in a set of variables, for example, variables representing policy choices, would reverberate through the market.

THE CASE FOR SELF-GOVERNMENT

One argument for restricting prediction markets to purely informational functions (such as collaborative economic modeling) rather than decisional functions (such as legislating) is that individuals have a preference for self-government. Opposition to colonialism may be based in part on dissatisfaction with the policies of colonizers, but many of the colonized would prefer to make the law themselves even if they believed that this would produce inferior policy results. Some of the more radical possible implementations of prediction markets, such as a government based entirely on self-resolving prediction markets, reduce self-government. If the citizenry came to believe that market participants were seeking to advance the interests of the population as a whole rather than their own special interests, they might still prefer to control policy decisions themselves. In part this is because people distrust elites and generally believe that their political instincts are the best ones, and in part this is because some people enjoy democratic participation.

In practice, however, the alternative to market-based government often will not be direct democracy but rather indirect republican governance. The success of representative democracy, or at least its general popular acceptance, suggests that people do not view indirect approaches to advancing the public good as inherently suspect. It is plausible that someday many people might prefer a system in which markets anticipate the policies that will satisfy collective preferences to a system in which the people must select leaders to act on their behalf. Many members of the public feel that special interests control decision making,[13] and they might come to appreciate the ability of prediction markets to reduce the effects of special interests. Some of the more populist versions of prediction markets described in this book might have particular appeal (see Chapter 6), whatever their merits as effective policy makers.

Enthusiasm for market-based government seems unlikely, however, to become a general sentiment for a long time, if ever, in part because of a bias toward status quo. Many Americans idealize the Constitution, supporting it not on the basis of a careful comparative assessment but rather because it is the basis of the government of our country, which has prospered under it. A remarkable feature of popular constitutional argumentation in the United States is that people on both sides of divisive issues such as abortion believe that the Constitution, properly interpreted, supports their position. Virtually no one (certainly not me) would support replacing the U.S. Constitution, even if prediction markets turned out to meet all expectations. In theory, the market-based legislature could be modified fairly easily to perform the task of drafting constitutions, but fundamentally changing a national form of government is inherently risky. There would be little need to do it merely to accommodate prediction markets, which should be able to function effectively within the existing constitutional framework.

A healthy appreciation for the importance of self-government leaves room for many possible applications of prediction markets. Most of the general public does not care about how policy is made in many obscure areas of the law. That self-government may be critical as a general matter and perhaps also for certain types of decisions does not mean that it is a vital value even in relatively technical areas. We may care about due process for many kinds of cases, but such concerns seem like a poor basis for opposing a legislative assistance market (see Chapter 8), at least if prediction markets are the only plausible means by which such a program can be implemented. Nonetheless, concerns about self-government could lead to an exaggerated focus on potential problems with prediction markets, such as the danger of manipulation. Even if the overall level of manipulation is relatively low, the public is likely to pay disproportionate concern to the issue because it seems to be a direct subversion of democratic decision making. The public might not consider whether the manipulation in prediction markets is less than the manipulation effected by special interests in political markets.

PREDICTION MARKETS FOR
DICTATORIAL REGIMES

Given concerns about the compatibility of prediction markets with democratic self-government, prediction markets might well be more plausible as decision making devices in nondemocratic countries. Markets could, after all, be designed to strengthen totalitarian regimes. One difficulty that a dictator faces is an inability to monitor the many decisions that must be made by other governmental officials. A dictator might, however, promise to review some subset of decisions, and conditional prediction markets could be used to forecast whether the dictator would agree or disagree with the decisions. The power of markets could thus be harnessed to help the dictator identify government officials who appear to be acting contrary to his preferences.

Recognizing the possibility that his preferences could be misunderstood, a smart dictator might focus on punishing those whose decisions are predicted to be disagreeable to the dictator, rather than punishing the few whose decisions he happens to review and dislike. With a strong dictator, the predictable result would be that decision makers would defer considerably to prediction markets, and there might not be any dissent or need for punishment at all. There would thus be no need for the dictator formally to yield decision making power to the prediction markets. A dictator might, however, also make prediction markets that anticipate his preferences decisive, limiting the need for a large decision making bureaucracy.

Prediction markets might advance undemocratic governments in other ways as well. For example, prediction markets might be used to advance the cause of censorship. China in recent years has sought to aggressively censor the Internet, blocking content including political dissent and pornography.[14] It would not be difficult to create a prediction market to perform this task. Members of a governmental panel could review a randomly selected subset of Web pages and vote on whether the content is permissible or impermissible. Participants in the market would anticipate the ex post assessments of panel members, and the market predictions would control whether pages would be censored.

If the head of state worries about the loyalty of the panel, then he might in turn review a sample of the panel's decisions. For each Web page randomly selected for inspection by a member of the panel, a conditional probabilistic prediction market could be established to determine whether the head of state would approve or disapprove of the page. Meanwhile, prediction markets could anticipate his ex post assessments of their decisions. Members of the panel who flout the predictions of the markets could be dismissed. As the example shows, conditional markets can be stacked one on top of another to allow a head of state who reviews only a tiny percentage of relevant decisions a great deal of control.

This system could help China reduce the danger of renegade Internet censors. It also might have other advantages. One problem with China's approach is that China needs at least to have its own censors seek out content deemed undesirable. This increases the extent to which members of the public will generally be aware of the censorship and the danger of information trickling out from the censors to the general population. With a decentralized prediction market, China could rely primarily on individuals outside the country to perform the censorship for it. The prediction market approach might also have the advantage of stimulating outsiders to develop more efficient means of accomplishing censorship, such as using artificial intelligence to analyze Web pages.

The possibility that prediction markets might be used to consolidate power in undemocratic regimes suggests that they may pose significant dangers. And yet it is also possible that prediction markets eventually could help liberalize such countries. China has taken the position that it should pursue democracy at its own pace.[15] Indeed, the abrupt adoption of democratic institutions might promote instability, as arguably was the case in post-Soviet Russia.[16] Prediction markets potentially could allow a transition path to gradual democratization. Initially, prediction markets might simply be used to consolidate power, but the head of state might later occasionally select others to serve as ex post decision makers. Gradually, they might become a democratically elected body, yet the structural foundation of the government would not change. It would not be so easy to design seamless transitions using more traditional institutions.

Prediction markets, in any event, might appeal to benevolent heads of undemocratic states. Let us assume that the Chinese government, for example, genuinely believes that the country is not ready for democracy. It nonetheless might hope that many critical decisions concerning the design of economic, financial, and other legislation should be based on the best possible advice. It is not easy, however, to staff a bureaucracy with competent people, ensuring that lower-ranking officials pursue the state's agenda while guarding against self-interested or incompetent decisions by higher-ranking officials. Prediction markets can ease the task considerably, because the government would simply need to select a small number of trusted individuals to serve as ex post decision makers. Such prediction markets would be no less democratic than existing alternatives, and, if the ex post decision makers are selected carefully, could improve the general quality of decision making.

MARKET-BASED EXECUTIVE POWER

The possibility that undemocratic regimes might use prediction markets to improve a head of state's ability to monitor decision making shows that prediction markets can assist in executive as well as in legislative and judicial decision making. But could prediction markets in principle supplant executive decision making? Surely they could perform some tasks commonly viewed as executive, for example, with predictive cost-benefit analysis or a text-authoring market used to enact regulations. Other tasks, such as the power to veto legislation, are not present in all governmental systems anyway. And still others might be outsourced with the help of prediction market mechanisms. For example, one might use prediction markets to decide which civil and criminal cases to bring, and one might use market-based reverse auctions to assign these tasks to particular agents, whether individuals or private groups (see Chapter 5).

Whether or not such changes would be desirable, it might still seem that there are many decisions that must be left to the power of a single chief executive. One reason might be that there are accountability benefits. This might justify great executive power in our present scheme of government, given the danger that special interests might influence decision making. Special interests can influence the president too, but it may be easier for the public to monitor that individual's good faith. Prediction markets, however, might minimize the effects of special interests, making this justification somewhat less powerful. Presumably, we care about accountability not because we want to punish bad decisions but because we hope that the prospect of such punishment will lead to good decisions. Whether the incentives that accountability provides are greater or less in magnitude than the financial incentives provided by prediction markets is an empirical question.

Another reason is that the government must conduct some decision making in secret. Prediction markets, however, might be used to delimit who has access to different classes of secret information. Those individuals might make recommendations based on their access to secret information without revealing it. Prediction markets in turn might make decisions based on these individuals' reputations and based on their statements of how strongly they feel. While government currently delegates power to individuals who have access to confidential information, the prediction market system would provide flexibility for participants to discount those individuals' assertions.

Alternatively, one could imagine allowing only individuals with access to classified information to trade on (and later, to resolve the payouts in) a prediction market. This approach gives a direct financial incentive to the individuals with access to that information. The strategy is analogous to the proposal considered in Chapter 2 of allowing individuals with access to classified information to trade on prediction markets so that the government can make credible predictions to the public.

A related concern, applicable particularly in the military context, is the need for surprise. If the object sometimes is to surprise an enemy, it does not make sense to debate and announce that surprise on the Internet. For this problem, the first of the strategies discussed above will not work, but the second would. The ex post decision maker would assess the wisdom of any surprise decision, but the prediction market would approve of a surprise decision only when it seemed wise to have a surprise action. If it makes sense sometimes to make decision making truly random (as it probably does for a baseball manager or football coach who aims to keep the opposition off guard), then the prediction market might predicate a decision on consultation of a random number generator. The market in turn would anticipate whether such consultation was wise, not whether it was good that a particular number was generated.

All of these concerns are relevant, of course, not only in imagining the unlikely prospect of market-based government but also because many private organizations rely to some degree on executive power. Many may feel that an organization needs a leader, though this may sometimes be a reflection of weaknesses in alternative existing decision making approaches. Accountability, secrecy, and surprise are all reasons why public prediction markets that vet all decisions might not be in an organization's interests. But even in these cases, prediction markets can limit the degree to which a single individual is invested with power. And if it is wise to assign some decisions to individuals, the same person need not always be assigned the same decision. Prediction markets can determine whether it is and who should be granted which parts of executive authority.

FEDERALISM AND INTERNATIONAL COORDINATION

One challenge of designing markets for governmental tasks that does not have a straightforward analogue in the private sector is the need to manage the interests of people in different states. The federalist system in the United States, for example, preserves separate though overlapping spheres of control for the state and federal governments. Meanwhile, international institutions are also limited in power and face the need to balance the interests, including the autonomy interests, of member states' governments. I have assumed so far that prediction markets would be used within the context of a particular government, such as a locality, a state, or a national government. It is possible, however, that prediction markets might facilitate cooperation among different governments.

Robin Hanson makes the interesting point that in a futarchy, governments could enter into covenants that explicitly agree to take each other's interests into account.[17] (Presumably, futarchy itself would approve of some such agreements, recognizing them to be in each state's interest.) For example, the United States and Canada might agree to make decisions that would maximize the GDP+ of the two countries combined. Market-based legislatures could also facilitate such agreements. For example, the United States could agree to pick a Canadian as an ex post decision maker some percentage of the time for its market-based legislature if Canada will do the same. The exact percentages might vary between countries, depending in part on their relative bargaining strength. Of course, New York and New Jersey might enter into similar agreements.

Even with such arrangements, it seems likely that in equilibrium, most jurisdictions would want their prediction markets mostly to be predicting their own decisions. After all, a major theoretical defense of federalism is that it allows groups in different jurisdictions to pursue their own collective preferences.[18] If New Yorkers prefer to have one kind of school system and New Jerseyans prefer to have another, whether because they have different views about ends or about means, then federalism allows them to have it. Some decisions made in New York, however, might have spillover effects on New Jersey, and vice versa, and prediction markets would allow each state some voice in the other's affairs. Especially if the market incorporates intensity of preferences (see Chapter 9), this might prevent New York from doing something that provides it a slight benefit at great cost to its neighbor.

A justification for national government, however, is that individuals sometimes have preferences about policy in other jurisdictions. If this were not so, then proposals to make uniform policies would generally be defeated, at least outside of commercial contexts, where there may be a benefit to policy harmonization. After all, a majority of the people in each state would conclude that they will end up in the majority on whatever the issue is in that particular state. Often, however, the national majority wants to ensure that its preferred policy also is applied in other states. At times, this can serve as a justification even for constitutional rights. If the vast majority of states have decisively rejected execution of juvenile murderers, for example, then arguably the collective welfare is advanced by establishing a uniform policy.[19]

Prediction markets could easily decide not only the content of decisions but also their scope. For example, a prediction market might make a policy that is nationwide in scope, with the exception of a few states in which countervailing sentiment is particularly strong. The challenge, however, is determining how much weight to place on local preferences. If a prediction market is anticipating the ex post decision of a member of the broad national constituency, that might bias the market in the direction of a national policy. According to this theory, it is important to maintain constitutional limitations on federal (and on international) governments as a means of preserving local autonomy.

Prediction markets, however, might reduce the need for such arrangements to some extent. Recall again the point that ex post decision makers are more likely to make decisions in a conscientious way, vindicating higher principles even when they would prefer that those principles yield in a particular case. In this context, an ex post decision maker who would rather impose a national solution on a particular problem would recognize that this ex post decision would not actually have any effect anyway. And so he or she might be somewhat more likely to consider as an abstract matter the degree to which the decision is of the type that should be decided locally rather than nationally. This tendency could be emphasized by bifurcating the issues for prediction market decision making: first using a market to determine whether a particular issue should be decided locally or on some broader level, and second, only if the latter results, resolving the issue with a national market.

The theoretical possibility that prediction markets might succeed in developing principled balances between local and national interests does not mean that all governments should want to yield authority to broader prediction markets, however, apart from issues of transition and uncertainty. After all, some governments might recognize that they will lose under a prediction market regime. The costs to the citizens of this government from having their autonomy curtailed may be less than the benefits of the system's curtailing the autonomy of others in directions they might prefer. This will especially be true of jurisdictions in which popular preferences differ greatly from those of other jurisdictions. And so, even in a hypothetical world in which prediction markets became commonplace, we should not be optimistic that governmental entities will cede their authority.

Nonetheless, prediction markets sometimes might help facilitate international coordination and thus encourage states to yield some of their sovereignty over discrete issues to international bodies. Prediction markets provide a relatively simple framework for allocating authority across member states. Each state can simply be given the right to appoint a particular number of ex post decision makers. States, of course, will still bicker about how these numbers should be determined, but prediction markets reduce the need for more complex structural arrangements.

Moreover, we have seen that supermajority rules may be less burdensome in the market-based legislature, which limits strategic bargaining and its tendency to prevent broadly beneficial legislation. This may be particularly important for supranational institutions, because there is often a need to induce voluntary participation from a large number of nations in order for a supranational institution to be successful. Assurance that legislation will be passed only if there is very high majority agreement may make it easier to induce countries to participate. Even with such a requirement, a market-based institution could eliminate much of the intractability associated with multilateral treaty negotiation.

THE ROAD TO PREDICTOCRACY

A predictocracy is a government whose foundational institutions are all controlled by prediction markets. Prediction markets might create institutions to serve as ex post decision makers or in some cases ex ante decision makers. The prediction markets themselves, however, would serve as the source of authority for the creation of these institutions, retaining the power to abolish them. Just as prediction markets can take many forms, so can predictocracy. The essence of predictocracy is that decisions are made on the basis of the market's anticipation of whether they will (or, with self-resolving markets, would) be approved of later.

From the vantage point of today, predictocracy is political science fiction. Like most science fiction, it presents a vision that might be seen as either promising or dark, either providing a solution to pragmatic problems of governmental organization or reducing our collective control of our legal destinies. And like most science fiction, it seems extraordinarily unlikely to happen. Far more likely is the possibility that prediction markets will make niche contributions to public and private decision making. Indeed, predictocracy may be more fanciful than most science fiction, which anticipates technological rather than legal development. Legal change is far slower than technological change.

And yet concerning the distant future, legal change is difficult to anticipate. Our legal system has evolved considerably in the past one hundred years and even more so in the past thousand or ten thousand years. Thomas Malone has argued that decreases in the costs of communications have allowed much more centralized decision making but that we are arriving at a point at which further decreases in those costs might facilitate more decentralized decision making.[20] Though Malone focuses on the workplace, the same could be true of government. Perhaps the Internet will reduce the need to rely on centralized leaders to make decisions on our behalf. Prediction markets might serve as one means of decentralizing decision making, though other approaches, such as increased use of initiatives and referenda, are possible.

It would be hubristic to make any predictions about what the legal system will look like in hundreds of years, especially given uncertainty about what our society will be like. Some theorists, most notably Ray Kurzweil,[21] anticipate that computers will within the lifetimes of some now living be trillions of times more intelligent than people. If this is so, and even if Kurzweil's timeline is off by hundreds of years, there might be little need someday for predictocracy. A major argument for prediction market governance, after all, is that it economizes on the costs of making decisions without allowing a small group of individuals too much control. If computers can cheaply assess the consequences of legislation better than we can, then we could have large decision making bodies (consisting, for example, of people who can consult their computers for recommendations) tackling very large numbers of decisions. That might reduce the need for predictocracy, so one scenario that sounds like science fiction can make another seem less likely. On the other hand, one might want to use prediction markets that anticipate human decisions to ensure that the computers continue to work for rather than against us.

The claim of this book is that if prediction markets indeed can overcome various obstacles, such as the danger of manipulation, then predictocracy might be an attractive world, perhaps more attractive than existing alternatives. The potential desirability of an end point, however, neither means that we will go there nor that we should. Transition costs are real, because each additional step toward predictocracy brings uncertainty. Moreover, transition brings the possibility of destabilization. Perhaps the most important feature of Western democracies is that they are generally accepted, that there is a "rule of recognition" that leads individuals to follow the laws that they produce.[22] The project of governance is in essence a giant focal point coordination game, and perhaps one of the most important goals of government should be to avoid the danger that competing focal points will arise and undermine stability. Increasing reliance on prediction markets at some point might produce uncertainty about the ultimate source of government power.

This book is a technical manual, not a manifesto. I have included radical examples to illustrate the power of prediction markets as building blocks in decision-making institutions, not to argue that we should or will displace our existing institutions. Whatever their flaws, our democratic governments serve us well, and many flaws could be reformed with modest solutions. Some of these solutions, this book suggests, might involve the use of prediction markets as auxiliary aids to other forms of decision making. And yet it is possible that if prediction markets work effectively, they could gradually assume greater importance over the decades and centuries. Perhaps society will rely increasingly more on prediction markets and then entrust ever more decisions to them. And someday, a government might decide to grant prediction markets the authority to decide whether to displace other nonmarket institutions with new prediction market institutions. If that day should ever come, then a predictocracy will have arrived.

Afterword

Suppose that someone were to invent a magic crystal ball in which a user could see a provisional future. Someone who did not like that future could decide to make small or large changes in conditions and behavior that would elicit a different vision presented in the crystal ball. As a society, we might want to prevent use of the crystal ball to foresee our individual destinies. Surely, however, we would decide to use it at least for some limited purposes. The crystal ball could tell voters what the world would look like if different candidates for office were elected. Corporations and other businesses could avoid investing in products in which consumers would have no interest. Trial judges might rely on the crystal ball to write decisions that would not be reversed. Administrative agencies and legislatures could improve their planning through a better understanding both of aspects of the future that are beyond their control and the effects of different decisions.

We will never have so wonderful a crystal ball that, true to its purposes, reliably depicts the future, but let us imagine weakening the crystal ball in a few ways. Suppose first that the crystal ball shows not the future but rather probability distributions indicating the likelihood of different possible futures. Then suppose that although the crystal ball will work for free, it will work more effectively if society invests money in it and has a stake in the outcomes. And suppose that the probability distributions are not necessarily perfect; they can be said only to represent estimates of the future that in general (though perhaps not always) will be at least as accurate as could be produced by spending the same amount of money in any other way. And, finally, suppose that there is some risk that individuals might try to manipulate the crystal ball into making worse predictions but that such efforts in general will backfire about as often as they will succeed. Even this weaker crystal ball would still be extraordinarily useful, allowing individuals and institutions to improve their decision making.

We might well be on the verge of having as many of these weak crystal balls as we might like to use. This book has used the phrase *prediction markets* to refer to these weak crystal balls, and my claim is that we ought at least to experiment with them. Whatever the merits of particular designs and proposals that I have suggested, my aim has been to show how careful thinking about the incentives of market participants can overcome virtually any limitation of prediction markets that otherwise might make them less powerful than the weak crystal ball. Prediction markets can aggregate the best available forecasts of particular events, can encourage individuals to generate better information about those forecasts, can lead people to share such information with others, can assess the consequences of possible decisions, can aggregate disparate opinions of normative issues into consensus forecasts, can create collaborative texts, and can be structured in a web that shows the relationship of each prediction market to every other. Prediction markets have not yet been implemented to test all these possible applications, but I hope that this book will inspire implementation of novel prediction market designs.

The more ambitious aim of the book has been to argue that bets may often be the best building block for institutions. An alternative means of resolving playground disputes, the vote, has emerged as the much more common building block of existing institutions. Voting regimes are structured in countless ingenious ways to reflect decision-making needs of different institutions. In corporations, shareholders vote and directors vote; in democracies, citizens vote and their elected representatives vote, as do such indirectly elected office holders as judges and administrative agency officials. Across all of these contexts, voting has certain well-understood limitations. When shareholders or voters choose their representatives, they cannot be assured that those representatives will look after the voters' interests. Voters of all types may have imperfect incentives to become perfectly informed about relevant issues.

Sometimes voting resolves disagreements that are largely predictive in nature. For example, a committee that is planning reconstruction of a city that has been severely damaged in a hurricane might disagree about the probability that a particularly severe hurricane will strike again. Committee members might then vote either to establish a particular working assumption or to resolve the ultimate issue of which precautions to take. Members of a board of directors might disagree about whether introducing a new product will increase a corporation's stock price, and they might vote on whether to introduce the product. Members of a legislature, in voting on whether to authorize the use of military force, might disagree about the threat posed by an enemy. This book has explored the ways in which prediction markets can be useful for resolving predictive disagreements of any kind, generating incentives for those who are best able to make the forecast to reveal their true beliefs.

At other times, voting resolves disagreements about normative issues, providing a means of aggregating preferences and views. A person's preferences (or those he or she would have if given time to consider particular issues) constitute a type of information. Prediction markets can effectively aggregate this information, too. For example, a prediction market can be used to forecast what someone randomly selected from a group would decide if given a chance to consider an issue in detail. Participants in the market will then have an incentive to take into account the actual and hypothetical views of all members of the group. A prediction of whether a randomly selected member would approve of a decision comes close to an assessment of what a median member, and thus the group as a whole, would decide. This forecast itself can serve as the decision, with the randomly selected decision maker's opinion serving only to provide the number that determines whether participants in the prediction market make or lose money.

It might seem silly to use a prediction of a decision to resolve an issue rather than simply waiting for the decision itself. After all, prediction markets are only weak crystal balls, not entirely accurate ones. At times they might make mistakes in assessing the preferences of a particular group. We have seen, however, that prediction markets can sometimes produce more representative decisions and better-informed decisions than could be obtained by having only a few members of the broader group vote. Prediction markets may even be cheaper, because those participating will tend already to be knowledgeable about the relevant topic. Prediction markets are more scalable than many existing approaches to decision making. Prediction markets also can produce better normative decisions than can voting regimes because an ex post decision maker is in a different position from decision makers in voting institutions. An ex post decision maker will have no reason to allow personal sympathies to cause deviation from general rules if he or she believes that in general those rules ought to be followed.

At the same time, it may be less necessary to use rules to constrain him or her, because this person's decision does not directly affect policy. And so prediction markets can make it much more feasible to generate consistent decisions on the basis of general standards. In addition, it may be easier to insulate an ex post decision maker from pressures by special interests, who will have no incentive to lobby once the prediction determines what will happen. Finally, relying on predictions of decisions reduces the danger that impasse will block useful decisions. Traditional decision making can produce strategic bargaining as parties seek to maximize their portion of the gains from political trade, but this seems less likely with retrospective decision making. In short, although experimentation is necessary, predictive decision making approaches that use ex post decision makers have many potential advantages over approaches based on voting.

To date, political conservatives have shown more enthusiasm for prediction markets than have political liberals. Conservatives generally have more confidence in market mechanisms. Distrust in the efficiency or equity of markets for goods and services, however, should strengthen the case for prediction markets. If they can effectively aggregate information, they can make government intervention cheaper and less prone to error. The better the decision-making institutions of government, the stronger the case for using those institutions to correct market failures. Those who wish to use the machinery of government more should be sympathetic to proposals to make that machinery work more efficiently. Prediction markets, then, can help political liberals achieve many of their aims. Prediction markets enhance the case for an activist government, albeit a market-oriented one.

Notes

PREFACE

1. James Surowiecki, The Wisdom of Crowds: Why the Many Are Smarter Than the Few and How Collective Wisdom Shapes Business, Economies, Societies, and Nations (2004).

CHAPTER 1: THE MEDIA

1. A study supporting this view is John McMillan and Pablo Zoido, *How to Subvert Democracy: Montesinos in Peru,* J. Econ. Persp., Fall 2004, at 69. The authors show that in Peru, the secret police paid much higher bribes to media organizations than to politicians.

2. *See, e.g.,* Frederic Schauer, Free Speech: A Philosophical Enquiry 15–16, 35–37 (1982) (stating that the "predominant and most persevering" justification for freedom of speech is the argument that it leads to the discovery of truth).

3. Abrams v. United States, 250 U.S. 616, 630 (1919).

4. *See* Anthony Downs, An Economic Theory of Democracy 214–16 (1957) (arguing that there are limits on the quantity of information that it is rational to acquire).

5. *See generally* Louis Phlips, The Economics of Imperfect Information (1989) (providing an overview of the field).

6. *See* Bryan Caplan, *Systematically Biased Beliefs About Economics: Robust Evidence of Judgmental Anomalies from the Survey of Americans and Economists on the Economy,* 112 ECON. J. 436, 441 (2002).

7. It is unclear whether media exposure in fact is to blame for the public's perceptions of the effects of trade. Caplan also notes that "there are topics that elicit emotional rather than analytical responses" from nonexperts, so prejudice against foreigners might lead to biased views of trade policy. *Id.* at 455.

8. *See* MICHAEL X. DELLI CARPINI AND SCOTT KEETER, WHAT AMERICANS KNOW ABOUT POLITICS AND WHY IT MATTERS 417 (1996).

9. *See, e.g.,* SAMUEL L. POPKIN, THE REASONING VOTER: COMMUNICATION AND PERSUASION IN PRESIDENTIAL CAMPAIGNS (2d ed. 1994) (suggesting that voters can process commercials and sound bites effectively).

10. These markets typically are computerized. For an early paper examining the efficiency of computerized continuous double-auction markets, see Arlington W. Williams, *Computerized Double-Auction Markets: Some Initial Experimental Results,* 53 J. BUS. 235 (1980).

11. Saul Levmore explains how this can provide an advantage of markets over voting regimes. *See* Saul Levmore, *Revisiting the Mechanisms of Market Efficiency: Simply Efficient Markets and the Role of Regulation; Lessons from the Iowa Electronic Markets and the Hollywood Stock Exchange,* 28 IOWA J. CORP. L. 589, 597–98 (2003).

12. *See* JAMES SUROWIECKI, THE WISDOM OF CROWDS: WHY THE MANY ARE SMARTER THAN THE FEW AND HOW COLLECTIVE WISDOM SHAPES BUSINESS, ECONOMIES, SOCIETIES AND NATIONS xi–xiii (2004).

13. *See* Cass R. Sunstein, *Group Judgments: Statistical Means, Deliberation, and Information Markets,* 80 NYU L. REV. 962, 976 (2005).

14. After September 21, 2004, the Iowa Electronic Markets split the shares, so that there were two Democratic contracts, one corresponding to the case in which the Democrat wins with more than 52 percent of the vote, one corresponding to the case in which the Democrat wins with less than 52 percent of the vote, and two corresponding Republican contracts. The discussion and figure 1.1 add up the prices from these two contracts for the sake of simplicity.

15. A similar definition for the 2000 election meant that Al Gore "won" the IEM as a result of winning the popular vote. According to Joyce Berg, the IEM defined the contract this way rather than with respect to the winner of the Electoral College because it would be more interesting for research purposes.

16. For a portion of this period, two shares were traded for each candidate, one corresponding to the possibility that the candidate would win with more than 52 percent of the two-party vote and one corresponding to the possibility that the candidate would win with less than 52 percent of the two-party vote. For the sake of simplicity, the last trading price of both of the contracts corresponding to each candidate are added together in figure 1.1. For example, if the share corresponding to the possibility that Bush would receive more than 52 percent last traded at thirty cents and the share corresponding to the possibility that Bush would receive less than 52 percent last traded at twenty cents, this was reported as a 0.5 percent chance of Bush's winning.

17. The source of the data is http://www.realclearpolitics.com/Presidential_04/bush_vs_kerry_historical.html (last visited June 27, 2006). The data listed are for the last day of the polling period for each poll.

18. *See* Justin Wolfers and Eric Zitzewitz, *Five Open Questions About Prediction Markets, in* INFORMATION MARKETS: A NEW WAY OF MAKING DECISIONS (Robert W. Hahn & Paul C. Tetlock, eds., 2006).

19. This may seem to be a trivial point, but it provides an empirical answer to Charles Manski, who developed a theoretical model demonstrating the possibility that prices might significantly differ from probabilities. *See* Charles F. Manski, *Interpreting the Predictions of Prediction Markets* (NBER Working Paper No. 10359, 2004). Subsequent scholars have offered theoretical models in which the equilibrium price will be equal to the mean belief of traders, weighted by budgets. *See* Steven Gjerstad, *Risk Aversion, Beliefs, and Prediction Market Equilibrium* (2005), *available at* http://www.aeaweb.org/annual_mtg_papers/2006/0106_1015_0701.pdf (last visited June 27, 2006); Justin Wolfers and Eric Zitzewitz, *Interpreting Prediction Market Prices as Probabilities* (2005), *available at* http://faculty-gsb.stanford.edu/zitzewitz/Research/interpreting.pdf (last visited June 27, 2006). A critical difference in the theoretical models is that Manski assumes risk neutrality, whereas the others assume risk aversion.

20. *See* Richard Borghesi, *Underreaction to New Information: Evidence from an Online Exchange* (2006), *available at* http://www.business.txstate.edu/users/rb38/Research/Underreaction%20to%20News%20Events.pdf (last visited June 27, 2006).

21. Shares of TradeSports pay out ten dollars if the predicted event occurs. TradeSports currently charges a commission of four cents per trade (but only two cents per trade for trades below five cents or above ninety-five cents). This commission is charged to the party that places the order that results in the trade, not to the party that initially placed a limit order on the bid or ask queue. TradeSports also currently charges four cents when a contract expires. Thus, the total commissions amount to at most eight cents on a ten-dollar contract, or less than 1 percent. *See* http://www.tradesports.com/aav2/rulesAndFaqs.jsp?helpPage=rules&rules=rates-fees (last visited June 27, 2006).

22. A useful illustration of a similar incentive comes from Mark Cuban's proposal to start a sports gambling hedge fund, which would use advanced analytical techniques to place sports bets. Carl Bialik, *Billionaire NBA Owner's Gamble on a Hedge Fund Faces Long Odds,* WALL ST. J. ONLINE, Dec 9, 2004, *available at* http://online.wsj.com/article/0,,SB110244506243393408,00.html (last visited June 27, 2006). Cuban eventually abandoned the idea, but the point remains that if people are willing to make bets on the basis of incomplete analysis, there will be some profit incentive to develop additional analysis.

23. *See* Emile Servan-Schreiber et al., *Prediction Markets: Does Money Matter?,* 14 ELECTRONIC MARKETS 243 (2004). Servan-Schreiber is the CEO of NewsFutures. *See also* David M. Pennock, Steve Lawrence, Finn Arup Nielsen and C. Lee Giles, *Extracting Collective Probabilistic Forecasts from Web Games, in* PROCEEDINGS OF THE SEVENTH ACM SIGKDD INTERNATIONAL CONFERENCE ON KNOWLEDGE DISCOVERY AND DATA MINING 174 (2001).

24. *See* Justin Wolfers and Eric Zitzewitz, *Prediction Markets,* 18 J. ECON. PERSP. 107, 113–14 fig. 3 (2004).

25. In a system of decimal odds, the payout is said to be eighteen dollars per dollar bet. In a racetrack using fractional odds, the original bet is returned to the winners, and the payout is then said to be 17:1.

26. *See, e.g.,* Stephen Figlewski, *Subjective Information and Market Efficiency in a Betting Market,* 87 J. POL. ECON. 75 (1979). Commentators have noted that independent pari-mutuel pools sometimes show slightly disparate odds, but the differences are not so great as to provide incentives to arbitrage given the need to pay commissions. *See* Marshall Gramm and Douglas H. Owens, *Inefficiencies in Pari-mutuel Betting Markets Across Wagering Pools in the Simulcast Era, available at* http://irving.vassar.edu/MIEC/GrammOwens.pdf (last visited June 27, 2006).

27. *See generally* Bruno Jullien and Bernard Salanie, *Estimating Preferences Under Risk: The Case of Racetrack Bettors,* 108 J. POL. ECON. 503 (2000).

28. For an empirical study that suggests that the favorite-longshot bias is attributable in part to misperceptions of probability, see Erik Snowberg and Justin Wolfers, *Explaining the Favorite-Longshot Bias: Is It Risk-Love, or Misperceptions?, available at* http://bpp.wharton.upenn.edu/jwolfers/Papers/Favorite_Longshot_Bias.pdf (May 17, 2005).

29. Marco Ottaviani and Peter Norman Sørensen, *Late Informed Betting and the Favorite-Longshot Bias* (Discussion Papers, Institute of Econ., Univ. of Copenhagen 03–33, 2003).

30. *See* Thomas Gilovich et al., *The Hot Hand in Basketball: On the Misperception of Random Sequences,* 17 COGNITIVE PSYCH. 295 (1985).

31. *See* THOMAS GILOVICH, HOW WE KNOW WHAT ISN'T SO 16 (1991).

32. *See generally* SCOTT A. HAWKINS AND REID HASTIE, HINDSIGHT: BIASED JUDGMENTS OF PAST EVENTS AFTER THE OUTCOMES ARE KNOWN, 107 PSYCHOL. BULL. 311 (1990) (providing an overview of the hindsight bias).

33. *See* Amos Tversky and Daniel Kahneman, *Judgment Under Uncertainty: Heuristics and Biases,* 185 SCIENCE 1124 (1974) (introducing the availability error and two other heuristics).

34. Timur Kuran and Cass R. Sunstein, *Availability Cascades and Risk Regulation,* 51 STAN. L. REV. 683 (1999).

35. *Id.* at 727–28.

36. *See* Linda M. Woodland and Bill M. Woodland, *Market Efficiency and Profitable Wagering in the National Hockey League: Can Bettors Score on Longshots?,* 67 S. ECON. J. 983 (2001); Linda M. Woodland and Bill M. Woodland, *The Reverse Favourite-Longshot Bias and Market Efficiency in Major League Baseball: An Update,* 55 BULL. ECON. RES. 113 (2003).

37. Paul C. Tetlock, *How Efficient Are Information Markets? Evidence from an Online Exchange* 16–21 (2004) (on file with author).

38. *Id.* at 24–30.

39. The original version of this figure appears in Erik Snowberg et al., *Information (In)efficiency in Prediction Markets, in* INFORMATION EFFICIENCY IN FINANCIAL AND BETTING MARKETS 366, 376 (Leighton Vaughan Williams ed., 2005), based on trading data provided by TradeSports.

40. Joyce Berg, Robert Forsythe, Forrest Nelson and Thomas Rietz, *Results from a Dozen Years of Election Futures Markets Research, available at* http://www.biz.uiowa.edu/iem/archive/BFNR_2000.pdf.

41. Taking the price at midnight might seem to give the market an unfair advantage, because polls must conclude earlier. Tallying the average market price in the week before each election, weighted by volume, produced only a slightly larger error, 1.58%.

42. In a separate paper, Berg and coauthors assess the long-term accuracy of the markets and develop a measure of forecast standard errors, analogous to confidence intervals with polls. *See* Joyce Berg, Forrest Nelson and Thomas Rietz, *Accuracy and Forecast Standard Error of Prediction Markets* (2003), *available at* http://www.biz.uiowa.edu/iem/archive/forecasting.pdf (last visited June 27, 2006).

43. *See* Oleg Bondarenko and Peter Bossaerts, *Expectations and Learning in Iowa,* 24 J. BANKING AND FIN. 1535 (2000).

44. Robert S. Erikson and Christopher Wlezien, *Are Political Markets Really Superior to Polls as Election Predictors?* (2005), *available at* http://www.nuffield.ox.ac.uk/Politics/papers/2005/EriksonWlezien,%20WAPOR%202005,%20Nuffield.pdf (last visited June 27, 2006).

45. *See, e.g.,* John O'Brien and Sanjay Srivastava, *Dynamic Stock Markets with Multiple Assets: An Experimental Analysis,* 46 J. FIN. 1811 (1991).

46. *See* Joyce E. Berg and Thomas A. Rietz, *Longshots, Overconfidence and Efficiency on the Iowa Electronic Market* (2002), *available at* http://www.biz.uiowa.edu/iem/archive/Longshots_2002January.pdf (last visited June 27, 2006).

47. Robert Forsythe et al., *Anatomy of an Experimental Political Stock Market,* 82 AM. ECON. REV. 1142, 1146, 1155–56 (1992); *see also* Kenneth Oliven and Thomas A. Rietz, *Suckers Are Born but Markets Are Made: Individual Rationality, Arbitrage, and Market Efficiency on an Electronic Futures Market,* 50 MGMT. SCI. 336 (2004).

48. *See, e.g.,* S. G. Kou and Michael E. Sobel, *Forecasting the Vote: A Theoretical Comparison of Election Markets and Public Opinion Polls,* 12 POL. ANALYSIS 277 (2004).

49. *See* Saul Levmore, *Revisiting the Mechanisms of Market Efficiency: Simply Efficient Markets and the Role of Regulation; Lessons from the Iowa Electronic Markets and the Hollywood Stock Exchange,* 28 IOWA J. CORP. L. 589, 601 (2003) (noting that as stakes rise, the potential for manipulation may increase).

50. *See, e.g.,* Roger B. Myerson and Robert J. Weber, *A Theory of Voting Equilibria,* 87 AM. POL. SCI. REV. 102, 102 (1993) (noting the existence of a "bandwagon effect").

51. See Erica Klarreich, *Economists Explore Betting Markets as Prediction Tools,* 164 SCI. NEWS 251 (Oct. 18, 2003), *available at* http://www.sciencenews.org/articles/20031018/bob9.asp (last visited June 27, 2006) ("Buchanan prices briefly spiked, but well-informed traders then seized the opportunity to profit off the manipulative traders and by the end of the day, the effect of the investments had virtually vanished").

52. *See* Paul W. Rhode and Koleman S. Strumpf, *Manipulating Political Stock Markets: A Field Experiment and a Century of Observational Data* 3–7 (Feb. 2006), *available at* http://www.unc.edu/~cigar/papers/ManipNBER.pdf (last visited June 27, 2006).

53. These markets are discussed in more detail in an earlier paper. *See* Paul W. Rhode and Koleman S. Strumpf, *Historical Presidential Betting Markets,* 18 J. ECON. PERSP. 127 (2004).

54. Rhode and Strumpf, *supra* note 52, at 7–20.

55. *Id.* at 20–27.

56. *See* Robin Hanson et al., *Information Aggregation and Manipulation in an Experimental Market* (Sept. 21, 2004), *available at* http://mason.gmu.edu/~roprea/manipEX1.pdf (last visited June 27, 2006); Robin Hanson et al., *Manipulators Increase Information Market Accuracy* (July 2004), *available at* http://hanson.gmu.edu/biashelp.pdf (last visited Nov. 8, 2006).

57. *See* Martin Strobel, *Are Prediction Markets Robust Against Manipulation? A Lab Experiment* (PowerPoint presentation, Feb. 2005), *available at* http://dimacs.rutgers.edu/Workshops/Markets/slides/strobel.ppt (last visited Nov. 8, 2006).

58. A typical poll found 42 percent of Republicans and 0 percent of Democrats predicting that the war in Iraq would help the Republicans in the 2006 midterm elections. *See generally* http://nationaljournal.com/insiders.pdf (last visited June 30, 2006) (providing the most recent poll).

CHAPTER 2: POLICY ANALYSTS

1. For example, in 1984, when asked whether taxes on pollution represent a better approach than imposition of pollution ceilings, 32.0 percent of economists surveyed indicated general agreement and 35.3 percent indicated general disagreement. *See* Bruno S. Frey, *Consensus and Dissension Among Economists: An Empirical Inquiry,* 74 Am. Econ. Rev. 986, 988 (1984). Concerning the propositions attracting the most agreement, a minority disagreed. For example, 10.3 percent of economists generally disagreed with the proposition "tariffs and import quotas reduce general economic welfare." *Id.*

2. For a laboratory experiment illustrating the efficiency of markets for contingent securities in which different market participants have different information, see Charles R. Plott and Shyam Sunder, *Rational Expectations and the Aggregation of Diverse Information in Laboratory Security Markets,* 56 Econometrica 1085 (1988).

3. Economic models suggest that rational actors' assessments ultimately should converge, even if their initial assessments are based on different information. *See* John D. Geanakoplos and Heraklis M. Polemarchakis, *We Can't Disagree Forever,* 28 J. Econ. Theory 192 (1982).

4. *See* http://volokh.com/archives/archive_2005_07_17–2005_07_23.shtml#1121797428 (last visited June 27, 2006).

5. *See* http://volokh.com/archives/archive_2005_07_17–2005_07_23.shtml#1121819891 (last visited June 27, 2006).

6. TradeSports instead awards interest on money it is holding. *See* http://www.tradesports.com/aav2/rulesAndFaqs.jsp?helpPage=banking#16 (last visited June 27, 2006).

7. Jan Pieter Krahnen and Martin Weber, *Marketmaking in the Laboratory: Does Competition Matter?* 4 Experimental Econ. 55 (2001).

8. *See* U.S. Patent No. 5,950,176 (filed Mar. 25, 1996); U.S. Patent No. 6,505,174 (filed Nov. 2, 1998). http://patft.uspto.gov/netacgi.

9. A complication is that multiple traders might have offers at the same price at the front of a queue. Ordinarily, in this case, an offer accepting the price would be fulfilled first

with those who made the offers first. An alternative is to give credits to all of those who have offers at the front of the queue and fill orders in proportion to the amount that these individuals have at risk. This should be straightforward in an on-line exchange, which can allow fractional share ownership.

10. This history is adapted from a combination of news reports and from a Web site created by Robin Hanson: http://hanson.gmu.edu/policyanalysismarket.html.

11. *See* http://www.acq.osd.mil/sadbu/sbir/solicitations/sbir012/darpa012.htm (last visited June 27, 2006).

12. Robin Hanson, *Could Gambling Save Science? Encouraging an Honest Consensus,* 9 Soc. Epistemology 3, 7–9 (1995).

13. Adam Clymer, *Threats and Responses: Electronic Surveillance,* N.Y. Times, Feb. 12, 2003, at A1.

14. David Johnston, *Iran-Contra Role Brings Poindexter 6 Months in Prison,* N.Y. Times, June 12, 1990, at A1.

15. United States v. Poindexter, 951 F.2d 269 (D.C. Cir. 1991).

16. Elizabeth L. Deeley, Note, *Viatical Settlements Are Not Securities: Is It Law or Sympathy?* 66 Geo. Wash. L. Rev. 382, 386–87 (1998).

17. Joseph E. Stiglitz, Op-Ed, *Terrorism: There's No Futures in It,* L.A. Times, July 31, 2003, at B17.

18. *See* Robin Hanson, *Designing Real Terrorism Futures* (Aug. 2005), *available at* http://hanson.gmu.edu/realterf.pdf (last visited June 27, 2006).

19. Stiglitz, *supra* note 17.

20. Feist Publ'ns, Inc. v. Rural Tel. Serv. Co., 499 U.S. 340, 343 (1991) ("That there can be no valid copyright in facts is universally understood").

21. Cara Granklin, *Virtual Las Vegas: Regulate or Prohibit?,* 2001 Duke L. Tech. Rev. 0021, ¶ 8 ("Online gambling is banned completely by specific legislation in three states— Nevada, Louisiana, and Illinois. Four states—Minnesota, New York, Missouri, and Wisconsin—have actually taken steps to litigate against parties involved in online gambling by means of already existing state laws").

22. 18 U.S.C. § 1084 (2000 and Supp. 2004); Christine Hurt, *Regulating Public Morals and Private Markets: Online Securities Trading, Internet Gambling, and the Speculation Paradox,* 86 B.U. L. Rev. 371, 414 (2006) ("The federal government, which has traditionally left the regulation of gambling to the individual states, has taken the position that internet gambling is illegal under federal law under the Wire Act") (citation omitted). *But see* In re Mastercard Int'l Inc. Internet Gambling Litig., 313 F.3d 257, 263 (5th Cir. 2002) (noting that the Wire Act does not prohibit non-sports Internet gambling).

23. See Tom W. Bell, *Gambling for the Good, Trading for the Future: The Legality of Markets in Science Claims,* 5 Chap. L. Rev. 159, 165–66 (2002).

24. Finster v. Keller, 96 Cal. Rptr. 241, 246 (Cal. Ct. App. 1971), *cited in id.* at 166.

25. *See generally* Earl L. Grinols, Gambling in America: Costs and Benefits 131–74 (2004) (discussing some of the negative social consequences of gambling).

26. Bell, *supra* note 23, at 168.

27. Security and Accountability for Every Port Act of 2006, Pub. L. No. 109–347, 120 Stat. 1884 (codified at 31 U.S.C. §§ 5361 et seq.).

28. *See, e.g.,* Stuart Weinberg and Angela Pruitt, *Despite Ban, Web Gamblers Play On,* WALL ST. J., Nov. 1, 2006, at B3D (noting difficulties in enforcing the statute).

29. Bell considers this issue in depth. *See* Bell, *supra* note 23, at 169–77.

30. 7 U.S.C. § 1a(4) (2000).

31. Bell, *supra* note 23, at 170–72.

32. 7 U.S.C. § 1a(13); *see* Bell, *supra* note 23, at 172–74.

33. One such hurdle is that prediction markets would need to count as excluded commodities entered into by "eligible contract participants in an electronic trading facility" to escape regulation. The CFA typically construes "eligible participants" as financial institutions, financial professionals, and individuals with at least five million dollars in assets. *See* Bell, *supra* note 23, at 172–74 (citing 7 U.S.C. § 2(d)(2)).

34. *See Street Sleuth: Firm Offers Hedging on a Small Scale,* WALL ST. J., Oct. 22, 2004. For a discussion of HedgeStreet's application, see Robert W. Hahn and Paul C. Tetlock, *A New Approach for Regulating Information Markets,* 29 J. REGULATORY ECON. 265, 273 n.58 (2006).

35. *See id.* at 276 and n.66.

36. 7 U.S.C. 2(a)(1)(C) (2000).

37. *See* http://tradesports.com/aav2/misc/commission.pdf (last visited June 27, 2006).

38. 17 C.F.R. § 35.1(b)(2)(vi)(A) (2006).

39. Letter from Andrea M. Corcoran, director, Division of Trading and Markets, C.F.T.C., to Iowa Electronics Markets (June 18, 1993), *available at* 1993 WL 595741.

40. The Iowa Electronic Markets no-action letter makes this explicit: "We do not render any opinion as to whether the operation of the Political Markets violates the provisions of any state law and our position does not excuse non-compliance with any such law." *Id.* at *3.

41. Hahn and Tetlock, *supra* note 34, at 274.

42. David Barboza, *Ogre to Slay? Outsource It to Chinese,* N.Y. TIMES, Dec. 9, 2005, at A1. Based on the real-money prices for virtual currency, an economist estimated the GNP per capita of the on-line world Norrath as falling between those of Russia and Bulgaria. *See* Edward Castronova, *Virtual Worlds: A First-Hand Account of Market and Society on the Cyberian Frontier* (CESifo Working Paper Series No. 618, 2001), *available at* http://papers.ssrn.com/abstract_id=294828 (last visited June 27, 2006).

43. *See* http://www.ideosphere.com (last visited June 27, 2006).

44. U.S. CONST. art. II, § 1, cl. 5 ("No Person except a natural born Citizen . . . shall be eligible to the Office of President").

45. *See* David M. Pennock, Steve Lawrence, C. Lee Giles, and Finn Årup Nielsen, *The Power of Play: Efficiency and Forecast Accuracy in Web Market Games* (NEC Research Technical Report 2000–168, 2001).

46. Emile Servan-Schreiber, telephone interview with author, May 24, 2006.

47. According to government ethics standards, an employee of the executive branch may not disclose information to further a private interest that she knows or reasonably should know is nonpublic. 5 C.F.R. § 2635.703 (2006).

48. *See* O'Grady v. Superior Court, 44 Cal. Rptr. 3d 72 (Ct. App. 2006).

49. *See* Alorie Gilbert, *Why So Nervous About Robots, Wal-Mart?, available at* http://news.com.com/2061–10790_3–5779674.html (last visited June 27, 2006).

50. A critical legal question is whether entry of a prediction market forecast would count as the "purchase or sale of any security" for the purpose of Rule 10b-5. 17 C.F.R. § 240.10b-5 (2006). This is unlikely. A case interpreting the word *security* is Great Lakes Chemical Corp. v. Monsanto Co., 96 F. Supp. 2d 376 (D. Del. 2000). Although the statutory definition of *security* is long—*see* 15 U.S.C. 77b(a)(1) (2000)—the case identifies the key questions as being whether an instrument qualifies as "stock" or an "investment contract." A prediction market security is unlikely to count as stock, in part because it provides no voting rights and cannot necessarily be negotiated. *Monsanto Co.,* 96 F. Supp. 2d at 385 (citing United Hous. Found. v. Forman, 421 U.S. 837 (1975)). Meanwhile, an "investment contract" involves an investment of money "in a common enterprise." *Id.* at 384–85 (citing SEC v. W. J. Howey Co., 328 U.S. 293 (1946)). But a prediction market security does not represent an investment in an enterprise in the usual sense of that term.

51. CHRISTOPHER WILLIAMS, CONG. BUDGET OFF., ECONOMIC AND BUDGET ISSUE BRIEF: WHAT IS A CURRENT-LAW ECONOMIC BASELINE? 1 (2005) ("The requirement that CBO's economic baseline must embody current law can explain some differences between CBO's and other forecasters' predictions for the economy").

52. CATO INSTITUTE, CATO HANDBOOK FOR CONGRESS: POLICY RECOMMENDATIONS FOR THE 107TH CONGRESS 53 (2001); Flemming v. Nestor, 363 U.S. 603, 611 (1960) (holding constitutional a decision by Congress to change the amount of Social Security payments).

53. *See* Refet S. Gürkaynak and Justin Wolfers, *Macroeconomic Derivatives: An Initial Analysis of Market-Based Macro Forecasts, Uncertainty, and Risk* (2005), *available at* http://www.nber.org/books/ISOM05/gurkaynak-wolfers9-20-05.pdf (last visited June 27, 2006).

54. Roe v. Wade, 410 U.S. 113 (1973).

CHAPTER 3: BUSINESSES

1. *See* State St. Bank and Trust Co. v. Signature Fin. Group, Inc., 129 F.3d 1368, 1375 (Fed. Cir. 1998).

2. Downloads are currently available at http://sourceforge.net/projects/zocalo (last visited June 27, 2006).

3. *See, e.g.,* Steve Lohr, *That Nation: "Ka-Ching"; Maybe It's Not All Your Fault,* N.Y. TIMES, Dec. 5, 2004, at D1 ("[C]redit card marketers employ the most advanced computer technology to track spending patterns. . . . They employ intricate data-mining systems, neural networks and business intelligence software—high-tech sleuthing tools similar to those used by national security agencies"); John Markoff, *Thinking Machines to File for Bankruptcy,* N.Y. TIMES, Aug. 16, 1994, at D4.

4. *See, e.g.,* William M. Grove and Paul E. Meehl, *Comparative Efficiency of Informal (Subjective, Impressionistic) and Formal (Mechanical, Algorithmic) Prediction Procedures: The Clinical/Statistical Controversy,* 2 PSYCH. PUB. & LAW 293 (1996) (showing that mechanical statistical approaches almost always beat human judgment); Nigel Harvey, *Improving Judgment in Forecasting, in* PRINCIPLES OF FORECASTING: A HANDBOOK FOR RESEARCHERS AND PRACTITIONERS 65–66 (J. Scott Armstrong ed., 2001) (summarizing the literature).

5. David Dunning et al., *Self-Serving Prototypes of Social Categories,* 61 J. PERSONALITY & SOC. PSYCHOL. 957 (1991); Marsha T. Gabriel et al., *Narcissistic Illusions in Self-Evaluations of Intelligence and Attractiveness,* 62 J. PERSONALITY 143 (1994); P. M. Lewinsohn et al., *Social Competence and Depression: The Role of Illusory Self-Perceptions,* 898 J. ABNORMAL PSYCHOL. 203 (1980).

6. *See, e.g.,* Valerie A. Clarke et al., *Unrealistic Optimism and the Health Belief Model,* 23 J. BEHAV. MED. 367, 372–74 (2000).

7. *See* Peter Harris, *Sufficient Grounds for Optimism? The Relationship Between Perceived Controllability and Optimistic Bias,* 15 J. SOC. & CLINICAL PSYCHOL. 9 (1996).

8. *See* Linda Babcock and George Loewenstein, *Explaining Bargaining Impasse: The Role of Self-Serving Biases,* 11 J. ECON. PERSP. 109 (1997); Oren Bar-Gill, *The Success and Survival of Cautious Optimism: Legal Rules and Endogenous Perceptions in Pre-Trial Settlement Negotiations,* J.L. ECON. & ORG. (forthcoming) (arguing that aspects of the legal environment, such as rules on fee shifting, might affect the degree to which litigants are optimistic).

9. Each monologue of Keillor's *A Prairie Home Companion* concludes: "That's the news from Lake Wobegon, where all the women are strong, all the men are good-looking, and all the children are above average." PETER A. SCHOLL, GARRISON KEILLOR 136 (1993).

10. Gregory Mitchell, *Cautious Optimism in Law Students* (FSU College of Law Public Law Research Paper No. 55, 2002).

11. *See* Aviad Heifetz and Yossi Spiegel, *On the Evolutionary Emergence of Optimism* (Northwestern U. Ctr. for Mathematical Studs. in Econ. and Mgmt. Sci. Discussion Paper No. 1304, 2000), *available at* http://kellogg.northwestern.edu/research/math/papers/1304.pdf (last visited June 27, 2006).

12. ZUR SHAPIRA, RISK TAKING: A MANAGERIAL PERSPECTIVE 73 (2005).

13. *See* Stuart C. Gilson, *Management Turnover and Financial Distress,* 25 J. FIN. ECON. 241 (1989).

14. Avishalom Tor, *The Fable of Entry: Bounded Rationality, Market Discipline, and Legal Policy,* 101 MICH. L. REV. 482, 561 and n.331 (2002) (citing Milton Friedman, *The Methodology of Positive Economics, in* ESSAYS IN POSITIVE ECONOMICS 3, 21–22 [1953], and Robin M. Hogarth and Melvin W. Reder, *Introduction: Perspectives from Economics and Psychology, in* RATIONAL CHOICE: THE CONTRAST BETWEEN ECONOMICS AND PSYCHOLOGY 1, 6 [Robin M. Hogarth and Melvin W. Reder eds., 1986]).

15. For a study showing how feedback mechanisms can reward overconfident predictions, see Magne Jørgensen, *Better Sure Than Safe? Overconfidence in Judgment Based Software Development Effort Prediction Intervals,* 70 J. SYS. & SOFTWARE 79 (2004).

16. *See* J. B. Heaton, *Managerial Optimism and Corporate Finance,* FIN. MGMT., Summer 2002, *available at* http://papers.ssrn.com/sol3/papers.cfm?abstract_id=71411 (last visited June 27, 2006).

17. *See* Neil D. Weinstein and William M. Klein, *Resistance of Personal Risk Perceptions to Debiasing Interventions, in* HEURISTICS AND BIASES: THE PSYCHOLOGY OF INTUITIVE JUDGMENT 323 (Thomas Gilovich et al. eds., 2002). For a discussion of the possibility of using legal interventions to accomplish debiasing, see Christine Jolls and Cass R. Sunstein, *Debiasing Through Law,* 35 J. LEGAL STUD. 199 (2006).

18. *See* James G. March and Zur Shapira, *Managerial Perspectives on Risk and Risk Taking,* 33 MGMT. SCI. 1404, 1410 (1987).

19. *See* David M. Pennock, A Dynamic Pari-Mutuel Market for Hedging, Wagering, and Information Aggregation, *in* PROCEEDINGS OF THE 5TH ACM CONFERENCE ON ELECTRONIC COMMERCE 170 (2004).

20. *See* U.S. Patent Application No. 20050171878 (filed Feb. 3, 2004). http://patft.uspto.gov/netacgi.

21. Pennock, however, has subsequently concluded that the formulas provided in the paper contained an error. E-mail from David Pennock to Michael Abramowicz (Jan. 18, 2006).

22. *See* Pennock, *supra* note 19, at 174, 176.

23. *Id.* at 175.

24. *See* U.S. Patent Application, *supra* note 20, ¶ 46.

25. *See* http://buzz.research.yahoo.com (last visited June 27, 2006).

26. The incentive is only approximate because the rules specify that "cash out events occur at long term intervals," and at cash out events, all money in the markets is allocated in proportion to buzz scores. Presumably, the purpose of this is to allow Yahoo! to close out particular markets and create new ones. The phrase "long term intervals" is undefined, but conceivably the duration might affect market behavior. For example, if a week were a long-term interval, there would be no incentive for market players to take a longer time horizon.

27. For a study using traditionally designed prediction markets to forecast the success of new products, see Thomas S. Gruca et al., *The Effect of Electronic Markets on Forecasts of New Product Success,* 5 INFO. SYS. FRONTIERS 95 (2003).

28. E-mail from David Pennock to Michael Abramowicz, *supra* note 21.

29. *See* http://buzz.research.yahoo.com/dm/info/help.html (last visited June 27, 2006).

30. Richard Roll, *Orange Juice and Weather,* 74 AM. ECON. REV. 861 (1984).

31. *See* http://hurricanefutures.miami.edu (last visited June 27, 2006).

32. Jack Hirshleifer, *The Private and Social Value of Information and the Reward to Inventive Activity,* 61 AM. ECON. REV. 561 (1977).

33. Even with the optimal amount of investment, at any given time, the market will be in disequilibrium; otherwise, there would be no incentive to invest. *See* Sanford J. Grossman and Joseph E. Stiglitz, *On the Impossibility of Informationally Efficient Markets,* 70 AM. ECON. REV. 393 (1980).

34. ROBERT J. SHILLER, THE NEW FINANCIAL ORDER: RISK IN THE 21ST CENTURY (2003).

35. George Akerlof, *The Market for "Lemons": Quality Uncertainty and the Market Mechanism,* 84 Q.J. ECON. 488 (1970).

36. *See* KENNETH S. ABRAHAM, DISTRIBUTING RISK: INSURANCE, LEGAL THEORY, AND PUBLIC POLICY 15 (1986) (describing adverse selection as "the process by which low-risk insureds tend to purchase less coverage, and high-risk insureds tend to purchase more coverage than they would if prices were more accurate").

37. Peter Siegelman, *Adverse Selection in Insurance Markets: An Exaggerated Threat,* 113 YALE L.J. 1223, 1226, 1266 (1970).

38. Steve P. Calandrillo, *Eminent Domain Economics: Should "Just Compensation" Be Abolished, and Would "Takings Insurance" Work Instead?,* 64 OHIO ST. L.J. 451, 528–30 (2003).

Takings insurance might be useful not only as a replacement for the Takings Clause but also as a supplement if the observation that just compensation typically leaves people worse off is true. *See* RICHARD EPSTEIN, TAKINGS: PRIVATE PROPERTY AND THE POWER OF EMINENT DOMAIN 185 (1985) ("[T]oday a large number of doctrines set benchmarks for compensation below market value, especially when cost or previous value is used as the benchmark").

39. *See generally* Lloyd's "About Us" Page, http://www.lloyds.com/About_Us/ (last visited June 27, 2006). Mutual insurance companies work on an analogous principle. *See generally* Antonio Cabrales et al., La Crema*: A Case Study of Mutual Fire Insurance,* 111 J. POL. ECON. 425 (2003) (assessing pricing incentives in one mutual insurance scheme).

40. *See, e.g.,* Robert Franciosi et al., *Fairness: Effect on Temporary and Equilibrium Prices in Posted-Offer Markets,* ECON. J., July 1995, at 938.

41. Kay-Yut Chen and Charles R. Plott, *Information Aggregation Mechanisms: Concept, Design and Implementation for a Sales Forecasting Problem* 5 (Cal. Inst. of Tech. Soc. Sci. Working Paper No. 1131, Mar. 2002).

42. *Id.* at 3.

43. *Id.* at 10.

44. *Id.* at 3.

45. Chen and Plott conclude that in theory, the markets presented a possibility for earning profits from arbitrage, but taking advantage of these opportunities would have been complicated and potentially risky, requiring individuals "to execute multiple trades when fluctuations of prices were substantial." *Id.* at 16.

46. *Id.* at 15.

47. *See, e.g.,* David McAdams and Thomas W. Malone, *Internal Markets for Supply Chain Capacity Allocation* (MIT Sloan Sch. of Mgmt. Working Paper No. 4546–05, June 2005).

48. For a discussion of prediction markets at Google, see Ian Austen, *At Google, the Workers Are Placing Their Bets,* N.Y. TIMES, Sept. 26, 2005, at C5.

49. Russ Juskalian, *Google: An Interesting Read on a Powerhouse Company,* USA TODAY, Nov. 14, 2005, at B5.

50. *See* http://blog.commerce.net/?p=233 (last visited June 27, 2006) (reporting comments from a designer of the Google markets at a conference on prediction markets).

51. *See* http://googleblog.blogspot.com/2005/09/putting-crowd-wisdom-to-work.html (last visited June 27, 2006).

52. Robin Hanson, *Foul Play in Information Markets, in* INFORMATION MARKETS: A NEW WAY OF MAKING DECISIONS (Robert W. Hahn and Paul C. Tetlock eds., 126, 132).

53. THE NAT'L COMM'N ON TERRORIST ATTACKS UPON THE UNITED STATES, THE 9/11 COMMISSION REPORT 171–72 (2004), *available at* http://www.9–11commission.gov/report/911Report.pdf.

54. Hanson cites one example involving a PaineWebber employee who caused computer destruction after betting against the company's stock. *See* Hanson, *supra* note 52, at 132 n.33 (citing Andy Geller, *Pained Webber: Geek Tried to Sink Stock with Cyber Bomb,* N.Y. POST, Dec. 18, 2002). The perpetrator was caught. Of course, it is possible that some individuals have engaged in sabotage undetected.

55. *See* Robin Hanson, *Designing Real Terrorism Futures* 16–17 (Aug. 2005), *available at* http://hanson.gmu.edu/realterf.pdf (last visited June 27, 2006) (noting the possibility of hiding prices from market participants).

CHAPTER 4: COMMITTEES

1. The Quotations Page, http://www.quotationspage.com/quotes/Robert_Copeland (last visited June 27, 2006).

2. JÜRGEN HABERMAS, BETWEEN FACTS AND NORMS: CONTRIBUTIONS TO A DISCOURSE THEORY OF LAW AND DEMOCRACY (William Rehg trans., MIT Press 1996) (1992).

3. *See, e.g.,* James Bohman, *Complexity, Pluralism, and the Constitutional State: On Habermas's Faktizität und Geltung,* 28 L. & SOC'Y REV. 897, 921 (1994).

4. CARLOS SANTIAGO NINO, THE CONSTITUTION OF DELIBERATIVE DEMOCRACY (1996).

5. *See* JAMES S. FISHKIN, DEMOCRACY AND DELIBERATION (1993).

6. *Id.* at 1.

7. *Id.* at 35 (citing THE FEDERALIST No. 71 (Alexander Hamilton)).

8. *Id.* at 36; *see also* HABERMAS, *supra* note 2, at 322–25.

9. BRUCE ACKERMAN AND JAMES S. FISHKIN, DELIBERATION DAY (2004).

10. *Id.* at 226.

11. *Id.* at 16.

12. *Id.* at 24–25.

13. *Id.* at 34–35.

14. *Id.* at 3.

15. JAMES S. FISHKIN, THE VOICE OF THE PEOPLE: PUBLIC OPINION AND DEMOCRACY 178 (1995).

16. *See generally* MICHAEL X. DELLI CARPINI AND SCOTT KEETER, WHAT AMERICANS KNOW ABOUT POLITICS AND WHY IT MATTERS (1996).

17. *See, e.g.,* Cass R. Sunstein, *Deliberative Trouble? Why Groups Go to Extremes,* 110 YALE L.J. 71 (2000). For an overview of the social psychological studies of the phenomenon, see ROGER BROWN, SOCIAL PSYCHOLOGY 200–48 (2d ed. 1986).

18. Sunstein, *supra* note 17, at 74.

19. *See, e.g.,* LEON FESTINGER, A THEORY OF COGNITIVE DISSONANCE (1957).

20. ACKERMAN and FISHKIN, *supra* note 9, at 63.

21. *See* http://uchicagolaw.typepad.com/faculty/2006/02/deliberation_da.html (last visited June 27, 2006) (providing a preliminary account of this experiment).

22. IRVING JANIS, VICTIMS OF GROUPTHINK: A PSYCHOLOGICAL STUDY OF FOREIGN-POLICY DECISIONS AND FIASCOES (1972).

23. *See, e.g.,* Won-Woo Park, *A Comprehensive Empirical Investigation of the Relationship Among Variables in the Groupthink Model,* 21 J. ORGANIZ. BEHAV. 873 (2000).

24. William Safire, Op-Ed, *The New Groupthink,* N.Y. TIMES, July 14, 2004, at A23.

25. *See, e.g.,* Harold A. Linstone, *The Delphi Technique, in* HANDBOOK OF FUTURES RESEARCH 273, 274–75 (Jib Fowles ed., 1978) (providing a ten-step overview of the Delphi approach).

26. *Id.* at 275.

27. *See, e.g.,* Irene Anne Jillson, *The National Drug-Abuse Policy Delphi: Progress Report and Findings to Date, in* THE DELPHI METHOD: TECHNIQUES AND APPLICATIONS 1, 5 (Harold A. Linstone and Murray Turoff eds., 1975) (reporting a study sponsored in part by the National Institute of Drug Abuse and the National Coordinating Council on Drug Education); J. F. Preble, *Public Sector Use of the Delphi Technique,* 23 TECH. FORECASTING & SOCIAL CHANGE 75 (1983) (providing an overview).

28. Norman Dalkey and Olaf Helmer, *An Experimental Application of the Delphi Method to the Use of Experts,* 9 MGMT. SCI. 458, 459 (1963).

29. *Id.*

30. *Id.* at 461.

31. *Id.* at 466.

32. Gordon Welty, *Problems of Selecting Experts for Delphi Exercises,* 15 ACAD. MGMT. J. 121 (1972).

33. *See* Harold A. Linstone and Murray Turoff, *Introduction* to THE DELPHI METHOD: TECHNIQUES AND APPLICATIONS, *supra* note 27, at 1, 5.

34. *Id.* at 121.

35. *Id.* at 124 (citing Nicholas Rescher, *A Questionnaire Study of American Values by 2000 A.D., in* VALUES AND THE FUTURE (K. Baier and N. Rescher eds., 1969)).

36. Linstone, *supra* note 25, at 286.

37. *See generally* HAROLD SACKMAN, DELPHI CRITIQUE (1975) (offering a systematic critique of the Delphi Method). Sackman argues: "The Delphi method typically measures very small sample attitudes toward future events at a given time. It does not measure the events themselves, nor does it incorporate systematic hypotheses and empirical feedback from such events. The leap from raw opinion to future events under these conditions is strictly an act of faith." *Id.* at 15. Even advocates of the technique have conceded that there are insufficient data to establish its success as a forecasting tool. *See* Harold A. Linstone and Murray Turoff, *Evaluation: Introduction, in* THE DELPHI METHOD: TECHNIQUES AND APPLICATIONS, *supra* note 27, at 227, 231.

38. *See* Roger J. Best, *An Experiment in Delphi Estimation in Marketing Decision Making,* 11 J. MKTG. RESEARCH 448, 449 (1974).

39. *Id.* at 450.

40. For another study along these lines, see George T. Milkovich et al., *The Use of the Delphi Procedures in Manpower Forecasting,* 19 MGMT. SCI. 381 (1972), which uses a Delphi to forecast the amount of labor that a particular firm would require.

41. *See* Norman W. Mulgrave and Alex J. Ducanis, *Propensity to Change Responses in a Delphi Round as a Function of Dogmatism, in* THE DELPHI METHOD: TECHNIQUES AND APPLICATIONS, *supra* note 27, at 288, 290.

42. *See* Robert I. Mehr and Seev Neumann, *Delphi Forecasting Project,* 37 J. RISK AND INS. 241, 244 (1970) (noting conflicting results).

43. For a notable exception, see GAZING INTO THE ORACLE: THE DELPHI METHOD AND ITS APPLICATION TO SOCIAL POLICY AND PUBLIC HEALTH (Michael Adler and Erio Ziglio eds., 1995). The authors acknowledge that since the mid-1970s "there have been no major publications which have sought either to address fundamental theoretical, method-

ological and practical issues relating to the Delphi Method or to describe new applications of the technique." Michael Adler and Erio Ziglio, *Preface* to Gazing into the Oracle, *supra,* at ix.

44. The expected values can be calculated by multiplying the payouts by the probability of their occurrence, so $0.625 = 0.75 \times 0.75 + 0.25 \times 0.25$.

45. *See, e.g.,* Morris H. DeGroot and Stephen E. Fienberg, *The Comparison and Evaluation of Forecasters,* 32 Statistician 12, 20 (1983) (discussing strictly proper scoring rules and noting that even they may produce dishonest forecasts where participants' utility is not a linear function of wealth).

46. Let E_1 through E_n represent the various outcomes that are possible, and let each r_i represent the forecaster's announced probability estimate of the probability of the corresponding event E_i. Suppose that in fact the event that occurs is j. Then, the quadratic scoring rule would pay $2r_j - \Sigma r_i^2$, where the summation is across all the events. *See, e.g.,* James E. Matheson and Robert L. Winkler, *Scoring Rules for Continuous Probability Distributions,* 22 Mgmt. Sci. 1087, 1088 (1976).

47. Using the same notation as in the preceding footnote, the payoff of the spherical scoring rule equals $r_j / (\Sigma r_i^2)^{0.5}$. *See id.*

48. *See* Carl-Axel S. Staël von Holstein, *A Family of Strictly Proper Scoring Rules Which Are Sensitive to Distance,* 9 J. Applied Meteorology 360 (1970).

49. *See* Robert L. Winkler, *Evaluating Probabilities: Asymmetric Scoring Rules,* 40 Mgmt. Sci. 1395 (1994).

50. *See* Robert L. Winkler, *Scoring Rules and the Evaluation of Probability Assessors,* 64 J. Am. Stat. Assoc. 1073 (1969).

51. *See* Robert G. Nelson and David A. Bessler, *Subjective Probabilities and Scoring Rules: Experimental Evidence,* 71 Am. J. Agric. Econ. 363 (1989).

52. Robin Hanson, *Combinatorial Information Market Design,* 5 Info. Sys. Frontiers 107, 110 (2003).

53. *See* Michael Abramowicz, *The Hidden Beauty of the Quadratic Market Scoring Rule: A Uniform Liquidity Market Maker, with Variations,* J. Prediction Markets (forthcoming).

54. Hanson, *supra* n. 52, at 115, 117.

55. For a more complete discussion, see Michael Abramowicz, *Deliberative Information Markets for Small Groups, in* Information Markets: A New Way of Making Decisions 101 (Robert W. Hahn and Paul C. Tetlock eds., 2006).

56. *Compare* Robert A. Prentice, *The Inevitability of a Strong SEC,* 91 Cornell L. Rev. 775 (2006) (arguing that the provisions of the Sarbanes-Oxley Act that promote a strong Securities and Exchange Commission are necessary and beneficial), *with* Roberta Romano, *The Sarbanes-Oxley Act and the Making of Quack Corporate Governance,* 114 Yale L.J. 1521 (2005) (arguing that the benefits of the act do not outweigh the costs).

57. *See* William H. Widen, *Lord of the Liens: Towards Greater Efficiency in Secured Syndicated Lending,* 25 Cardozo L. Rev. 1577, 1629 (2004) ("Even in light of legal reform, such as the Sarbanes-Oxley Act, comparative advantages should accrue to firms that can provide credible assurance that their managers will not misuse firm assets").

58. *See* Prentice, *supra* note 56, at 829.

59. *See id.* at 808–10.

60. *See* Kay-Yut Chen, Leslie R. Fine, and Bernando A. Huberman, *Forecasting Uncertain Events with Small Groups, available at* http://papers.ssrn.com/abstract_id=278601 (last visited June 27, 2006).

61. Richard L. Revesz, *Litigation and Settlement in the Federal Appellate Courts: Impact of Panel Selection Procedures on Ideologically Divided Courts,* 29 J. LEGAL STUD. 685 (2002).

62. Some studies of bias already exist in discrete contexts. *See, e.g.,* Joel Waldfogel, *Aggregate Inter-Judge Disparity in Sentencing: Evidence from Three Districts,* 4 FED. SENTENCING REP. 151 (1991).

63. *See, e.g.,* Micheal W. Giles et al., *Picking Federal Judges: A Note on Policy and Partisan Selection Agendas,* POL. RES. Q., Sept. 2001, at 623; LEE EPSTEIN AND JEFFREY A. SEGAL, ADVICE AND CONSENT: THE POLITICS OF JUDICIAL APPOINTMENTS 124–29 (2005).

64. *See* 5 U.S.C. § 553 (2000).

65. *See* David Fontana, *Reforming the Administrative Procedure Act: Democracy Index Rulemaking,* 74 FORDHAM L. REV. 81 (2005).

66. *See generally* MANCUR OLSON, THE LOGIC OF COLLECTIVE ACTION: PUBLIC GOODS AND THE THEORY OF GROUPS (2d ed. 1971) (providing the seminal work on collective action and the legislative process).

67. *See, e.g.,* Lars Noah, *Scientific "Republicanism": Expert Peer Review and the Quest for Regulatory Deliberation,* 49 EMORY L.J. 1033, 1045–46 (2000) (noting that some have equated peer review with the scientific method but observing some limitations of the peer review process).

68. Peter M. Rothwell and Christopher N. Martyn, *Reproducibility of Peer Review in Clinical Neuroscience: Is Agreement Between Reviewers Any Greater Than Would Be Expected by Chance Alone?* 123 BRAIN 1964 (2000).

69. Thomas O. McGarity, *Peer Review in Awarding Federal Grants in the Arts and Sciences,* 9 HIGH TECH. L.J. 1 (1994).

70. David F. Horrobin, *The Philosophical Basis of Peer Review and the Suppression of Innovation,* 263 JAMA 1438 (1990).

71. *See, e.g.,* Daniel Engber, *Quality Control: The Case Against Peer Review,* SLATE, June 27, 2005, http://www.slate.com/id/2116244 (last visited June 27, 2006).

72. *See* Alan D. Sokal, *Transgressing the Boundaries: Towards a Transformative Hermeneutics of Quantum Gravity,* 46–47 SOCIAL TEXT 217 (1996). For a discussion of the hoax, see Stanley Fish, *Professor Sokal's Bad Joke,* N.Y. TIMES, May 21, 1996, at A23.

73. *See* Susan van Rooyen et al., *Effect of Open Peer Review on Quality of Reviews and on Reviewers' Recommendations: A Randomised Trial,* 318 BRITISH MED. J. 23 (Jan. 2, 1999). The authors conclude that the benefits of open review, such as transparency, nonetheless argue in favor of it.

74. David Dobbs, *Trial and Error,* N.Y. TIMES MAGAZINE, Jan. 15, 2006, at 18.

CHAPTER 5: REGULATORY BODIES

1. *See, e.g.,* Jon D. Hanson and Kyle D. Logue, *The First-Party Insurance Externality: An Economic Justification for Enterprise Liability,* 76 CORNELL L. REV. 129 (1990) (advancing the case for enterprise liability regimes).

2. *See generally* EMBRACING RISK: THE CHANGING CULTURE OF INSURANCE AND RESPONSIBILITY (Tom Baker and Jonathan Simon eds., 2002).

3. This might not be the case if rules are complex or obtuse. *See generally* Peter H. Schuck, *Legal Complexity: Some Causes, Consequences, and Cures,* 42 DUKE L.J. 1 (1992).

4. FREDERICK SCHAUER, PLAYING BY THE RULES (1991).

5. *Id.* at 47.

6. *Id.* at 31–34.

7. *Id.* at 94.

8. *Id.* at 45.

9. *Id.* at 151.

10. As the probability of a condition's occurrence nears zero, the market dynamics become similar to those of the self-resolving prediction market described in Chapter 10.

11. For a more complete discussion of predictive decision making, see Michael Abramowicz, *Predictive Decisionmaking,* 92 VA. L. REV. 69 (2006).

12. 304 U.S. 64, 69–90 (1938).

13. Travelers Ins. Co. v. 633 Third Assocs., 14 F.3d 114, 119 (2d Cir. 1994).

14. *See, e.g.,* Arthur L. Corbin, *The Laws of the Several States,* 50 YALE L.J. 762 (1941).

15. Einer Elhauge, *Preference-Estimating Statutory Default Rules,* 102 COLUM. L. REV. 2027 (2002).

16. Where current preferences are not ascertainable, Elhauge suggests that judges instead should select the interpretation that is most likely to lead the legislature to resolve the issue, thus possibly overruling the court. *See* Einer Elhauge, *Preference-Eliciting Statutory Default Rules,* 102 COLUM. L. REV. 2162, 2165 (2002).

17. Elhauge, *supra* note 15, at 2049–56.

18. *See, e.g., id.* at 2039 (arguing that each legislature would rather have its preferences control current courts as to all legislation than to have its preferences control all future courts but only as to legislation that it enacted).

19. *Id.* at 2107.

20. *Id.*

21. An incremental step in this direction would be to require disclosure of the price paid for insurance. *See, e.g.,* Sean J. Griffith, *Uncovering a Gatekeeper: Why the SEC Should Mandate Disclosure of Details Concerning Directors' and Officers' Liability Insurance Policies,* 154 U. PA. L. REV. 1147 (2006).

22. For a discussion of insurance risk classification, see Kenneth S. Abraham, *Efficiency and Fairness in Insurance Risk Classification,* 71 VA. L. REV. 403 (1985).

23. *See* Kenneth E. Scott and Thomas Mayer, *Risk and Regulation in Banking: Some Proposals for Federal Deposit Insurance Reform,* 23 STAN. L. REV. 857, 864–66, 893 (1971).

24. *Id.* at 895.

25. 29 U.S.C. §§ 1001–1461 (2000).

26. Michael Schroeder, *Pension Agency's Director Resigns,* WALL ST. J., Mar. 24, 2006, at A2.

27. Ergonomics Program, 65 Fed. Reg. 68,262 (Nov. 14, 2000).

28. *See* Kathy Chen, *Effort to Kill Workplace Ergonomics Rules Gains Steam as Bush Gives Endorsement,* WALL ST. J., Mar. 7, 2001, at A3.

29. S.J. Res. 6, 107th Cong. (2001); *see also* Steven Greenhouse, *House Joins Senate in Repealing Rules on Workplace Injuries,* N.Y. TIMES, Mar. 8, 2001, at A19.

30. *See, e.g.,* Thomas A. Lambert, *Avoiding Regulatory Mismatch in the Workplace: An Informational Approach to Workplace Safety Regulation,* 82 NEB. L. REV. 1006 (2004).

31. 42 U.S.C. § 2210 (2000).

32. *See generally* T. H. TIETENBERG, EMISSIONS TRADING: PRINCIPLES AND PRACTICE (2d ed. 2006).

33. *See generally* W. KIP VISCUSI ET AL., ECONOMICS OF REGULATION AND ANTITRUST 330–83 (1992).

34. *See* Harold Demsetz, *Why Regulate Utilities?,* 11 J.L. & ECON. 55, 63 (1968).

35. *See* VISCUSI ET AL., *supra* note 33, at 390–92.

36. The proposal, however, could not be permitted to include any commitment to ensure that the ex post assessment by the government would exceed at least some level. Otherwise, the proposed regulator would be precommitting to seeking to influence the decision maker ex post.

37. *See* Stephen Calkins, *Perspectives on State and Federal Antitrust Enforcement,* 53 DUKE L.J. 673, 726 (2003) (arguing that the Department of Justice and Federal Trade Commission should "continue to use and develop" their powers to challenge mergers).

38. *See* ROBERT H. BORK, THE ANTITRUST PARADOX 217–24 (1978).

39. U.S. DEP'T OF JUSTICE AND FED. TRADE COMM'N, HORIZONTAL MERGER GUIDELINES (1992, rev. ed. 1997), *reprinted in* 4 Trade Reg. Rep. (CCH) ¶ 13,104 (1992), *available at* http://www.usdoj.gov/atr/public/guidelines/hmg.pdf (last visited June 27, 2006).

40. *Id.* § 0.1.

41. 21 U.S.C. 355(a) (2000).

42. *See, e.g.,* HENRY I. MILLER, M.D., TO AMERICA'S HEALTH: A PROPOSAL TO REFORM THE FOOD AND DRUG ADMINISTRATION (2000); Michael I. Krauss, *Loosening the FDA's Drug Certification Monopoly: Implications for Tort Law and Consumer Welfare,* 4 GEO. MASON L. REV. 457 (1996).

43. For a mathematical approach to this test crafted by Judge Richard Posner, see American Hospital Supply Corp. v. Hospital Products, Ltd., 780 F.2d 589, 593 (7th Cir. 1985).

44. For an example of a lengthy district court opinion considering whether to issue a preliminary injunction, see Northwest Airlines, Inc. v. American Airlines, Inc., 989 F.2d 1002 (D. Minn. 1993).

45. For an analysis and a comparison of private and public prediction mechanisms in this context, see Eric Helland and Alexander Tabarrok, *Public Versus Private Law Enforcement: Evidence from Bail Jumping,* 47 J.L. & ECON. 93 (2004).

46. *See* Doug Smith and Jeffrey L. Rabin, *Mulish Budget Battle Unique: California Lawmakers Remain Stuck in Costly Partisan Gridlock While Legislatures in Other States Find Ways to Compromise,* L.A. TIMES, June 2, 2004, at B1.

CHAPTER 6: ADMINISTRATIVE AGENCIES

1. *See* Harold Hotelling, *Stability in Competition,* 39 ECON. J. 41, 54 (1929).

2. Kenneth O. May, *A Set of Independent Necessary and Sufficient Conditions for Simple Majority Decision,* 20 ECONOMETRICA 680 (1952) (introducing what has come to be known as May's Theorem).

3. Heather K. Gerken, *Second-Order Diversity,* 118 HARV. L. REV. 1099 (2005).

4. Heather K. Gerken, *Dissenting by Deciding,* 57 STAN. L. REV. 1745, 1749 (2005).

5. Indeed, Gerken recognizes that variance in jury decision making may have costs as well as benefits. *See* Gerken, *supra* note 3, at 1165–66.

6. *See generally* Dan Simon, *A Third View of the Black Box: Cognitive Coherence in Legal Decision Making,* 71 U. CHI. L. REV. 511 (2004) (arguing that premises and facts affect individuals' conclusions, but conclusions also affect premises and factual assessments).

7. 5 U.S.C. § 706(2)(A) (2000).

8. Greater Boston Television Corp. v. FCC, 444 F.2d 841, 851 (D.C. Cir. 1970).

9. *Id.*

10. 15 U.S.C. §§ 1381 et seq. (1976 and Supp. IV 1980).

11. *See* Motor Vehicle Manufacturers Ass'n v. State Farm Mutual Auto. Ins. Co., 463 U.S. 29 (1983).

12. *See* Thomas O. McGarity, *Some Thoughts on "Deossifying" the Rulemaking Process,* 41 DUKE L.J. 1385, 1411–25 (1992).

13. For a more complete discussion of predictive cost-benefit analysis, see Michael Abramowicz, *Information Markets, Administrative Decisionmaking, and Predictive Cost-Benefit Analysis,* 71 U. CHI. L. REV. 933, 997–1018 (2004).

14. *See, e.g.,* Frank Ackerman and Lisa Heinzerling, *Pricing the Priceless: Cost-Benefit Analysis of Environmental Protection,* 150 U. PA. L. REV. 1553, 1560 (2002).

15. *See* OFFICE OF MANAGEMENT AND BUDGET, CIRCULAR NO. A-94 REVISED (Oct. 29, 1992), *available at* http://www.whitehouse.gov/omb/circulars/a094/a094.html (last visited June 27, 2006).

16. *See, e.g.,* Lisa Heinzerling, *Risking It All,* 57 ALA. L. REV. 103, 114 (2005).

17. *See* Robert H. Frank and Cass R. Sunstein, *Cost-Benefit Analysis and Relative Position,* 68 U. CHI. L. REV. 323 (2001).

18. *See* Thomas J. Kniesner and W. Kip Viscusi, *Why Relative Economic Position Does Not Matter: A Cost-Benefit Analysis,* 20 YALE J. ON REG. 1 (2003).

19. *See generally* CONTINGENT VALUATION: A CRITICAL ASSESSMENT (Jerry A. Hausman ed., 1993).

20. *See, e.g.,* Frank B. Cross, *Restoring Restoration for Natural Resource Damages,* 24 U. TOLEDO L. REV. 319, 330–31 (1993) (discussing the phenomenon of "embedding").

21. Eric A. Posner, *Controlling Agencies with Cost-Benefit Analysis: A Positive Political Theory Perspective,* 68 U. CHI. L. REV. 1137 (2001).

22. *See* 5 U.S.C. § 706(2)(E) (2000) (requiring the court to approve the agency's factual findings if supported by "substantial evidence").

23. Chevron U.S.A., Inc. v. Natural Resources Defense Council, Inc., 467 U.S. 837 (1984).

24. 515 U.S. 687 (1995).

25. Endangered Species Act, 16 U.S.C. § 1532(19).

26. For a case illustrating the distinction between purely legal issues and mixed questions of law and fact, see NLRB v. Hearst Publications, Inc., 322 U.S. 111 (1944).

27. Adrian Vermeule and Jacob Gersen have independently recognized the possibility that *Chevron* analysis might be based on the percentage of judges who would prefer one interpretation to another, rather than on whether a majority of judges believe that a statute is ambiguous. *See* Jacob E. Gersen and Adrian Vermeule, Chevron *as a Voting Rule,* 116 Yale L.J. 676 (2007). Their approach runs inevitably into the law of small numbers, however. A statute might genuinely be ambiguous even if all three judges on a three-judge panel prefer a particular interpretation. An advantage of the normative prediction market approach is that it averages the range of possible views of a diverse group of potential ex post decision makers.

28. *See, e.g.,* Linda Greenhouse, *A Deeper Dimension: The Senators, Judging Bork, Try to Define Conservatism,* N.Y. Times, Oct. 11, 1987, at D1 (discussing the views of senators concerning the nomination of Judge Robert Bork to the Supreme Court).

29. *See, e.g.,* David S. Clark, *The Selection and Accountability of Judges in West Germany: Implementation of a* Rechtsstaat, 61 S. Cal. L. Rev. 1795 (1987–88).

30. 5 C.F.R. § 930.203(b) (2006).

31. *See* Epstein and Segal, *supra* note xx, at 108–13.

32. For a discussion of this issue in the context of recent developments in U.S. campaign finance, see Richard Briffault, *The 527 Problem . . . and the* Buckley *Problem,* 73 Geo. Wash. L. Rev. 949 (2005).

33. *See, e.g.,* Michael S. Kang, *Democratizing Direct Democracy: Restoring Voter Competence Through Heuristic Clues and "Disclosure Plus,"* 50 UCLA L. Rev. 1141, 1167 (2003) ("[G]overnment reporting of campaign finance information remains too far removed from public information to reach many voters").

34. *See* Ian Ayres and Jeremy Bulow, *The Donation Booth: Mandating Donor Anonymity to Disrupt the Market for Political Influence,* 50 Stan. L. Rev. 837 (1998).

35. 524 U.S. 417 (1998).

36. The Court found that because the president had been given the power to cancel legislation, the statute violated the Presentment Clause. *Id.* at 436–41.

37. *See, e.g.,* 145 Cong. Rec. S534–35 (1999) (introductory remarks of Sen. McCain).

38. *See* Maxwell L. Stearns, *The Public Choice Case Against the Item Veto,* 49 Wash. & Lee L. Rev. 385 (1992).

39. *See, e.g.,* Trade Act of 1974, 19 U.S.C. § 2192 (2000).

40. *See* Press Release, The Bank of Sweden Prize in Economic Sciences in Memory of Alfred Nobel (Oct. 11, 2004), http://nobelprize.org/economics/laureates/2004/press.html (last visited June 27, 2006).

41. *See* Finn E. Kydland and Edward C. Prescott, *Rules Rather Than Discretion: The Inconsistency of Optimal Plans,* 85 J. Pol. Econ. 473, 477–80 (1977).

42. *See, e.g.,* Katherine S. Neiss, *Discretionary Inflation in a General Equilibrium Model,* 31 J. Money, Credit, & Banking 357, 359 (1999).

43. *See* Kenneth Rogoff, *The Optimal Degree of Commitment to an Intermediate Target,* 100 Q.J. Econ. 1169 (1985).

44. *See, e.g.,* Milton Friedman, A Program for Monetary Stability 9 (1959).

45. For a proposal along these lines, see Robin Hanson, *Shall We Vote on Values, But Bet on Beliefs?* (Sept. 2003), http://hanson.gmu.edu/futarchy.pdf (last visited June 27, 2006).

46. *See generally* Todd J. Zywicki, *The Rule of Law, Freedom, and Prosperity,* 10 Sup. Ct. Econ. Rev. 1, 3–15 (2003) (identifying the major attributes of the "rule of law").

47. Shankar Vedantam and Dean Starkman, *Lack of Cohesion Bedevils Recovery: Red Tape, Lapses in Planning Stall Relief,* Wash. Post, Sept. 18, 2005, at A1.

48. *Id.*

49. Robert E. Pierre and Ann Gerhart, *News of Pandemonium May Have Slowed Aid,* Wash. Post, Oct. 5, 2005, at A8.

50. Spencer S. Hsu, *Waste in Katrina Response Is Cited; Housing Aid Called Inefficient in Audits,* Wash. Post, Apr. 14, 2006, at A1.

CHAPTER 7: PUBLIC CORPORATIONS

1. *See* Thomas W. Malone, The Future of Work: How the New Order of Business Will Shape Your Organization, Your Management Style, and Your Life (2004).

2. Michael C. Jensen and William H. Meckling, *Theory of the Firm: Managerial Behavior, Agency Costs and Ownership Structure,* 3 J. Fin. Econ. 305 (1976).

3. *Id.* at 308.

4. *See, e.g.,* Kam-Ming Wan, *Independent Directors, Executive Pay, and Firm Performance* (2003), available at http://papers.ssrn.com/ abstract_id=392595 (last visited June 27, 2006) (finding that the presence of independent directors had little impact on executive pay and did not produce stronger corporate performance).

5. *See, e.g.,* Broz v. Cellular Info. Sys., Inc., 673 A.2d 148 (Del. 1996) (applying Delaware's conflict-of-interest principles).

6. *See, e.g.,* Phillippe Aghion and Jean Tirole, *Formal and Real Authority in Organizations,* 105 J. Pol. Econ. 1 (1997) (offering a model in which increasing an agent's real authority increases the effort of the agent).

7. For a brief overview of Delaware law, see Sean J. Griffith, *Good Faith Business Judgment: A Theory of Rhetoric in Corporate Law Jurisprudence,* 55 Duke L.J. 1, 13–14 (2005).

8. *See, e.g.,* Robin Hanson, *Combinatorial Information Market Design,* 5 Info. Sys. Frontiers 107, 112 (2003).

9. *See* Lance Fornow, Joe Killian, David M. Pennock, and Michael P. Wellman, *Betting Boolean-Style: A Framework for Trading in Securities Based on Logical Formulas,* Electronic Commerce (Proceedings of the 4th ACM Conference on Electronic Commerce) 144 (2003).

10. *See* Henry G. Manne, Insider Trading and the Stock Market (1966).

11. Henry G. Manne, *Insider Trading: Hayek, Virtual Markets, and the Dog That Did Not Bark* (ICER Working Paper No. 7–2005, Mar. 2005), *available at* http://papers.ssrn.com/abstract_id=679662 (last visited June 27, 2006).

12. Alexei Barrionuevo, *2 Enron Chiefs Are Convicted in Fraud and Conspiracy Trial,* N.Y. Times, May 26, 2006, at A1.

13. *See* Sean J. Griffith, *Unleashing a Gatekeeper: Why the SEC Should Mandate Disclosure of Details Concerning Directors' and Officers' Liability Insurance Policies* (U. Pa. Inst. for Law & Econ. Res. Paper No. 05–15, 2005), available at http://papers.ssrn.com/abstract_id=728442 (last visited June 27, 2006).

14. Robin Hanson has observed this possibility. *See* Robin Hanson, *Shall We Vote on Values, But Bet on Beliefs?* (Sept. 2003), http://hanson.gmu.edu/futarchy.pdf (last visited June 27, 2006) ("To avoid this distortion, we can . . . put market estimates directly in control of decisions, rather than making such estimates advisory").

15. *See* Lucian A. Bebchuk, *The Case for Increasing Shareholder Power*, 118 HARV. L. REV. 833, 844–46 (2005).

16. *See* 17 C.F.R. § 240.14a-8(i) (2006).

17. *See, e.g.,* Lovenheim v. Iroquois Brands, Ltd., 618 F. Supp. 554, 556 (D.D.C. 1985) (assessing excludability of a shareholder proposal phrased as a call to the board to "form a committee to study" a particular issue).

18. Bebchuk, *supra* note 15, at 880–82.

19. *Id.* at 878.

20. *Id.* at 879–80.

21. *See, e.g., id.* at 844–50 (providing an overview of U.S. law).

22. Milton Friedman, *The Case for Flexible Exchange Rates, in* ESSAYS IN POSITIVE ECONOMICS 157 (1953).

23. The classic study is Eugene F. Fama, *Efficient Capital Markets: A Review of Theory and Empirical Work*, 25 J. FIN. 383 (1970).

24. *See* Alan J. Ziobrowski et al., *Abnormal Returns from the Common Stock Investments of the U.S. Senate*, 39 J. FIN. & QUANT. ANALYSIS 661 (2004).

25. *See, e.g.,* Eugene F. Fama, *Efficient Capital Markets: II*, 46 J. FIN. 1575, 1575 (1991): an "economically more sensible version of the efficiency hypothesis says that prices reflect information to the point where the marginal benefits of acting on information (the profits to be made) do not exceed the marginal costs."

26. *See, e.g.,* ROBERTO MANGABEIRA UNGER, FALSE NECESSITY: ANTI-NECESSITARIAN SOCIAL THEORY IN THE SERVICE OF RADICAL DEMOCRACY 491–96 (1987).

27. William N. Goetzmann and Massimo Massa, *Daily Momentum and Contrarian Behavior of Index Fund Investors* (NBER Working Paper No. 7567, 2000).

28. ROBERT J. SHILLER, THE NEW FINANCIAL ORDER: RISK IN THE 21ST CENTURY 14 (2003).

29. *Id.*

30. Robert J. Shiller, *Bubbles, Human Judgment, and Expert Opinion* 7 (Cowles Foundation Discuss Paper No. 1303, 2001).

31. *See, e.g.,* Gregory A. Brauer, *Closed-End Fund Shares' Abnormal Returns and the Information Content of Discounts and Premiums*, 43 J. FIN. 113 (1988) (assessing this anomaly).

32. Kenneth R. French and Richard Roll, *Stock Return Variances: The Arrival of Information and the Reaction of Traders*, 17 J. FIN. ECON. 5, 17 (1986).

33. *See* Colin Camerer and Keith Weigelt, *Information Mirages in Experimental Asset Markets*, 64 J. BUS. 463 (1991).

34. *Id.* at 481.

35. *See* J. Bradford De Long et al., *Noise Trader Risk in Financial Markets,* 98 J. Pol. Econ. 703 (1990).

36. *See* Dwight R. Sanders et al., *Noise Traders, Market Sentiment, and Futures Price Behavior* (May 1997).

37. Robert J. Shiller, *From Efficient Markets Theory to Behavioral Finance,* 17 J. Econ. Persp. 83 (2003).

38. *See* Eli Ofek and Matthew Richardson, *DotCom Mania: The Rise and Fall of Internet Stock Prices,* 58 J. Fin. 1113 (2003).

39. *See* Robert Battalio and Paul Schultz, *Options and the Bubble* (Mar. 2004), *available at* http://www.fdewb.unimaas.nl/finance/zipfiles/upload_papers/upload3081.pdf (last visited June 27, 2006).

40. Andrei Shleifer and Robert W. Vishny, *The Limits of Arbitrage,* 52 J. Fin. 35, 37 (1997).

41. *See* Ravi Dhar and William N. Goetzmann, *Bubble Investors: What Were They Thinking?* (Yale ICF Working Paper No. 05–01, Feb. 2005).

42. *See* J. Bradford De Long et al., *The Survival of Noise Traders in Financial Markets,* 64 J. Bus. 1, 5 (1991).

43. *See* Robin Hanson, *Markets for Telling CEOs to Step Down,* http://hanson.gmu.edu/dumpceo.html (last visited June 27, 2006).

CHAPTER 8: COURTS

1. Charles Nesson, *The Evidence or the Event? On Judicial Proof and the Acceptability of Verdicts,* 98 Harv. L. Rev. 1357 (1985).

2. *See* Michael Abramowicz, *A Compromise Approach to Compromise Verdicts,* 89 Cal. L. Rev. 231, 258–59 (2001).

3. *See* Charles Silver, *Does Civil Justice Cost Too Much?* 80 Tex. L. Rev. 2073 (2002).

4. *Id.* at 2082.

5. *Id.*

6. Robert H. Mnookin and Lewis Kornhauser, *Bargaining in the Shadow of the Law: The Case of Divorce,* 88 Yale L.J. 950 (1979) (arguing that settlements track changes in legal doctrine).

7. Silver, *supra* note 3, at 2083.

8. In theory, a court can block discovery where "the discovery sought is unreasonably cumulative or duplicative, or is obtainable from some other source that is more convenient, less burdensome, or less expensive." Fed. R. Civ. P. 26(b)(2)(i). In practice, increasing the other party's litigation expense can be an effective litigation tactic and difficult for the courts to distinguish from discovery designed primarily to obtain information.

9. *Compare.* Steven Shavell, *The Level of Litigation: Private Versus Social Optimality of Suit and of Settlement,* 19 Int'l Rev. L. & Econ. 99, 101 (1999) (concluding that with information asymmetry, there will be a socially excessive incentive by both litigants to go to trial rather than to settle, at least unless trial provides a deterrent effect above that of settlement). Shavell notes that the overall level of litigation may be suboptimal, because plaintiffs do not take into account that their lawsuits provide deterrence benefits to third parties, *see id.* at 100, but this is a separate question from the level of spending

within litigation. Shavell does not directly consider the possibility that at any given stage of litigation, each party will have excessive spending incentives. It is possible that high plaintiff expenditures, by increasing deterrence, may be optimal or suboptimal, but it will still generally be the case that lowering both plaintiff and defendant expenditures could improve social welfare.

10. *See* Norman R. F. Maier and James A. Thurber, *Accuracy of Judgments of Deception When an Interview Is Watched, Heard, and Read,* 21 Personnel Psychol. 23 (1968).

11. Paul D. Carrington, *Virtual Civil Litigation: A Visit to John Bunyan's Celestial City,* 98 Colum. L. Rev. 1516 (1998).

12. *Id.* at 1525.

13. *Id.* at 1525–26.

14. *Id.* at 1527.

15. *Id.* at 1529–31.

16. *Id.* at 1536–37.

17. *See* Fed. R. Civ. P. 56 (providing the standard for an award of summary judgment).

18. In his original paper about prediction markets, Robin Hanson briefly suggests the possibility of such an approach wherein judging is expensive. *See* Robin Hanson, *Could Gambling Save Science? Encouraging an Honest Consensus,* 9 Soc. Epistemology 3, 7–9 (1995) (discussing "audit lotteries"). In an audit lottery, many prediction market contracts would be combined into a pot and most would be randomly cancelled.

19. *See* http://www.humanitiesweb.org/human.php?s=I&p=c&a=q&ID=36 (last visited June 27, 2006). Frost repeated the phrase "trial by market" in a poem. *See* Robert Frost, *Christmas Trees,* in Complete Poems of Robert Frost 132 (1964).

20. *See* ABA Model Code of Judicial Conduct Canon 3E(1)(d)(iii) (2004).

21. *See* Richard A. Posner, Overcoming Law 109, 110–11 (1995) (noting that this generally provides only a small incentive).

22. For a fuller development of these ideas, see Michael Abramowicz, *Trial by Market: A Thought Experiment* (GWU Law School Pub. Law Research Paper No. 180, 2006), *available at* http://papers.ssrn.com/abstract_id=873475 (last visited June 27, 2006).

23. *See* John E. Coons, *Approaches to Court Imposed Compromise—The Uses of Doubt and Reason,* 58 Nw. U. L. Rev. 750 (1964).

24. For an argument that proportional damages should be applied only in the middle of the probability spectrum, see Abramowicz, *supra* note 2.

25. Such limitations on fee-shifting have been proposed in conjunction with conventional fee-shifting mechanisms. *See, e.g.,* H.R. 988, Attorney Accountability Act of 1995 (1995).

26. *See, e.g.,* Steven Shavell, *Suit, Settlement, and Trial: A Theoretical Analysis Under Alternative Methods for the Allocation of Legal Costs,* 11 J. Legal Stud. 55 (1982).

27. For a comprehensive comparison of ex ante and ex post fee-shifting, see Michael Abramowicz and Omer Alper, *Ex Ante Penalties for Frivolous Litigation* (2006) (on file with author).

28. *See* Ethan Katsh, *Bringing Online Dispute Resolution to Virtual Worlds: Creating Processes Through Code,* 49 N.Y.L. Sch. L. Rev. 271 (2005).

29. *See* F. Gregory Lastowka and Dan Hunter, *The Laws of the Virtual Worlds,* 92 Cal. L. Rev. 1, 50–51 (2004).

30. *See* http://www.squaretrade.com (last visited June 27, 2006).

31. For an analysis of how the gathering of individuals into networked communities facilitates regulation, see Amitai Aviram, *Regulation by Networks*, 2003 B.Y.U. L. Rev. 1179 (2003).

32. *See, e.g.,* CAL. CIV. PROC. CODE 116.710(b) (West 2002) ("The defendant . . . may appeal the judgment to the superior court in the county in which the action was heard").

33. *See, e.g.,* WILLIAM M. LANDES AND RICHARD A. POSNER, THE ECONOMIC STRUCTURE OF TORT LAW (1987). For a critique, see J. M. Balkin, *Too Good to Be True: The Positive Economic Theory of Law*, 87 COLUM. L. REV. 1447 (1987) (reviewing LANDES AND POSNER, *supra*).

34. *See generally* Eleanor Roberts Lewis and Harry J. Connolly Jr., *Trade Adjustment Assistance for Firms and Industries*, 10 U. PA. J. INT'L BUS. L. 579 (1988) (providing a historical and legal overview of U.S. trade adjustment assistance programs).

35. For a discussion of the criteria of Kaldor-Hicks and Pareto efficiency, see RICHARD A. POSNER, ECONOMIC ANALYSIS OF LAW 12–17 (5th ed. 1998).

36. *See, e.g.,* Lawrence Blume et al., *The Taking of Land: When Should Compensation Be Paid?*, 99 Q.J. ECON. 71 (1984) (discussing the problem of moral hazard in the takings context).

37. *See, e.g.,* FED. R. CIV. P. 11.

38. *See, e.g.,* Physicians Multispecialty Grp. v. Health Care Plan, 371 F.3d 1291, 1294 (11th Cir. 2004) (concluding that a claim was not frivolous because it depended on an issue of first impression).

39. *See, e.g.,* United States v. Miller, 771 F.2d 1219, 1230 (1985) (finding error in a trial judge's refusal to conduct an *in camera* examination of grand jury materials requested by the defendant).

40. *See* George B. Shepherd, *Failed Experiment: Why Broad Pretrial Discovery Should Be Eliminated* (2005) (on file with author).

41. *See, e.g.,* Paul Milgrom and John Roberts, *Relying on the Information of Interested Parties*, 17 RAND J. ECON. 18 (1986).

42. *See* Elizabeth Mertz and Kimberly A. Lonsway, *The Power of Denial: Individual and Cultural Constructions of Child Sexual Abuse*, 92 NW. U. L. REV. 1415, 1427 & n.38 (1998) (noting that there is some research suggesting that adults may be able to influence children such that they "remember" events that never occurred).

43. Richard A. Devine, *Clemency Reviews Take Time*, CHI. SUN TIMES, Sept. 9, 2002, at 29 ("Those on Death Row are there because judges and juries have found them guilty and because appellate courts—several appellate courts—have affirmed those decisions").

CHAPTER 9: LEGISLATIVE BODIES

1. *See* http://www.noveltwists.com (last visited June 27, 2006).

2. *See* http://www.glypho.com (last visited June 27, 2006).

3. *See, e.g.,* A. SCOTT BERG, MAX PERKINS: EDITOR OF GENIUS (Riverhead 1997) (exploring the influence of editor Max Perkins on writers such as F. Scott Fitzgerald, Ernest Hemingway, and Thomas Wolfe).

4. *See, e.g.,* David Luban, *Reason and Passion in Legal Ethics,* 51 Stan. L. Rev. 873, 895–96 (1999).

5. *See* Stefanie A. Lindquist and Frank B. Cross, *Empirically Testing Dworkin's Chain Novel Theory: Studying the Path of Precedent,* 80 N.Y.U. L. Rev. 1156 (2005).

6. http://www.wikipedia.org (last visited June 27, 2006).

7. *See* http://en.wikipedia.org/wiki/WP:3RR (last visited June 27, 2006) ("Do not revert any single page in whole or in part more than three times in 24 hours. Or else an Administrator may suspend your account") (emphasis and links omitted).

8. According to Wikipedia, 65 percent of edits in February 2005 were attributable to the one thousand most frequent contributors. *See* http://en.wikipedia.org/wiki/ Wikipedia:List_of_Wikipedians_by_number_of_edits (last visited June 27, 2006).

9. *See* Jim Giles, *Internet Encyclopaedias Go Head to Head,* 438 Nature 900 (2005).

10. *See* Encyclopedia Britannica, Inc., *Fatally Flawed: Refuting the Recent Study on Encyclopedic Accuracy by the Journal* Nature (Mar. 2006), http://corporate.britannica.com/ britannica_nature_response.pdf (last visited June 27, 2006).

11. *See* http://en.wikipedia.org/wiki/Wikipedia:Wikipedia_Signpost/2006–04–24/Job_board (last visited June 27, 2006).

12. *See* Yochai Benkler, The Wealth of Networks 94 (2006) (summarizing the results of research indicating that, "under some circumstances, adding money for an activity previously undertaken without price compensation reduces, rather than increases, the level of activity").

13. *See* http://www.digitaluniverse.net (last visited June 27, 2006). The Web site indicates that eventually experts, named "Stewards," will be paid with revenue from site programs. *See* http://collab.digitaluniverse.net/steward/index.php/FAQ#Q:_Will_I_have_ to_register_to_contribute.3F__Will_I_have_to_purchase_ISP_or_any_other_services.3F (last visited June 27, 2006).

14. *The Wiki Principle,* Economist, April 22, 2006, at 10.

15. *Compare., e.g.,* John F. Duffy, *Rethinking the Prospect Theory of Patents,* 71 U. Chi. L. Rev. 439 (2004) (explaining how policies ending patent races at a relatively early point can stimulate earlier development of technologies).

16. *See generally* Michael Abramowicz, *Perfecting Patent Prizes,* 56 Vand. L. Rev. 115 (2003) (providing an overview of these proposals).

17. *See* Robin Hanson, *Shall We Vote on Values, But Bet on Beliefs?* (Sept. 2003), http://hanson .gmu.edu/futarchy.pdf (last visited June 27, 2006).

18. *Id.* at 9–10. In an earlier version of the paper, Hanson suggests that the GDP+ function might itself be based on a prediction market assessment of which function would produce the "smallest error rate" in assessing legislators' rank of "hypothetical test choices." *See* http://web.archive.org/web/20030409122906/http://hanson.gmu.edu/futarchy.pdf (last visited Nov. 8, 2006). This comes close to the prospect of using a normative prediction market, but it is only to discipline a nonnormative market, and it relies on test cases rather than on unconstrained welfare assessments.

19. Hanson, *supra* note 17, at 14.

20. *Id.* at 21.

21. *Id.* at 22.

22. *Id.* at 24.

23. *Id.* at 22.

24. *See* U.S. Const. art. II, § 2, cl. 2 ("[T]he Congress may by Law vest the Appointment of such inferior Officers, as they think proper, in the President alone, in the Courts of Law, or in the Heads of Department").

25. *See* Kenneth Arrow, Social Choice and Individual Values (1951).

26. *See* Maxwell L. Stearns, Constitutional Process: A Social Choice Analysis of Supreme Court Decision Making 93 (2000).

27. *See, e.g.,* Gerald H. Kramer, *Sophisticated Voting Over Multidimensional Choice Spaces,* 2 J. Mathematical Sociology 165 (1972).

28. The term is coined in Kenneth A. Shepsle, *Institutional Arrangements and Equilibrium in Multidimensional Voting Models,* 23 Am. J. Pol. Sci. 27, 36 (1979). For further discussion, see Kenneth A. Shepsle and Barry R. Weingast, *Structure-Induced Equilibrium and Legislative Choice,* 37 Pub. Choice 503 (1981).

29. *See* Stearns, *supra* note 26, at 157–211.

30. *Id.* at 249–301.

31. Saul Levmore, *Public Choice Defended,* 72 U. Chi. L. Rev. 777, 779 (2005).

32. For a response to such arguments, see Donald E. Campbell, *Social Choice and Intensity of Preference,* 81 J. Pol. Econ. 211 (1973).

33. *See, e.g.,* Herbert Hovenkamp, *Arrow's Theorem: Ordinalism and Republican Government,* 75 Iowa L. Rev. 949, 955 (1990).

34. *See, e.g.,* Francesco Parisi, *Political Coase Theorem,* 115 Public Choice 1 (2003).

35. For a social choice model of a welfare function that considers legislators' relative preferences concerning two issues, see Frank DeMeyer and Charles R. Plott, *A Welfare Function Using "Relative Intensity" of Preference,* 85 Q.J. Econ. 179 (1971).

36. *See, e.g.,* Restatement (Second) of Torts (1977).

37. *See* Alan Schwartz and Robert E. Scott, *The Political Economy of Private Legislatures,* 143 U. Pa. L. Rev. 595 (1995).

38. *Id.* at 597.

CHAPTER 10: PREDICTOCRACY

1. *See, e.g.,* Goodwin v. Agassiz, 186 N.E. 659 (Mass. 1933) (failing to impose liability for insider trading).

2. *See generally* Robert G. Bone, *The Boundaries of the Dispute: Conceptions of Ideal Lawsuit Structure from the Field Code to the Federal Rules,* 89 Colum. L. Rev. 1 (1989).

3. Kyoto Protocol to the United Nations Framework Convention on Climate Change art. 17, Dec. 11, 1997, U.N. Doc. FCCC/CP/1997/L.7/Add.1 (entered into force Feb. 16, 2005), *reprinted in* 37 I.L.M. 22, *available at* http://unfccc.int/resource/doc/convkp/kpeng.pdf (last visited June 27, 2006); *see also* Gary C. Bryner, *Carbon Markets: Reducing Greenhouse Gas Emissions Through Emissions Trading,* 17 Tul. Envtl. L.J. 267 (2004) (surveying the evolution of carbon trading systems).

4. Ronald H. Coase, *The Federal Communications Commission,* 2 J.L. & Econ. 1 (1959).

5. For Coase's own account of the reception he received, see Ronald H. Coase, *Comment on Thomas W. Hazlett: Assigning Property Rights to Radio Spectrum Users: Why Did FCC License Auctions Take 67 Years?* 41 J.L. & Econ. 577, 579 (1998).

6. *See* Robin Hanson, *The Informed Press Favored the Policy Analysis Market* (Aug. 8, 2005), http://hanson.gmu.edu/PAMpress.pdf (last visited June 27, 2006).

7. *See* http://www.inklingmarkets.com (last visited June 27, 2006).

8. Thomas C. Schelling, The Strategy of Conflict 56 (1979).

9. John Maynard Keynes, General Theory of Employment, Interest, and Money 156 (1936).

10. *Id.*

11. *See* Teck-Hua Ho et al., *Iterated Dominance and Iterated Best Response in Experimental "p-Beauty Contests,"* 88 Am. Econ. Rev. 947 (1998).

12. *See* Nicholas Chan, Ely Dahan, Adlar Kim, Andrew Lo, and Tomaso Poggio, *Securities Trading of Concepts (STOC)* (2002), *available at* http://www.anderson.ucla.edu/faculty/ely.dahan/content/chan_dahan_lopoggio.pdf (last visited June 27, 2006).

13. In the Attitudes Toward Government Survey, conducted for the Council for Excellence in Government in February 1997, 50 percent of respondents said "the influence of special interests" was a "very major" cause of reduced confidence in government. For the complete survey report, see http://www.excelgov.org/admin/FormManager/filesuploading/juy97fullreport.pdf (last visited June 27, 2006).

14. *See* Clive Thompson, *Google's China Problem (And China's Google Problem),* N.Y. Times Magazine, Apr. 23, 2006, at 64.

15. *See* Orville Schell, *China's Hidden Democratic Legacy,* Foreign Aff., July–Aug. 2004, at 116.

16. Tjasa Redek and Andrej Susjan, *The Impact of Institutions on Economic Growth: The Case of Transition Economies,* J. Econ. Issues, Dec. 1, 2005, at 995 (noting that the Russian GDP fell 40 percent and the volume of official measured industrial output fell 56 percent between 1990 and 1994).

17. *See* Robin Hanson, *Shall We Vote on Values, But Bet on Beliefs?* 14–15 (Sept. 2003), http://hanson.gmu.edu/futarchy.pdf (last visited June 27, 2006).

18. *See, e.g.,* Michael W. McConnell, *Federalism: Evaluating the Founders' Design,* 54 U. Chi. L. Rev. 1484, 1493 (1987) ("[D]ecentralized decision making is better able to reflect the diversity of interests and preferences of individuals in different parts of the nation").

19. The U.S. Supreme Court has found the execution of juveniles to be a cruel and unusual punishment under the Eighth Amendment, relying in part on the fact that most states and foreign countries have barred such executions. *See* Roper v. Simmons, 543 U.S. 551, 564–78 (2005).

20. *See* Thomas W. Malone, The Future of Work: How the New Order of Business Will Shape Your Organization, Your Management Style, and Your Life 8–11 (2004).

21. *See* Ray Kurzweil, The Singularity Is Near (2005).

22. *See* H. L. A. Hart, The Concept of Law 13–17 (2d ed. 1994).

Index